SHAWMUT

SHAWMUT

150 Years of Banking
1836–1986

Asa S. Knowles

with the editorial collaboration of
Antoinette Frederick and William H. Schoeffler

Boston

HOUGHTON MIFFLIN COMPANY

1986

Library of Congress Cataloging in Publication Data

Knowles, Asa S. (Asa Smallidge), 1909–
Shawmut : 150 years of banking, 1836–1986.

Includes index.
1. Shawmut Bank of Boston, N.A. — History. 2. Banks
and banking — Massachusetts — Boston — History.
I. Frederick, Antoinette. II. Schoeffler, William H.
III. Title.
HG2613.B74S415 1986 332.1′223′0974461 85-18101
ISBN 0-395-38375-7

Printed in the United States of America

V 10 9 8 7 6 5 4 3 2 1

Acknowledgments

This history of Shawmut from its founding in 1836 to December 31, 1982, has been in preparation over a span of three years. During this time numerous former and present officials of the Shawmut Bank of Boston, N.A., the Shawmut Corporation, and affiliated banks and subsidiaries have contributed information, reports, records, and documents on which the history is based.

Special thanks are due to John P. LaWare, Chairman and Chief Executive Officer of the Corporation and the Shawmut Bank of Boston, N.A., not only for authorizing the preparation of the history and for contributing information, but also for his encouragement of work in progress.

Warren Berg, Senior Vice President for Corporate Relations of the Corporation, has given unstintingly of his time to assist those preparing the history by helping to define the project at its outset, guiding the author and his staff in their research and writing, and reading and making suggestions on the contents of chapters of the history.

Former Chairman and Chief Executive Officer of the National Shawmut Bank and Shawmut Association, Inc., Lawrence H. Martin, has been a major source of information in the writing of the history, particularly beginning with the Bucklin administration, and has given valuable advice on persons and records to be consulted. He also reviewed and criticized parts of the manuscript and prepared numerous memoranda of great value in giving direction to research efforts.

D. Thomas Trigg, former Chairman and Chief Executive Officer, has given generously of his time in providing sources of information relative to the Devonshire Financial Service Corporation, the Shawmut Association, the Corporation, and facts relating to the period when he served as an officer in various capacities and as President of the National Shawmut Bank and later as Chairman and Chief Executive Officer of the Shawmut Bank of Boston, N.A., and the Shawmut Corporation.

John K. Benson, former Vice Chairman of the Shawmut Bank of Boston, N.A., and former President of the Shawmut Association, Inc., prepared memoranda that aided greatly in gaining perspectives on events of historical importance which occurred during his long period of service as an officer.

David Currier, Senior Vice President, was a significant source of information on the Martin and Trigg administrations and particularly on the planning, construction, and occupancy of the Shawmut headquarters building at One Federal Street.

Thanks are also due to F. Thayer Sanderson, Executive Vice President and head of the Trust Division; and Robert L. Hussey, Executive Vice President of Community Banking. Both served as conferees and consultants on various aspects of the history, particularly those related to their own areas of responsibility.

Paul A. Miller, Executive Vice President and Treasurer of the Corporation, was a source of considerable information for this history. He wrote special materials contained in some chapters and gave generously of his time to read and criticize various chapters in the process of development. James Nix, Vice President and Deputy Controller of the Corporation, was a frequent source of valuable information on bank organization and auditing.

Neal F. Finnegan, Executive Vice President, was especially helpful in providing information concerning the merger and integration of the Worcester Bank Corporation and the Shawmut Corporation.

Dorothy Reardon, secretary to the author in his capacity as Chancellor of Northeastern University, was of great assistance during the preparation of the manuscript, typing drafts of chapters and other materials contained in the history. She assisted also in making preliminary editorial corrections on the manuscript.

Thanks are extended to Mrs. Wilfred Stanley Lake for providing access to her late husband's unpublished doctoral dissertation "The History of Banking Regulations in Massachusetts 1784–1860."

John J. Green, Executive Vice President and Chief Loan Officer, assisted greatly in providing information on the names and locations of existing branches and offices of the Shawmut Corporation, the history and development of involvement of the Corporation and its affiliates in New England Bankcard Association with the offering of credit card services, including the services and functions of the Credit Division of the Shawmut Bank of Boston, N.A.

Charles M. Bush, Senior Vice President and head of the Personnel Division of the Shawmut Bank of Boston, N.A., was particularly helpful in giving the author and his staff access to personnel records of former officers and staff when they were needed for purposes of the history. He and his staff also prepared a brief and comprehensive statement on the policies and ongoing operations of the Personnel Division.

The examination of official records and minutes of meetings of the directors of the Shawmut Association, Shawmut Corporation, Shawmut Bank, Shawmut National Bank, National Shawmut Bank, and Shawmut Bank of Boston, N.A., entailed spending many hours on the part of the author and staff in the vaults located at One Federal Street building of the Shawmut Bank of Boston, N.A. The vault staff was most cooperative and helpful in making available documents and records. These were Robert H. Peterson, Marjorie Curry, Evelyn J. Moleca, and Alma A. Tower. Special mention must be made of Richard E. Fischer, Cashier of the Shawmut Bank of Boston, N.A., who was continuously helpful in locating documents and records in the vaults, in areas where records are stored, and in the Leahy Archives.

Thanks are also extended to Thomas J. Killeen, Editor of *Shawmut News*, who made his files available to us, and to Lawrence J. Lynch, Assistant Vice President of Corporate Relations, who helped immeasurably in the accumulation of graphics and in publication arrangements.

Catherine L. O'Connor, former Secretary to Chief Executive officers Lawrence H. Martin and D. Thomas Trigg and now serving as Assistant Clerk and Assistant Secretary of the Corporation, was most helpful as a source of information on Bank records and policies and as a reviewer of the contents of some chapters of the history.

I would also like to give special thanks to Patricia Strange, who typed the final manuscript and, with patience and good nature, made all the numerous revisions that completing such a project entails.

This book would not have been possible without the additional assistance of Raymond Abdella, Herbert P. Almgren, Donald Armitage, Lincoln Barber, Jr., James F. Botelho, Jr., Eric D. Bradlee, Margaret K. Browning, Joseph A. Bruno, James T. Chamberlain, Eileen M. Chapman, David W. Dailey, William J. Deane, Jr., Robert W. Dobson, P. Clarke Dwyer, John G. Fallon, Donald F. Geary, Helen Gegerias, George H. Goodwin, Jr., John J. Gould, George G. Greene, Timothy J. Hansberry, Carter H. Harrison, Merry K. Howe, C. Keefe Hurley, Jr., John H. Kalchbrenner, Margaret F. Kane, Arnold I. Kappel, John J. LaCreta, Barrie H. MacKay, Paul A. MacKinnon, Paul M. Maniff, David A. Marcoux, William S. McLaughlin, Marguerite Meserve, Andrew A. Orrock, John B. Pierce, Jr., Amy Ribuoli, Anne B. Riley, Hilda Roberts, Powell Robinson, Jr., Betty J. Samuel, Anne Crowley Sandonato, William Schmink, William C. Schrader, Eugene B. Smith, Francis Smith, Leo F. Swift, Horace C. Sylvester, Alma A. Tower, John Wallace, John Warren, Myron O. Wilkins, Richard A. Williams, Gerald C. Woodworth, John T. Worcester.

Sources

In preparing this book, I have relied heavily on the minutes, records, publications, including the annual reports, correspondence, and general files of the Shawmut Bank of Boston, Shawmut Association, Shawmut Association, Inc., and the Shawmut Corporation. All this material is available in the Shawmut Library and archives at the Shawmut Bank of Boston, One Federal Street.

Other financial information was derived from publications of the Federal Reserve Bank of Boston and the Federal Reserve Board.

Supplementary research has been performed at the following local repositories: Baker Library, Graduate School of Business Administration, Harvard University; Boston Public Library; Brookline Public Library; Dodge Library, Northeastern University; Massachusetts Historical Society; Massachusetts State Archives; Massachusetts State Library; Mugar Library, Boston University; and the Registries of probate and deeds in the counties of Essex, Middlesex, Norfolk, Plymouth, and Suffolk, in Massachusetts.

I have also relied heavily on a number of standard reference works relating to the entire period covered.

Asa S. Knowles
December 1982

Since this manuscript was originally submitted, I have updated the appendices and added the John LaWare chapter.

A. S. K.
Fall 1985

Contents

Illustrations
following page 268

Benjamin T. Reed, President, 1836–1848
Exchange Coffee House
John Gardner, President, 1848–1853
Albert Fearing, President, 1853–1854
William Bramhall, President, 1854–1868
Shawmut bank notes
The Shawmut Indian as it appeared on bank notes in the 1850s and 1860s
The standing Indian used in the late 1800s
The Shawmut Indian as it appeared at the turn of the century
A brass engraved image placed on the marble floor at Water Street
The bust of Obbatinewat as we know him today, created by Adelbert Ames, Jr., in 1910
Contemporary logo, introduced in April 1975
A studio showing the production of Shawmut commercials for television, 1947
Calendar used during Shawmut's 100th anniversary year
National Shawmut Bank 1964 auto loan ad
John C. Cummings, Jr., President, 1868–1898
James P. Stearns, President, 1898–1907
Shawmut's 60 Congress Street headquarters, rebuilt in 1874 after the Great Boston Fire of 1872 and occupied until 1907
William A. Gaston, President, 1907–1917
Alfred L. Aiken, President, 1918–1923
40 Water Street, Shawmut's headquarters from 1907 to 1975
Bank floor of 40 Water Street, 1907
Main lobby of 40 Water Street, 1940s
Walter S. Bucklin, President, 1923–1952; Chief Executive Officer and Chairman, 1952–1956

The Shawmut Story

This is the story of the Shawmut's growth and development from its founding in 1836 to the present time. Originally a small state bank, it has become one of the largest financial institutions in the United States — a major New England banking organization with affiliated banks and offices throughout the Commonwealth of Massachusetts and offices in financial centers of the United States and overseas. Its combined assets today exceed $5 billion, and the Shawmut organization now employs more than five thousand people.

Founded just before the Panic of 1837, Shawmut has survived and even prospered during several periods of recession, financial panics, and business conditions adverse to the welfare of many banks and financial organizations.

Among the banks of Boston and New England, Shawmut has been a leader in financing progress and change in the industrial and commercial economy of Massachusetts, New England, and the nation. As industry has grown and developed, with new industries being financed to replace old ones, the community has benefited and so has the Bank.

In its earliest days, Shawmut contributed to the financing of shipping and trade carried on by the merchants and ship owners of Boston, who founded the Bank. As New England developed its manufacturing capabilities, Shawmut was involved in financing warehouses for raw cotton and wool and the manufacture of finished cotton and woolen textiles. Of equal significance was its later role in providing loans to the tanning, leather manufacturing, and boot and shoe industries, which became major staples of the New England economy in the late nineteenth and early twentieth centuries.

Throughout its history, Shawmut has also been a source of financing for transportation. In the 1830s and 1840s, as inland travel began to develop and shifted from the stagecoach to the steam railroad, Shawmut supplied funds to help lay track and to sustain the railroad companies that operated services between Boston and many major New England towns. At the same time the Bank also contributed to the introduction of steam power in coastal and overseas shipping.

As the years passed Shawmut further extended its interests in transportation. During the late nineteenth century it began to participate in the development of railroads nationwide, and with the advent of the twentieth century, became one of the first United States banks to provide funds not only for the manufacture of automobiles but also for their purchase on an installment plan. In this way the Bank helped to promote a new industry of national importance and to put America on wheels.

In the first decades of the twentieth century, Shawmut expanded its loans to utility companies and began to finance installment plans for the purchase of electrical appliances, thus contributing to the growth of the electric utilities industry. When American Telephone and Telegraph was organized, Shawmut staff and directors were involved, and the Bank became an important source of funds for this new form of communication. Shawmut's activities in these areas foreshadowed its current role in financing the electronics and computer industries, which are dominant elements of the New England economy in the 1980s.

Over the years Shawmut has grown increasingly national in service. It has played a significant role in providing resources for national and international businesses that have been the foundation of America's huge industrial economy, and in contributing to the ever rising standard of living of the American people. It also has had a distinguished record of assisting in national causes. Shawmut participated in financing the Civil War and the two world wars, providing funds for war-industry production and promoting the sale of government bonds.

As Shawmut's role has expanded so has its physical presence. In 1836 it began operations in a rented room on the second floor of an office building on State Street in Boston; today its headquarters is a thirty-eight-story high-rise in the heart of Boston's financial district. This building is headquarters for both the Shawmut Bank, now designated as the Shawmut Bank of Boston, N.A., and the Shawmut Corporation, the name of the holding company that controls and supervises all the Shawmut-affiliated banks and subsidiary organizations.

The story of Shawmut, then, is the story of a constantly changing financial organization. Many of its traditions — its basically conservative policies and dedication to the welfare of its city, state, and region — even some of its dominant financial interests, can be traced to its origins in Boston in the early nineteenth century. Yet no one person has dictated its shape; no one decade has determined its course. Over the years, as the nation's banking system has changed and as the concept of community has broadened to include not only the immediate environs but the nation and finally the globe, these traditions and interests have been modified, expanded, and augmented. Shawmut's story is that of many dedicated persons working within the context of their particular time to assure the continued growth and development of a strong and responsive financial institution.

For these reasons we chose to tell much of Shawmut's history chronologically, beginning with a summary of the historical conditions that existed when the Bank began and which first affected the shape and direction it would take. The second chapter focuses on how the Bank was founded. The story then moves forward through time, with chapters named according to various administrations. These divisions, however, should not be understood to imply that the development of Shawmut can in any way be neatly segmented, or that any one chief executive officer was ever more than a guide or mentor for the institution that preceded his tenure and continued after. In the last three chapters we abandoned the chronological format in favor of broad overviews on particular aspects of Shawmut's story.

No single book can, of course, tell the whole story. Inevitably, some details of Shawmut's growth that one reader considers important have been left out, while other events that another considers trivial have been included. Our intent, however, is to show how one small, local banking institution profited from its past and came to be a major New England banking institution. To the extent that this aim is fulfilled, this history will be successfully told.

PART ONE

The
Chronological Story
of Shawmut

Chapter 1

As It Was

The Boston Scene at the Time of
the Founding of the Original Shawmut

Eighteen thirty-six, the year in which the Shawmut
Bank was born, was a pivotal year for the young republic of
the United States. It was a time marked by frantic business
activity, high production, high employment, record investments, bustling trade, and perhaps most important, by a record
circulation of multicolored, multisized bank notes that were
the currency of the time — the symbol and expression of the
new nation's prosperity. Eighteen thirty-six was the apex of a
quarter century of almost uninterrupted expansion. Paradoxically, it was also the prelude to a recession that would grip
the country well into the next decade.

In the spring of that year little evidence of future decline
overshadowed the busy port of Boston. In its protected harbor
at the foot of Massachusetts Bay rocked a forest of masts, as
schooners, brigs, packets, and sloops threaded their way among
the greening harbor islands to deposit and take on again cargoes, which bore stamps of origin from as far away as Russia,
China, and India and from as close to home as New Haven,
Hartford, New York, Richmond, Savannah, New Orleans, Columbus, and St. Louis. Here, along the eastern shore of the
town, thronged a crowd of pigtailed sailors, Irish dockhands,
and men of commerce in tall beaver hats and frock coats, shoul-
dering one another aside in the noisy tumult that was the rush

of daily trade. Above them on a staff that topped Central Wharf — a half-mile-long pier filled with shops and businesses and piled high with bales and barrels — snapped a semaphore of flags announcing the comings and goings of various ships. Around them echoed the shouts of longshoremen, the babble of auctioneers, the whisper of entrepreneurs, and the steady thunder of wooden-wheeled carts careening from dockside to dockside. The very smell was overwhelming — molasses, pitch, Malaga raisins, oranges from Sicily, drying fish. Here and in the adjacent marketplace throbbed the heart of the city's economy and, by extension, much of the nation's.

Boston in 1836, however, was no mere port town whose economy, culture, and appearance were exclusively dictated by its waterfront. In the course of its 206-year history, it had developed a sophisticated network of businesses and industries, a way of doing things, and a physical presence which, if they were not typical of the country at large, were the product and source of much of its vitality.

1

Historically, of course, Boston was a shipping and trading town. Located on a tiny peninsula thrust like a clenched fist into the sea and connected to the mainland by only a thin natural causeway, the town had little arable land, forests, or game that were the mainstays of so many early colonial economies. It had instead the sea, and here Bostonians turned for survival, rapidly developing a lively economy that centered on the construction of ships, the manufacture of related goods, and the provision of supporting services.

Within decades the half-moon harbor bristled with the skeletal hulks of ships under construction; several downtown areas were festooned with duck and linen, set out to weather before being cut into sails, while rope walks — tar-covered paths where cord and hemp were twisted into rigging — presented the constant threat of fire. Providing service to these enterprises was a host of small businesses. Hanging wooden signs suspended above cobbled streets announced the presence of lodging

houses, taverns, provisioners of victuals, printing shops, smith-
eries, apothecaries, and most common of all, tiny shops that
retailed the manufactured wares of England and the wooden
ware, dry goods, and groceries of the New England region.
The one essential trade service that the colonial town could
not provide, however, was banking. Indeed, any form of financial service was severely frowned upon. British law forbade the
colonists from printing their own currency or from establishing
their own banks, and although some rudimentary attempts were
made to circumvent the law, they were largely ineffective.

Nevertheless, despite these restrictions, Boston grew quickly
and by the mid–eighteenth century was not only the largest
port in the British colonies — boasting some 16,000 inhabitants
as contrasted with Philadelphia's 13,000 and New York's
11,000 — but was also the second largest community in the
entire British domain. A cosmopolitan commercial capital,
closely tied by shipping and trade as well as by financial laws
to the Old World, its society and culture reflected those bonds.

At the top of the social ladder the Royal governor and representatives of the Provincial Government presided. Sharing their
prominence were men of means, usually the younger sons of
wealthy British families who, cut off from inheriting ancestral
estates at home, parlayed Old World connections into New
World fortunes. There was also a handful of newly minted merchant princes, generally men who had begun their careers before the mast, accumulated gold from the shared profits of
the cargoes, and then come ashore to buy their own ships and
goods. Around this group, and often of it, circled a large bour-
geoisie of artisans, craftsmen, shopkeepers, educators, and
transplanted clergymen. Few of these were without worldly am-
bition; many reaped worldly rewards. On the lowest rung of
the social ladder stood a small group of unskilled laborers,
retained to do the limited heavy work of the settlement. To a
large extent the proportions of this populace were inverse to
those of many other colonial settlements, where profit depended on muscle and the production of goods for exchange.
In Boston, wealth depended far more on wit and connections,
and greater profits were extracted from the process of exchange
than from the production of goods themselves.

Out of this amalgam emerged a unique society, one dominated by English manners and customs and by a cosmopolitan cast of mind that came from daily intercourse with the world beyond the colonies. It was by and large a rational, educated society: Harvard College on its outskirts was in operation by 1636, religious freedom was secure by 1691. The very ties, however, that gave Boston its strength also made it vulnerable. When the Revolution came it devastated the town as much, if not more, than any settlement in the colonies. During the war the population plummeted to 10,000. Trade and shipping came to a virtual halt, and the community, once the commercial and cultural capital of the country, found itself reduced to little more than an island enclave.

The city into which the Shawmut was born was largely a nineteenth-century creation, a world significantly different from the past and yet significantly similar. Boston of 1836 was the product of new commercialism, industrialism, and expansion that began to sweep the nation in the wake of the Revolution and accelerated rapidly in the first four decades of the new century; it was also a place where the expression of these trends was uniquely shaped by the particularities of its own history.

2

Certainly a major factor in shaping nineteenth-century Boston was the revival of its shipping and trade and their related industries. These recreated enterprises were no mere mirrors of the past. New demands presented new needs, and in form, substance, quality, and quantity important innovations developed.

Colonial restrictions and the Revolution had taught hard lessons that the Jefferson embargo and the War of 1812 reinforced: to trade with western Europe was not enough, to be confined to exporting raw materials and importing manufactured goods was to lose vast profit potential. The story of the new city is very much the story of the development of new markets both overseas and at home. It is also the story of the increasing diversity of products that were distributed to these markets.

During the colonial era commerce had largely been confined to the exchange of goods with the mother country and the

West Indies. The war cancelled these restrictions, and in 1787 two of Boston's own vessels set sail for Canton, China, via the seal- and otter-rich West Coast. In 1790 the first of these vessels, the *Columbian,* returned to its home port laden with a cargo of teas and silk. The China trade, which Boston came to dominate, had begun. In the ensuing years other Far East and Asian markets developed: by 1803 the town was sending thirty-eight ships a year to Russia; by 1833 it was exporting ice some 20,000 miles to Calcutta.

During the same period domestic trade also increased. In 1790 there were thirteen states; by 1836 there were twenty-three. Westward expansion was a hallmark of the era, particularly in the decades of the 1820s and 1830s: old states filled to their westernmost borders, while new territories opened for settlement. Accelerating this expansion was an increase in total population from 4 million in 1790 to 13 million in 1830 to 17 million in 1840. Simultaneously, the introduction of new modes of transportation — toll roads, canals, steamboats — forged links between isolated communities that expedited not only new settlement but also the transfer of goods from and to these areas.

Much of the new transportation affected Boston only indirectly: the opening of the Erie Canal in 1825 actually diverted some trade in the western half of Massachusetts from the state's capital to New York. Nevertheless, the overall consequences of population growth, westward expansion, and new modes of transportation were vast increases in both supply and demand, and a related increase in the total volume of trade goods that eventually filtered through the port of Boston. In 1820 the taxable value on both foreign and domestic goods passing through the port was $38 million; in 1840 it was $95 million.

As the markets expanded, so also did the diversity of products. New modes of transportation meant new access to agricultural products and to natural resources whose distribution had been previously limited. By the 1830s, grain and cattle from the Ohio valley, rice and tobacco as well as raw sugar from the South, and wheat and dairy products from upper New York state were appearing in far greater volume on Boston's wharves than ever before. New England's own vegetables and fruits and Boston-dried fish were far more likely to be served in Charleston and Savannah than they would have been even a few decades earlier. Furthermore, as the rich agricultural potential of the West began to be tapped, farmers in soil-poor New England began to look for more profitable ways to use their land: raising sheep became a new occupation, and wool became a major New England resource.

But the wealth of the new republic lay not only in its agriculture and raw materials. The country, of course, had never been quite the agrarian paradise extolled by Jefferson: "While we have land to labor, let us never wish to see our citizens occupied at a workbench or twirling a distaff." It was not until the nineteenth century, however, that manufactured goods became an important component of the total economy.

Boston's own manufacturing capability was, of course, severely limited by space, but this did not prevent it from playing an important role in the development of manufacturing. In 1812 the town's own native son, Francis Cabot Lowell, whose immediate family had made a fortune in the China trade, returned from England with the plans for Britain's cotton spinning machines firmly committed to memory. (The exportation of machine parts or plans was forbidden.) The following year young Lowell, in conjunction with his brother-in-law, set up the Boston Manufacturing Company, with a capital of $400,000, for the express purpose of applying the spinning machine to the manufacture of textiles, and in 1813 the country's first real factory opened in Waltham, Massachusetts, six miles west of Boston. Nine years later, in 1822, Boston Manufacturing opened the now famous Lowell Mills, and shortly after, similar operations began in Manchester, New Hampshire. As early as 1817 Boston Manufacturing was paying dividends of 20 percent, and by 1831 it had been joined by many similarly successful corporate enterprises located throughout New England but backed by Boston capital.

While the new manufacturing system placed the country on the verge of a dramatic change that would eventually alter the entire economy and bring new revenues to the city, other manufacturing enterprises, designed along more conventional lines, were also flourishing. Iron, supplied from nearby Saugus, and copper were readily available and provided the base for four manufacturing corporations headquartered in and paying taxes to the city.

Meanwhile, the sea continued to supply raw materials, of which silica derived from sand was an important element. Boston boasted three major companies devoted to glass production. Other major concerns that had their roots in Boston's early manufacturing and paid substantial city revenues in the nineteenth century were soapstone makers and brewers. During this period the shoe and leather industry, ultimately a central feature of Boston's economy, also began to appear.

Expanded trade, shipping, and manufacturing, however, were not the only elements that figured in the formation of 1836 Boston. As the population increased throughout the rest of the country, so also it increased in the port city. In 1790 there had been a mere 10,000 Bostonians; in 1830 there were 62,000; by 1840 there would be 98,000. A good portion of this growth was provided by newcomers. In the 1830s annual immigration to the United States was 50,000. This was small contrasted with the 100,000 that would come annually only a few years later; nevertheless, the numbers were substantial. Although the vast majority of these new arrivals moved on, contributing to the settlement of the West and to the subsequent land boom in that area, others remained in the East.

Of the early nineteenth-century immigrants remaining in Boston, most were Germans whose ideals, education, and industry were in sympathy with the prevailing culture. They were rapidly absorbed. By the 1830s, however, Irish immigration had become an important factor in the make-up of the population. Between 1836 and 1845, an average of 5500 Irish came to make their homes in the city each year. Largely unskilled and uneducated, lacking the wherewithal to move on, and separated by their culture and religion from a mainstream still dominated by English manners and mores, they formed small, isolated enclaves. An insight on their impact is provided by a contemporary real estate agent, one Amos Cotting, who in the late 1830s warned some of his Brahmin clients of the adverse effect this group might have on property values. In 1847 he spelled out his warning explicitly: "The change [in value] of your Federal Street property is owing in part to some owners letting their estates to the Irish who have got such control that they drive good tenants away."

In toto, the overall explosion in population, trade, shipping, and manufacturing might well have created what Henry Adams would later scathingly call "a new Bristol in America." The term, with its connotation of a swarming waterfront, throbbing shipyards, tumultuous marketplace, and heterogenous citizenry stoutly devoted to the business of making a daily living, was not without its aptness as a description of the city in 1836. It was, however, only a small part of the complete picture, for Boston of that time was not merely a strident, second-rate port. Although it would never again be the country's major port city — in 1830 New York with 197,112 inhabitants and Philadelphia with 80,462 had both surpassed it — its physical appearance, its culture, and most important, its leadership role in shaping the attitudes of the new country made it among the most influential of nineteenth-century cities.

With the departure of the Provincial Government, Boston had faded as a political center. After the Revolution, as the headquarters of the Federalist party, it briefly regained some of that stature. Its citizens were instrumental in shaping the new confederacy, while two of the first six presidents, John Adams and John Quincy Adams, could both claim a Boston connection. However, after the latter's defeat in 1828 by the Jacksonian Democrats, much of the city's control of national politics evaporated.

Although Boston continued to have some political influence throughout the nineteenth century — and the founding of the Whig party there in the 1830s was no small part of that influence — in general, the city's interests were those of eastern business, which Jackson did not represent. Indeed, when Josiah Quincy, president of Harvard College, courageously determined to confer an honorary doctor of law degree on Jackson, many, including John Quincy Adams, were outraged. The arrival of Old Hickory to receive the honor in May 1833 was anticipated with dread. Jackson was the first President to come from what was then considered the West and had been held up to Bostonians as the symbol of the rough frontier, its uncouth energy, its unpredictable wildness, or as one contemporary would later record, "the name of Andrew Jackson was indeed one to frighten naughty children with."

As the story goes, when Jackson rode along Beacon Street on his way to Cambridge that May morning, merchants and their families huddled inside. One well-known Brahmin, whose home was adjacent to what is now the Somerset Club, was apparently curious enough to peer reluctantly out the window to see the reputed "wild man" president for himself. What he expected is not reported; what he saw was an erect, slender, white-haired, well-dressed figure whose innate dignity and aristocratic bearing were so unmistakable that the amazed Beacon Street nabob called impulsively: "*Do* someone come here and salute the old man!" And as the younger Josiah Quincy recorded in his *Figures of the Past,* the merchant's "little daughter was thrust forward to wave her handkerchief to the (hitherto) terrible personage" of Andy Jackson. The incident suggests that Jackson's appearance was at least somewhat less formidable in reality than in anticipation.

Even as Boston was losing its political clout, however, it was establishing itself more firmly as the cultural leader of the country. In the 1830s Boston presses, which in pre-Revolutionary times had devoted their attention to commercial pamphlets, political brochures, and matters of parochial interest, began to turn their attention elsewhere, and in this decade the town became the acknowledged publishing center of New England, wresting that honor from the previous leader, Hartford. In addition, although the Loyalists had departed even before the first volley of shots was fired at Concord, upper-class English manners and mores had remained the accepted standard of behavior. In his history *The Problem of Boston,* Martin Green notes that the concept of "responsibility" was the key to Boston society and finds its source in the British ruling class rather than in New World puritanism. Green goes on to cite Bronson Alcott's 1828 comment on contemporary culture: "It is a city set on high. It cannot be hid. It is Boston. The morality of Boston is more pure than that of any other city in America."

Such morality, or at least the confidence that it existed, prompted Bostonians to support more humanitarian and philanthropic organizations than could be found anywhere else in the new republic. Between 1810 and 1830, thirty benevolent institutions were established, including Massachusetts General Hospital and Perkins Institute for the Blind. It was also during this period that David Sears set up his famous Fifty Associates. An early real estate trust and a delightful combination of community, family, and business interests, Fifty Associates was designed to distribute its profits equally among the Overseers of the Poor, the Sears' heirs, and money-making real estate ventures.

The same responsibility and morality syndrome contributed to an unprecedented faith in the efficacy of educational and cultural institutions. While other communities found the three R's to be sufficient and often touted shrewdness as a more useful tool than knowledge, Boston continued to support Harvard and to institute such notable educational facilities as the Massachusetts Historical Society, 1791, and the Boston Athenaeum, 1807. (The Athenaeum was one of three libraries in the country, the others being the City Library of Philadelphia and the Harvard University Library.)

Boston's cultural preoccupations were sophisticated and well rooted in a long tradition of liberal, cosmopolitan taste. While citizens of other communities delighted in gambling, barn raising, and square dancing, Bostonians attended the Federal Street Theatre, which opened February 3, 1794, learned the gavotte from an imported Italian dancing master, and attended free lectures on science, religion, or literature at the Lowell Institute, the fund for which was established in 1836.

But perhaps no single factor so substantially contributed to the unique character of 1836 Boston as the massive efforts to reconstruct the tiny peninsula so that it might more graciously accommodate the new demands of a new time.

During the first years of settlement, Boston's insular topography, with its single narrow path to the mainland, had been largely viewed as a security asset. In the latter years of the seventeenth century and the early years of the eighteenth, when Boston's eyes were turned toward the mother country, such limited access was still perceived as inconsequential. The closing of the ship lanes during the Revolution and the later Jeffersonian embargo, however, put a new construction on the matter. As inland trade began to grow, the one narrow means of ingress and egress was recognized as a liability, and post-Revolutionary Boston began a time of stretching outward. In 1786 the town fathers chartered a corporation to construct a bridge and toll road that would span the Charles River to Charlestown and open the way northward to foot and vehicular traffic. In the course of the next several years, Boston corporations constructed three more bridges, each topped with a generous highway: West Bridge to Cambridge (1793), South Bridge to Dorchester Neck (1805), and Craigie, or Canal Bridge, to Lechmere (1809). The most enterprising undertaking, however, did not occur until 1817, at the height of the national turnpike boom. This was a mile-and-a-half toll road that ran atop a mill dam, cutting across what was then literally a back bay. The road, connecting the corners of Charles and Beacon Streets at the northwest edge of the peninsula to the mainland at Sewall Point (now Kenmore Square), opened in 1820.

In the meantime, to spur further expansion of the Lowell Mills, Boston capitalists planned and had dug the Middlesex Canal, which in the late 1820s connected the mill complex with the port facilities of Boston. This provided an efficient means of transportation for carrying raw materials from the city to the mills and returning finished products to Boston for distribution from its port.

By 1836 Boston already had six major roads radiating from its center and the canal, all supplementing its sea lanes as conduits for trade goods coming to and from the port. Adding to these spokes and giving substance to Boston's nickname, the Hub City, was the construction of railway lines.

Although Boston did not have the first steam railroad in the U.S. (that honor was Baltimore's), it triumphantly opened three lines in 1835: the Boston and Lowell, the Boston and Worcester, and the Boston and Providence. In 1836 it added still a fourth, the Eastern, which ran into East Boston. None of these lines, it is true, penetrated very far into the countryside — in 1836 the Worcester ran only as far as Newton, twelve miles away — but if the growth of rail traffic as a significant part of the economy lay in the future, the promise of what it could accomplish was already providing a stimulus to investors. Even more promising was the breakdown of Boston's insularity. By the 1830s the city was looking not only east across the Atlantic but also west toward the opening frontiers.

Despite new modes of transportation and growth of inland markets, shipping, particularly by sailing vessels, remained dominant. (The development of transatlantic steam travel began in the 1830s but would not become important to Boston until the next decade.) To accommodate increased nineteenth-century trade, Bostonians undertook several massive projects designed to improve their waterfront. These included the construction of new streets and granite warehouses along the harbor, the addition of new wharves, including the half-mile Central Wharf, and in 1825, the extension of land into the harbor at Faneuil Hall to facilitate the erection of the Quincy Market complex. This last complex served as a heart of trade and commerce for generations and recently has regained its former vitality as a vibrant focal point.

Further contributing to the new shape of the nineteenth-century city were massive land and architectural changes that occurred farther into the peninsula. On January 11, 1798, the now familiar domed State House, designed by Charles Bulfinch, replaced the old "lion and unicorn" landmark as the seat of state government. Moving the seat of government away from the market to what had been previously a rural outpost of farms and orchards focused new attention on Beacon Hill. In the meantime, various projects in other parts of town were transforming the topography and substantially altering the character of the city.

In 1836 Boston confronted the world in a far more sophisticated garb than it had a mere fifty years earlier. No longer a small, homogeneous town, its very physical presence bespoke a new and more vital prosperity. The wharves and markets were still the center of commercial activity, but new highways and railroads to the mainland supplemented the shipping lanes as avenues for trade. The town's profile of sharp, empty hills had also been modified: the peaks were blunted and on the slopes substantial homes began to appear. It was, moreover, a place of juxtaposed contrasts: of masts and church spires and green elms; of the copper-domed Quincy Market and the pewter-domed State House; of hundreds of new shops and businesses and, a mere few steps away, quiet residential neighborhoods reminiscent of London's Belgrave Square. Here, in solid brick and granite mansions, a new class of merchant prince found the appropriate expression of its own solidity.

Most of these merchant princes had ridden the crest of the nineteenth-century expansion into prosperity, and the sources of their wealth were as many and as varied as the opportunities of their time. Whatever the source of new fortunes, however, all had one common denominator: none could have flourished had it not been for the introduction of Boston's newest major industry, the banking business. So vital, in fact, was the development of banks to nineteenth-century Boston that the story deserves a section to itself.

3

During the colonial period, the British Crown, which was well aware of the importance of financing to the development of trade, had deliberately curtailed colonial independence by forbidding colonists to print their own currency or establish their own banks. Corn was the only legal tender "except money and beaver be expressly named," and there were no New World banks.

In the earliest and virtually self-sustaining agricultural settlements, which were able to get by on simple barter — room and board for labor, wheat and corn for sugar, raw materials for finished goods — these restrictions were no more than an inconvenience. In Boston, which was dependent on trade, the British restrictions were a heavy burden. A colonial merchant could secure a captain and crew on the promise of profit from a returning cargo, but he could not build his ship or fill the hold without substantial capital. Such capital, however, was most often furnished by the Bank of England, and these loans were limited to borrowers and enterprises that the Crown smiled upon. It was a device that effectively handcuffed the colony to the mother country, and Bostonians protested, albeit ineffectively.

By the mid–seventeenth century, a variety of gold and silver coins — mostly Spanish doubloons, pieces of eight, and bits of British sterling — were circulating in the colony, but these were hardly sufficient for any extensive trade. To augment these resources, the Massachusetts General Court authorized the minting of twelve-, six-, and three-penny pieces in 1652. Printed with a pine tree on one side, they became popularly known as the Pine Tree Shilling. Unfortunately the denominations were too small to be really useful, and this, in combination with the Crown's opposition, doomed the operation to failure. Although the mint survived twenty-five years, it was finally closed in 1677.

The second attempt to develop colonial currency was only marginally more successful. It began in 1690, when Sir William Phips, then Provincial governor, returning from an expedition to Canada, found there was not enough money to meet the military payroll in the Treasury. At his direction the Massachusetts General Court authorized the issue of paper bills, which declared on their face that the notes would be equal in value to a specified amount of specie and would be accepted by the Treasury for all public payments. Two years later the scope of these bills was expanded, making them equivalent to money for payments of any sort.

The issuance of paper currency on government credit continued for the next fifty-eight years but never proved either a satisfactory or stable medium for exchange. Its value was subject to the whim of government; the public regarded the notes with justifiable suspicion, and problems were compounded when Connecticut, New Hampshire, and Rhode Island, following Massachusetts' lead, began issuing their own currency. By 1751 the situation had become so chaotic that the British Parliament issued an edict forbidding Massachusetts from printing any bills of credit except those that might be needed to meet the expense of government.

In the meantime, Massachusetts merchants, whose needs were by no means satisfied even by the growing circulation of provincial notes, had taken matters into their own hands. As early as 1686, or at least so the story goes, a bank had been set up on the peninsula. No records of the operation remain, however, and the first verifiable institution, a Bank of Credit, was not established until 1714. Unchartered and unauthorized, it enjoyed only a brief existence and closed within a year. The next efforts were made in 1733 and 1739. The first of these, called the Private Bank, was based on specie. The second used property rather than specie as security for its notes. Neither venture met with favor from the Royal governor and both were closed.

With the advent of the war the problem of currency accelerated. To meet war obligations, the colonial government authorized the printing of new notes, but there was little gold to back them, and it was not until the founding of the first bank in the new republic, the Bank of North America, which opened in Philadelphia in January 1782, that they were accorded a semblance of stability. Capitalized for $400,000, the new bank was designed to meet the war obligations of the government. The problem of merchants' credit remained unaddressed, but not for long. In 1784 the Massachusetts Bank, the first such institution locally chartered, opened its doors. Banking in Boston had begun.

The significance of the Massachusetts Bank to banking is in some ways analogous to the importance of Lowell Mills to manufacturing. The latter poised the country on the edge of new industrialism; the bank poised it on the edge of great financial growth.

With the founding of the Massachusetts Bank, New England merchants could, for the first time, obtain business loans from a state-chartered corporation. Granted, the provisions of the charter, which had been modeled on those of the Bank of North America, were relatively broad. Nevertheless, in tandem with the Act to Prevent Fraud in Massachusetts Banks, passed by the legislature at roughly the same time, it established an important precedent to regulate the industry and make banking safe.

The provision of the temporary credit needed to sustain business was a landmark event and one that brought new prosperity not only to the bank's borrowers but also to its stockholders. By 1791 the Massachusetts Bank was returning 16 percent per annum on the par value of its stock, and it is little wonder that others would soon seek to enter the field. In 1791 the Boston Tontine, later called the Union Bank, was opened, and the next year, it was followed by a third institution, the old Boston Bank. That the competition in the private sector was not more fierce was largely due to still another development in the industry.

As the new republic began to take shape under the Constitution, the secretary of the Treasury, Alexander Hamilton, proposed the founding of the Bank of the United States. Modeled on the Bank of England and chartered by the federal legislature, the Bank of the United States was designed to implement policies that would establish the new country on a firm financial footing, stemming specie attrition and providing a government-backed currency. This currency was needed to realize the country's real wealth — abundant labor, raw materials, and an agricultural and manufacturing potential. Bostonians were ardent in their support of the project, and in 1791 the First Bank of the United States opened in Philadelphia, with a branch established in Boston in 1803.

Although the First Bank of the United States substantially accomplished the goals set for it by Hamilton, it was not an unqualified success. Detractors asserted that its federal charter and power to demand specie in payment of state bank notes gave it an unfair competitive edge over private institutions, that its policies had too restrictive an impact on the circulating medium, and that it was arbitrary in its lending — favoring some eastern investors, ignoring others. As a consequence of these arguments, as well as difficulties in management, the twenty-year charter of the bank was not renewed. In 1811 its funds were distributed to state institutions, and the bank closed.

At first it appeared as if the naysayers were correct. In the seven years between the founding of the Massachusetts Bank and the establishment of the First Bank of the United States twenty-nine private banks had been opened in the country. Eighteen of these were in New England, where trade was an essential element of the economy; seven were in Massachusetts, and three were in Boston. With the establishment of the First Bank of the United States, the organization of private banks came to a virtual halt, but in 1811, it started up again. Between 1811 and 1814, 120 new banks opened their doors. Two of these, the New England Bank (1813) and the Manufacturers and Mechanics (1814), called Tremont since 1830, were located in Boston. At the same time circulation increased by some $30 million.

Unfortunately not all bankers were equally reputable, and much of the capitalization of the notes was illusory. How and if the situation could have corrected itself is a matter of speculation. With the advent of the War of 1812, new debts accumulated and new and massive investments became a necessity. In 1816 the Second Bank of the United States, with a new twenty-year charter, was established. By this point the credit needs of the country had increased to such a degree that private initiative was curtailed, although it was not completely stifled. By 1830, when the renewal of the Second Bank of the United States again arose as a political issue, there were some 329 private banks in the country with a total circulation of some $102 million.

Not all currency issued by these institutions was of equal repute. The words of a European traveler in 1829 provide an instructive insight on the situation:

> The greatest annoyance I was subjected to in travelling was in exchanging money. It is impossible to describe the wretched state of the currency — which is all bills issued by private individuals; companies; cities and states; almost all of which are bankrupt; or what amounts to the same thing they cannot redeem their issues. All of their bills are at discount, varying from ten percent to fifty percent; and such rags of bills too. . . . It is true that there is in Charleston, New York, and some of the Eastern cities, good money issued by private banks that can be converted into specie at sight.

Of these eastern cities, the one with perhaps the best reputation was Boston, which by 1830 had firmly established itself as a major financial center. Extending credit to local merchants and traders — and thereby making possible the great expansion in shipping, trade, and manufacturing — were a host of private institutions. These included not only the banks mentioned above but also the Suffolk (1818), the City Bank of Boston (1825), the North Bank (1825), the Bunker Hill Bank (1825), and the Atlantic Bank (1828). It was not simply the plethora of these institutions, however, but their stability that made Boston second only to New York as a financial capital.

In 1830 Boston banks held approximately $4.5 million in specie, about half of the total capitalization of all banks in New England. It was, however, providing only 25 percent of the notes in circulation. Nor was there, at first, any way of telling if an out-of-town note had any backing at all or was in fact as "wretched" and unredeemable as the traveler quoted above declared.

The problem was simply the lack of enforceable regulations limiting the ratio of note issue to specie. Although the acquisition of a state charter demanded at least the appearance of capitalization, it was not unknown for a banker to borrow gold for just as long as was required to attain a charter, and then, returning the gold, go happily about printing notes with no backing whatsoever. Even where there was not overt fraud, there was frequent mismanagement. Situations where upcountry bankers sustained their operation in the hope that their notes would circulate so far afield that no one would be presumptuous enough to attempt redemption were all too familiar.

To Boston's merchants and traders, whose very fortunes depended on the dependability of currency, such practice was regarded with high disfavor. To control the situation and assure the soundness of the notes coming into the port, the New England Bank, followed in 1818 by the Suffolk, set itself up to collect non-city-issued notes and return them to the point of origin for redemption. The competition between the two institutions for this business was fierce until 1824, when seven of the major Boston banks, forming an association, selected the Suffolk as the agent for their note redemption.

The introduction of the Suffolk System was a landmark in the development of the banking industry, and Boston entered the 1830s secure in its position as a financial leader. Events on the national scene, however, would profoundly affect even the solid foundation of Boston's State Street institutions.

As the decade began, arguments were building on the validity of continuing the Second Bank of the United States. The major opposition to renewing the charter came largely from westerners who wanted to avail themselves of new investment opportunities, particularly in land, and, therefore, desired a freer currency not subject to redemption by the national bank. The major proponents of continuing the charter were the eastern merchants and traders whose fortunes depended on a stable currency, one recognized in Europe and at home as a valid means of exchange. In 1832 the situation came to a head when Congress, under the influence of the powerful Nicholas Biddle, president of the Bank of the United States, passed the charter only to have it vetoed by Jackson. State Street drew in its breath and shivered.

Although the Second Bank of the United States would not actually close its doors until 1836, the effect of Jackson's veto was immediate. In 1833, the year after the veto, there was $102 million worth of notes in circulation; in 1837, the year after the Bank of the United States was phased out, there was $149.2

million. At the same time, the number of banks more than doubled to reach 788 by 1837. In Massachusetts the figures jumped from 69 to 126. In Boston, which had added 2 new institutions in 1831, the Merchants Bank and the Traders Bank, the total went from 15 to 30.

The immediate effects of the growth in circulation and banks were unquestionably efficacious. Never before had so much money been available to so many, and business boomed. In Boston the wharves were jammed, the shipyards worked at full capacity, and manufacturers struggled to keep pace with demand. Certainly one beneficiary of the boom was the insurance industry. An important trade service, it was founded in the town in 1724 to provide protection for the fishing industry and for merchants' cargoes. The industry's growth had closely paralleled that of the entire economy, and by 1831 one-sixth of the city's major corporations was devoted to assuring that its merchant princes would not suffer unduly from storms, fires, and other unfortunate circumstances. Paradoxically, one stipulation of the laws regulating this industry was a restriction on where it could invest. Bank stock was among its few legitimate outlets, and one by-product of the demise of the Second Bank of the United States was a rise in bank holdings by insurance firms and, in turn, a rise in the number of banks that were established to act as vehicles for insurance investment.

The 1830s explosion in prosperity, however, was not without its darker side. By 1836 the new flood of currency had stimulated such a burst of land speculation in the West that Jackson was finally forced to promulgate an edict declaring that all land must be paid for in specie. But the pronouncement was too little, too late. The flood had seeped into almost all aspects of the economy, and in the following year it became clear that land development and hundreds of other enterprises had been built not on gold but on unredeemable paper, causing the economy to come crashing down.

4

Americans, it has been said, have always traded in futures. The Pilgrims traded the known problems of the old world on the off chance that the unknown problems on the coast of Massachusetts would be more conducive to creating a City of God. The Revolutionists traded the security of their colonial status on the off chance that the insecurity of independence would be more amenable to their political and economic development, and in the nineteenth century more and more Americans began to trade their current prosperity on the off chance that investments in new ventures would increase that prosperity in the future.

Serving as both the ticket to and expression of that faith in the future were the notes of the nation's banks. The gold in these banks was much less in amount than the face value of circulating notes. The men who managed the banks, however, counted on the fact that such bills would stimulate the development of the nation's natural wealth, which would, in turn and in time, bring into the country, either through foreign trade or investment, the very specie that would give the notes their expressed value. If such a system suggests a kind of legerdemain, a willing suspension of disbelief and a wishful faith in the future, few would argue that it was an ill-conceived idea, particularly for a young country poor in gold and rich in other resources.

In Boston in 1836, such faith seemed particularly well founded. Between the rocking masts at its waterfront to the trails of steam on its western horizon, its citizens and its energies were poised to stride into tomorrow.

Chapter 2

Founding the Warren Bank
(1836)

As merchant interests throughout the nation anticipated a significant banking upheaval in 1836, when the federal charter of the Second Bank of the United States expired, a flurry of petitions for new state bank charters appeared in several state legislatures. In Massachusetts, one such petition began with these words:

> The undersigned, citizens of Boston, respectfully represent that in their opinion the wants of the mercantile community in this city require a considerable increase of Bank Capital therein; that they are many of them stockholders in the Warren Insurance Company and in the Fishing Insurance Company, institutions now incorporated under the authority of the Commonwealth.

After reciting the legal requirements governing investment of insurance capital in Massachusetts, the petitioners closed with the following request:

> Your petitioners therefore pray, that for the promotion of the public convenience, and for the purpose of affording the said Insurance Companies the legal means of investing a portion of their capital, they may be incorporated for the purpose of establishing a Bank, in the city of Boston, to be called the "Warren Bank" . . . and with a Capital Stock of Five Hundred Thousand dollars.

This petition was submitted to the state legislature in February 1836, and within two months the Warren Bank charter was granted. Hardly a year later this new bank adopted the name Shawmut. Thus began the 150-year history of the Shawmut Bank of Boston, N.A., and the Shawmut Corporation.

When the subscribers for the stock of the Warren Bank gathered for their first meeting on May 6, 1836, they elected the full complement of twelve directors allowed by state law:

William Bramhall	John Gardner
Gardner Brewer	Jairus B. Lincoln
John D. Bridge	Benjamin T. Reed
Nathaniel Dana	Josiah Reed
John L. Dimmock	Aaron Rice
Albert Fearing	Horace Scudder

These men were leading proponents of the new bank and most of their signatures appear on the petition to the legislature for its bank charter. Why these men formed the Shawmut Bank (as the Warren Bank) and how they came together, is a matter of interest. Describing the typical organizers of new banks, an American economist in the next generation wryly observed, "It has come to be a proverb that banks never originate with those who have money to lend, but with those who wish to borrow money." The Shawmut founders seem to be the exception proving the rule. Unlike typical bank promoters, these men apparently did have money to lend. Many who signed the Warren Bank petition were not only stockholders but directors of the two insurance companies, and by state law insurance companies were limited in the types of investments they could make.

Stock in Massachusetts state banks was the only legally authorized investment for fully one-third of all insurance capital in the Commonwealth. Provisions in the law allowed the remaining two-thirds of that capital to be invested in real estate mortgages and on pledges of bank stock (presumably meaning loans secured by bank stock), but the extent of insurance capital that had to be invested in bank stock must have created pressures in that market.

These pressures were particularly felt by the Warren Insurance Company and the Fishing Insurance Company, according to the petition for the Warren Bank charter. The petitioners asserted that, "it has been found extremely difficult, not to say impracticable to invest satisfactorily even the one-third part of the capital stock [of the insurance companies] in the manner required by law." In addition, they identified the recent "increase of insurance capital, made necessary by the unexampled prosperity of commerce" as another factor prompting their petition for a new bank charter.

Who were these Boston citizens who petitioned for and organized the Warren Bank? The petition attracted forty-three signatures, including twenty-four individuals and nineteen firms. Four were directors of the Fishing Insurance Company, and no fewer than eight were directors of the Warren Insurance Company. Although these two insurance companies were the only ones named in the text of the petition, among the signers were directors of at least four others, representing an additional $900,000 of Boston's insurance capital.

This obvious common interest in insurance matters was just one of the many ties linking the petitioners for the bank charter. They also shared many commercial and political connections. Most of their businesses were concentrated on Central Wharf or nearby Long Wharf at the heart of the old Boston waterfront. Seventeen of them were commission merchants, and seven others were merchants in West Indies goods — together more than half the total number of petitioners. Among the remaining nineteen were the two insurance company presidents, two dry goods merchants, two importers, two weighers, one sea captain, one stationer, one crockery merchant, one lumber merchant, one pump and block manufacturer, one druggist, and the proprietor of the *Boston Commercial Gazette*. Four counselors-at-law, including Warren Insurance Company solicitor Theophilus Parsons, completed the group. Many of the Warren Bank petitioners also shared interests in Whig Party politics. Two men who would take a leading role in organizing the Warren Bank, John L. Dimmock and Benjamin Tyler Reed, were both successful Whig candidates in the 1834 campaign for the Massachusetts legislature. Whig politics that fall seemed to fuse the group of men who would become Shawmut directors. A campaign group called the Whig Young Men of Boston was organized one month before the election in 1834 to support the Dimmock and Reed candidacies. This group included William Bramhall, Gardner

Brewer, John D. Bridge, Albert Fearing, and John Gardner, all rising merchants in their early thirties. Bramhall, Brewer, and Bridge signed the petition for the Warren Bank charter.

Gathering signatures for the bank charter petition was only one preliminary step on the path to establishing the Warren Bank. The petition had to be shepherded through the Massachusetts legislative process. Only one petition had been granted in the previous two years, but suddenly the legislature was more receptive to such requests, and on April 8, 1836, the Warren Bank charter was approved. Endorsed by the Council Chamber one day later, it officially authorized the incorporators to proceed with the organization of the bank.

"Edward D. Peters, John L. Dimmock, and Aaron Rice, their associates and successors, are hereby made a corporation by the name of 'the President, Directors, and Company of the Warren Bank' to be established in the city of Boston." Thus read the new charter. But more than just a document is needed to bring a bank to life. Next, the three incorporators had to find subscribers for the bank stock who would contribute the $500,000 capital needed to commence operations. While the legislature had allowed an increase of only $50,000 in the banking capital in the whole state during the prior two years, its new receptivity resulted in the authorizing of $3,350,000 new banking capital in Boston alone, and this put competitive pressures on the incorporators seeking to attract the necessary stock subscribers.

Under such conditions, the character and standing of the men sponsoring a new venture counted heavily. Peters, Dimmock, and Rice, all Boston merchants who had come from out of town, were well respected, and they filled their subscription list of five thousand shares within a period of three weeks. Other banks of similar size starting up that spring took months longer to attain the same response.

As early as April 28, 1836, the incorporators could run the following advertisement in the Boston newspapers:

WARREN BANK. Subscribers to the Stock of the Warren Bank are notified to meet at the Exchange Coffee House on FRIDAY, the 6th of May, at 3½ o'clock P.M., to accept the Act of Incorporation, choose Directors, and transact any other business that may properly come before them.

Edw. D. Peters ⎫ persons named in
John L. Dimmock ⎬ the Act of
Aaron Rice ⎭ Incorporation

As the date of this first organizational meeting, May 6 has taken on a special meaning at Shawmut Bank. Years later it would become the date designated for the actual reorganization of the Bank's relationship to its present holding company and corporate parent.

The hour of the meeting, "3½ o'clock P.M.," reveals something of the habits of the day. Each morning the Boston merchant would walk from home to the head of State Street, where he would stop in the central lobby of City Hall (now the Old State House) to get his mail from his private post office box or from the delivery window of the post office, which opened on the lobby. From the lobby, he would usually go to the basement, where in the merchants' reading room he could glance over the newspapers or examine the latest handwritten entries in one or more of the seven large books that kept up-to-date general news, port and shipping news, names of important visitors — everything, in short, to bring the merchant abreast of the day.

Next the merchant would go down State Street to his counting room on Central Wharf, or elsewhere on the waterfront. There he stayed until noon, when he retraced his way up State Street to "go on 'Change" — that weekday gathering of top-hatted men on the State Street sidewalk from Kilby to Congress, during the hours of twelve to two.

At two o'clock the crowds on 'Change thinned as the merchants went to dinner at home (if they lived nearby, as most of them did) or at the Exchange Coffee House or other hostelry. After dinner they returned to the counting room again, to end their business day at any time from three-thirty on.

So the time of "3½ o'clock," named for the meeting of May 6, was admirably suited both to the schedule of the Exchange Coffee House and the customs of the day. At "3½ o'clock," dinner was over, the banks and the Custom House were closed, and the business day was just about done. The group of Warren Bank stockholders assembled at the Coffee House, relaxed and unhurried in that familiar, comfortable setting, and with Theophilus Parsons guiding the legal steps, accepted the act of incorporation, ordered bylaws prepared, and elected the first directors.

At that time the law stipulated that no bank could have less than five directors, nor more than twelve. In the Exchange Coffee House on that May afternoon, the stockholders elected the full quota. Edward D. Peters, busy just then in the Maine "land fever," and necessarily absent from the city at times, felt he could not undertake the regular attendance then needed from the directors on the "discount days" each Monday and Thursday, when applications for loans were reviewed and acted upon. But the other two incorporators, John L. Dimmock and Aaron Rice, agreed to serve as members of that founding group of twelve, listed at the beginning of this chapter.

Although Dimmock had taken the lead in creating the Warren Bank, when the newly elected directors first met to organize the enterprise, they elected Benjamin Tyler Reed as their president. Reed was well known to many of them as a fellow director of the Warren Insurance Company, Central Wharf merchant, and Dimmock's Whig colleague in the 1835 legislature. More important, he was a man with strong banking experience, having already served on the board of the Tremont Bank, and this background made him a reasonable and commendable choice. Apparently the only college man on the Warren Bank board, Reed had graduated from Harvard in 1821 with such illustrious classmates as Ralph Waldo Emerson, Josiah Quincy, John Lowell Gardner, and George Washington Adams, eldest son of John Quincy Adams.

Prominent relatives were of some benefit to Benjamin T. Reed's early development. Born about 1801 in Marblehead, he bore the same name as his sea captain grandfather and shipowning father, who was recorded as employer of seventy-five seamen in 1813. Reed's mother was the niece of William Gray, one of the leading Salem and Boston shipping magnates of his day and first president of the State Bank in Boston. After college, Reed had gained invaluable business training in Gray's Boston counting room. There, according to his *Boston Globe* obituary, Reed "obtained that excellent knowledge of mercantile affairs which distinguished him through life." Meanwhile, his father's sister had married into the noted Hooper family of Marblehead. At family gatherings Reed probably met his aunt's niece, Elizabeth T. Hooper, whom he married in 1825, four years out of Harvard. This drew Reed even more closely into a family of remarkable banking acumen. His bride's father was president of the Marblehead Bank, and her brothers assumed important positions in several Boston banks. One brother, Samuel Hooper, achieved early prominence in banking and on several insurance company boards, was frequently Reed's partner in later business ventures. He went on to serve in the United States Congress, where he chaired the House Banking and Currency Committee at the time it formulated the Civil War–era legislation, creating the national banking system that survives to this day.

In the year of Reed's marriage, William Gray died, so Reed joined with William Ropes to form the merchant firm Ropes, Reed and Company, setting up shop at 27 Central Wharf. The new firm engaged largely in commerce and navigation, carrying on an extensive trade with Russia and other countries. But Benjamin T. Reed was too vigorous to be merely one member of a partnership: he spent three years with Ropes and then in 1828 went into business for himself at 45 Central Wharf. Soon Reed had extended his commerce to include the Pacific and the East Indies. Perhaps the business interests of Ropes and Reed had gone separate ways (although the obituary suggests the firm continued for many years), but their friendship apparently remained strong.

Reed's business interests began to burgeon into several different fields in the late 1820s. In 1828 he became a member of the board of the Columbian Insurance Company, where he remained a director until 1832. He gained first-hand banking exposure when he was elected a director of the Manufacturers and Mechanics Bank in 1830, at the time it assumed the name Tremont Bank. Reed's father died in 1829, leaving an estate of over $30,000, which may well have made him an attractive addition to any board. His family ties to the Hoopers no doubt helped, too. At any rate, Reed's interests in banking intensified, and in 1831 he was among the original stockholders of the Mercantile Bank, which became the Granite Bank in 1833.

Reed's political activities during the 1834 Whig campaign and his resulting service in the 1835 Massachusetts legislature have been noted already. That year he was, of course, one of the original directors of the Warren Insurance Company, which played such a prominent role in creating the Warren Bank. At the May 6, 1836, organizational meeting of the Warren Bank, Reed was elected its first president. In addition, he was busy completing preparations for establishment of the Eastern Railroad Company, which would be formally organized on May 10 in Salem. Within weeks, he was elected its first treasurer, a position deemed most important at the time since the railroad president merely presided over board meetings.

Some men might have been overburdened by assuming the responsibilities of treasurer of a new railroad and president of a new bank, but Benjamin Tyler Reed was not such a man. Young, alert, and impressive, he seemed to thrive on the duties, and was without doubt the most vigorous and versatile member of the Bank's founding group. As his later career would demonstrate, Reed was a visionary in his day. He spent the next several years quickly establishing both new enterprises and guiding them through the disastrous financial times of their early years.

Chapter 3

The Reed, Gardner, and Fearing Years
(1836–1854)

WHEN Benjamin T. Reed accepted the presidency of Warren Bank at the May 6, 1836, meeting of stock subscribers, he confronted a formidable array of tasks. Little more than the framework for the bank had actually been established, and several problems waited to be resolved before the Warren could even open its doors to the public. Among the most immediate problems were the selection of a location for the banking rooms and the hiring of staff members. Furthermore, the national economic picture was uncertain, and Reed would have to work hard to build a firm foundation for the Bank to assure its future success.

One major step was the choice of a cashier — in those days the only bank officer whose position required a bond regulated by Massachusetts law. By mid-July the Boston papers carried the announcement that Thomas Drown had been selected cashier by the Warren Bank. Just twenty-eight years old, Drown already had seven years experience in banking, having served as the Atlantic Bank bookkeeper since 1829.

Cashier Drown took up his duties on August 1, 1836, when he began organizing a staff and gathering the supplies required by the Bank. Temporary quarters were found at 16 State Street, facing the Old State House, which then served as Boston's City Hall and Post Office, and just across the way from the Warren Insurance Company at 13 State Street. Reed and Dimmock, the Warren Insurance Company president, had already made arrangements for permanent quarters at the corner of State Street and Merchants' Row, however, and the Bank moved into these later in the year.

By the time October arrived, the month designated by state law for the annual meeting of all banking corporations, the preliminary details had been met, and all that remained was for the capital to be paid in by the stock subscribers. The first annual meeting was held at the 16 State Street office on October 3, 1836, and the next Tuesday, October 6, was determined as the day when the capital stock was due. Massachusetts required that half of the authorized capital be paid in the form of specie, the gold and silver coins of the day, and remain deposited in the vaults of the bank, primarily serving as a reserve against the banknotes the bank would soon issue. So long as half the authorized capital was paid in the form of specie, a bank did not have to receive the full total. Nonetheless, Warren's stockholders did pay in the full amount of $500,000 capital at this first call, making Warren the first bank of its size to commence business that year with its capital fully paid in. From the start, a conservative approach to the business of banking guided the conduct of the Warren directors. This fundamental soundness served Warren well in the coming months.

When the Warren Bank opened its doors to the public, it joined a well-established fraternity of Boston banks. At the beginning of 1836, twenty-eight banks were active in the business community and six other newcomers were competing with the Warren Bank, each trying to carve a niche for itself in the commercial affairs of the active port. Warren Bank's ties to the insurance company of the same name strongly suggests its early interests were closely linked to the seafaring trade and the needs of the commission merchants lining Boston's busy wharves.

Boston's position as the primary port of New England was firmly established by other developments in the transportation industry, particularly by the development of the railroads. As Warren Bank president Benjamin Tyler Reed was also treasurer of the newly established Eastern Railroad, his first duties for that company included supervising the construction and track laying of the road from East Boston to Salem. Undoubtedly, the Eastern Railroad was a major early customer of the Warren Bank.

Eighteen thirty-six was an eventful year and the Warren Bank quickly took a modest, but sound, position in the banking arena of the day. Wherever its customers came from, and no matter how the Warren Bank positioned itself, it had to fit into the existing banking structure. A major feature of this structure was the Suffolk Bank System, the origins of which were noted in Chapter 1.

According to this system all out-of-town notes, which had once been redeemable only at the issuing bank, could now be redeemed at one central location, the Suffolk Bank in the city of Boston. To implement this service, the Suffolk Bank arranged to have each New England bank maintain a deposit with it or another Boston bank that would act as a redemption agent for the outlying bank. Any bank that balked at this arrangement faced the prospect of Suffolk clerks arriving with a large hoard of its notes, all taken out of circulation in Boston. Before long, most every bank in New England arranged to maintain deposits for redemption purposes in one of the Boston banks. This local and relatively easy redemption in Boston increased the value each note commanded in the market, reducing to a minimum note discounts, which were figured on the cost an individual would incur if he desired to take a note back to the issuing bank. Thus, where 4 percent had once been considered a fair norm, after the Suffolk System took root, discounts soon dropped to mere fractions of a single percentage point. This system gave New England bank notes a relatively sure value in the region, and a reputation that made them attractive throughout the country.

The new Warren Bank enjoyed the advantages of the Suffolk System from the time it opened for business. Within a few years, its statements suggest, the bank was serving as an agent for outlying banks and holding large deposits from them, carried on its books as "due to other banks." Meanwhile, its notes were met with the high regard of any sound bank participating in the Suffolk System.

Bank note issue was the grist of the banking industry during this period. Unlike the modern practice of depositing money in the account of the borrower when extending a loan, early nineteenth-century bankers issued a stack of bank notes in the amount of the loan to the borrower. These bank notes were then spent by the borrower and circulated until they eventually were redeemed at the issuing bank or through the Suffolk System. Demand-deposit accounts subject to checks remained to be discovered by future bankers and merchants. Reserve requirements imposed by law were rudimentary at best and laxly enforced, so the impact of the Suffolk System's redemption operation was the only real limit on any bank's note issue. It was an effective limit though, because the Suffolk Bank kept a close watch on the statements of the various participating banks, and steps it took with regard to any one bank's notes had a dramatic impact on their acceptability.

In this atmosphere of hundreds of state banks issuing thousands of bank notes, a stable bank's paramount concern was to maintain a distinct identity so its notes would not suffer from confusion with the notes of weaker banks. When the Warren Bank began its operations, it was named after the Warren Insurance Company, which in turn honored General Joseph Warren, a prominent colonial Boston doctor and patriot who died in the Battle of Bunker Hill. Two other banks had the same Warren name, including one in Warren, Rhode Island, which was in poor shape in early 1837 and finally suspended operations in May of that year. It was no surprise, then, when Reed's Warren Bank petitioned the Massachusetts legislature for a new name in April 1837, to create an identity distinct from this failing bank. The directors selected Shawmut as the new name, an inspired choice.

In early colonial times, Shawmut was an Indian name associated with the Boston peninsula. Historians posited that it meant "land accessible by water" and "land with living fountains." Either could be applied to the Boston peninsula, which had a good natural harbor and several fresh water springs. The name "Shawmut" had fallen into disuse in the immediate Boston area, but several ships sailing out of Salem were so christened, suggesting that President Reed may have proposed it. Another possibility stems from a popular George Bancroft history of Boston that appeared in 1834, renewing Bostonian interest in the colonial heritage. Whether Reed proposed the new name or merely accepted it, he took the name to heart. In 1843 when the Eastern Railroad imported a massive new engine from England, the largest in the railroad at the time, Reed named it "Shawmut." By July 1837, the Warren Bank stockholders con-

firmed the name change to Shawmut, and Cashier Drown immediately published official notice of the change. The new name
drew instant attention in business circles, for that very day this
advertisement appeared:

SHAWMUT BANK

Checks on the Shawmut and other banks, printed in the hand-
somest style, can be had at this office at the shortest notice or
at Henry P. Lewis, 22 Congress Street, upstairs.

The Warren Bank founders did not dispassionately abandon
their original name. In designing the new Shawmut Bank notes,
they included an engraved view of State Street depicting the
business sign of the Warren Insurance Company. Also appearing on the banknote was an Indian — a forerunner of today's
renowned logo — and a second engraving portraying the Boston harbor with Central Wharf clearly visible. These engravings
on the Shawmut banknotes graphically displayed the marine
and insurance company origins of the Bank's founders.

The baptism of the Shawmut Bank took place just as the
country was plunged into the Panic of 1837, the longest and
most devastating depression of the nineteenth century. It was
truly a baptism of fire. The crash shattered the rosy appearance
of 1836, which had generated so much optimism. As that year
ended, prices were rising and financial stringency increased.
Indications that trouble lay ahead can be seen in the February
10, 1837, New York food riots. In late March Boston received
news that a New Orleans cotton brokerage had recently failed.
As corresponding failures quickly followed among New York
merchants, a Boston newspaper expressed the prevalent concern: "How far these stoppages will affect our Boston merchants
is not at present known, but considerable gloom and anxiety
pervades the whole community." Boston counted 168 business
failures in six months while New York suffered 250 within sixty
days.

As fears took hold about the risks involved in lending and
the ability of any firm to repay, specie took on a premium value,
and the notes of all businesses, including banks, suffered. Interest rates on even the best commercial paper, payable in three
to six months, jumped from a prevailing 15 percent annual
rate to the 30 percent level by April. The financial crisis was

in full swing by early May, and the number of failures caused a rash of concern about the advisability of banks doing business with these merchants. When one New York bank actually failed, a resulting run on specie held by other New York banks removed more than a million dollars in specie in two days. These banks were forced to suspend redeeming their notes for specie on May 10, 1837. News of the suspension reached Boston the next day, and to preserve their own specie, Boston bankers decided that evening to follow suit the next morning, May 12.

Circumstances surrounding the decision by Boston bankers to suspend specie payments were dramatic. On the very evening of May 11, 1837, several men arrived from New York bearing notes and drafts which they intended to present for specie the next morning; their presence made the danger of losing specie to New York City, or other trading centers, a harsh reality. So, at the meeting at which the bankers decided to suspend specie payments, they also appointed a committee of seven to address the problems of operating without specie transactions. On Saturday, May 14, this committee recommended that the various banks join together in an ad hoc organization called the Associated Banks of Boston, a novel and brilliant effort to maintain public confidence in the banking system. Each Associated Banks member would accept the bank notes of all other members and the group would strive to prevent excessive issue of bank notes and bank credit.

All but one of the thirty-five Boston-area banks participated in the Associated Banks of Boston, and Shawmut's own Thomas Drown gained the distinction of being named clerk to the group's Board of Commissioners, which included one director or cashier from each member bank. As clerk, Drown was the man who signed every public statement issued by the Associated Banks, and the statistics about the state and condition of the Boston banks compiled by this group, and published over Drown's signature, have been credited with easing the difficulties that otherwise would have been caused by the suspension of specie payment. Businesses were able to continue operating, bank notes continued to circulate, and the weekly examinations by the Associated Banks shored up public confidence.

Shawmut managed to survive this period of dismal economic conditions, but it was a struggle. The earliest known statement of the condition of the Bank is the annual report to the secretary of the Commonwealth, dated October 1, 1837. Shawmut had been in operation almost one year and reported assets totalling $889,533.

The banking crisis fomented by the Panic of 1837 became acute by the winter months of 1838. The secretary of the Commonwealth found it necessary to call for a special report on the condition of all Massachusetts banks as of February 10, 1838. The devastating severity of the crisis is apparent in Shawmut's own report, which indicates a shrinkage of 25 percent in the assets in just four months. Assets amounted to only $660,000, barely enough to keep the Bank operating so that it could cover its expenses and pay a modest dividend. Every aspect of the Bank's operation was at a minimal level. Bank notes, the lifeblood for banks of the day, stood at only $47,554, indicating that things were indeed very quiet at Shawmut's 72 State Street office.

Despite the efforts of the Associated Banks of Boston, state legislators felt the public would be better served by a state banking commission, so one was established in April 1838 to supervise the banks in Massachusetts. Its reports to the state legislature reveal fascinating glimpses into contemporary banking practices and Shawmut's own stature. The 1840 report, for instance, discloses that only thirteen Boston banks were engaged in discounting commercial paper payable in Massachusetts outside the city of Boston. Shawmut was one of these, and its schedule of exchange rates indicates it was also actively discounting paper payable in the cities of New York, Philadelphia, and Baltimore. Already in a league above the purely local Boston banks, Shawmut had an extensive banking business in the Northeast.

As the conditions of 1837 settled into a long term depression, one that lingered for more than six years, their toll on businesses throughout the nation was severe. Massachusetts did not escape, nor did its banks: in 1844, only 103 Massachusetts banks survived of the 126 in operation when the panic began.

By 1843 business reached such a standstill that demand for money dropped to a new low. Several banks seriously considered surrendering their charters because the return on their stockholders' invested capital was so anemic. Despite the difficulties of these times, Shawmut forged ahead. It was one of the weaker Boston banks to survive this trying period, as both its stock prices and dividend rates seem to indicate, but survival alone was quite an accomplishment for such a new bank when three of the other six begun in 1836 closed before the end of 1839. Through it all, Shawmut remained capitalized at $500,000 and managed to maintain a solid record of dividend payments. Only a single semiannual dividend payment was missed, in April 1840, during a period when every third bank in the city folded, and of the twenty-four Boston banks that did survive, seven missed two or more dividends.

In this prevailing gloom, Shawmut experienced several internal changes, including attrition in the number of its directors. Josiah Reed died during 1840, and two other directors, Gardner Brewer and Horace Scudder, resigned to pursue other interests in 1843, leaving only eight of the original twelve founding directors on the board. At this time, only one man was elected as a replacement. He was William Whitney, who served until 1849.

The difficulties of the Panic of 1837 obviously made it trying to carry on a new banking business, but the individual directors also suffered in their personal business ventures. One of them, Nathaniel Dana, served nine years on the Shawmut Board of Directors, from its founding until 1845. He was born in Natick, Massachusetts, in 1787 but began his business career in Portland, Maine. His marriage in 1813 to a Boston girl drew him to the city by 1830, although he continued his business house in Portland, too. In Boston, Dana took on a partner, Philip Greely, Jr., a native of Portland, who was more than twenty years his junior. We learn of Dana's financial setbacks in a letter Greely wrote to his Cambridge landlord in July 1837:

> You have no doubt heard before this that owing to the failure of a house in Portland with which my partner Mr. Nath'l Dana was connected, and numerous other losses and disappointments, our house of Dana, Greely, & Co. was obliged some time since to suspend payment, and in this respect shares the fate of many others among us who have been more deserving perhaps of a better lot. We have the satisfaction of knowing that we have been reduced from comparative affluence to poverty and bankruptcy by no fault of ours and shall pay off our debts to the full extent of our means. For myself, I am a young man and it

only remains for me to endeavor to retrieve my fallen fortunes by untiring industry and attention to business and the strictest prudence and economy.

Dana, of course, was not so young and his subsequent fortunes after this setback are difficult to trace. He was fifty years old at the time of the Panic of 1837, he remained on the Shawmut board another eight years, but what he did for the rest of his life is uncertain. Greely continued on a successful career as a West Indies merchant in Boston, eventually heading Dana's old firm at the head of Central Wharf under the new title Greely, Guild and Co. Well connected politically, in 1849 Greely was appointed collector of the Port of Boston by President Zachary Taylor, a position he held through the Taylor and Millard Fillmore administrations but had to relinquish upon the election of Franklin Pierce. Greely had connections to the banking business, too, for his uncle Eliphalet Greely was president of the Casco (Maine) Bank from 1825 through 1855.

Philip Greely also played an interesting role in the transition between Shawmut's first and second cashiers. In 1836, Thomas Drown had been appointed cashier and had served Shawmut well for several years. In July 1844, however, a new man, Stephen G. Davis, came into the Bank as the receiving teller, and Reed apparently found him a more attractive man for the cashier's post. During the next two years Davis earned salary increases, while Drown did not. By October 1846, Davis was assigned the title and duties of cashier, as Drown's successor. When Drown received his final pay on December 10, 1846, Philip Greely served as a go-between on Drown's behalf, obtaining the amount due him, amid indications there may have been hard feelings. Stephen G. Davis then became the focal point of Shawmut activities. Forty-three years old at the time he was elected cashier, Davis held the post for the next thirty years, until he retired in 1876.

With the recession abating, expansion was the order of the day. In 1846 Reed moved the Shawmut Bank across the street to offices in 39 State Street, near the corner of Congress Street and just two doors away from the new Merchants' Exchange Building, which had just recently opened at 53 State. The new quarters were a prime location in the very heart of Boston's financial center.

By 1847, late in the Reed administration, Shawmut reported total assets of $1,212,729. Banknotes outstanding stood at $247,632, almost half the Bank's capital and a tremendous increase over the $47,000 of just a few years before.

Gradual and steady growth in the Massachusetts banking system characterized the rest of the 1840s, a period when bank dividends averaged 5.55 percent per annum. This was slightly below the average for the preceding twenty-five years. Shawmut's own record on dividends was barely below this norm, despite the passed dividend of 1840, for its ten year average from 1836 through 1845 stood at 5.2 percent.

Investor interest in bank stocks revived by 1848 as earnings increased. Bank stocks yielded an average 7.27 percent that year, the highest levels since the War of 1812, and they remained that high through the next several years. Shawmut stock was an even better investment. The Bank increased its own dividend to 7.5 percent in 1848, and beginning in October 1849, Shawmut paid a regular dividend of 4 percent every six months for the next decade.

In the meantime, in the months following the October 1847 annual meeting, Benjamin Tyler Reed resigned as president of the Shawmut Bank and John Gardner was elected to take his place on May 22, 1848. Reed remained devoted to Shawmut affairs and active on the Board of Directors for another twenty-seven years.

1

John Gardner's election to the presidency of Shawmut Bank came in the midst of a minor "rich man's panic" that unsettled the banking world but did not trigger any depression like the one just survived. Political turmoil abroad had created economic problems that were further exacerbated by extensive crop disasters. During the year, stock and commodity prices dropped by 20 to 30 percent, and discount rates in Boston and New York fluctuated between 12 and 18 percent in markets more accustomed to rates in the range of 5 to 8 percent.

When Gardner took the Shawmut helm, this was the nature

of the crisis he faced. During his administration, the Bank began to develop its interests in the burgeoning wool and cotton trade, so prominent in New England at that time. The selection of Gardner was indicative of this interest. Originally a retail hardware dealer, Gardner dropped out of that business when he was elected treasurer of the Hamilton Woolen Company on April 14, 1846. Hamilton Woolen Company financial records, now at the Harvard Business School Manuscript Library, indicate transactions with Shawmut Bank. His involvement in this woolen business continued long after his resignation from Shawmut, and he remained a director of the Hamilton Woolen Company for the rest of his life.

Among the most important occurrences during the Gardner tenure was the discovery of gold in California. Reams have been written about the forty-niners and the lure of gold nuggets, but the impact the new gold had on the financial condition of the nation and on the world's commerce has not been highlighted to the same extent. Almost overnight, gold production skyrocketed from an annual rate of $9 million to $133 million. It was the largest disruption of the world specie base since the Spanish conquest of Latin America 250 years before. The uncertainty fomented by such a massive jolt to the economic foundation of the day prompted Shawmut to continue the conservative approach to banking practices it had pursued under Reed, practices that apparently paid off.

By January 1853, the Bank was stronger than ever. An examination of the Shawmut Bank, taken by the State Banking Commission on February 25, 1853, revealed that loans had broken the million-dollar level and stood at $1,031,578. Total assets had reached $1,226,405; in five years Gardner had restored Shawmut to its hearty self.

2

In early 1853, Gardner resigned the Shawmut presidency. To fill the vacancy, the Shawmut directors elected Albert Fearing to that office in February 1853. Another founding director of the Bank, Fearing had been a successful ship chandler for many years. Among the supplies he carried was cotton duck produced by two separate manufacturers, the Plymouth Cordage Company and the Lawrence Duck Company. Both companies were managed by Fearing, his partner Isaac Thacher, and his cousin David Whiton, who was elected to the Shawmut Board ten years later. Apparently, their cotton duck was of superior quality, for it had earned the silver award at a merchants' exhibition in the Faneuil and Quincy Hall Markets in September 1847. A native and lifelong resident of Hingham, Massachusetts, Fearing was elected to the Warren Insurance Company Board, from 1838 through 1851, serving shortly after helping to organize the Shawmut Bank.

After his election as president of Shawmut, Fearing held the office only twenty months, the shortest term of any chief executive officer in the history of the Bank. During his brief administration, though, he engineered the first capital increase in Shawmut's history. This increase took place during a period called the "bank mania" of 1853 and 1854. Renewed high returns on capital invested in bank stocks had made them an attractive investment once again, and everyone seemed to want to join in. Between 1850 and the spring of 1854, the state legislature received a flood of petitions for new banks and capital increases in existing banks. Among these was a January 18, 1854, petition from Shawmut asking to double its capital to $1 million. Late in March the legislature authorized a $250,000 increase, provided the new capital was fully paid in by May 1, 1855.

The fourteen-month deadline allowed much more time than Shawmut needed to raise the new capital. Well before the limit specified by the legislature, Shawmut directors certified that the entire $250,000 had been received before the end of August 1854. At the end of 1854, the "bank mania" came to an abrupt halt when the State Banking Commission recommended against any further capital increases in Massachusetts. Concerned that the banking industry might overexpand and suffer a fate similar to the debacle brought on by the Panic of 1837, the commissioners had turned off the flow of new capital and clamped down on the existing banks.

No sooner had the capital been received by Shawmut then another minor panic developed in the fall of 1854. Several business firms failed in Boston, while banks throughout the Midwest suffered similar fates. Banks in New England apparently held their own, but the year marked a major transition in banking interests. American shipping began to slip for the first time in its history. Major storms disrupted the coastal trade and severe losses strained the marine insurance business during the next three years. Many of Boston's marine insurance companies paid out claims totaling more than their actual capital in each of the three years. By this time only John L. Dimmock and Jairus B. Lincoln, among Shawmut's original directors, remained on the board of the Warren Insurance Company. Reed, Bramhall, Rice, and Fearing had all left the Warren board in the years prior to 1854.

Albert Fearing's administration of Shawmut affairs must have been impressive, for it attracted the attention of at least some of his Boston banking peers. On November 9, 1854, he was elected to the board of the new, but more prominent, Webster Bank, at a time when state law did not permit individuals to sit on more than one bank board. Accordingly, Fearing resigned from the Shawmut presidency and Board of Directors. At the time of his departure in 1854, Shawmut was eighteen years old and still very much in the control of the original group who founded the Bank in 1836. All seven directors on the board in 1854 had been members of the original 1836 board.

Just ten days before Fearing was elected to the Webster board, Shawmut held its nineteenth annual meeting on October 31, 1854. Newspapers of the day stated that the Shawmut president had been reelected. Presumably this referred to Fearing, although by November 6, 1854, William Bramhall signed a deed as president of the Shawmut Bank.

Chapter 4

A Changing System
and the Rise of National Banks
William Bramhall (1854–1868)

Late in 1854, at fifty-seven, William Bramhall became Shawmut's fourth president and the last of the original founders to hold the office. A native of Plymouth, Massachusetts, he first appeared in the Boston city directory in 1830, when he was already a commission merchant in partnership with Thomas Howe, under the firm name Bramhall and Howe. The firm dealt in West Indies goods, primarily the brandy trade, and their counting room was at 34 Long Wharf. Common interests drew Bramhall to John L. Dimmock and Benjamin Tyler Reed, and he was one of the organizers of the Whig Young Men of Boston, which successfully supported their candidacies for the Massachusetts legislature in 1834. While Dimmock and Reed were serving in the state legislature in 1835, Bramhall joined them in organizing the Warren Insurance Company and then helped establish Shawmut as the Warren Bank in 1836. He remained a director of the Bank until his death on April 4, 1871.

While serving as a director in the Bank's first decade, Bramhall seems to have concentrated his energies on his own merchant firm, which soon expanded beyond handling West Indies goods to engaging in the coastal trade with a packet line serving the port of City Point, Virginia. Over the years, Bramhall became a prominent ship owner as well.

Bramhall's interest in the Warren Insurance Company

flagged during the financial difficulties of the late 1830s, and he left its board of directors in 1839. But it would not be the end of Bramhall's connection with Boston insurance concerns. In 1853 the Equitable Safety Marine and Fire Insurance Company elected Bramhall to its board, one year before he became president of the Shawmut Bank. Two other insurance companies followed suit by 1856, when Bramhall was also a director of the U.S. Insurance Company and the Alliance Insurance Company (of which future Shawmut director Henry H. Crocker was already a board member). Undoubtedly a successful and attractive businessman, Bramhall also was recruited sometime between 1856 and 1859 by the Robbins Cordage Company to be its treasurer. He accepted the post, and the company subsequently moved its office to Bramhall's 40 State Street location.

In the meantime, Bramhall's two sons had grown up and entered the Boston business world with interesting Shawmut connections. William T. Bramhall worked in the newly thriving leather district at 93 Pearl Street, the very building where John Cummings, Jr., and Company located its Boston sales office in the 1860s. Cummings later became a Shawmut director, succeeding Bramhall as president, and his partner's father was Leonard B. Harrington, destined to serve twenty years on the Shawmut board. These developments on Pearl Street captured the imagination of President Bramhall, and in 1858 he purchased a property there that remained in the family throughout the nineteenth century. His second son, Thomas M. Bramhall, was the Shawmut Bank collection clerk for several years.

The Bramhall family lived on Purchase Street in Boston during the early 1840s, as neighbors of Jairus B. Lincoln, a Shawmut and Warren colleague. Not long after, Bramhall moved his family to suburban Brookline. There his daughter Elizabeth met and eventually married a young lieutenant, James P. Stearns, who was the son of a Brookline neighbor. Two years after their 1865 wedding, Stearns began a life-long career at the Bank. Beginning as a clerk, he moved on to become cashier, vice president, and finally president. Ultimately he was elected Shawmut's first chairman of the board.

As Back Bay was being filled and developed, Bramhall was one of the prominent merchants who purchased a townhouse along the extended Beacon Street, as was Benjamin T. Reed. Bramhall's interest in the sea also continued, and he chartered his ships out to various parties throughout the time he was Shawmut president. During this period he was one of the two Shawmut founders to increase substantially his stockholdings in the Bank. When he died in 1871, the inventory of his estate included 250 shares of Shawmut Bank, valued at $31,000. In one final note reflecting how Bramhall's later life centered around the Shawmut Bank, both his 1865 will and 1866 codicil were witnessed by Shawmut Bank employees.

During Bramhall's administration many striking changes transformed Shawmut Bank. Among these were the establishment of the Boston Clearing House, a new understanding of the role of deposits, a shift to the use of checks in lieu of bank notes as a means of payment, and the founding of the Bank of Mutual Redemption. It was also during this period that the control of Shawmut passed from the original group of founders to a new group of directors with ties to the shoe and leather industry. Finally, there was the coming of the Civil War and the National Banking System, which Shawmut joined late in 1864.

1

Almost a year after Bramhall began serving as the Shawmut president, plans for a major improvement in Boston banking practices began to be formalized. The rising use of checks drawn against demand deposits, which businessmen found easier and more convenient to use than bank notes, was straining the ability of the banks to process the daily volume of these checks. In September 1855 Boston bankers began to organize the Boston Clearing House to provide a more efficient and safer method of clearing the checks. Up to this point, each bank in the city had sent messengers to all the banks on which it had received checks during the day. These messengers would collect the proceeds of checks and return with specie settlements to their own bank. Even with most of the fifty Boston banks concentrated within a two-block stretch of State Street, the process had proved tedious and an invitation to dangerous thugs. The new clearing operation allowed each bank to send two messengers to one central location with checks drawn on all participating banks. There they could meet messengers of other banks at an appointed hour, deliver all the checks, and tally up a balance sheet indicating whether their bank owed money to the pool or would receive money from it. The clearing house arrangement eliminated the multitude of separate settlements between banks and allowed the messengers to settle with the pool in a single specie transaction later in the day. Thus simplified, the check-clearing process became more attractive than ever for the banks and their customers.

Twenty-nine city banks, including Shawmut, joined the Boston Clearing House on its first day of operation, March 29, 1856, when $2.7 million in checks were exchanged, though only $384,000 in specie had to change hands. In developing this clearing house, Boston bankers could claim no ingenuity. New York City bankers had adopted a clearing house system three years earlier, itself based on the London operation that was formalized early in the century. Even so, as other cities began to establish similar clearing house associations, the Boston Clearing House was noted as a model operation.

The interest in clearing houses, and the need to establish them, coincided with the growing shift from bank note loans to demand deposit loans. Though deposit banking had existed for a long time, it was used almost exclusively as a safeguarding service for which the depositor paid a service fee. Bankers quickly recognized, however, that specie held by a bank on deposit could be as useful to them as the specie paid in as capital. Soon banks began competing for these deposits, service fees disappeared, and interest payments eventually were offered for the use of the specie left on deposit.

Almost two decades after the Suffolk System began, and seven years after Shawmut Bank opened its doors under the Warren name, an obscure provision in an 1843 Massachusetts banking statute further contributed to changing the existing banking conditions. The 1843 act provided that banks in Massachusetts could pay out only their own bank notes and not the notes issued by any other bank. Excluded from paying out other bank notes, Massachusetts banks faced various alternatives. The most popular alternative remained the Suffolk System, which amounted to processing the bank notes in much the same manner we think of clearing checks. As similar as these two functions may seem to us today, bankers did not then readily recognize the similarities.

One reason this similarity was not recognized immediately was that the Suffolk Bank acted as a middleman in the note-redemption service. Its back-room nature obscured the actual process, as bankers simply delivered their daily intake of bank notes to the Suffolk and received credit for the deposits. Later in the day, they were charged for the notes issued by them that came in during the deliveries. Few bankers actually considered the process or the extent of the cost their non-interest-bearing deposits were subsidizing. Of course, complete understanding was further hampered by the fact that many New England banks did not deal directly with the Suffolk but relied on agent Boston banks to act for them. The size of deposits Shawmut held for other banks suggests strongly that it was one such agent bank.

Eventually some country banks realized how much their compensating balances contributed to the profitability of Suffolk's redemption activities. These banks were disturbed by the inordinate power that Suffolk, because of its monopoly position in note-redemption activities, wielded over the reputations of every bank in New England. By 1854 a number of disconcerted New England bankers contemplated a mutual bank to perform these same redemption functions so that they could share the actual costs and profits rather than pay Suffolk for the service.

This group of country bankers presented the Massachusetts legislature with a petition for just such a mutual bank, and the charter was granted in 1855, a special exception to the legislature's stringent new policy against issuing bank charters that year. The charter contained several special provisions designed to suit the unusual needs of a banker's bank.

When the Bank of Mutual Redemption opened on August 23, 1858, its participating banks withdrew their deposits from Suffolk and expected to redeem their outstanding notes through the new bank. Instead, Suffolk greeted the new competitor by treating it just like any other bank. Suffolk demanded the same compensating balance maintained by other Boston banks acting as redemption agents, and it refused to deal with the new bank until it established such a balance.

Never as successful as hoped, the Redemption Bank could not attract the number of participating banks originally anticipated. This was due in part to the shaky, controversial start it got. But it was also caused by the prevailing shift to the use of checks as a means of payment and the virtual disappearance of state bank notes from circulation, when the federal tax provisions of the National Banking Act of 1865 took effect.

2

While these changes were transforming the business of banking and, by extension, the nature of Shawmut's business, the Bank was also undergoing several internal changes. In the eighteen years before Bramhall was elected president, only one man who was not a founder joined the Board of Directors. This was William Whitney, who served from 1843 to 1849. In the decade between 1854 and 1864, however, eight new men were elected to the board, although no more than nine men ever served at any one time.

The first new man to join Shawmut's board during Bramhall's administration was Barnabas Davis, who was elected at the annual meeting on October 31, 1854, and served thirty-one years until his death on December 16, 1885. As an honorary member of the Boston Marine Society, Davis was known to Lincoln, Dimmock, and Bramhall. He was also well known to Horace Scudder, his lifelong business partner and an in-law ever since both men married sisters in the Bacon family, a well-to-do Barnstable family related through marriage to the Crockers and Sears. This extended family group would produce several future Shawmut directors. Included among these was Henry H. Crocker, a first cousin of the Scudder and Davis wives, who was elected to the Shawmut board in 1856. Only thirty-six at the time, Crocker was already Bramhall's colleague on the Alliance Insurance Company's board of directors. He served on the Shawmut board only two years before his business interests took him to New York City.

Upon Crocker's departure, the Shawmut stockholders elected two new directors in 1858, George Johnson and John C. Abbott. Little is known of Johnson, but Abbott would emerge as a crucial figure in Shawmut's midcentury transition. A leather dealer and insurance company executive, Abbott was the first Shawmut director connected to the leather industry and undoubtedly was responsible for attracting to Shawmut three other leather dealers who, with him, would dominate the Bank's affairs through the 1870s and 1880s. The three dealers were the future president, John C. Cummings, Jr., his partner's father, Leonard B. Harrington, and Silas Potter.

Listed in the 1855 Boston city directory as a commission merchant on Central Wharf, John C. Abbott first came to attention as a prospective director when he was elected to the Warren Insurance Company board at least three years before the death of John L. Dimmock in 1856. There he served together with Dimmock and Jairus B. Lincoln. Furthermore, in 1854 he was a town selectman in Brookline, where Bramhall then lived. In 1857 Abbott married Lincoln's cousin and the following year was elected to the Shawmut board at the annual October meeting. By then, Abbott was also president of the Shoe and Leather Dealer's Fire and Marine Insurance Company, which included Harrington and Potter on its board.

Shawmut had grown as a state bank by the time these new directors took their seats on the board. Its business was widespread, reaching far beyond the bounds of New England even at that early date, before the Civil War. The annual report of 1859 of the Massachusetts Banking Commission provides an intriguing glimpse at the extent of Shawmut's transactions. For years the commission had fought against the banking practice of assessing exchange charges on paper payable at a distant location. By 1859 Shawmut was one of the banks making no such charge against paper payable in New York City, Philadelphia, or Baltimore, even though other banks persisted in the practice. Shawmut's schedule of exchange charges reflects activity in discounting paper from a variety of cities throughout the Mississippi River Valley, including Mobile, New Orleans, Louisville, St. Louis, Cincinnati, and Chicago, as well as cities in New England and New York State.

The examination of Shawmut that year took place on February 10, 1859, and showed that total assets were above $1.5

million. Deposits were approximately half the $750,000 capital figure, standing at $375,000, and the circulation amounted to almost $135,000. In view of today's operating costs, an interesting figure provided in the examination is the annual expense of the Bank, which then amounted to $13,000, including rent and salaries.

In the months following the outbreak of Civil War hostilities, unprecedented financing demands called for new vigor from bank directors. At Shawmut, the new vigor was expressed in the addition of three new directors at the November 1861 annual meeting. This election of D. Waldo Salisbury, Prentiss W. Scudder, and Edward Wyman marked the largest single transformation of the board before the 1898 mergers. Wyman served for seven years and appears to have been an active member of important committees. Salisbury and Scudder both represented strong ties to the original board. Salisbury was a first cousin of the former president, John Gardner, who remained yet another two years on the board, and Scudder was a nephew of the late Horace Scudder. Salisbury and Scudder were active directors on the Shawmut board, serving together almost thirty years, into the 1890s.

As 1861 drew to a close, with the Civil War creating financial demands on a scale unknown before, nine directors were guiding the twenty-five-year-old Shawmut Bank. Four were founders, three were new directors, and the other two had three and seven years experience respectively on the Shawmut board. The nine directors were the following:

Name	Age	Year elected
President William Bramhall	64	1836
Former President Benjamin T. Reed	60	1836
Former President John Gardner	58	1836
Jairus B. Lincoln	69	1836
Barnabas Davis	54	1854
John C. Abbott	50	1858
D. Waldo Salisbury	44	1861
Prentiss W. Scudder	33	1861
Edward Wyman	n.a.	1861

One final change in the Shawmut board came in the midst of the war, when John Gardner resigned during 1863 at age sixty. To his Shawmut vacancy, the stockholders elected David

Whiton, a second cousin of a former director and president, Albert Fearing. These directors governed Shawmut Bank affairs through the difficult years of the Civil War, which were the last years of Shawmut's existence as a state bank chartered under the laws of Massachusetts.

3

The United States Government's pressing needs to finance the Civil War produced by far the most significant changes in the structure of the banking system. The existing state bank system was inadequate to meet these needs, and Abraham Lincoln's secretary of the Treasury, Salmon P. Chase, recognized the difficulties early. When the Lincoln administration took office in 1861, the United States was served by 1642 state banks. In place of this cumbersome and uncertain system, Chase proposed a system of national banks that would operate under federal law and that could issue national bank notes to serve as United States currency. No such national currency then existed.

Suggested as a means to reform the currency circulating in the nation, Chase's proposal also included several features designed to simplify efforts of the U.S. Government to finance the Civil War. Critics bitterly opposed Chase's plan, and Congress would not even consider it until several other financing arrangements had been attempted and proved unsatisfactory.

Political expediency governed the early fund-raising measures adopted by Congress. When the conflict began, it was perceived as likely to be of short duration, but by the summer of 1861, the continuing need for new sources of funds had become apparent, and Congress passed the first of several acts authorizing the government to borrow by issuing notes.

The first act, dated July 17, 1861, authorized "greenback" demand notes and interest-bearing three-year notes, which had attached coupons for the interest payable every six months. A flood of new paper currency soon followed. Government figures indicate the total volume of state bank notes in circulation was $130 million when the first $60 million worth of greenbacks were issued. Before the Civil War ended, over $450 million in greenbacks alone were issued. As Congress became aware of the impact its issues created on the money market and circulation, it tried to correct earlier flaws by tinkering with the terms and conditions in later note issues. Only after trying all of these funding measures, and learning several monetary policy lessons along the way, was Congress willing to experiment with the more drastic changes in the U.S. banking system proposed by Secretary Chase.

By 1863 further need for currency reform was clear, and Congress became receptive to the more stable and orderly national currency promised by Chase's proposal for a national banking system. On February 25, 1863, it signed into law a national banking act, the first of three relating to national banks enacted during the remaining two years of the war. The National Bank Act of 1863 had an impact more far-reaching than any relating merely to war financing. Its national bank note features remained in effect for seventy years, but even more important, the act established the system of national banks that serves to this day as the primary commercial banking institution in the United States.

As originally passed, the National Bank Act of 1863 did not immediately transform the banking system. Although dozens of new banks were organized under the act, most state banks were reluctant to convert. One reason for their reluctance was that they had to give up their established names for anonymous numbers (e.g., the Third National Bank of Hometown), and this meant forgoing the recognition and reputation those names had built up over the years. To make national status more attractive, Congress adopted a revised version of the act on June 3, 1864.

In most respects, the National Bank Act of 1864 was similar to its predecessor, but some important corrections were added, including one provision allowing state banks to retain their familiar names simply by adding the word *National* rather than by requiring the shift to an anonymous number. Whether this provision prompted Shawmut to change its own status is unknown. What is known is that by the fall of 1864 the Bank directors had determined to put the question of whether Shawmut should become a national bank to the stockholders at their regular annual meeting, held that year on November 3. Formal notice of the outcome of this vote was published in the *Boston Daily Advertiser* on November 10, 1864, and three weeks later, on November 22, 1864, the Comptroller of the Currency in Washington, D.C., issued Shawmut's federal charter. This charter was Certificate 582, indicating that Shawmut National Bank was among the first 35 percent of the almost 1650 national banks existing at the end of 1865 to join the system.

Shawmut was not the only Boston bank to change its status at this time. Most of the city's state banks had taken up the same question of conversion at their own annual meetings, and on the first business day of 1865, January 2, ten, including Shawmut, had formally completed the transition and opened for business as national banks.

As far as Shawmut's customers were concerned, the transformation was merely a legal formality. Outwardly, the only difference was the addition of the word *National* to the Shawmut name. Shawmut National Bank remained the same size, performed the same services, had the same personnel, and was located in the same State Street offices. Internally, however, several adjustments had occurred.

Part of Shawmut's necessary reorganization process entailed rendering a report of its final financial position as a state bank to Massachusetts authorities. Naturally enough, Shawmut had to cease issuing state bank notes, and the directors also voted to distribute the undivided state bank profits in a special 10 percent dividend approved in March 1865. The state bank commissioners then published official notices on June 28 announcing "the issue of circulating notes of the Shawmut Bank was discontinued on February 7, 1865, and the liability of said bank to redeem its outstanding circulation will cease February 7, 1868." To its credit, Shawmut National continued to honor these state bank notes long after the period required by law.

Shawmut's own records from this period are woefully inadequate to support even a guess about the number of accounts it handled, so it is virtually impossible to draw any comparison between the Shawmut National Bank and other Boston banks. However, the numbers that do survive suggest that Shawmut was rising both in prestige and profitability. Although Shawmut was one of the youngest, perhaps weakest, of the Boston banks to survive the rigors of the 1837–1843 depression, it had grown steadily from that time onward. Improved business conditions and returns on banking investment had encouraged the formation of a number of new banks during the 1850s, including several larger than Shawmut, but by 1868 Shawmut National Bank was one of the senior institutions among the forty-eight national banks in Boston. And its increasing prominence in the local community was greatly enhanced by Bramhall's successor as president, John C. Cummings, Jr.

Chapter 5

The Introduction of Modern Banking
John C. Cummings, Jr. (1868–1898)

W̲HEN John C. Cummings, Jr., became president of the Shawmut National Bank on January 11, 1868, America was still a relatively homogeneous and underdeveloped country. Seventy-five percent of its 38 million people lived on farms or in tiny isolated towns. Most goods were still made at home, and businesses were still family affairs run by owners who could be counted on to remember employees' birthdays, marriages, and anniversaries. Time was measured by sunlight and seasons, the demands of the farm; space by the distance a good horse could travel in one day.

When John Cummings relinquished office in 1898, the population was 78 million, 10 million of whom were foreign born. The rural population had dropped to 60 percent. Railroads, America's first big business, linked village to village in a vast network of steel threads. Time was measured by factory shifts, by the fulfillment of production goals, while Chicago was now only a day's distance from New York by steam engine. In thirty years of industrialization, big business and the railroads had altered the shape of America.

Even in retrospect it is difficult to assess the impact of such change. Certainly, the blessings were not unalloyed. Large corporations, presided over by faceless tycoons whose major concern was to extend their corporate empires, had come to dominate America's work scene. The triumph of these enterprises

had been accompanied by social, economic, and political upheavals that left bloodstains on the landscape. Immigrants and
uprooted farm workers, surging into urban centers to fill the
labor needs of new industrial enterprises, often found themselves inhabitants of jerry-built company towns or urban ghettos
where six to ten in a room was not uncommon. Sordid conditions, low wages, and long hours of labor gave rise to violent
strikes, which extended from Marshall, Texas, to Homestead,
Pennsylvania; from Buffalo, New York, to Haymarket Square,
Chicago.

There was, however, another side of the story. If mass industrialization brought poverty to some and fortunes to others
(by 1891, 1 percent of the population owned more wealth than
the other 99 percent), to millions of others it brought a new
standard of living. Indoor plumbing, sewing machines, coal
stoves, gaslight, and ready-made clothes were only a few of
the amenities that provided new leisure time, some of which
went into the development of cultural opportunities previously
untapped.

In Boston, the Museum of Fine Arts moved into new and
elaborate facilities to the south of Copley Square (1876); Major
Henry Lee Higginson founded the Boston Symphony Orchestra
(1881); the Public Library designed by McKim, with murals
by Puvis de Chavannes, opened its doors to the public (1895).
While Italians and Irish crowded ever more thickly into the
North and South Ends, from whence the latter fought their
way to control of City Hall, the "older" families retained control
of the middle ground. Along State Street the great investment
houses — Lee, Higginson and Company, Estabrook and Company, Kidder, Peabody and Company — gained new stature,
trading now in the investments and securities of businesses,
with national scope. The merchant princes, who had begun
their ascent in the 1820s, 1830s, and 1840s in shipping, textiles,
and leather, solidified their gains, moving into railroads, mining,
and utilities in the 1870s, 1880s, and 1890s. And in the evening
they strode home across the Common and the Garden to the
brownstone and brick mansions they had built on the sunny
side of Commonwealth Avenue and the water side of Beacon
Street; while across the avenue on the shady, or land, side,
the second in command gave heartfelt thanks that they had

snatched the few remaining lots in the now completed Back Bay.

Within this tumultuous context, the business of banking also changed. It was a change that can be roughly divided into two periods. During the first period, 1867–1879, financing was still dominated by the effects of the Civil War. Industry was beginning to grow and the importance of deposits and investments was beginning to be recognized, but major financial attention had to be paid to reducing inflation and the stock of money in circulation, both of which had increased dramatically during the war. The years immediately following the war were largely ones of transition, in which the problems of the past remained to be settled while the way to the future was prepared.

During the second period, 1879–1897, the modern era truly began. These seventeen years saw the essential completion of continental settlement, a population growth of approximately 2 percent per year, and the consolidation of vast railroad empires, which linked not only all the major cities but the intervening small towns as well. As a consequence of these conditions, markets multiplied and manufacturing surged ahead, with the gross national product topping $17.3 billion by 1897. Keeping pace with this growth was the rapid expansion of the commercial banking system, which experienced not only a large increase in the number of institutions but a substantial change in their operations.

To keep abreast of these changes became the charge of John C. Cummings, Jr. Few men could have been better suited to the task. Under his guidance the Shawmut became a "modern" bank: its operating procedures were streamlined and rendered more efficient; its capital swelled from $750,000 to $1 million; its deposits expanded greatly and became primary income earners; loans grew in size and diversity; investments became a major consideration, with railroad securities becoming an important part of the portfolio; and the influence of the Bank, founded to serve local needs, spread beyond the narrow confines of New England. Finally, in response to its increasing size and status in the community, the Bank moved out of its tiny headquarters on State Street to a new and much more substantial home in the heart of the business district at 60 Congress Street. In 1865 Shawmut had been twenty-fourth in size of assets among Boston's forty-two banks. Thirty-three years later it stood fifth among the city's sixty banks. That this growth should have been accomplished in the face of two major recessions, several business cycle constrictions, a fire that decimated much of the downtown area, and within a context of general social, political, and economic unrest stands as a testament to the leadership of John Cummings.

1

In light of Cummings's accomplishments, it is unfortunate that credit cannot be given to the person who brought him into the Bank. What is clear is that, although in May 1866 he was not even listed as a stockholder, by January 1867 he had been elected a director. In all probability, what happened was that several members of the Shawmut board, particularly John C. Abbott, an executive in the leather business, anticipating Jairus B. Lincoln's retirement and aware of Cummings's reputation as a local businessman and community leader, recruited him to replace Lincoln. That the choice was a good one soon became clear. Despite his status as a novice director, Cummings was almost immediately elected to the Bank's all-important Exchange Committee. This committee, which had the power "to discount and purchase bills, notes and other evidences of debt, and to buy and sell bills of exchange" and which was essential to the operation of the Bank, consisted of only three members — the president, the cashier, and a single director. That Cummings should have been chosen was indicative of the high regard in which his peers held him. Even more illustrative of that regard was their choice of Cummings to act as president pro tem, in December 1867, when ill health prevented William Bramhall from fulfilling his presidential duties.

If such a rapid acquisition of responsibilities is unusual, given the character and imposing presence of Cummings, it was not surprising. Born October 12, 1812, in Woburn, Massachusetts, at eight he was already demonstrating an extraordinary capacity for work — at least legend has it that by this time he was already gainfully employed, driving a team of horses to bring bricks from Medford to Woburn. Asked to confirm this story many years later, an old-timer curtly responded, "Well, I don't know how old he was but he couldn't reach the tailgate of the wagon."

By the time he was a teen-ager, Cummings had given up brick transportation for helping his father in the tanning and currying business. Nor were either of these jobs dictated by family need, for the Cummings were apparently well off. His great grandfather was a pioneer in developing the leather industry for New England, and by 1775 he had sufficient capital to purchase a large tract of land in Woburn, which operated as a working farm well into the twentieth century. Leather, however, remained the mainstay of the Cummings family, and the business started by the great grandfather continued through four generations. The Shawmut president's father, in fact, merited inclusion in *Who Was Who in America* for his contribution in promoting "chaise leather," a component used in carriages and a lucrative outlet for a material previously used almost exclusively for shoes and boots.

Despite the family's financial and social position — Cummings's mother was Maria Richardson, a member of "one of the most numerous, prominent, and well-connected families of New England" — young John did not go on to Harvard but was, in the words of Francis Amasa Walker, president of Massachusetts Institute of Technology, "largely self-taught." A college education was not, of course, considered essential at that time, except for ministers. It was probably quite clear that young Cummings needed no polish of Latin or Greek to develop his natural talents. Thus, after attending Warren Academy in Woburn and later a school in South Reading, he moved into his father's business, assuming total direction of it in 1847, when the elder Cummings retired. Under the son's direction the enterprise expanded, and in 1852 two partners were added — John B. Alley and Charles Choate — and the name changed to Alley, Choate and Cummings. In 1857 Alley retired, but the partnership went on with the two remaining members.

The next several years were ones of great importance for the leather industry. In 1860 the invention of the power machine for pegging boots and shoes and for sewing soles vastly increased production capacity. At the same time the advent of the Civil War, which brought orders for army footgear, as well as the steady growth of the population, increased consumer demand. By the mid-1860s the leather industry had become a central element in the New England economy. Responding to this expansion, Cummings once again reorganized his business, creating two new companies — John Cummings and Company and Harrington and Cummings. Both did well, contributing to the continued increase in leather production, which had reached an aggregate value of $9,984,467 in 1870. The role of Cummings in this development, as well as the respect of his peers for his talents, is perhaps best attested by the fact that in 1869 he was elected vice president of the newly formed New England Shoe and Leather Manufacturers Association — which became Boston's first Board of Trade — and in 1872 became its president.

Cummings's management abilities were quite clear by the time he became a member of the Shawmut board. Further enhancing his attractiveness for a bank dedicated to community service was his role as a leader of that community. As early as 1862, Cummings had become active in the affairs of the Boston Society of Natural History, for which he promoted the idea of instituting lecture courses for the benefit of local school teachers. The plan, which was promptly implemented, met with considerable success and continued for a number of years with "all expenses generously paid by Mr. Cummings."

It was also during the 1860s that Cummings's association with Massachusetts Institute of Technology began. Although he was not one of the original incorporators of that institution when it was approved by the Massachusetts legislature, on April 10, 1861, he did join the governing body in 1866, serving in that capacity until 1872, when he became the third treasurer of the institute. As a member of the corporation he proved himself anything but passive, taking a leadership role in fending off the overtures of Harvard when it attempted to absorb the school. As treasurer he was also active, transcending the role generally associated with the office, and M.I.T. historians unanimously credit him with saving the school during a severe financial crisis between 1875 and 1878, when "he pledged his personal credit for large sums" owed the school's creditors.

In 1889 Cummings relinquished the post of treasurer and again became a member of the corporation, which he served until his death in 1898. In the meantime, in 1889, and in recognition of his services, "Mr. Cummings's name was applied in perpetuity to the laboratories of Mining, Engineering and Metallurgy." At this time the president of the institute remarked that it was "to his courageous acceptance of responsibility and his strong financial support, the friends of the school largely attribute its rescue from pecuniary embarrassment and its subsequent remarkable development." It might also be noted here that during his lifetime Cummings gave two substantial gifts of $10,000 each to M.I.T. But this is to anticipate. In 1867 it was simply clear that here was a man of considerable business acumen, vision, and determination — qualities which the Shawmut directors recognized and promptly put to good use.

2

When Cummings officially assumed the presidency of Shawmut on January 11, 1868, the shadow of theft by a teller, Bryant Henry, still hung over the Bank. In late 1867 Henry had absconded with $52,000, no small sum considering the Bank's total capitalization was $750,000, and the event had prostrated William Bramhall. Cummings, however, very wisely did not allow the incident to overshadow his own administration, and when Henry was discovered in Havana, the new president quickly and calmly supported a settlement worked out by two directors, Benjamin T. Reed and D. Waldo Salisbury. Even more important, when in March the bank examiner discovered that the entire affair had reduced the Bank's earnings from the previous September high of $69,000 to $22,000, Cummings still advised that the Bank pay its regular 5 percent semiannual dividend. Although the dividend exceeded earnings by 65 percent, the decision underscored Cummings's faith in the future and his belief that past events were best forgotten in the interest of more immediate business. And certainly there was more immediate and important business to which the new president gave priority, for his first year in office proved a whirlwind of activities.

One of his first projects was the implementation of new personnel policies. In 1868 the national economy was still reeling from the effects of an 1866 money panic and continuing inflation. In response to this situation, the new administration began to modernize its payroll practices. By the end of January 1868, it had already voted to pay officers on a monthly basis instead of the quarterly basis that had prevailed for thirty years. Further, Cummings authorized the cashier to advance to any employee "who might desire it, an amount not to exceed one half month's salary." These actions were characteristic of Cummings's sensitivity to staff needs, and one of his chief contributions to the Bank would be the enlightened attitude he brought to personnel practices and his unwillingness to be fettered by tradition when current events demanded a new approach. It was an unwillingness dramatically underscored in 1885, when the Shawmut became the first national bank to employ a woman. Her name was Jane Draper and she was appointed to a responsible post as assistant head teller.

If Cummings was farsighted in his personnel policies, he was equally farsighted in his economic policies. Although the Henry affair had caused the Bank's earnings to drop precipitously, nevertheless, Cummings had supported a continuation of the regular dividend, and the courageous move soon proved justified. The next six months saw net earnings rise to $47,800, nicely covering the 5 percent dividend declared in October 1868. The dividend decision, however, was by no means the only one of that first year in which the new president demonstrated his financial courage and his grasp of economic realities.

In November 1868, eleven months after he took office and even before the economy began to rally from the effects of the war, Cummings sponsored an increase in the Bank's capital from $750,000 to $1 million, and further stipulated that the stockholders should pay the full extent of their commitment by January 1869. The deadline proved fortuitous. In the fall of 1869, Jay Gould's strategy to corner the gold market came to a head. By 11:25 A.M. on September 24, a day thereafter referred to as "Black Friday," Gould had succeeded in driving the price of gold up to $164 an ounce. At this point the government ordered the Treasury to sell $5 million in gold, and in fifteen minutes the market dived twenty-five points. Brokers tumbled over each other in attempts to get out, and the ensuing panic reverberated across the country. After Black Friday, the Shawmut's capital stock would have been difficult to sell had it not already been distributed, and the impact of the Gould maneuver on the Bank was minimal.

Keeping pace with the financial expansion initiated by Cummings during his first year was the physical expansion of the Bank. In 1868 the Shawmut was still a second-floor bank at 20 State Street, where it had been located for ten years. A month after the announcement of the capital increase, the board authorized the president to lease stores at 62 through 68 Water Street, and plans were laid to occupy the new headquarters in January 1870.

Thus, within the first twelve months of John Cummings's administration, the payroll had been modernized, the capital increased, and the stage set for the Bank to move into new and much larger rooms. Characteristically and appropriately, it was Benjamin T. Reed, Shawmut's first president, who quickly appreciated the new man's value, and in June 1869, he introduced a motion to increase Cummings's salary from $1500 to $2500 a year.

3

As the new decade opened, the future looked bright. The Shawmut was now a million-dollar enterprise and clearly anticipated continued growth. Evidence of this anticipation was shown in actions taken by the Board of Directors on January 17, 1870. At this meeting the board authorized Cummings to sign additional leases for 60, 70, 72, 74, and 76 Water Street, virtually giving the Shawmut the entire block east of Congress Street. It also allocated funds for repairs and alterations to the property, including a new entryway at 50 Congress Street, and it was this address that the Bank gave for its next annual meeting in January 1871.

Throughout 1870, 1871, and 1872, earnings were stable, rising to $60,503 in September 1872, while the semiannual dividend remained at a consistent 5 percent. Then within twelve months two catastrophic events occurred — a fire and a financial

panic. Either might have scuttled a less secure institution. That
neither did was a tribute both to past and current management.

The first of these events, the Boston Fire, began at 7:00 P.M.,
Saturday, November 9, 1872, in a four-story building at 87
Summer Street. A combination of delay in sounding the alarm,
an epidemic that had sorely reduced the number of fire horses
available to haul equipment, and a severely inadequate water
supply hampered efforts to control the blaze. Panic and looting
broke out, martial law was declared, and finally, in a last ditch
effort to stem the flames, Mayor William Gaston (father of a
later Shawmut president) ordered the demolition of several
buildings to serve as a fire break. By Sunday evening the fire
was over, but sixty-five acres of downtown Boston had been
devastated and 776 buildings, including 50 Congress Street,
lay in wreckage. An eyewitness account, related in April 1875
to the cashier of the Shawmut, gave the details:

> On Sunday morning, November 10, at about 4 A.M., the building
> occupied by the Bank at 50 Congress Street was burned and
> all the fixtures, furniture, and stationery blanks outside the vault
> were totally destroyed. All the Bank's notes, cash, and securities
> in the vault were saved in good order, nothing being injured.
> When the building was thoroughly on fire, it was blown up by
> the Fire Department. On the 11th, after a labor of six hours,
> the vault was entered by moving a portion of the top and all
> the most valuable property of the Bank together with a number
> of trunks and boxes belonging to depositors, which had been
> placed there for safekeeping, were removed to the new quarters,
> number 43 State. On the 13th the remaining property of the
> bank and of its depositors was taken from the vault and removed
> to that place.

An amusing insight on the values of contemporary bankers
is provided by the minutes of the Board of Directors, November
14, 1872. Herein no mention of the fire or the move to 43
State Street is made, but the business of discounting notes is
simply recorded as usual. It is not until March 3, 1873, when
the board voted to contribute $500 to a new merchants' ex-
change and newsroom, which outside sources reveal was devastated by the fire, that there is any hint that the disaster affected
business. And it is not until May 26, 1873, when the minutes
show that "the President in connection with the Massachusetts

Bank is authorized to employ George Snell, Esq., architect, to prepare and present plans for a fireproof building to be erected on the land leased to the Shawmut National Bank by George Howe at the corner of Congress and Water," that there is any concrete evidence that the Bank was affected at all.

But there was, for example, the matter of a new building, and on August 25, 1873, the minutes show a vote to authorize Cummings "to cause to be erected . . . at the corner of Congress and Water Streets . . . a building suitable for banking and other purposes . . . provided that the cost of the building to the Shawmut National Bank shall not exceed $25,000 excepting only as it is understood that in addition to the $25,000 . . . the bank shall pay one-half of the expenses of constructing six extra safe vaults, said amounting to $1800."

Further, on September 24, 1874, the following year, the minutes show a "charge to Profit and Loss of $25,000 being loss on Bank interest in building on Congress and Water Street destroyed by fire 9–10 November 1872, also loss by same fire on fixtures and furniture $2500."

But if the fire brought losses, they were nowhere as profound as those resulting from the next cataclysmic event — the Panic of 1873. Three months after the conflagration, the Bank showed six-month earnings of $62,774, a record for the ten-year period, and a regular-dividend payment of 5 percent. Six months later, however, on September 22, earnings dropped to $56,811, and more important, the dividend was cut to 4 percent. Thereafter, steady attrition followed, with earnings slipping to $41,325 by March 1875. These were not fire-engendered losses but rather the consequences of a severe recession that began September 18, 1873, and did not relinquish its hold on the economy until well into 1878.

Historians today still argue the genesis of the 1873 financial crisis. Some attribute it to the inelasticity of the currency, which was one by-product of the national banking acts; others feel that the overall atmosphere of laissez-faire government and the excesses of business and corruption in high places were the major causes. Certainly the previous years had seen excessive speculation and overbuilding, particularly of the railroads — a situation of which Cornelius Vanderbilt himself remarked, "Building railroads from nowhere to nowhere at public expense is not legitimate business." Whatever the cause, the precipitating incident was the failure of the nation's largest investment firm, Jay Cooke and Company, which in a tight-money economy had nonetheless floated a $100 million bond issue in support of the Northern Pacific Railroad. On September 18 a million-dollar note came due. Cooke could not pay and closed its doors. The New York Stock Exchange promptly collapsed, and for the first time in that institution's history, trading was suspended, not to be resumed for ten days. In the course of the next five years thousands of businesses failed, including one-fifth of the rail investment in the country, which were sold under foreclosure.

It was during this trying period in the country's financial history, when one might assume that a bank president had enough to occupy his attention, that Cummings decided to run for the state legislature. In 1873–1874 he was the representative of Woburn in the legislature. In 1876 he was elected senator from his own district, carrying every town within its boundaries. In both houses he served as chairman of the Committee on Banks and Banking, and as a senator he also worked on the Treasury Committee. That such an opportunity to see and understand the overall banking situation helped Cummings in the formulation of wise policies for the Shawmut is undoubtedly true, but it is also true that his constantly growing reputation as an astute banker made him the appropriate person to select for such a post. In any event, the Shawmut, unlike many of its sister banks, rode out the depression without severe damage, although there is no question that the 1870s, which has been noted as a decade of "disturbance of industry," demanded a full reserve of management skills.

The toll that these economic disturbances took on the Shawmut, and the way that Cummings contrived to minimize that toll, is suggested by the following facts. Between 1873 and 1876 gross earnings for the bank were generally low. In March 1876, however, they surged upwards to a record $162,000 for a single six-month period. This figure, representing 16 percent of the capital, included $85,000 in interest and profits on U.S. government securities. Ironically, at this point the Shawmut lowered its dividend to 3 percent. Such an action might at first seem baffling — after all, why shouldn't shareholders profit from this ostensible windfall? What Cummings perceived, however, was that conditions were still unstable in 1876 and that building reserves against the future was a wiser course than raising dividends. His policy proved well founded. After a brief respite, the economy slipped again. Earnings dropped in 1877 and again in March 1878, when the dividend was reduced to 2.5 percent. The history of these dividends may also be understood to reflect not simply hard times but also the changing value of the currency. By 1875 the cost of goods and services in the country had been deflated to a point that justified congressional passage of the Specie Redemption Act, which went into effect January 1, 1879. In other words, the value of money, pegged once again to specie, was actually greater than a decade earlier, and in terms of purchasing power, a dividend of 3 or even 2.5 percent represented a return not much smaller than the earlier 5 percent.

The latter part of the 1870s also saw heavy write-offs of dubious loans. Specifically, these were $40,000 in September 1876, $65,000 in 1877, and $98,000 in 1878. Some of these, of course, were not the result of immediate problems but were simply loans held over from an earlier time and deliberately not discharged until the promise of recovery was clear. Finally, on January 1, 1879, the country returned de facto to the gold standard, although silver was also considered specie, and a new era began for the economy.

4

In the introduction to this chapter some of the characteristics of the seventeen years between 1879 and 1897 have been identified. The period was a time of considerable expansion, although such expansion was in no way steady or even dependable. As Milton Friedman and Anna Schwartz have pointed out in their excellent and comprehensive *A Monetary History of the United States 1867–1960*, the relative stability and confidence in the economy, which in general characterized the financial world between 1898 and 1914, were still in the future. The challenge for bankers was to anticipate what might happen and to choose from a plethora of uncertain opportunities those that might best serve the interest of their institution for the long run. Again Cummings proved himself a master of such decisions.

Probably the greatest change during this period concerned the role of deposits in relation to the successful operation of a commercial bank. An appreciation of this resource had actually begun in the 1850s, but even after passage of the National Bank Act of 1864, it was still assumed that note issue and discounts were essential to the success of commercial banks. Many state banks had converted to national status to secure national bank notes, and when in 1865 the government imposed a tax on state bank note circulation, still other state banks quickly converted. By 1868, however, it was becoming clear that demand deposits, transferable by check, which could be used as money, presented another alternative to notes. Even so it was not until the 1880s and 1890s that deposits truly began to rise at a significant rate. Contributing to the change was the increased availability of checking facilities and the growth in real income, which prompted more companies and wealthy individuals to substitute deposits for currency. Indications of the growth are demonstrated in figures cited by Friedman and Schwartz, who note that in 1879 "the public held $2 of deposits for every dollar of currency and in the end (1897) they held $4." During this time, then, bankers began to vie with one another for the acquisition of deposit accounts. How successful the Shawmut was in this area can be seen from a few comparative figures. In 1865 the Shawmut had little over $500,000 in deposits. Sixteen years later, in 1881, it had almost four times that amount, $1,987,184. A mere three years later the number had almost doubled again to $3,182,789, and in 1897, the Bank passed $9 million in deposits, a growth of over 1500 percent since 1865.

As deposits grew, the character and size of loans also began to change. In the earliest days, Shawmut had focused its attention on local borrowers and local enterprises. During the 1880s and 1890s it continued to support these firms, providing funds particularly to textile, shoe, leather, wool, and cotton enterprises. It also began to extend loans to companies, the focus of whose enterprises lay far afield. The railroads were one such kind of enterprise. Most of these companies did have Boston offices and their directors were well known to those at the Bank. Indeed, Cummings himself served on the boards of the Boston and Maine, the Boston and Albany, the Concord and Montreal, and the Eastern. To some extent, these lines might be considered local firms; but other lines — even those with executive offices in and around State Street — were essentially western or midwestern concerns. Nevertheless, the Bank proved receptive to their demands, particularly in the late 1880s and 1890s.

The fact is worth noting, if for no other reason than that many other institutions, stung by the poor showing of the railroads between 1873 and 1879, hesitated to renew railroad investments. Cummings, however, had no reservations and in this regard proved more farsighted than many of his colleagues. Among the loans he supported, in addition to those to New England lines, were those to the Kansas City, Fort Scott and Memphis line and the Chicago, Burlington and Quincy line. Not all such investments proved to be without problems. The percentage of those that were good, however, seems to have justified his policies and added not only to the Bank's earnings but also to its status as an institution capable of responding to national and regional concerns.

A third and very important change that occurred during this span of years was the growing emphasis on the Bank's investment portfolio as an income earner. Prior to Cummings's administration, indeed prior to the 1880s, investment securities held by the Bank were primarily those of the U.S. Government and were largely paper that the Bank was required to deposit with the U.S. Treasury, as collateral against the issue of national bank notes. By 1886, however, it was clear that these bonds could also serve as major income-earning investments. Providing a stimulus to this recognition was the appointment of the Shawmut as special depository for U.S. postal funds in February 1884. (Apparently the Shawmut replaced the old Boston National in this role.) Indeed, February 1884 might be considered the beginning of Shawmut's focus on investment funds. At any rate, the bank began that year with $1 million in United States 4.5 percent bonds. By 1886 it was adding railroad bonds to its portfolio. Some of these were acquired as collateral against loans, but others appear to have been purchased outright and paid substantial yields of 5, 6, and 7 percent.

By 1890 the Shawmut's earnings from securities were exceeding its earnings from loans and discounts. By March 1892, they had almost doubled the loan income as shown in the following statement:

Interest from loans		$16,200
Interest from U.S. bonds	$12,500⎤	
Interest from railroad bonds	18,824⎦	31,324
Total Interest		$47,524

The Panic of 1893 was in the making, but as loans decreased, investment income carried the Bank forward.

All of these changes had their effect on the management of the Bank. In 1884, the same year that the Shawmut became a special depository for U.S. postal funds, Cummings's salary as president was raised to $5000; three years later it was raised again to $7000, and on March 20, 1891, the Shawmut Board voted unanimously to make the president's salary $10,000 per year, retroactive to April 1, 1889. Although those moves must be interpreted as a tribute to Cummings's role in promoting Shawmut growth, in a sense they are more important as a reflection of the changing concept of the presidential office itself. In the earlier years, when loans and discount were the chief income earners, the cashier, on whom the responsibility for handling this business largely fell, was unquestionably a pivotal officer. As the Bank expanded, however, and as investments became increasingly important, more and more responsibility fell upon the shoulders of the president himself. Under Cummings the notion of the Bank's president as chief executive officer took hold. It was also during his administration that the need for a vice president arose, and in 1894 James Stearns, who had been appointed cashier in 1876 and who had served the Bank for twenty-six years, was the first person appointed to hold that office. (See Chapter 6.) The move proved fortuitous.

In March 1896, when Cummings was eighty-four, he attended his last board meeting. Thereafter, age and illness kept him confined to his home in Woburn. The fifth president's active period ran from 1868 to 1895 — a total of twenty-eight years. In those years Shawmut's net earnings on a capital of $1 million, totaled $2,634,052 — out of which the stockholders received a total of $1,832,500 on their 10,000 shares. Nor was a single semiannual dividend missed.

The record was remarkable. It was achieved in spite of postwar inflation, of currency agitation, and of tremendous social and economic unrest, including the Populist and Greenback movements, the free silver campaign, the deadly Homestead riots, and the panics of 1873, 1884, and 1893. Furthermore, it was achieved when banking competition increased Boston's commercial banks from forty-two to sixty in number.

Although much of the credit for the Bank's accomplishments must be attributed to the intelligent leadership of Cummings, the role of the board in recognizing and approving his actions cannot be overlooked, and the changes in this body between 1865 and 1895 were important. During Cummings's administration fourteen new directors were elected to the Shawmut board, although, because of retirements, this increased the total membership by only three. Of the fourteen, half had some connection with the leather industry. The first of the new directors were Leonard B. Harrington, Cummings's own business partner, who joined in January 1869, and Silas Potter, whose business was boots and shoes and who succeeded the former president, William Bramhall, upon his death in 1871. During the great Panic of 1873, it was these three of the leather industry — Cummings, Harrington, and Potter — who played a major role in guiding the Shawmut through that troubled time.

Other Shawmut directors with connections to the leather industry were Charles Coburn Bills (1879–1889), a wholesale leather dealer, Moses N. Arnold (1889–1898), a North Abington shoe manufacturer, George Coburn (1889–1903), a boot and shoe manufacturer, Micajah P. Clough (1892–1933), who at the time of joining the Shawmut was associated with Lynn Gas and Electric and the Essex Trust Company but who had at one time been in the shoe business, and Nehemiah W. Rice (1896–1898), an importer of hides.

The remaining appointments — Horatio J. Gilbert (1874–1902), William Bassett (1883–1898), James P. Stearns (1886–1922), William S. Spaulding (1892–1925), and William E. Russell (1896) — represented a variety of interests, including railroads, banking, hardware, sugar refining, and politics. In fact, William E. Russell had been governor of Massachusetts.

In 1897 Cummings suffered a paralyzing stroke, and in July 1898 James P. Stearns was appointed acting president. The next few months were to see a flurry of activity culminating in the merger of Shawmut with nine other Boston banks. Although Cummings could not participate in this merger, it was unquestionably his astute guidance that had placed the Bank in a position to assume the central role in it.

In 1889, at the time of the dedication of the Cummings laboratories at M.I.T., the president of that institution had remarked:

> Mr. Cummings' remarkable disinterest in public life, his severe integrity, combined with great kindliness in personal intercourse, his powerful intellectual grasp, and strong Scotch-American sense, have made him one of the most useful citizens of his native Commonwealth.

It was a tribute that could be applied with equal appropriateness to John C. Cummings's career as Shawmut's fifth president.

Chapter 6

A Time of Mergers

The National Shawmut Bank and the Administration of James P. Stearns

(1898–1907)

I N 1893, five years before John C. Cummings, Jr., officially left the presidency of the Shawmut, he was eighty-one years old. Although nothing in the minutes of the Board of Directors indicates that he was anything but his usual robust self, 1893 had been a year in the history of the United States economy that could easily have shaken a much younger man. Reckless expansion, the continued race among overcapitalized industries to outdo each other, a constantly accelerating production of goods regardless of the country's ability to consume such products, the swallowing of small enterprises by monstrous trusts that avoided restrictions of the 1890 Sherman Antitrust Act with casual unconcern — all these finally culminated in a panic that rivaled that of 1873.

Railroads, including the Erie, the Baltimore and Ohio, Northern Pacific, Union Pacific, Reading, Santa Fe, and 149 others, capsized with a crash that sent shudders through the financial community. Fifteen thousand factories and commercial houses went out of business and 500 banks plunged into bankruptcy. A panic-induced hoarding of gold made heavy inroads on the Treasury. But although Coxey's famous "industrial army" of the unemployed marched on Washington to protest the condition of workers, the captains of industry — the Morgans, the

Vanderbilts, the Rockefellers — went about their business un-
fazed, buying up defunct enterprises, whose demise they had
frequently manipulated.

Throughout this turmoil the Shawmut had remained remarkably steady. It continued to pay dividends of 2.5 percent; its
earnings continued to grow; its surplus was undepleted. Nevertheless, it was a situation calculated to try the nerves of the
most stalwart, and although there is no evidence that the ex-
tremes of 1893 affected John Cummings's health, it is probably
no coincidence that in 1894 the Board of Directors at the Shawmut decided to create the Bank's first vice-presidency. If nothing
else, the move recognized that the increasing complexities of
management justified some sharing of responsibilities. To this
office they appointed James P. Stearns, a man who had been
with the Bank since 1867 and whose rise through the ranks
was only one testament to his many qualifications.

How wide a range of responsibilities Stearns actually assumed
at the moment of his appointment is difficult to determine.
We do know that he presided at the annual meeting in January
1897, that in the summer of 1897 Cummings suffered a paralytic
stroke, and that in January 1898 Stearns again presided at the
annual meeting. Further, in June 1898 the board voted that
from "July 1, 1898, the salary of John Cummings be reduced
to $5,000 per year and the salary of J. P. Stearns, vice president
and acting president, be increased $5,000 making his salary
$12,000." Six months later, when the Shawmut National was
reorganized as the National Shawmut Bank, Stearns became
president of that institution.

The specific date that James P. Stearns assumed the duties
of the Shawmut presidency, however, is of less import than
the fact that he began acting in that role at almost exactly the
time the national economy began to rally. In 1896, following
a vicious national campaign, William McKinley, the choice of
big-business interests, had been elected president of the United
States. It was not McKinley's election so much as the coincidence of other events that sent the country once more on the
path to prosperity.

Much of the presidential campaign had been spent in bitter
wrangling over monetary issues. Since the Bland-Allison Act
of 1878, the Treasury Department had been buying large quan-

tities of silver. The country was in fact on a bimetal standard. Businessmen, charging that this had largely precipitated the 1893 depression, demanded a return to the gold standard. Angrily opposed to this position were Democrats and Populists, who contended that the problem lay in a lack of circulation and that, if the business point of view prevailed, workers would be "crucified on a cross of gold." Just before the election, however, came the discovery of new sources of gold in the Klondike, the invention of a new and much more efficient process of extracting the precious metal from ore, and a banner year in wheat production that coincided with a shortage of wheat in Europe, India, and South America. These events promised to, and indeed did, resolve the problem of scarce money.

However, the first priority of the McKinley administration was not the bimetal standard — circulation had taken care of itself — but the tariff problem, which was resolved by imposing a higher protective tariff than any previous one. Under the changed circumstances, business began to flourish again. Finally stimulating expansion was the explosion of the American battleship *Maine* in Havana Harbor on February 15, 1897, an event that launched the Spanish-American War. Initially the war industries, by providing employment, gave impetus to economic growth. Far more important in the long run were the consequences of the war, which gave the United States control over the Philippines, Puerto Rico, Guam, and Hawaii. By 1898 the country could claim 124,000 square miles that it had not possessed a year earlier and a host of new markets for its products. In the spirit of Teddy Roosevelt's charge up San Juan Hill, business, industry, and financial institutions began to charge toward new peaks of prosperity.

1

For the Shawmut the age would be one of unprecedented expansion. The Bank had always been fortunate in choosing a president suited to the times. In its early days, when establishing a firm foundation was the most important consideration, it was blessed by the guidance of Benjamin T. Reed, John Gardner,

Albert Fearing, and William Bramhall. John C. Cummings, Jr., was a visionary at a time when vision was needed. Stearns in his turn might be more aptly characterized as an enterprising man who was willing to make rapid, bold, and sometimes risky decisions at times when a slow and more cautious approach might have meant simply missing the boat altogether. His contemporary, Andrew Carnegie, remarked, "Europe moves at a snail's pace, the Republic is like an express train rushing by." That Stearns was capable of catching that express is aptly borne out by the record of his achievements at the Shawmut.

The son of a well-to-do Brookline, Massachusetts, family with considerable property holdings in that town, the young Stearns showed his adventurous spirit early. Having graduated from the Boston preparatory school Chauncey Hall, in 1856, he enrolled at Harvard but evidently found the excitement of military service more enticing. A member of the Company K State Militia, he left Harvard at the end of his freshman year to serve the army full-time and was commissioned second lieutenant of Company K, Twenty-second Massachusetts Volunteers, on October 1, 1861. In this role he served at the siege of Yorktown in the spring of 1862 and at the battles of Hanover Court House, Mechanicsville, and Gaines Mill. During this last encounter, he was wounded and taken prisoner to Libby Prison in Richmond, Virginia. Exchanged in July, young Stearns was promoted to first lieutenant but would not see active service at this rank. The wound inflicted at Gaines Mill had not healed, and in September 1862, his left leg was amputated. This handicap does not seem to have daunted Stearns's patriotic fervor, for although he was discharged for disability in February 1863, he promptly joined the Veterans Reserve Corps and served out the rest of the conflict as a first lieutenant at Hartford, then New Haven, and finally at David's Island in New York Harbor.

During this period, and probably while on leave to Brookline, where his family moved in the same social circles as the Bramhalls, he made the acquaintance of Elizabeth Shaw Bramhall, daughter of Shawmut's president, William Bramhall. The two were married in June 1865. A year and a half later, on December 26, 1867, shortly after Bryant T. Henry's departure left a vacancy in the Bank's six man staff, Stearns went to work at Shaw-mut.

If William Bramhall was responsible for getting James P. Stearns his first job at the Shawmut, it was Stearns himself who molded that job into a triumphant career. In March 1868, by which time Bramhall had been succeeded by Cummings, Stearns's employment as collection and discount clerk at a salary of $800 retroactive to his December employment date was con-firmed by the Board of Directors. Eight months later he was given a raise to $1000 and in January was given another $200 per annum. At that time the cashier received $5000 and the paying tellers $2500 each. Stearns's salary was thus proportion-ately large, and one can only assume that it reflected the direc-tors' respect for his services.

In 1870 Stearns was made discount clerk at a salary of $1500 and in 1872 advanced to $1800. A year later he began to act as assistant cashier but was not given a title until the end of January 1876, when the cashier, Stephen G. Davis, then seventy-two and suffering from ill health, resigned after thirty years in office. Stearns moved into the position and also took over the task of transcribing the minutes of the meetings of the Board of Directors. In 1886, at forty-six, Stearns became a Bank director, the first to come from the staff; in 1894 the board created the position of vice president for him. In 1898, in recog-nition of his acting as president, his salary was raised to $12,000, and in November of that year he officially became president of the National Shawmut Bank.

The energies that propelled James P. Stearns through the ranks to the presidency were to be amply demonstrated in his handling of the executive office. Cummings had made the posi-tion the most important in the Bank's hierarchy; Stearns would use that power to reorganize and transform the institution into a major financial house embracing several other banks, with a much larger and more powerful Board of Directors and consid-erable investment in the country's transportation, communica-tions, and utilities industries.

Of all changes that took place under the sixth president, however, certainly the most dramatic was his first action — the reorganization of the Bank in the interest of merging with it nine other Boston banks, the groundwork for which he had laid before he officially became president.

2

The impetus that culminated in the Shawmut mergers in 1898 can be traced to forces in the economy that were coming into place much earlier. The latter decades of the nineteenth century were a time of a great many mergers and consolidations. Although many of them were accomplished by an individual seeking control of a particular industry, this was by no means the only pattern.

In the instance of the Shawmut mergers, the instigator was not the Bank seeking to swallow its competitors but Massachusetts savings banks, which had a large portion of their resources invested in Boston national banks. The problem for these savings banks was that Boston simply had too many national banks. As a consequence, there was too much capital in relation to the commercial needs of the city. Money could be borrowed at a very low rate of interest, which meant that the investor received a limited return on his investment. In addition, representatives of the savings banks contended that a low money market was conducive to extravagant and unnecessary borrowing. Consequently, not only the dividends but also the value of the stocks of many national banks in Boston were threatened. Altogether, the situation was not good for savings banks, which by law were limited in those areas in which they could invest their resources.

Representatives of the savings banks, feeling that the welfare of their depositors demanded that something be done "to recover as nearly as possible the principal invested in the securities of national banks," approached the private investment firm of Kidder, Peabody and Company in 1897. It was the idea of these savings institutions that the investment firm should effect a merger of several of Boston's national banks, consolidating them into a new corporation. The banks selected included some of Boston's oldest: the Boston National (1853), the Columbia National (1822), the Hamilton National (1832), the Howard National (1853), the Market National (1832), the National Bank of North America (1850), the National Eagle (1822), the National Revere (1859), and the North National Bank (1825), not to mention the Shawmut National itself.

Kidder, Peabody and Company was amenable to the idea,

and on September 21, 1898, a formal agreement was signed between the committee representing the savings banks and the investment firm. According to stipulations of the agreement, the savings banks would sell their shares in the aforementioned banks to Kidder, Peabody at twelve dollars above market price. The investment firm would then undertake the liquidation of these corporations and form a new bank for the purpose of taking up part of their business. The successor institution was not named, although a condition of the agreement was that it must have a capital of at least $3 million but not more than $5 million, in contrast to the combined $8,550,000 in the existing banks.

At this point Kidder, Peabody proceeded to the next step which was to form and underwrite a syndicate that would agree to furnish funds to buy up controlling shares in the nine banks and ensure their placement in the successor corporation. By the end of October, twenty-seven underwriters had been found, all but five of whom came from Boston. Of these five, three were Kidder, Peabody affiliates; the other two were the New York City firms of Price McCormick, which underwrote approximately $2.5 million, and J. P. Morgan and Company, which underwrote $1 million. Kidder, Peabody itself provided $3 million. Other Boston participants with large commitments included F. S. Moseley and Company and R. L. Day and Company, both of which contributed $1 million; Lee, Higginson and Company, $750,000; and Brown Brothers and Company, $300,000.

In the meantime, on September 30 Kidder, Peabody sent out notices to all stockholders of the nine banks offering to buy the outstanding shares for twelve dollars above market price. According to other provisions of the program, Kidder, Peabody would continue to buy these shares until it held at least two-thirds, at which point it would withdraw the offer. It would write the president of each bank asking him to hold a stockholders meeting at which liquidation would be put to a vote; it would reorganize an existing bank that would inherit the business of the liquidated institutions; finally, it would carry out liquidation proceedings and settle with the syndicate and savings banks. It was not until all these steps were accomplished that an announcement appeared in the newspapers of October 5, 1898, declaring that a reorganized Shawmut was to be the successor bank.

Exactly why or when the Shawmut was selected for this role is a matter of speculation. Did Stearns approach Kidder, Peabody or did representatives of the investment firm solicit the Bank? Either is possible. Although there were no official notices of the plan until September 29, 1898, when the *Boston Evening Transcript* and the *Boston Daily Advertiser* carried the story of the merger, citing it "as one of the biggest financial deals" of the period, members of the banking community must have been well aware of what was afoot long before that time. Stearns may have even had more information than most, for his son, William Bramhall Stearns, was coincidentally a member of the Kidder, Peabody firm. The younger Stearns was only thirty at the time, and it is doubtful that he had any position of influence. But he might easily have heard office rumors of the proposed consolidation and confided them to his father. The latter, as he demonstrated in some of his later actions for the Bank, was not the sort of person to let an opportunity slide by. It is easy to envision him at a meeting of the Bankers Association letting appropriate persons know that, if such a consolidation were in the offing, Shawmut would be interested. It is not necessary, however, to rely on such a theory to explain the choice. By 1898 Shawmut was the fifth largest bank in the city, and although it was smaller than some of the banks to be liquidated, it had a solid record of having paid 6 percent dividends to its stockholders for the past five years. It was a record not to be matched by any of the merging banks, only two of which had managed to pay 6 percent in 1893 and one of which had paid 2 percent in 1897. According to either scenario, Stearns was obviously a willing participant.

On October 11, 1898, Stearns called a meeting of the Board of Directors at 60 Congress Street, and at this time it was voted that "the directors of this institution recommend to their shareholders the reorganization of this bank under the direction of James P. Stearns into an institution of increased capital to bear as nearly as possible the name of the Shawmut National Bank." Two weeks later on October 25, the stockholders of that institution received a notice:

> Gentlemen: In connection with several of the National Banks of Boston, it is proposed to establish a bank with large capital and paid up surplus, which bank will be practically a reorganization of the present Shawmut National. Such a bank it is believed

will succeed to a substantial part of the business of the liquidating banks and by reason of its resources and connections will be one of the strongest in New England.

The reorganization itself was accomplished by liquidation of the Shawmut National Bank and its prompt rechartering as the National Shawmut Bank with a capital of $3 million and paid-in surplus of $1.5 million. On November 25, 1898, a meeting of the stockholders of Shawmut National was held at 11 A.M. at which time it was voted 177 to 10 that the "Shawmut National Bank be placed in voluntary liquidation." James P. Stearns and Frederic E. Snow were appointed agents of liquidation. Shareholders in the old bank had the right to subscribe to shares in the new institution in proportion of four to five, with the expectation that the proceeds of liquidation would be more than sufficient to pay in full for stock in the new bank.

In the meantime, on November 14, 1898, an association charter for the new National Shawmut was drawn up. According to its stipulation, the board should consist of not less than five or more than twenty-five members. Five came from the old institution: Micajah P. Clough, George M. Coburn, Edward D. Hayden, William S. Spaulding, and, of course, James P. Stearns. Of the twelve new directors, four were presidents of the merging banks: Horatio Newhall, who served the new corporation as secretary, of Columbia National; Alfred S. Woodworth, of National Eagle; Daniel B. Hallet, of Boston National; and Jeremiah Williams, of North National. Three were associated with Kidder, Peabody and Company: Robert Winsor and Frank G. Webster were partners of that firm, and Edmund D. Codman represented it as a lawyer. The eighth director, Henry S. Howe, was an influential figure in a growing firm, AT&T. The ninth, Eben S. Draper was a manufacturer. Finally, Henry L. Higginson and Frederick S. Moseley were both members of prominent investment banking houses participating in the syndicate organized by Kidder, Peabody. The twelfth new director, William A. Gaston, was an attorney with Gaston Snow, which had represented the Shawmut during the merger. On November 16, Charles Dawes, United States Comptroller of the Currency, approved the articles of association and authorized the National Shawmut Bank to commence business on Saturday, November 26, 1898.

During the next few weeks final settlement was made with eight of the nine merging banks. Not all were equally pleased at the prospect of the merger, but only the Howard Bank presented complex problems. Not only did it protest the merger, but it also overstated its asset value in reports to the Comptroller of the Currency. A series of events then followed in which the Howard officers turned over deposit accounts and note discounts to the National Bank of the Republic, the Howard Bank president suffered a nervous collapse, and the bank teetered at the edge of receivership. Only a loan from the National Bank of the Republic prevented that event. Eventually the Howard was acquired by Shawmut, although its assets were not what the syndicate had originally been led to expect.

The impact of the reorganization of the Shawmut National into the National Shawmut cannot be overestimated. Although technically this was a new bank with its own charter, continuity had been provided by the presence of the five directors of the Shawmut National on the board of the new institution. That Stearns was elected president underscored this continuity, as did the fact that the balance of deposits, as they stood on the books of the Shawmut National at the close of the banking day, November 25, were automatically transferred to the new National Shawmut. To the man on the street, the change undoubtedly appeared to be simply one of a shifted adjective. To those in the banking community, the change was more complex. Though the new institution was smaller than the sum of its merged parts, it had a capital stock of $3 million, which meant thirty thousand shares at $100 apiece. The capacity of the Bank to do a great deal more business is implicit in these figures. The kind and quality of that business were of major importance for the entire financial community.

3

The rebirth of the Shawmut National as National Shawmut was only the first step in what was to be almost a full decade of unimpeded growth for the Bank. Aiding in the expansion of the newly organized institution was a combination of several factors, including the growing national prosperity and the adventurous spirit of Stearns. He seems to have had an ability to perceive an opportunity as soon as it arose and the courage to take advantage of that opportunity, often to the dismay of the bank examiners, a Mr. Neal and a Mr. Evans. (Periodically, these gray eminences appeared at the Shawmut, and periodically they reported to the U.S. Comptroller of the Currency that the Bank was overstepping itself.) Further contributing to expansion was the high proportion of persons who either served or had served as directors, trustees, or officers of other large investment institutions. In addition to those company affiliations mentioned above, for example, Frank G. Webster was a director of the Boston Safe Deposit and Trust Company, and Robert Winsor was a director of the First National Bank of Boston. Later this system of interlocks among key money institutions gave rise to the allegation that the nation's economy was controlled by a small, tightly inbred, and all-powerful group. In the meantime, the advantages for those who had connections with such a group were undeniable.

Under Cummings, the Shawmut National had begun to understand the importance of deposits as a source of funds for its other banking activities and to appreciate the earnings potential of its investments in bonds. It had begun to depend more on these bonds than its traditional loans and discounts for its earnings. Under Stearns the full potential of that shift was realized. Contributing to this end was Stearns's appointment of Moseley, Winsor, and later Howe to the Executive Committee of the Board of Directors of the Bank, on which they served with him, Gaston, and Clough. The function of the committee was largely to approve loans and investments, and it is hardly surprising under the circumstances that many of the interests of the Shawmut paralleled those of major investment houses, particularly Kidder, Peabody, or reflected interests of members of the new board.

One of the more interesting of Shawmut's involvements during these years perfectly illustrates how such interlocking concerns worked. In 1899 Kidder, Peabody became one of the first major houses to develop a national and international market for AT&T bonds, negotiating an issue of collateral trust bonds for $15 million between 1899 and 1902. Kidder, Peabody also helped in the reorganization of the Erie Telephone and

Telegraph Company, which not only "extended AT&T facilities but, more important, virtually eliminated its most powerful rival, the Telephone, Telegraph and Cable Company . . . that had sought to use the Erie Company to challenge the Bell's dominance of the telephone business." By 1904, Kidder, Peabody was serving as the principal Boston banker of AT&T and in 1905, together with Baring Brothers, won a bid for $25 million of AT&T bonds, $5 million of which Kidder, Peabody sold privately.

In light of this, it is instructive to note the March 27, 1902, statement of Shawmut earnings, which shows, under "extraordinary profits," returns from Erie Telephone and Telegraph (underwriting syndicate), $1421; from Erie Telephone and Telegraph, 5 percent note $1000; from AT&T, $7500. Furthermore, on August 17, 1905, a letter from the Comptroller of the Currency, dated August 15 and commenting on the examination of the Bank for July 26, declared certain loans to be in excess of the limit prescribed by Section 5200 USRS. Among the loans cited for criticism was one of $1,018,750 to AT&T. In addition, the Comptroller pointed out that the Bank held $761,000 in bonds of AT&T, an investment that the Comptroller felt was "not only excessive but out of proportion to the capital of the Bank which with the bond liability is entirely too large for your bank to carry with one interest." The Bank, undeterred by this criticism, responded that the loans would be repaid at their maturing date. This was evidently not entirely satisfactory to the Comptroller, who in February 1906 again found the Shawmut generosity to AT&T excessive. However, the notes must have come to maturity, for this was the last time the Comptroller faulted the Shawmut on that score.

The Bank also shared a great many other interests with Kidder, Peabody. During the first decade of the twentieth century, the investment firm played an active role in promoting certain railroads, gas and electric utilities, and mining companies, and it negotiated several loans with foreign countries. Records indicate that Shawmut was involved with very similar properties.

From the summer of 1903 on, the bonds of the Chicago, Burlington and Quincy syndicate, which both Kidder, Peabody and Lee, Higginson were instrumental in reorganizing, consistently show themselves as the source of "extraordinary profit" for Shawmut Bank. Shawmut also shared the investment house's interest in the Santa Fe, in which Kidder, Peabody had been heavily involved since 1889.

The utilities and mines in which Shawmut's interests overlapped those of the investment firm were New England Gas and Coke Company, Massachusetts Gas Companies Purchase Syndicate, Pennsylvania Coal Purchasing Syndicate, and Reading Coal and New Jersey Central Syndicate. The Bank's assistance to the Massachusetts Gas Syndicate, incidently, became another source of conflict with the Comptroller of the Currency, who evidently felt that the Shawmut's loan of $500,000 to this syndicate was in "excess of prescribed limits."

Another close tie with Kidder, Peabody involved foreign investments. In the early years of the new century, when foreign governments began borrowing in the United States, the investment firm was active in these operations. In 1901, Kidder, Peabody and Company, together with J. P. Morgan and Drexel and Company, distributed millions of British consols. It is no coincidence that in 1903 Shawmut shows "extraordinary profits" from British consols. Further, in 1905 Robert Winsor, a president of Kidder, Peabody and a Shawmut director, was "authorized to subscribe on behalf of this bank [Shawmut] for 4.5% bonds of the new Japanese loan to any amount not to-exceed $350,000."

The majority of Shawmut's loans and investments, of course, do not show the influence of its new investment-house-affiliated directors. The point is simply that many did and that the addition of the new directors was in general advantageous to the Bank, solidifying financial interests in a way that would later give rise to political opposition. In the early part of the century the situation was seen as simply a step in the evolution of the banking industry.

Loans and investments were not, however, the only source of growth for the National Shawmut. During this same period, and in the continued interest of reducing competition and increasing the dividends for investors in bank stocks, the trend toward consolidation of national banks, which had resulted in the formation of the National Shawmut, was continuing. On November 18, 1901, at a special meeting of the Board of Directors, it was voted "that a committee of three be appointed by the president from the Board of Directors with full power to negotiate with Kidder, Peabody and Company for the acquirement of the assets and property of the National Bank of the Commonwealth." This bank was subsequently merged with Shawmut at the end of the month. At the same time negotiations were underway for the Third National to be liquidated, with its business to be transferred to the National Shawmut. The Executive Committee was authorized to buy the assets of the Third National for $1 million, and the deal was consummated on December 3, 1901.

By the end of that year, business at the Shawmut had increased so considerably that a meeting of the stockholders was called to see whether they would authorize an increase in capital stock from $3 million to $3.5 million. This represented 24,173 shares, and the increase was unanimously approved. In January 1902, at the annual meeting and in recognition of the growing commitments of the Bank, it was also voted to increase the number of directors to twenty-five. New members were Henry B. Endicott, Francis B. Sears, Joseph B. Russell, and Moses Williams. All were directors of the Third National, Moses Williams having also served as that bank's president. From the National Bank of the Commonwealth came William A. Tower, F. A. Foster, and Oliver Ames. The eighth new director, who served for one year, was W. Murray Crane, then governor of Massachusetts. It was also at this meeting that the Shawmut Bank executive staff was reorganized to include three vice presidents. In 1900 E. Hayward Ferry had been elected to the board to replace Eben S. Draper. At that time Ferry was also selected as National Shawmut's first vice president, although Stearns, of course, had been vice president of Shawmut National. At the 1902 meeting two more vice presidents were added, Francis B. Sears and Abram T. Collier. The latter was not a member of the board.

The merger of these banks with the Shawmut evidently whetted Stearns's appetite for more bank business. In Bank minutes for March 1903 there appears the comment that the Executive Committee loaned to the Colonial National Bank $395,180 against 2500 shares of that institution's stock. Stearns went on to add that the Colonial would allow Shawmut interests to obtain up to 4000 shares, and he invited directors to participate.

The statement suggests that Stearns would have supported a merger with this bank, but whatever his intentions, a merger did not occur, and in 1904 the Colonial National Bank was taken over by the Commonwealth Trust Company. Other merger attempts, however, were more successful. In December 1906 the National Shawmut absorbed the National Exchange Bank.

In the meantime, the business of the Bank was brisk. In 1901 a committee of directors appointed to examine loans and investment reported:

> We think the business of the bank is conducted in an admirable manner. . . . It seems to us that the assets of the bank are in very healthy condition and we desire to compliment the President of the bank and the Executive Committee on their excellent judgment in making loans, and the officers of the bank on its admirable system of accounts.

Two years later a similar committee, this time composed of Henry B. Endicott, Henry S. Howe, and Alfred S. Woodworth, was slightly more critical, suggesting that loans, particularly to friends, might be reduced, although the Bank showed a steady record of good investments and growing earnings. Part of this triumph must be attributed to the presence of Ferry, who on coming to the Shawmut introduced the Bank's first systematized credit operation in 1900. Seven years later, on his resignation, the directors applauded his contribution, stating that it was "chiefly due to him [Ferry] and to the credit system that he introduced that the bank has made no losses on any of its loans for the past three years and that its losses were so insignificant during the earlier years of Mr. Ferry's service."

The Stearns administration was one of expansion. Dividends climbed steadily, rising from 1.25 percent quarterly at the time of the 1898 merger to 1.5 quarterly in December 1900 and then to 2 percent quarterly in December 1905. New banks were added, the loans-and-investments portfolio grew, and the Board of Directors became increasingly representative of both industrial and financial institutions. Between 1905 and 1907, four new persons were added to the Shawmut board. In 1905 Robert Bacon, who had been with the Lee, Higginson and J. P. Morgan companies, was appointed to replace William A. Tower, who died November 4, 1904. Bacon served for a year, leaving to assume a position in government, but returned as a director in 1912. Three others elected in 1905 were E. Pierson Beebe; Charles F. Choate, an attorney, then also a director of the Merchants National Bank and later a director of both the New York, New Haven and Hartford Railroad and AT&T; and Frank B. Bemis, a member of the firm of Estabrook and Company. In 1907 an additional six were elected to the board. Included among them were two Bank officers, Walter Swan and Harold Murdock. Murdock had served as a cashier at the National Exchange and now became a vice president at the Shawmut. Also added that year were Charles K. Cobb, attorney; Charles A. Locke, of Locke, Tolman and Company; George W. Wells, an optical goods manufacturer with connections to Worcester banks; and Harold J. Coolidge, a specialist in trust properties with the law firm of Loring, Coolidge and Noble.

The year 1907 was to be another fateful one in the annals of American economic history. A decade of almost unobstructed prosperity ended on October 21, 1907, with a run on the Knickerbocker Trust Company of New York. After one and a half days, the bank's reserves gave out. Other banks throughout the country were forced to close, and panic was averted only by the timely intervention of J. Pierpoint Morgan and a group of businessmen, who combined resources to import $100 million of gold from Europe. That the Shawmut felt the impact of these problems is attested by the minutes of December 1907, when it was moved to "approve the liberal and courageous policy adopted by the bank in the present troubled times." This commended policy, however, was not so much the work of J. P. Stearns as of William Gaston, for on May 2, 1907, Stearns "having served the bank in various capacities since 1867 asked 'relief from the active duties of my position.'" Perhaps with that ability to assess the future, which seemed to have characterized so many of his decisions for the Bank, he had sensed the coming difficulty and knew that the future now required the energy of a younger man. He did not, however, step out, for at that same meeting the directors voted that a chairman of the board be created, to which position Stearns was unanimously elected.

4

National prosperity, the enterprising spirit of Stearns, the reduction in competition through the merger of other banks into the Shawmut, and interlocking directorates of major financial institutions all contributed to the expansion of the National Shawmut Bank between 1898 and 1907. Reflecting this growth were changes in the internal management and structures of the Bank itself.

The mergers had brought new divisions, departments, and officers into the Bank, and new ways of management. Among the most important of these was the Credit Department. E. Hayward Ferry first introduced the idea of a systematized credit operation, and to him is attributed much of the success of the scheme. Sharing in this honor also was Norman I. Adams. Adams had been with the Boston National Bank and joined the Shawmut in 1898, at the time of the mergers. Initially connected with the Receiving Teller Department, in 1900 he organized the Analysis Department, which he manned with two employees. Out of this emerged Shawmut's Credit Department in 1903, one of the first such departments to be developed in the country. In 1907 Adams became the Bank's credit manager, and his contributions in this department were recognized in 1916, when he was appointed a vice president.

At the time of the mergers, several other officers also came into the Shawmut from the merging institutions. In addition to the vice-presidential appointments noted above, other major officers included Horatio Newhall, secretary, from the Columbia National. Wallace S. Draper, Henry T. Smith, and Arthur P. Stone all served as assistant cashiers during the Stearns administration and all came from merged banks. The measure of change is perhaps best attested, however, by contrasting the number of major officers in 1895, the last full year of Cummings's active presidency, with the number in 1907, when James P. Stearns resigned. In 1895 there were four major officers: the president, John C. Cummings, Jr.; the vice president, James P. Stearns; the cashier and paying teller, J. G. Taft; and one assistant cashier, F. H. Barbour. In 1907 there were nine major officers: the president, James P. Stearns; four vice presidents: E. Hayward Ferry, Francis B. Sears, Harold Murdock, and Abram T. Collier; the secretary, Horatio Newhall; the cashier, Frank H. Barbour; and two assistant cashiers: Wallace S. Draper and Henry T. Smith. (Arthur Stone had resigned in 1904 and was not replaced until 1908.) This list does not take into account the large number of new personnel, many of whom came from merged banks and who helped the Shawmut handle a greatly increased volume of business. Such men included Joseph Smith in the Check Tellers Department, from the Columbian Bank, and George Woods in the Loan Department, from the National Bank of the Commonwealth. Both men served the Shawmut for over thirty years.

It was also during the years of the Stearns administration that the Bank began to add new positions that in some ways reflected even more aptly its expanding business. In 1898 Shawmut retained its first special officer to oversee visitors coming through the building's rear door and also hired its first bench boy, that member of the staff charged with delivering all of the Bank's messages. In 1901, it petitioned the Board of Police of the city of Boston to appoint guard John Shaw as a special police officer, with police powers, to serve in and about the premises. Shaw dutifully patrolled and kept safe the premises for the next several years. In 1906 the Bank appointed its first clerk of the works, J. Albert Cole, at a salary of $36 per week.

Operational procedures also became increasingly sophisticated in the first years of the new century. Under Cummings the first typewriter and first telephone had been introduced, the latter sitting on Cashier James Stearns's desk. During the Stearns administration other phones, adding machines, and an addressograph were added. Although from the point of view of the 1980s such technology may seem primitive, it did make a substantial difference in the ability of the Bank to handle increasingly complex business transactions.

Between 1898 and 1907 the Shawmut became big business. But in many ways, despite its growth, the methods of conducting its affairs were still relatively informal. A perfect image expressing this informality is that of kettles perking behind the screens of the central banking office: while no one was allowed to leave the premises during banking hours, it was considered perfectly acceptable for the teller to brew his own tea. Also, cheese and crackers were always available to allay a clerk's sudden hunger.

At this time, of course, the space occupied by the Bank in rented rooms at 60 Congress Street was relatively small. Although the rooms had been more than adequate, in fact almost palatial, when the Shawmut first occupied them after the fire of 1873, by the time of the mergers, it was clear that more suitable quarters would have to be found. However, Shawmut's lease at Congress Street ran until 1907, and thus, initially at least, remodeling took precedent. In 1901, $14,830 was spent toward this end, and by the close of the year the central banking room had been reequipped and furnished in white mahogany, "the last word in equipment."

In the meantime, plans went ahead for more permanent facilities, although a special committee to study future location of banking rooms was not appointed until April 7, 1904. From this point on events moved swiftly, and in March of the following year a meeting was called to examine plans for a proposed new bank building to be located on Water Street between Congress and Devonshire. By April 6 the final plan had been selected, and by May the architect and contractor were engaged.

As the new building moved ahead, its plan became increasingly elegant, in keeping with the growing status of the Shawmut. Granite and bronze plating were authorized over cheaper limestone and cast iron as appropriate exterior materials. Interior facilities included ninety boxes for safe-deposit purposes, as well as a considerably more commodious central banking room. Altogether, the facility was a far cry from the second-story rented room on State Street that was home for the first Shawmut operation. Instead the new building, the first owned outright by the Bank, stood as an impressive and appropriate symbol of the importance the institution had achieved in the Boston financial community.

5

When the new bank building opened late in the spring of 1907, James P. Stearns had already resigned as president. His term had spanned an expansive period in American history. The great titans of industry had risen to prominence, and vast commercial enterprises — Standard Oil, AT&T, United States Steel — were now well launched into the twentieth century. Communications and utilities had vastly expanded. Chicago and New York were only eighteen hours apart on the Twentieth Century Limited and minutes away by telephone. Boston had also changed.

In 1867, when James P. Stearns first came to the Shawmut, the city boasted only 200,000 persons; by 1907 it had roughly 630,000. In 1867 business and residences still stood together in downtown Boston. By 1881 the Back Bay had been filled, and elegant brownstones, with bowed fronts and tall windows, overlooked what had been marshland. By 1907 some of Boston's most well-known buildings, the Boston Public Library (1895), the Christian Science Mother Church (1895), Symphony Hall (1899), and Isabella Stewart Gardner's famous palazzo in the Fenway (1900) extended the city to the west.

Throughout these changes the Shawmut kept pace. In 1867 the Bank was a quill-pen and high-stool operation, functioning in small rented quarters and illuminated by oil or gas on dark wintery afternoons. By 1898 it had already moved into larger quarters, though the dominant method of illumination was still gas. By 1907 the lighting was electric and the scratch of the quill pen had given way to the clatter of the typewriter and addressograph. If one listened hard, one might hear the rumbling of the subway, the first underground system in the country, completed in 1897. In 1907, however, there were also other rumblings that could be heard as the growing power of the banks and the concentration of monied interests began to give rise to a cry for government regulation. The ability of J. Pierpoint Morgan to rescue the country from panic in the fall of that year did nothing to quiet the protest. These sounds, however, were not problems for James P. Stearns but his successor. Stearns had guided the bank to a pinnacle of prosperity; it was up to William A. Gaston to secure it.

Chapter 7

Years of Regulation and War
The Gaston Administration
(1907–1917)

THE rash of corporate mergers at the beginning of the twentieth century gave rise to some alarm on the part of the general public. Although industrial titans could point to lowered prices and an improving standard of living as evidence that "bigness was not necessarily badness," an increasing sense of unease came to a head in the Panic of 1907. That a few individuals were able to avert a serious money crisis made clear what had previously been only suspected: the concentration of enormous economic power in the hands of only a few firms had profound social and political impact. Further contributing to the suspicion toward big business was the work of the "muckrakers." The term, first used in a modern context by Theodore Roosevelt, referred to writers who made it their business to expose the underside of American economic life. In 1903 *McClure's* magazine started the trend by employing Ida Tarbell to investigate Standard Oil Company. Her findings, published in 1912, conclusively shattered whatever white-knight image of big business remained. In the meantime, other writers, such as Lincoln Steffens and Upton Sinclair, whose 1906 novel *The Jungle* dealt with the meat packing industry, were hammering away at other abuses, and reform became the order of the day.

By 1907 the tide of sympathy for unbridled individualism in big business and the laissez-faire policies that supported it had already begun to ebb, and the problem confronting business leaders became not simply how to grow but how to respond to investigation, regulation, and reform. Again, the Shawmut was fortunate in having a leader suited to the times.

1

By nature and training, William A. Gaston was remarkably well suited to the kind of community-oriented vision that his age was coming to need and demand. On his mother's side, Gaston could claim kinship with the Beecher family of Connecticut, which included among its members the fiery clergyman Henry Ward Beecher and Harriet Beecher Stowe, author of *Uncle Tom's Cabin*. On the paternal side, Gaston's father, William, was a prominent Boston attorney, one-time representative in the state legislature, former mayor of Boston, and the first Democrat elected governor of Massachusetts since the Republican Party gained ascendancy in 1858. On another branch of the family tree was Judge William Gaston of North Carolina, associate justice of the state supreme court, a Catholic in a Protestant state, who, as a member of the state legislature in 1835, was instrumental in forming that state's constitution into a model of religious toleration. Generations earlier the patriarch of the dynasty was Jean Gaston, a Huguenot who preferred exile from his native France to the surrender of his religious principles. Respect for independent thought, leadership in reform movements, and public service were all very much part of William A. Gaston's heritage. It was a heritage that would stand him in good stead in the changing world of the early twentieth century.

Gaston's temperament was also well suited to respond to the challenges of his time. Self-assured and self-contained, he was predisposed to hold his ground, declare his intentions, and then remain firmly entrenched until his opponents came round. The success of such an approach had shown itself during his college years when as the "light-weight" boxing champion of Harvard he was matched against the heavyweight boxing champion, Raymond Guiteras. Although the latter had literally all the weight on his side, Gaston had the advantage of endurance. In a bout that lasted a record three rounds of ten minutes each, and with classmate and friend Theodore Roosevelt as his second, Gaston adroitly held his own until finally Guiteras simply wore out and threw in the towel.

This college event provides an appropriate analogy for a man who often found himself pitted against the weight of entrenched business interests, but whose ability to stand fast often gave him the victory. One of Gaston's chief contributions to the Shawmut was precisely this dedicated perseverance, duly channeled into the service of the community. Under Stearns the Bank had grown into a major financial institution; under Gaston it became a leader in supporting and promoting general practices that had far-reaching effects on the entire financial community. Under Stearns the policy of the Bank was that what was right for the Shawmut would in the long run prove right for the community at large; under Gaston the policy was that what was right for the community at large would in the long run prove right for the individual institution. At no time was this approach more clearly demonstrated than in the first months of his administration.

2

In March 1907, shortly before Stearns left office and Gaston took over, the stock market experienced a dramatic slump. The economy rallied, but October brought the now famous run on the Knickerbocker Trust Company of New York. The failure was followed by others as the shortage of available money made it impossible for banks and businessmen to realize their commitments. In the face of a panicky demand for gold, there was an equally panicky reaction on the part of many institutions to hoard their assets. Banks began to force payment of loans from businesses that were essentially healthy but that, cut off from funds to meet daily expenses, now teetered at the edge of bankruptcy. Gaston confronted impending disaster with commendable calm. Refusing to panic, he authorized a letter to be sent to every bank in the United States with which the Shawmut had financial relations. The letter, dated November 15, 1907, urged restraint in calling in loans and eloquently stated Gaston's contention that it was the duty of a bank to look beyond its own narrow interests and assume a stance of public responsibility:

THE NATIONAL SHAWMUT BANK

Capital $3,500,000   Surplus $4,500,000

Boston, Massachusetts, November 15, 1907

Dear Sirs: — In a period of such stringency of the money market as we are now experiencing, it is of the utmost importance that the banks shall renew, as far as it lies in their power, the notes which may be maturing of merchants and manufacturers and others who are worthy of credit.

In many cases it is utterly impossible for perfectly solvent business houses, either to borrow new money or to collect their receivables, which ordinarily are paid, or to sell their merchandise, and if they are forced unnecessarily by the banks to pay their notes, bankruptcy or receivership is sure to follow.

In order to restore business affairs to a normal state, a general liquidation of business must take place. This, we believe, every merchant is attempting to do to the extent of his ability, but the banks and trust companies must, in our opinion, do their share by extending maturing notes in whole or in part. The fewer the number of solvent merchants who are forced to pay their debts where it seems hardship, the fewer the failures, and consequently, the sooner a restoration of confidence and normal condition of the money market will ensue.

We therefore urge you, as far as is in your power, to help the serious mercantile situation in this way.

Very truly yours,
National Shawmut Bank,
William A. Gaston,
President

Not all of Shawmut's directors, of course, agreed with the president's position. Some quite justifiably contended that were the Bank to preach leniency to others, it would have to be equally lenient itself in calling in debts and thereby risk its own assets. Gaston's policy, however, prevailed and had an undeniable cooling effect on the overheated situation; it also benefited the Bank by creating good will in the business community. Years later, Thomas B. Durrell, head of the firm of Brown, Durrell Company, expressed that good will: "This act of Mr. Gaston as president of the National Shawmut was unprecedented as an extraordinary example of banking courage, common sense, and sympathy with the businessmen who were at the time being unwarrantedly driven to the wall." To assume that such praise did not have marketable value would be naive.

The values demonstrated by Gaston in this 1907 letter, namely, that community interest must take precedence over self-interest, characterized many of the financial decisions that he made for the Shawmut. Most notable among these were the positions he took in support of the Federal Reserve System.

Following the Knickerbocker failure, a move was made to begin studying the country's financial situation, with a view to preventing future panics. At the same time, and partially stimulated by the work of muckrakers, investigations began into the concentration of monied interests in this country. Both the impulse to come up with a structure more responsive to economic needs than the National Bank acts and the investigations proceeded apace. The first result was the passage of the Aldrich-Vreeland bill in 1908. The act, designed to make the immediate money situation of the country more elastic, did not pretend to any permanent solution of the currency problem. It did, however, provide for a congressional monetary commission to make an exhaustive study of the country's financial needs and resources. Senator Nelson W. Aldrich, a conservative Republican from Rhode Island, served as chairman of this National Monetary Commission. One result of its investigations was a plan, formulated in 1911, to establish a National Reserve Association. This association would have branches throughout the country and would coordinate and centralize financial efforts through its power to issue currency and discount commercial paper of member banks.

Although such a system might have resolved some of the country's current monetary problems, politically it was doomed. The proposal not only ignored popular fears that financial control was already too centralized in the hands of a few bankers, it exacerbated them. For one thing, Senator Aldrich was the father-in-law of John D. Rockefeller, and this connection alone was enough to alienate the general public. Furthermore, Aldrich had proposed that a board of directors made up almost exclusively of bankers should govern the National Association. The recommendation brought a cry of outrage from Democratic and Progressive politicians, most notably William Jennings Bryan, who hotly contended that big bankers would "then be in complete control of everything through the control of our national finances." Thus the Aldrich plan, although favored by many bankers, died aborning. It did, however, prepare the way for passage of later banking and currency reforms.

With the National Monetary Commission disbanded and the Aldrich plan shelved, the House Banking and Currency Committee set up a subcommittee in April 1912, "to obtain full and complete information of the banking and currency conditions of the United States for the purpose of determining what legislation was needed." Popularly known as the Pujo Committee in deference to its chairman, Arsene P. Pujo, a Louisiana lawyer and Democrat, this group conducted one of the most extensive and sensational investigations of banking in the nation's history. Pujo's investigative method was to invite representatives of several investment houses to appear before the committee and to request from national banks the answers to a series of probing questions. Not all were equally delighted by the invitations or the requests. In Boston a committee of the clearing house reported to its members in a letter, read aloud to the Shawmut Board of Directors on May 16, 1912, that the clearing house had been advised by counsel that Pujo had no right to demand from national banks the information he requested. "Counsel also doubts if the banks are at liberty to furnish such information, making public the private affairs and business of their customers, especially as the facts and data required are all to be acquired from the Comptroller of the Currency." The final decision of what to do, however, rested with the individual banks.

At the Shawmut the matter was referred to its Executive Committee which, under the guidance of Gaston, returned a recommendation that "the questions asked should be answered by the bank," and this was duly voted by the Board of Directors on June 6, 1912.

As the Bank cooperated in the work of the Pujo Committee, so also it cooperated in the founding of the Federal Reserve

System. Following the demise of the Aldrich Plan, Congress dragged its feet on the question of financial reform. It was still, however, very much a central issue, and much of the rhetoric of the 1912 presidential campaign was devoted to the problem of immobile reserves and an inelastic money supply. That a solution could be effected without resorting to a dreaded central bank under banker domination was the contention of Woodrow Wilson, Democratic and reform candidate from New Jersey.

The pledge won him popular support and contributed to his victory in November, but while the promise had been simple to make, political and economic realities made it more difficult to fulfill. Throughout the winter of 1912–1913 two chief presidential advisors, Congressman Glass of Virginia, who would later become chairman of the House Committee on Banking and Finance, and H. Parker Willis, later that committee's expert advisor and, in 1912, associate editor of the *New York Journal of Commerce*, struggled with the solution. By December 26, 1912, they had already devised a basic structure. According to their plan, Wilson would create twenty (the number was later reduced to twelve) privately controlled regional reserve banks, each of which would hold a portion of member banks' reserves, perform other central banking functions, and issue currency against commercial assets and gold. Coordinating the entire effort would be a public agency, the Federal Reserve Board. President Wilson contributed the idea of this board to the Carter Glass proposal and presented it to a joint session of Congress on June 23, 1913. Bankers felt Wilson's currency reform promised far too much government control, and the conservatives who represented them in the legislature were outraged.

Back in Boston, as in other major financial strongholds, events in Washington had loosed a swirl of controversy. The proposed currency reform, contended many of the leading bankers, was not to be countenanced, and in tones of bitterness, they denounced it as unwarranted intrusion on the laissez-faire economic policies that had traditionally prevailed.

That the government was setting itself up to regulate their industry through a board dominated by political appointees was not, however, the only aspect of the plan they opposed. Equally disliked, especially by bankers in the central reserve cities of Chicago, St. Louis, and New York, was the idea that henceforth only Federal Reserve banks would hold reserves. Still others with national charters protested the proposed compulsory membership in the Federal Reserve System, which they saw as an intrusion of the government on "private rights." And finally, many who were conservative and Republican saw the whole idea as a partisan political ploy designed to undermine their party and its interests.

Against this tide of opposition, the opinion of Gaston, as president of Shawmut, stood out in high relief. Gaston was by inheritance and conviction a Democrat. In 1888 he had taken time out from his law practice to work in the gubernatorial campaign of Democrat William Russell. And in 1890, when Russell was elected, Gaston had been appointed to his staff, an appointment he kept through Russell's next two victories. In 1912 he had supported Wilson for the presidency, and now he supported his currency reform proposal. It was not so much political sympathy, however, as economic conviction that formed Gaston's point of view. What he was able to perceive, although many of his peers could not, was that reform was mandatory, that the issue transcended partisan politics, and that the country must have the best law possible. To this end, and over the opposition of many of his colleagues, he traveled frequently to Washington to help perfect the plan.

In the meantime, President Wilson, well aware of the bankers' opposition and anxious to placate them, made some important modifications in the currency reform bill. These modifications included a provision stipulating that national bank notes be retired slowly, thus protecting the various banks' investments in the U.S. bonds that backed this currency; a provision for regional reserve banks allowing them to have more authority over the rediscount rate than was originally projected; and a provision calling for a federal advisory council, consisting of representatives of the banking community, to serve as a liaison between reserve banks and the Federal Reserve Board. Despite these concessions, most bankers remained adamant in their disdain for the system. Matters reached a crisis late in the summer of 1913, when the Boston Clearing House, anticipating a national meeting of banking associations, called together its own members to condemn the pending legislation. Gaston made it quite clear that he would not support any such condemnation, and the defection of the largest bank in Boston carried weight, although it by no means scuttled criticism.

Throughout the summer and into the late fall, the controversy raged. Partially as a result of the Pujo investigations, public opinion was largely on the side of Wilson, and on December 19, 1913, the Federal Reserve Bill narrowly passed in both houses of Congress. Four days later, on December 23, by which time minor differences between the House and Senate versions had been ironed out, the Federal Reserve Act was signed into law.

In the meantime, on December 22, in the board room of the Shawmut, the Executive Committee "on motion of the President . . . voted to recommend to the Directors of the Bank the immediate acceptance of the terms and provisions of the Federal Reserve Act now pending." On December 26 the entire Board of Directors "voted to accept the provisions of the Federal Reserve Act," and on January 1, 1914, the directors again voted "acceptance of this association of the terms of the Federal Reserve Act and intention to subscribe to capital stock of the Federal Reserve Bank." This it subsequently did, voting on April 16, 1914, to subscribe to 9000 shares at $100 par value of capital stock of the Federal Reserve Bank.

As time has proved, the Federal Reserve Act was a major step in providing the national community with a basis for sound economic development. To this extent Gaston's support of the scheme must be commended as an act of unselfish and disinterested foresight, but it also had other and perhaps somewhat less disinterested implications as well.

Gaston's staunch defense of national Democratic policies undoubtedly had an impact on the local Boston community. In its early days, city politics had been largely dominated by the Whigs and by those who came to be fondly known as the Boston Brahmins. The steady increase in the foreign population, particularly the Irish, the gradual, but decisive, growth in the power and wealth of the Roman Catholic Church, with which many of the immigrants were associated, and the withdrawal from active participation in municipal offices of the Brahmins had all served to change the power base of the city. In the thirty years between 1884, when Hugh O'Brien, a native-born Irishman, was elected mayor of Boston, and 1914, the Democrats won fourteen out of nineteen elections. Gaston's political stance, then, although it may not have endeared him to his Republican colleagues, certainly did not alienate him or his institution from the local community, and it is probably no coincidence that during his administration the Shawmut's reputation as the city's bank began to grow. Not only was it increasingly favored for municipal deposits, but also the archdiocese frequently turned to the Shawmut as a depository for its funds and as an institution that would be sympathetic to its needs for loans. So prevalent was the idea that the Catholic Church in Boston preferred to do business with the Shawmut that producers of a 1963 movie, *The Cardinal,* insisted that their protagonist use checks marked with the Indian logo.

Some of Gaston's detractors have asserted that he was simply a political pragmatist, who tailored his views to conform to the prevalent opinion in the city and enhance his own and his institution's reputation. They support their contention by pointing to the fact that, after leaving the Bank, Gaston ran for political office on the Democratic ticket. To charge that the Shawmut's president, whose father had served as a Democratic mayor and governor, tailored his policies for political expediency, however, seems specious. Much more likely is that the Board of Directors, knowing Gaston's political views and perceiving the mood of the country, deliberately chose a man whose sympathies, they recognized, made him the correct man for the times. After all, the Shawmut had always prided itself on being *the* bank of Boston business. In its early days it served the shipping merchants, and its policies and Board of Directors had reflected this concern. As the textile and railroad industries grew, the Bank reflected this interest. Now in the first decades of the twentieth century, the Bank continued to reflect its community. Indeed, at a time when NO IRISH NEED APPLY was still a popular sign in Boston, the directors at the Shawmut welcomed on the board two persons who were Irish: in 1915 John Joyce, a self-made businessman who had gained a small fortune in bottled soda before becoming vice president of Gillette Safety Razor, became a director of Shawmut; his partner in both enterprises, Maurice Curran, was appointed a director in 1917. Such evidence would seem to indicate that the Board of Directors, rather than the president, were the true pragmatists.

Two other financial decisions that Gaston proposed and the board supported, and which also had political implications, concerned the Gold Fund and the Cotton Pool. In the first instance a serious situation had arisen concerning a large quantity of gold being exported to Europe from the United States. In 1914, the federal government formulated a policy which, in essence, asked various banks, both state and national, to contribute a specified amount of their reserves to a central fund to augment Treasury resources. On September 4, 1914, in Washington, D.C., a conference of the Clearing House Associations of the Central Reserve and Reserve Cities appointed a committee to study the situation, and on September 19 the committee returned the recommendation that a gold fund of $100 million be set up with contributions coming from banks located in reserve cities. This recommendation was approved by the Federal Reserve Board, and on October 1, 1914, on a motion of President Gaston, the Shawmut Board of Directors voted to authorize "the President, the Vice President and the Cashier on behalf of this bank to subscribe $1,291,626 payable in gold or gold certificates to a Gold Fund."

Again, not all bankers were equally pleased by this move. Many who needed gold in various foreign countries to help meet their obligations abroad protested the idea on the principle that if a bank had reserves to spare, they should be at the demand of stockholders and depositors. Despite this opposition — and there is no indication that members of Shawmut's Board of Directors were so opposed — the Gold Fund was initiated. It proved instrumental in equalizing the exchange rate between Europe and the United States, and again, after the fact, few could find fault with either the fund or Shawmut's participation in it.

The problems surrounding Shawmut's role in the federally supported Cotton Pool, however, were somewhat more complex. With the onset of war in Europe, the market for raw cotton on the continent was sharply curtailed; bales began piling up in warehouses and prices plummeted. To forestall the possibility of bankruptcy throughout the South, the Wilson administration called for the banks of the country to form a pool that would allow the Federal Reserve Board to buy cotton and thus keep the price level. At the Shawmut opinion was divided. On the one hand, Moses Williams declared, "I can see no more reason logically for supporting the price of raw cotton than of the manufactured good." A more accommodating position was voiced by Charles Hayden: "I can see no reason why New England banks which have purchase of cotton for New England mills should loan money to the seller in the south . . . but if you don't think it will prevent accommodation of the mills and it is good advertising . . . I will support the pool." Gaston in his turn openly supported the idea, although exactly why is more difficult to pinpoint. Was his motive purely altruistic? Certainly the cotton subsidy served to sustain the industry and the jobs of those who depended on it. Or was his view, as his detractors would have it, simply an instance of currying political favor by supporting policies of the Democratic administration? Or was it, as is perhaps most likely, simply hard business sense?

Since the 1840s the Shawmut had played an important role in the textile industry. It lent funds to the cotton manufacturers and played a very important part in the development of the Lowell mills and numerous others throughout the Northeast. In fact, leading members of the Board of Directors still had close connections with the cotton manufacturing industry.

Assuming that their interests lay with keeping the price of cotton low, it seems odd that on November 12, 1914, they voted to go along with Gaston and give $1 million to the Cotton Pool. Was he simply that persuasive, or were other factors involved? Were "vested interests" perhaps not as simple as they appeared on the surface? It is most probable that the Shawmut's involvement with cotton went beyond manufacturing and extended to making loans for the transportation of the raw product and its warehousing in New England. It is safe to assume that the collateral for such loans was pegged to the price of a bale. For this reason, rather than altruism or politics, it was in the Shawmut's interest that the industry remain solvent. In the course of the next few years, several new members joined the board, all of whom were directly concerned with cotton manufacturing. It is hard to believe that any of these men would have felt friendly toward a bank that had supported an unreasonable cotton price.

Gaston's attitude and decisions in the 1907 panic, and his support of the Pujo investigations, Federal Reserve System, Gold Fund, and Cotton Pool, had national implications. That in most cases his positions corresponded with those of the Democratic administration is notable, but that such positions improved the condition not only of the Shawmut Bank but also of the banking industry as a whole is worthy of greater note.

3

Although some might conclude that the correspondence between William A. Gaston's point of view and that of the Democratic party made him a "radical" businessman, the evidence suggests the contrary. Gaston was undeniably intelligent and farsighted, and he was well able to perceive the consequences of certain, even unpopular, positions. He was, however, in no sense a radical — at least to the extent that that term implies a risk taker. The record of his policies at the Shawmut suggests one who was basically conservative and whose decisions reflected a careful study of the needs of his time. A glance at some of these policies and the conditions that affected them illuminates these generalities.

Impact of Federal Legislation

During the early years of his administration, the focus of Gaston's efforts was on the formulation of national policies that would contribute to the continued well-being of his own institution. Two federal acts were of profound significance in this regard. The first of these was the Federal Reserve Act, which established the Federal Reserve System and enlarged the scope of national banks, authorizing them to undertake certain operations from which they had previously been excluded. For instance, it allowed national banks to serve as trustees, executors, and administrators of trust funds. This was particularly relevant in Boston, where state chartered institutions, such as the Old Colony Trust Company, and private trustees dominated the lucrative field of trust funds. According to the Federal Reserve Act, commercial banks could now also perform these services.

Shawmut moved quickly to realize the advantages of the new law, and on April 1, 1915, permission having been granted by the Federal Reserve Board, the Bank established a separate Trust Department. Four months later the first Trust Committee of the Board of Directors was appointed to act on matters pertaining to investments and reinvestments of trust funds. Although the full impact of trust activities on the earnings of the Bank would not be felt until later, expansion into this area was one undeniable advantage to come from the new legislation. Other consequences of other bills were not so advantageous. Certainly one law that had at least mixed results was the Clayton Antitrust Act and its subsequent Kerr Amendment.

Much of the point of the new laws had been to diffuse the concentration of monied interests. In the case of trust activities, such diffusion operated in the Bank's favor. The Clayton stipulation and Kerr Amendment, however, which were designed to prevent interlocking directorates between investment banks, trusts, and other national banks, had a somewhat less salubrious effect. Specifically, these laws meant that many of the Shawmut's most respected directors could no longer serve the Bank and other financial firms simultaneously. In the spring of 1914, five members of the Board of Directors, who were partners in major investment houses, resigned. These were Frank G. Webster and Robert Winsor of Kidder, Peabody and Company; Frederick S. Moseley of F. S. Moseley and Company; Frank A. Bemis of Estabrook and Company; and Henry Lee Higginson of Lee, Higginson and Company. Higginson's letter of resignation expressed the situation of each: "Unwilling and in obedience to the orders of the United States laws, I resign my position as director of the National Shawmut Bank."

Two years later five others stepped down. On June 8, 1916, Edwin F. Atkins sent a letter to the Shawmut board: "Owing to the act of Congress last year [the Kerr Amendment] prohibiting interlocking directorates between national banks and trust companies I am obliged to hand you my resignation." He was followed in the fall by Oliver Ames, Moses Williams, F. C. Dumaine, and Charles Hayden, who wrote: "I have received notice from the Federal Reserve Board of Washington that as a private banker and member of the firm of Hayden, Stone and Co. I am not eligible under the Kerr Amendment of the Clayton Antitrust Act to be a director in any member institution of the Federal Reserve System." That Hayden had to be reminded to resign suggests the reluctance of these men to sever their connections with Shawmut; that the Bank felt the loss equally is also clear. A letter from the board to Winsor, on May 25, 1914, indicates the sentiment of the remaining members. Ironically, it also indicates the degree of indebtedness to certain board members that the antitrust acts had sought to reduce: "Mr. Winsor has served on the Executive Committee from the onset and in connection with many large enterprises has neglected no opportunity to bring profitable business to the Bank. Its growth and success have been greatly promoted by his untiring interest."

Although the new laws effectively cut the legal connection between the boards of institutions with overlapping interests, and although the Shawmut expressed regret at the loss of these men, their influence was not automatically dissipated, particularly in relation to the connection between the Shawmut and Kidder, Peabody and Company.

As noted in the previous chapter, the two institutions had been closely allied since 1898, when the investment firm managed the merger of nine banks into the National Shawmut. Throughout the Stearns administration they remained closely connected, and this continued under Gaston. For example, in November 1908 the Bank subscribed for 250,000 new-issue AT&T convertible 4 percent bonds, undoubtedly urged to do so by the investment house, which in 1906 had negotiated with J. P. Morgan, Kuhn Loeb, and Baring Brothers to distribute $150 million in convertible bonds. The issue was offered to the public over a two-year period with Kidder, Peabody in charge of New England sales.

Many of the Bank's railroad interests also continued to overlap those of the investment company. Bank records of March 1908 show Shawmut had at least $260,000 in bonds of the New York, New Haven and Hartford. April records make note of $178,000 on the "loan of the New York Central and Hudson Railroad 3.5 percents, and $55,000 on the loan of the New York, New Haven and Hartford." These figures become more interesting when one recognizes that in the decade between 1903 and 1913, there was a major attempt on the part of Charles Mellon, representing the New York, New Haven and Hartford, to gain control of all New England transportation, including waterways. During these years capitalization of the New Haven went from $93 million to $412 million, with Kidder, Peabody and Company playing an important role in much of the financing. How deeply involved the Shawmut was is difficult to ascertain, but we do know that as late as April 1914 the Executive Committee voted to underwrite its share of a syndicate formed to finance the New Haven, subscribing $660,000 for New England Navigation, $660,000 for New York, New Haven and Hartford, and $330,000 for Harlem River and Port Chester Railroad.

Underscoring the close affiliation between the Shawmut and Kidder, Peabody and Company was the disclosure by the Pujo Committee in 1912 that the investment house owned $679,200 par value stock in the Shawmut, almost 20 percent of the contemporary total. Although there was nothing illegal about this kind of stock ownership or complementary participation in projects, it was exactly the sort of concentration of power that the new laws had been designed to break up. To the extent that overlapping directorates were now forbidden, they succeeded in accomplishing their ends. In reality, however, the situation was not much altered. Certainly Gaston's policies show the continuing influence of his friend and classmate, Robert Winsor.

In relation to this, and although Webster and Winsor left the Shawmut prior to discussion of either the Gold Fund or the Cotton Pool, Gaston's position corresponded exactly with that of the Kidder, Peabody management. The investment house was a staunch supporter of the Gold Fund, contributing $3 million to it; further, the firm was actually summoned by William McAdoo, secretary of the Treasury, to help avert a financial crisis in the South and became one of the major architects of the Cotton Pool, to which the Shawmut had pledged its support.

Additional evidence of the continuing influence of investment banks on Shawmut is provided by a notation in the minutes of April 12, 1915: "The Executive Committee voted $825,000 par value as part of a syndicate to purchase 5 percent notes of N.Y., N.H., & H. according to the conventions outlined by Lee, Higginson, and Kidder, Peabody"; and another of April 13, 1916: "The Executive Committee voted the purchase of $577,000 4-percent, 14-year notes of the N.Y., N.H., & H. according to letters of Higginson and Kidder, Peabody." Throughout Gaston's administration, the Shawmut continued its interests in AT&T, in public utilities, and in syndicates, many of which issues were generated by the investment firm.

Impact of the War

If federal legislation was one force exerting influence on the Shawmut management under Gaston, United States involvement in World War I was another. The effects of this involvement on the Bank were many, but perhaps the most significant was the role it played in opening up opportunities for international investments. The Shawmut, of course, had always had interests abroad. In its early days it had provided loans for goods to be traded in the Far East and had consistently offered letters of credit to its clients. Under Stearns, the Shawmut subscribed to bond issues of various governments, including those of Japan, Russia, and Italy, and also played an important role in the financing of Mexican railroads. It was not until World War I, however, that the volume of the Bank's investments abroad warranted the separate attention of several of its officers, a focus that provided the foundation of what became the Bank's Foreign Department.

The first indication that the Shawmut intended to broaden its international commitments actually emerged several years before the war. It did, for example, participate in the financing of the Panama Canal, purchasing at least $50,000 in U.S. Panama Canal 2 percent bonds and making other loans of at least $250,000 toward the project. Although this was not, strictly speaking, a foreign investment but rather an investment in the United States, the very character of the enterprise did focus the Bank's attention outside United States borders. More important was the Bank's application in November 1913 to the secretary of war "for designation as a depository of funds belonging to and under control of the government of the Philippine Islands." The designation was duly granted, and shortly after, the Bank made note of $4 million in U.S. bonds "for securing circulation and part of a long term loan security for the Philippine War Department Loan."

The major thrust of the Shawmut's investments abroad, however, did not begin until the fall of 1915. The previous fall, the Wilson administration lifted its ban against private credits and loans to the combatants, which it had imposed at the beginning of the war. Between October 1914 and April 16, 1917, when the United States declared war on Germany, the warring nations received almost $2.7 billion in loans from American banks. Kidder, Peabody and Company was extremely active in underwriting and distributing many of these loans. Its dealings included loans to the Italian government, whose bank of deposit it had been since 1907; a $500 million Anglo-French loan; and a $50 million Russian loan negotiated with J. P. Morgan in 1916. It also assumed responsibility for loans to various French cities and for a Canadian bond issue in 1917.

During the same period Shawmut investments were similar. In September 1915 the Executive Committee voted to purchase $500,000 in 6 percent, one-year notes from the Italian government. On September 28 it voted to recommend underwriting $1.5 million in 5 percent notes from England and France; in June 1916 it subscribed to $1 million of the Russian 6.5 percent loan; in July the Shawmut accepted participation of $500,000 in American Foreign Security 5 percent notes of a syndicate offered by J. P. Morgan; and in August, it voted to subscribe $1 million to one- and two-year 5 percent secured loans of the United Kingdom and Ireland. Finally, on July 26, 1917, the board voted "at the suggestion of the President to accept participation of $250,000 in a syndicate" to sell 100 million Dominion of Canada two-year 5 percent gold notes dated August 1, 1917.

Still other foreign loans during the period included one of December 1915, when the Shawmut, in conjunction with several other banks, such as the National City Bank of New York, Bankers Trust, and the Guaranty Trust Company, voted to extend a line of credit to Messrs. Schneider and Company of Paris and Contour, France, to pay for exports to the United States. Two years later the Bank's participation in "new French export credit under the same terms as of December 27, 1915" was also approved.

Although Shawmut's participation in the above loans constituted a large part of its contribution to the war effort, also
important were loans and lines of credit extended to industries
engaged in the manufacture of war goods. Some of the leading
firms Shawmut dealt with at this time were U.S. Radiator Corporation, the United States Rubber Company, Winchester Repeating Arms Company, and the Remington Arms Company.

Still a third war-related service that the Bank performed was
selling United States war bonds. Between 1917 and 1919 five
bond drives were undertaken by the Treasury, and these collected a total of $20.5 billion. The first was launched in June
1917, at which time the Shawmut cashier was authorized "when
details of subscriptions are settled for Liberty Bonds, to fill
out forms required by the Secretary of Treasury." Two months
later the board approved "the action of its officers in borrowing
$870,000 of U.S. 3.5 percent Liberty Bonds." The approval
was by letter 96 of the Federal Reserve Board requiring a vote
of the Board of Directors for loans to directors and their companies fixing a specific amount to be loaned each individual. Directors were asked to make applications for the amounts to which
they would themselves and their companies be entitled. The
success of the first loan in Boston — the city ranked third in
overall subscriptions, led only by New York and Chicago —
was unquestionably due in large part to the enthusiastic support
of such men as William Gaston who, even after he had left
the presidency of the Bank, continued to speak out loudly for
continued purchase of these issues.

The impact of the war, of course, was not solely confined
to the financial actions of the Bank. Like all businesses, it experienced an attrition of personnel. In April 1917 three officers
left the Bank, having applied for commissions in the Officers
Reserve Corps. Others followed, some as volunteers, some as
a consequence of the draft law instituted in November. It was
in November that Gaston also stepped down from the presidency of the Shawmut. That his decision was motivated by a
desire to participate more closely in the war effort is nowhere
explicitly stated; nevertheless, it should be recognized that immediately after resigning the presidency, he was appointed
chairman of the Committee on War Efficiency, which was to
represent Massachusetts in all war labor problems.

Impact of the United States Spheres of Influence Policy

Closely related to the effect that World War I had on internationalizing the commitments of the Shawmut was the effect of the United States policy of "spheres of influence." This policy — which was largely the impetus for and consequence of the Spanish-American War — meant that the country had become increasingly involved in the domestic operations of certain nations that it felt were particularly important for its own welfare. In some cases involvement went beyond "interest" to the development of dependencies or insular possessions. Just such a possession was the Philippines, and Shawmut's application as a depository for Philippine funds, and its subsequent loans to that country, can be seen as a direct result of national policy.

Still other areas of national concern were the Caribbean and Central and South America. In June 1917, at the prompting of the Guaranty Trust Bank Company in New York, the Shawmut Board of Directors authorized the president to petition the Federal Reserve Bank for permission to invest in 2000 shares, at $125 per share, of the Mercantile Bank of America, Inc., which was duly allowed. Although the implications of this investment and the interest of Shawmut directors in Caribbean enterprises was not fully realized until later, it was under Gaston that the Bank began to turn its attention to this area of the world, an area that became increasingly important to the Shawmut.

Altogether, the years between 1912 and 1917 were ones of increasing foreign commitments for the National Shawmut. During this period the Bank began to develop its foreign loans, to extend many more letters of credit, and also to create "acceptances." All of these operations became major aspects of the Bank's continued growth. In this regard it is instructive to note that in the report of condition of the National Shawmut Bank, November 1, 1917, "Acceptances Purchased" and "Customer Liabilities Under Acceptances and Letters of Credit" had expanded greatly, amounting to $3,479,192 and $29,805,862 respectively.

Effect of Domestic Conditions on Bank Policy and Growth

By 1907, when William Gaston assumed the presidency of the Shawmut, the major period of bank mergers was already over. Between 1898 and 1906, the number of national banks in Boston dropped from sixty to twenty-eight. In the next five years, before passage of the Federal Reserve Act made consolidation less favored as a way to reduce competition and stimulate growth, the number dropped by only eight; of these the Shawmut absorbed two. In 1908 it took over the National Bank of the Republic, which the previous year had taken over the Freeman's National, and in October 1912 Shawmut absorbed the Eliot National, which had itself taken over the City National and Tremont National in 1898. In anticipation of this latter merger, the board voted in May 1912 to increase its capital stock from $3.5 million to $10 million and issue a corresponding 65,000 hundred-dollar par value shares. At this time, the banking capital of the twenty national banks in Boston was $271 million, with the Shawmut the largest — although its last consolidation was not an unalloyed blessing.

According to stipulations of the Shawmut-Eliot agreement, Harry L. Burrage, president of the latter bank, joined the Shawmut Board as a vice president, with at least one full year's compulsory service. The idea, of course, was that he would bring the business of the Eliot with him. In fact, the original agreement, later canceled, suggested that Burrage was to receive a "remuneration proportionate to the amount of Eliot Bank deposits beyond $5 million which I [Burrage] might succeed in retaining for the Shawmut." Such deposits never materialized, and by January 1914 Burrage had left the Shawmut and $307,500, which he owed the Bank, had been charged down.

In the meantime, other events had their effect on the Bank's internal affairs. Of these, the most important was the difficulty that business experienced between 1912 and 1914. During this period trading volume on the New York Stock Exchange dropped from 131.1 million shares to less than 83.5 million. Although many businessmen attributed the decline to the atmosphere of uncertainty, generated by a decade of reform efforts and exacerbated by Wilson's regulatory policies, that view is undoubtedly too simplistic. Whatever the cause, the effects were felt throughout the financial community and were reflected at the Shawmut by a decrease in dividends from the 3 percent quarterly that had obtained since 1907 to 2 percent in September 1912. These dividends did not rise again until 1915, when the board voted a 2.5 percent return.

Despite the setbacks or, more truly, the "holding pattern" of these two years, business at the Shawmut expanded steadily during Gaston's administration. Between March 1907 and November 1, 1917, assets rose from $65,024,959 to $187,064,671. The causes of this growth are varied and many of its aspects have been discussed above. There remains, however, one area of expansion that, in terms of innovation and ultimate effects, is most appropriate to conclude a discussion of Gaston's financial policies. This was the National Shawmut's decision to engage in automobile financing, thereby opening up a new avenue of growth that had a profound effect on American society.

The roots of the automobile industry in America can be traced to Massachusetts. In 1891 the first electricity-powered car produced in the United States was introduced by Holtzer-Cabot Company of Brookline. Two years later the first successful gasoline engine car was built by Duryea Brothers in Springfield, and in 1897 the Stanley Brothers of Newton brought out America's most popular steam-powered car, the Stanley Steamer. Massachusetts's interest in the automobile was further underscored in 1903 when it became the first state to issue numbered license plates. That same year the first school in America to offer courses for drivers and auto mechanics opened at the YMCA in Boston.

At the turn of the century, Massachusetts might well have become the automobile center of America had Henry Ford not decided to build his "Tin Lizzie" in Detroit. Car manufacturing did continue in the area. In Springfield there were the Duryea Brothers and the American branch of Rolls Royce, while in Stoneham, Massachusetts, a company called Shawmut Motors produced a gasoline-powered vehicle named "The Shawmut." But despite the similarity in name, there is no evidence that the Shawmut Bank ever contributed anything to the financing of this company. The first record of the Bank's considering a car manufacturing loan does not appear until August 1910, when the directors discussed a loan to Buick, and by this date the Shawmut Motors was already closed.

In the meantime, in 1909, the Shawmut car and Ford's Model T had participated in the country's first coast-to-coast race. First reports declared Ford the winner, but a later examination of results uncovered violations, and five months later the winner's cup was awarded to the Shawmut team. Had the company continued in business, the Bank might well have become one of its financial supporters, but in late 1909 the factory was decimated by fire and never rebuilt.

The loss of the Shawmut Motor Company was not the end of the Shawmut name in the automobile industry. Between 1900 and 1914, at which time the war slowed production, the number of cars in America catapulted from 4,192 to 2.5 million, while capital invested in their manufacture rose from around $8 million to $407.7 million. In spite of this growth, cars remained largely a rich man's toy, although by 1910 some effort was made to change this situation: a method of financing, initiated by the Morris Plan Banks, allowed those with small incomes to borrow for the purchase of cars. By 1913, however, there were only twelve Morris Plan Banks, and a more comprehensive solution had yet to be found.

Anxious to open new markets, Ford Motor Company sent letters to five major banks in 1913 inquiring whether it would be possible to sell cars on an installment plan. The Shawmut responded immediately with a plan that came to be known as Shawmut Bank Plan, the prototype for many automobile financing plans that exist today. According to its stipulations, the purchaser made a 20 percent down payment on the cost of the car, plus a service charge, with the balance paid in twelve monthly installments. The car itself served as collateral. The plan was enthusiastically accepted by Ford, and on July 13, 1916, the first loan was made to a Paul D. Ackerman for a small down payment and five notes of forty dollars each at 6 percent, all of which were secured by a chattel mortgage on a Ford car. It would be difficult to overestimate the impact of this first financing on American culture. Certainly it helped to make the automobile manufacturers' dream of mass production come true, and in this regard, it was also indirectly responsible for putting America on wheels, opening up the suburbs, and changing the landscape into a vast web of highways.

4

One month after Gaston became president of the Shawmut, in May 1907, the Bank's new building was dedicated. Located on Water Street between Devonshire and Congress streets, the granite structure, with its bronzed entranceway, suggested by its location and architecture the central position that the Shawmut had achieved in Boston's financial community. The time, of course, had long since passed when the Bank's functions could be accommodated in small quarters near the wharf's edge. The growth of business and industry had transformed the face of the downtown area, and multi-storied office buildings now dominated a district once given to red brick residences, kitchen gardens, and meandering cattle. It was an expansion bought at a price, but perhaps at no time was this price more apparent than on Sunday afternoons, when the captains and workers in the various businesses returned to their suburban homes and silence settled on the peninsula. This Sunday silence expressed the kind of disengagement between work and everyday life that was the inevitable consequence of growth, and with which Shawmut and all major businesses had to contend.

When Stearns had assumed office, the number of Bank officers and employees was only fifty-eight, by 1907 the personnel had increased to 158. Although it was still possible for all members of the staff to know one another and for problems to be dealt with on a one-to-one basis, this "family" atmosphere was rapidly eroding. One of the first issues facing the Gaston administration was to adapt its personnel policies to the needs of its expanded work force.

A major problem of growth was that of training. In the old days, when the functions of the Bank were few and uncomplicated, a willingness to assume any task could open the way to advancement. The career of an ambitious young man like Stearns was an example of this. Although such a possibility still existed, the increasing complexity of bank functions made it less available. Recognizing this, the American Bankers Association established the American Institute of Banking in 1900, which was designed "to place within the reach of every banking man and woman in America the opportunity to prepare for a better salary, for an ultimate position in the highest ranks of the financial world." To this end the institute offered courses "to qualify graduates for new positions and to acquaint them with the solution of problems continually facing bank executives." In 1909 the American Institute of Banking opened a chapter in Boston and became incorporated in 1914. The National Shawmut, which had always taken an interest in the institute's operations, promptly took out an annual membership in the new corporation, encouraged its staff to participate in its educational programs, which came under the supervision of Boston University, and later assumed half the cost of tuition for those of its staff who successfully completed the institute's final examinations.

Active participation in the American Institute of Banking was one demonstration of the Bank's concern for the professional welfare of its employees; other activities also made clear its concern for their economic welfare. On September 9, 1909, the Board of Directors voted that "the bank be authorized to establish in connection with the officers and clerks of the bank an arrangement for a pension fund to which they may contribute on behalf of this bank a sum not to exceed $10,000." The following year the president introduced a "Bylaws of A Shawmut Annuity System," which was adopted on November 25, 1910, "for the purpose of providing annuities or endowments for employees and officers of the National Shawmut Bank retiring from service of the bank on account of age." The annuity was allotted at retirement age (then sixty-five) or in case of retirement caused by ill health, at which time the employee received the whole amount, or one-tenth followed by nine other payments. The following year another pension plan was introduced. This one stated that a pension "shall be given to clerks (with fifteen years service) under the grade of Assistant Cashier." The amount awarded was to be 30 percent of the salary at the time of retirement.

Still another accommodation made toward the economic welfare of employees occurred on January 27, 1910. At this time the president was authorized "to purchase stock of this bank in such quantities as the Executive Committee may approve for the purpose of supplying such employees as may wish to buy shares of said stock and that it be sold to said employees at less than market price."

Professional and economic security did not define the limits of the Gaston administration's concern for employees. In May 1910 the Bank opened a vacation camp in Silver Lake, New Hampshire. The facility was described in the *Boston Sunday Globe,* July 31, 1910: "Any Young Man in Its [Shawmut's] Employ May Have Two Weeks Rest Amid Delightful Surroundings at a Total Cost of $12.30, Including Fares From the City and Return — An Interesting Experiment by New England's Largest Financial Institution." A year later a letter signed by National Shawmut Bank employees and addressed to Gaston expressed the employees' response:

> Dear Sir: We the undersigned wish to express to you our keen appreciation and gratitude for the wholesome rest and recreation which Shawmut Camp has afforded us and for your solicitation and liberal interest in its establishment and maintenance. To us it has become in fact "The Camp of Proved Desires and Known Delights."

5

On November 17, 1917, William Gaston resigned as president of the National Shawmut Bank. Two months later, at the annual meeting, he was appointed chairman of the Board of Directors, a post Stearns had resigned from the previous October. Between 1907 and 1917 both the country and the Bank underwent dramatic changes. Not only was the internal economic policy of the country altered by the introduction of the Federal Reserve System, but the United States' international position was also changed. Following World War I, and as a consequence of the role it had taken in financing the combatants, the country was no longer a debtor but a creditor nation. Within this context the Shawmut continued to grow, taking a leadership role in many of the major national issues of the day and developing new departments and new operations to meet new demands. It was up to the next Shawmut president to adapt the organizational changes to the needs of a postwar world.

Chapter 8

A Time of Adjustment
The Administration of Alfred L. Aiken
(1917–1923)

At the January 1918 annual meeting of the National Shaw-mut Bank of Boston, the Board of Directors confirmed the November 1917 election of Alfred L. Aiken as president. In the two preceding decades the Bank had experienced consistent growth. Under James P. Stearns and, later, William A. Gaston, it responded quickly to a series of difficult challenges. During a period characterized by corporate consolidations and the growth of big business, it grew through mergers and increased its participation in the financing of railroads, public utilities, and major industries. During a period of regulation and reform, the Shawmut became a leader in supporting reform, and when regulation gave way to war as the central national concern, it became active in the war effort, providing loans to combatant nations abroad and supporting Liberty Loan Act bond drives at home. But in some ways, the challenges confronting Aiken grew increasingly difficult, demanding great reserves of patience and perseverance.

Fulfillment of Shawmut's war commitments during the final year of conflict, readjustment to a postwar economy, and the depression of 1920–1921 were some of the challenges calling for such reserves. Furthermore, following the depression, the country embarked on a period of expansion so rapid and so intense that only those who enjoyed risks could confront them with ease. Alfred Aiken was by neither inclination nor training a financial buccaneer. It is a credit to his intelligence that he appeared to know this and that he resisted the temptation for hasty action. Restrained and analytical, his approach was to proceed cautiously and to react to circumstances rather than aggressively shape them. Within these limits — external circumstances, the brevity of his tenure, and his own personality — lay the strength and weakness of his administration.

1

In November 1917, when William Gaston retired, it was, in the words of one contemporary, "considered no easy task for the financial interests behind the bank to fill the vacancy . . . but when State Street heard of the selection of Alfred L. Aiken, it was satisfied that the tradition of the bank would be upheld and that there would be a continuance of the broad, progressive policy which had characterized the bank for three generations." Contributing to this "satisfaction" were, undoubtedly, the credentials of the new president, who both literally and figuratively stood out among his peers.

Six-foot-six, of impressive and gracious manner, Alfred Aiken came to Shawmut from the prestigious position of governor of the Federal Reserve Bank of Boston, a post he had filled since the Bank's founding in 1914. Nor was his success there surprising. Not only did Aiken serve as an advisor to Nelson Aldrich when the latter was chairman of the National Monetary Commission but, on the demise of Aldrich's bank plan, he became active in setting up the Federal Reserve System. Indeed, though Aiken was only forty-seven when he became president of the Shawmut, his banking experience already extended over two decades. It included the presidency of the Worcester National Bank, 1913–1914; the presidency of the Worcester County Institute for Savings, 1908–1913; treasurer of the latter institution, 1904–1908; and a host of other somewhat less august positions in major financial institutions.

Despite these credentials, however, Aiken's immediate knowledge of the Shawmut was limited. He was the first person appointed to the presidency who had not had some prior connection with the Bank. Nevertheless, and perhaps more important, he was well acquainted with the New England tradition of which the Shawmut was so much a part. His granduncle was Franklin Pierce, New Hampshire native, scion of a distinguished colonial family, and fourteenth president of the United States. His maternal grandfather was William Alfred Buckingham, governor of Connecticut in the 1860s and, later, a United States senator. His father was Brigadier General William A. Aiken, quartermaster general of Connecticut during the Civil War.

Alfred Aiken's personal connection with the Boston community was also extensive. As a young man five years out of college, he moved to the city to become assistant manager of the New England Department of the New York Life Insurance Company, 1894–1899. From there he went to the National Hide and Leather Bank, 1899–1901, as assistant cashier, a post he also filled at the State National Bank, Boston, 1901–1904. In addition, though a graduate of Yale, Aiken was appointed a member of the board of visitors of Harvard University Graduate School of Business Administration. He also served as a trustee of that most venerable Boston institution, the Boston Symphony Orchestra. Despite his experience and broad knowledge of both banking and Boston, however, his years at the Shawmut were not easy ones.

2

The first challenge confronting the Aiken administration was to maintain the well-being of the Bank in the face of an escalating European war. Although the United States entered into the conflict in April 1917, the tide did not immediately turn in favor of the Allies, and a year later, in April 1918, it seemed all too likely that the Germans would break through to Paris. Military experts believed that the next twelve months must be those of vast buildup in material and equipment preparatory to a major siege in 1919. One of the immediate consequences of these conditions was the continued attrition of Bank personnel. By October 1918 the situation had become so acute that the Shawmut directors authorized Aiken "to apply to local Boards for exemption from military service of such employees of the Bank as may be considered absolutely necessary and essential to efficient and proper conduct of the Bank." How such boards would have responded is a matter of speculation; the war ended six weeks later. Nevertheless the application indicates at least one kind of problem with which the new administration had to contend.

Of greater consequence, of course, were the problems of financial management, triggered by the United States' entry into the war and to which the Aiken administration fell heir. One of these problems was the sudden drop in assets that occurred during the first six months of Aiken's tenure. A comparison of the statements for November 1, 1917, and March 1, 1918, shows a plunge in assets of some $24 million, or a fall to $163 million from a previous $187 million. Such a sudden drop would seem to indicate a period of severe strain. But although these declines cannot be minimized, certain mitigating circumstances made their management less difficult to deal with than might be imagined, and the impact less difficult to absorb than might be expected.

The unstable state of the economy at the time contributed to some of the attrition. On February 21, 1918, the Executive Committee suggested a $400,000 charge down on the stock and bond account which reflected a general drop in stock market values. A far greater portion of the fall in assets, however, appears to have been anticipated, to have been provided for, and the challenge was simply to implement plans already made.

Between March 1915 and November 1917, Shawmut's deposits suddenly rose by some $51 million. During this period, allied war purchases reached an all-time high, inflating deposit liabilities of banks arranging payments for these orders. Such deposits were by their nature temporary, and it was the principle of banks enjoying them to keep on hand a large amount of cash and short-term, high-credit commercial paper, such as acceptances, that could be liquidated rapidly when the deposits were withdrawn. This is exactly what happened at Shawmut.

In November 1917, as plans for the spring campaign began to unfold, many foreign depositors began to withdraw funds to meet commitments elsewhere. By March 1918 Shawmut deposits had fallen $15 million while acceptances and letters of credit — that is, paper accepted by the Bank and relevant to foreign trade — dropped $5 million. On the resource side of the ledger, cash resources went down $12 million, and paper pertinent to foreign trade by $9.8 million. What occurred, however, was not so much a real loss as an anticipated adjustment and return to more normal conditions after a period of temporarily inflated figures.

At the same time the Bank experienced a decline in its assets, there was also a countermovement toward growth. This had actually begun in April 1917, when the United States entered the war and domestic industries began to gear up to meet war demands, but the full impact of growth was not felt until March 1918. From then on assets grew rapidly. Loans alone increased by $53 million in six months to reach $147 million in November 1918. Deposits showed a comparable expansion, reaching $143 million in November 1918. Contributing to deposit growth, although minimally, was Shawmut's acceptance as an Alien Property Custodian. In January 1918 the Board of Directors authorized the Bank "to act as depository for Alien Property Custodian under the provision of the Trading with the Enemy Act and confirm the designation of Alfred L. Aiken and William Burnham in signing for the Bank as depository of $1000." On August 8, 1918, the board agreed "to accept the designation as Alien Property Custodian."

The fluctuation in loans and deposits, which required constant vigilance, was only one war-related problem that occupied Aiken during his first year. Another important by-product of the conflict abroad was inflation. Although the War Industries Board placed a cap on prices that were rising most rapidly, holding the line at double the 1913 level, other prices soon caught up. At Shawmut such inflation was reflected in periodic reevaluation and upscaling of salaries and concurrent attempts to contain costs. During this period, the Bank also increased its participation in activities designed to help the war effort. In May 1918 the Board voted to subscribe $50,000 to the American Red Cross, and on November 18, a week after the war ended, it voted a contribution of $50,000 to the United War Work Campaign.

With the end of the war, many of the conditions that had

dictated the Bank's policies during the first twelve months of Aiken's administration also came to an end. Not all of the country's or the Shawmut's war-related activities, however, abruptly terminated. Some loans, particularly those to shipyards, were extended pending the completion of war contracts, whether the actual battleships ever saw service. The sale of Liberty Bonds, now called Victory Notes, also continued, the fifth and final drive taking place in June 1919. Again the Shawmut participated. This latter investment was one in which Aiken was particularly interested, having served as chairman of the First and Second Liberty Loan committees of New England.

Still another by-product of the war with which the Shawmut had to grapple was the spread of Spanish influenza. In February 1919 the minutes declared that "the Shawmut will contribute to a hospital for the outdoor treatment of influenza on the understanding that the National Shawmut Bank can nominate members of its staff to receive preferential treatment of such a hospital." But in general the sudden cessation of conflict introduced a new series of crises with which the Bank now had to contend.

3

National plans for the transition from war to peace were sketchy at best. The most immediate problem was the cancellation of government war contracts, which promptly followed the armistice and put many industries in serious straits. Though some contracts continued (the Bank, for example, continued to loan money and extend credit to Winchester Arms throughout Aiken's term), of $4 billion outstanding nationwide on goods not yet produced, $2.5 billion were cancelled within four weeks. The consequence of this situation introduced a new tumult of events.

One of the most immediate manifestations of the new conditions was a sudden drop in Shawmut's deposits at the end of 1918, a decline which continued into the following spring. The problem created by these withdrawals contrasted with those of the previous year. The latter had been anticipated and could be largely mitigated by cash reserves and easily liquidated acceptances; the immediate postwar withdrawals presented a more severe strain.

The cause of the new attrition was not hard to understand. Industries needed money to compensate for contract losses and to retool to meet postwar demands, hence they withdrew funds. But such withdrawals sharply curtailed the Bank's ability to lend funds, creating a new dilemma. It is no coincidence that the armistice was also followed by a drop in loans as a source of Bank income. Such loans went from $147 million in November 1918 to $129 million in December of that year. During the next six months, however, they began to rise again and by March 1919 reached $137 million, from which level they rapidly continued upward. The immediate ability of the Bank to increase these funds did not come from deposits — they were still decreasing and would not rise again for several months. Instead, some money came from a new expansion in foreign commitments. Indeed, the role of foreign markets in the postwar recovery of the United States and in the history of the Shawmut bears further attention.

During the war the United States became for the first time in its history a creditor, rather than debtor, nation. The value of exports more than doubled, while the value of imports rose by only some 40 percent. Directly after the armistice there was a sharp decline in foreign-market demands, which had been largely based on war needs. By the spring of 1919, however, as Europe adjusted to peace, it turned again to the United States as a source for goods and commodities it could not yet produce itself.

In 1919, after an initial falloff, the dollar volume of exports began to rise again, and by the end of the year, the excess of exports over imports reached about $4 billion, the highest in the country's history. All of these events affected the Shawmut, whose affairs were a microcosm of the national situation. On December 31, 1918, when foreign trade dropped in importance as a factor in the national economy, the Bank's statement of condition shows that acceptances as a source of earning assets went down some $6 million to 11 percent of total assets as compared with 14 percent the previous month. In the spring, as foreign trade revived, the situation at the Bank also changed, with acceptances rising to $30 million, again 14 percent of total resources. By December they were up to $34 million or 15 percent, corresponding to a trend noted in the eighth annual report of the Federal Reserve Board: "Acceptances [for member banks] reached a peak in December 1919."

If the story of the Shawmut in the immediate postarmistice months was typical of most commercial banks, it was not entirely so, for there were some long-lasting effects that were specific to the Bank itself, particularly in regard to the formation of its own Foreign Department.

The Foreign Department had initially been developed as a separate entity under Gaston, with the vice president, John Bolinger, assuming responsibility for overseeing international activities. It was not until June 1919, however, that the Bank, prodded by growing offshore activity, gave the unit recognizable administrative status. A new position, assistant manager of the Foreign Department, was added. The post was first filled by John Canfield. Shortly after, a second assistant manager of the Foreign Department position was created and taken by William Hartney. In the course of the next several years the names of the particular officers changed, but the recognition of the Foreign Department as an integral unit of Shawmut did not.

It was also in 1919 that a six-member Foreign Committee was appointed from the Board of Directors. The members were to serve three consecutive months, to meet every Thursday, and to report weekly to the board. A temporary rise in acceptances, the permanent formalization of the Foreign Department, and the founding of the Foreign Committee were not, however, the only effects that the United States' increased involvement in offshore markets had on Shawmut.

By April 1919, the United States had begun to recover from the transition to a peacetime economy, and for the next twelve months economic indicators, particularly production, wholesale and retail sales, and favorable balance-of-trade figures, continued to rise, creating a boom economy. Paralleling this boom was a rise in Shawmut's assets, and the Bank began to look for new ways to develop earnings.

Two of the most important ways it chose to do this were directly affected by the growing importance of international markets. To capitalize on these markets and to take advantage of a new federal law broadening commercial bank activities overseas, the Aiken administration conceived of Shawmut Corporation of Boston, a subsidiary wholly owned by the Bank and designed to carry on offshore banking transactions. The Bank also became involved in a new investment — the Caribbean Sugar Company — that subsequently influenced the administration of three Shawmut presidents. Because both these transactions, the one a subsidiary, the other a speculative investment, are important in Shawmut's history, they are discussed in detail below.

The Shawmut Corporation of Boston. The concept of a commercial bank forming an organization to manage and develop the growing business in acceptances and government bonds was by no means unusual. The Federal Reserve Act of 1913 included a section, 25(a), specifically authorizing national banks to form corporate subsidiaries "to engage in international or foreign banking or other international or foreign financial operations." It was not until after the war, however, that conditions made the formation of such corporations seem attractive, and they became a popular form of expansion. As the war in Europe had dragged on, trade with the continent became increasingly complex. As a consequence businessmen in the United States looked more and more toward the other Americas for new markets. In 1917 the First National Bank of Boston opened its first foreign branch in Buenos Aires, Argentina. The enterprise was successful almost immediately and was destined to become one of the most important branches of any United States bank in that area.

Not coincidentally, on June 21, 1917, the Board of Directors at the Shawmut authorized President Gaston "to petition the Federal Reserve Board for permission to invest in 2,000 shares at $125 per share of the Mercantile Bank of the Americas, Inc." Mercantile Bank was an enterprise promoted by Guaranty Trust in New York and designed to operate in the Caribbean and South America. A year and a half later, in the fall of 1918, by which time Aiken was in office, National Shawmut was given an opportunity, apparently by Guaranty Trust in New York, to extend its interest in Mercantile Bank. The total amount of stock to be issued this time was worth $1,000,000 at $140 per share. The amount allotted pro rata to Shawmut was

$75,000. The express purpose of the investment was to establish a bank in Cuba, the stock of which would be owned by Mercantile. Aiken consulted with Gaston and the latter approved the subscription.

Six months later, in the spring of 1919, the Board of Directors of the National Shawmut requested permission of the Federal Reserve Board to invest in the stock of a corporation "to be principally engaged in international or foreign banking," and on May 1, 1919, the Shawmut Corporation of Boston came into being. A year later, in March 1920, the Bank sold to its affiliate Corporation almost all its shares of Mercantile Bank of the Americas, Inc., and certain other shares in foreign banking corporations.

What the confluence of these factors suggests is that the Shawmut Corporation of Boston was established not so much to operate as an autonomous unit that would develop its own business but rather as an extension of National Shawmut Bank's own Foreign Department. It assumed responsibility for certain foreign banking affairs, particularly those focused in the Caribbean. That this was an area rich in potential had been made clear by the experience of the First National. Shawmut did not, of course, have a branch in the Americas, but in all probability, it hoped to develop competitive interests in that area through the Shawmut Corporation of Boston, which was tied to the Mercantile Bank and its proposed Cuban branch.

Whatever the particular motive for establishing the Shawmut Corporation of Boston, it did come into being in May 1919. The disposition of its stock was: 15,000 shares to the National Shawmut Bank; 2000 to the Guaranty Trust Company, New York; with another 2000 in blocks of 500 apiece held by Rhode Island Hospital Trust Company, Providence, Rhode Island; Worcester Bank and Trust Company, Worcester, Massachusetts; Merchants National Bank, Worcester, Massachusetts; and Union Trust Company, Springfield, Massachusetts. By the end of its first year it had a total capitalization of $1.9 million and a paid-in surplus of $380,000; the future looked bright indeed. Unfortunately, one year later the new Corporation was faltering badly, and stockholders were asked to pay additional funds in the form of a 40 percent assessment. By December 2, 1921, Shawmut Corporation was in serious trouble.

Why the Corporation foundered quite so badly is a matter

of speculation. In all likelihood it was a combination of several factors. Certainly the primary reason was the failure of two of its major investments, the Mercantile Bank and Foreign Bank and Share Corporation, both of which were discovered by the bank examiner in December 1921 to be "worthless." Unfortunately the Shawmut Corporation of Boston had little with which to cushion this failure. It did have substantial holdings in Caribbean Sugar Company, and though the bank examiner did not find these explicitly worthless, they were of little immediate value.

Behind this specific reason for disaster, however, lies a host of others. Included among these was the lack of diversity in the Corporation's investments, which can be attributed to its overly narrow focus. Shawmut Corporation of Boston had concentrated on simply extending the Bank's interests in the Caribbean by a series of overlapping investments and failed to develop any real business on its own. As a result, by December 1921 the net worth of the Corporation had sunk to $653,000, and the book value of the stock had depreciated to $34 per share.

To remedy the situation Aiken recommended that the Bank acquire all the stock of the Shawmut Corporation of Boston "so that it might be in a position to make a consolidated return of the income of the Bank and the Corporation," and this it subsequently did. However, the Corporation was not dissolved. A letter to the Shawmut Board of Directors from two National Shawmut vice presidents, John Bolinger and Robert S. Potter, both of whom were closely allied to the Corporation from its inception, indicates why: "It is our recommendation that the Corporation continue for the following reasons: 1) loss of prestige due to closing New York and Boston offices, 2) necessity for maintenance of an office in Boston to handle Caribbean Sugar and other overdue accounts, 3) necessity for maintenance of a New York office (justified on grounds that the rental contract would not run out until October 1924 and that the office was needed to handle other overdue accounts)."

Thus the Corporation continued, but its focus was changed. Originally the emphasis was on making investments on behalf of the Corporation; by March 1922 the directors had decided that attention should also be paid to the distribution of securities. The new focus was explicitly noted in the Corporation minutes of April 24, 1922: "It was the unanimous opinion of the Executive Committee that the Corporation should enter the Acceptances, Certificate of Indebtedness and Liberty Bond business." A list follows of the inventory to be retained: "A maximum portfolio of Acceptances, $2 million; U.S. Certificates, $500,000; Liberty Bonds, $1 million."

The change required no new application to the Federal Reserve Board. The bylaws, however, were modified to relax restrictions on certain signing procedures and to allow for the appointment of new officers, specifically assistant managers. Both organizational changes suggest the anticipation of new business, and by June the maximum portfolio had already been increased to allow for $5 million in acceptances and $2 million in Liberty Bonds. The Corporation had begun to move in a new direction that would be fully realized under the next Shawmut Bank president, Walter Bucklin.

The Caribbean Sugar Company. Closely related to the development of Shawmut Corporation, and indeed the crux of that organization's early problems, was the Bank's and subsequently the Corporation's investment in a Cuban sugar enterprise called the Caribbean Sugar Company.

It might at first seem strange that a Boston bank became involved in such a company, but traditionally the town had strong ties to the West Indies. Many a Boston Brahmin family could trace the roots of its first fortune to colonial triangular trade in which sugar played a major part. In the early nineteenth century such trade had faltered, but in the wake of the Spanish-American War, when Cuba acquired its independence, American businessmen again began to look south again. The passage of the Platt Amendment in 1902 allowed for a substantial tariff reduction on Cuban sugar, which promoted a rapid increase in its production. Production was further stimulated by an influx of New England capital. Shawmut's involvement with the Caribbean Sugar Company may thus be understood as simply part of a larger pattern.

The Bank's concern in the area began in March 1920 with a loan of $250,000 to a Cuban company called Macareno Associates. In July this firm was succeeded by a new company called

Caribbean Sugar. In the next month both the Bank and Corporation increased their commitment so that by mid-August they had an aggregate of $1,250,000 invested in Caribbean Sugar Company.

The impetus for this investment was the rising price of sugar, which between March and August 1920 climbed from 5.5 cents to 22.5 cents a pound. By September, however, the price collapsed and within six months was down to a ten-year low of 3.75 cents a pound.

Despite the collapse and Shawmut's own heavy exposure, the Bank did not call its loans. In fact, the board voted to extend its commitment in hopes that once the plant was fully operative it might be able to realize substantial recovery. An additional factor influencing Shawmut's response was the fact that well over half of Caribbean Sugar Company's 8 percent coupon notes were held not only by the Bank and the Corporation but also by Shawmut directors. To have liquidated the company in a depressed market would have incurred heavy losses all around.

It was a gamble watched with grim resolve in the Shawmut board room. But the gamble paid off, and on July 23, 1923, a Shawmut vice president, Frank C. Nichols, was able to announce "the Statement for Caribbean Sugar has been received . . . and indicated profits for the year available for interest on prior lien notes and 8 percent notes, etc. before depreciation of $662,000." The story of Caribbean Sugar, however, was by no means over and became an issue again in the next Shawmut administration.

4

The previous two sections have focused on two distinct sets of conditions which influenced the financial policy of the Bank during the first two years of Aiken's administration. In summary, these were: the conditions engendered by the final year of the war and the shift in priorities attendant on the United States' entry into that war, and the conditions created by the transition to a peacetime economy, culminating in the boom of 1919 and early 1920, when the National Shawmut began to organize Shawmut Corporation and invest in Caribbean Sugar. The environment however, soon began to change again.

The opening paragraph of the seventh annual report of the Federal Reserve Board for 1920 describes the conditions under which the Shawmut was operating:

> The past year has been essentially a period of reaction. The year immediately preceding was characterized by an unprecedented orgy of extravagance, a mania for speculation, overly extended business in nearly all lines and in every section of the country.

The report went on to recognize that "world events forced upon this country during a period of five years the greatest expansion it has ever known." Noting that it was universally realized that sooner or later there would be reaction and readjustment, the report concluded:

> While indications that the country was approaching a readjustment period were not lacking in 1919, it was not until the spring of 1920 that it became generally recognized that reaction had set in. This process of readjustment began almost simultaneously throughout the world . . . The process has been necessarily painful.

In 1919 the country produced more goods than domestic consumer need warranted, but the excess was easily exported. As Europe began to experience its own postwar recession, the market for American goods dried up. Production was cut back, prices fell, unemployment rose, and the consumer market shrunk even further. The pattern was classic, and it is worth noting here the new importance of the European market on domestic events. Many relate the 1920–1921 recession in the United States to the collapse of the Japanese silk market in the fall of 1919. This had, some economists claim, a domino effect on national economies that the war had inextricably linked together.

Whatever the precipitating cause, 1920 was a year of "painful" decline. The trend continued downward: "During 1921 there was, until December, an almost continuous decline in loans and earning assets of the Federal Reserve member banks," according to the eighth annual report of the Federal Reserve

Bank. Again, Shawmut serves as a microcosm of this larger world.

In December 1919 Shawmut's assets had stood at a postwar high of $258 million; its loan portfolio at $163 million. Two years later comparable figures were $164 million and $99 million. But if the Bank was at a loss to forestall the impact of external circumstances, it could and did make an attempt to mitigate them.

The policy that Aiken pursued during the recession was to go slow, resist the temptation to panic, and hold the line. This approach was manifest in both his loan and dividend policies.

He prevailed on the board to continue loans on the books as long as possible and, in some instances, to extend further credit even if repayment was doubtful. That some of the renewals were questionable was made clear by the extensive write-offs that the next administration had to make. The reasoning behind the renewals, or delaying strategy, however, was also clear, and it was based on two premises: when conditions get better the chance of a loan being recovered will improve; and if a particular loan does not improve, it is better to write it off during a period of affluence, when the loss can be more easily absorbed, than during a period of recession, when attrition in assets is likely to shake confidence.

The Bank had, of course, its own precedent for such a delaying strategy. In 1907 Gaston had enjoined his fellow bankers not to make a bad situation worse by hastily calling loans and demanding repayment when such repayment might seriously jeopardize a company temporarily in bad straits but essentially solid. The idea was then relatively new and gave rise to some criticism in the financial community. But by 1920–1921 it was an accepted practice, and in fact, the eighth annual report of the Federal Reserve took particular note of "frozen credits" as accountable for a distinction between the very bad state of business and the somewhat more sanguine picture indicated by bank loans:

> Frozen credit is credit carried beyond the time when the transactions which gave rise to the credit should normally have liquidated themselves. Because of the unliquid loans the member banks loan curve indicated a more gradual and moderate liquidation (than circumstances might have warranted).

Closely related to the Bank's freezing of credit during the recession was the equally prudential and, in a sense, optimistic attitude that it took toward dividends. The pattern of determining dividends during Aiken's administration began ordinarily enough. In December 1918, when assets rose to a new high, the board voted a quarterly dividend of 3 percent or $3 in contrast to the $2.50 that had obtained previously. Dividends remained at this level until June 1920, when, despite a six-month general decline, the board voted "a regular dividend of three percent, plus an extra two percent to be paid July 1, 1920." In September 1920, though assets had dropped further to $205 million, the quarterly dividend became 3.5 percent or $3.50 per share. Here, and in spite of a continuous decline in earning resources, the dividends stabilized for the next two years. Further, not until December 1922, when it was clear that the economy and the Bank's resources were improving, were dividends reduced and then by only fifty cents, to $3. The only way to explain this apparent anomaly is that the administration felt it important to show its faith in the economy and particularly in the Bank's finances and chose to do this by keeping the return on shares relatively high. Such a policy would have been dangerous, of course, unless those who implemented it had good reason to believe that the institution was solid and that the economy would right itself. Apparently Aiken was sure on both these points.

Certainly he knew that the Bank had a large and diverse portfolio and that it had not overextended itself in any one area. Paradoxically much of the evidence for this diversity comes from the number and variety of loans that his successor, Walter Bucklin, eventually wrote off. Bucklin chose to see these later write-offs as indicative of a previously weak loan policy, but viewed from another perspective, they may be taken as evidence that under Aiken the Bank had begun to extend its interests and to lessen its dependence on certain, specifically local aspects of the nation's economy. If Aiken is to be faulted for some poor loans, he must also be given credit for extending the Bank's loan portfolio beyond railroads, communication, textiles, and utilities into such diverse areas as farm equipment, drug development, and automobile manufacturing. Furthermore, within these new categories the Bank had extended credit to a variety of firms. For example, between 1917 and 1921 accounts were opened up or continued to Ford, Rolls Royce, Wills-St. Clair, Willys Overland, Packard, and Maxwell Motors. Given such a broad base of commitments, the administration had good reason to believe that, barring an apocalyptic disaster, the law of averages would operate in Shawmut's favor and that a proportionate number of businesses would weather the recession.

Furthermore, Aiken was a student of economic history. Although one can only speculate to what degree such historical perspective influenced his policy decisions during the recession, it is logical to assume that it did. In all likelihood, thanks to his awareness that history is a process, a series of recurring patterns, Aiken had confidence that business would right itself, making him more prone to passive holding policies than a president who saw each event as unique would have been. In any event, the Bank avoided precipitous moves and maintained an outward calm, generally optimistic approach throughout the recession.

Time, of course, proved Aiken's attitude well founded. Business did improve, and although Walter Bucklin might later be irritated to write off loans contracted by his predecessor, making his own accumulation of assets seem less spectacular, it can be well argued that the courage and confidence of men like Aiken, their willingness to hang on, to follow through, and to assert their faith in recovery actually brought about the rapid resurgence of the economy.

By late 1921 business conditions were already improving, and according to the annual report of the Federal Reserve Board, 1922 saw "almost continuous recovery from disorganized markets and depressed business conditions resulting from the abrupt decline of 1920." True, Shawmut's own recovery lagged somewhat behind that of the nation. In March 1922 assets dropped to a postwar low of $155 million, but this was largely because of delayed write-offs, and from then on, they began to rise rapidly.

The final year and a half of Aiken's administration was marked by a general return to prosperity. During this period particular attention was paid to further diversification of the loan portfolio. Some characteristic new loans of the period included $100,000 to W. R. Hearst (November 1922); a million-dollar line of credit to Henshaw Motors, secured by Dodge cars at wholesale price

(December 1922); $500,000 to Mitsui Bank, secured by Imperial Japanese Bonds (March 1923).

The latter loan is of particular interest, for one by-product of the recession was a change in the character of Shawmut's foreign transactions and in the components of its resources as a consequence of this change. In December 1919, as noted above, acceptances peaked at $38 million or 15 percent of total resources. Then they declined rapidly as a consequence of the overall decrease of foreign trade. In terms of percentages, though, acceptances still remained an important resource. As the country began to get back on its feet, however, the Bank shifted its focus away from acceptances. By December 1922 they constituted only 10 percent of total resources, and nine months later, when Aiken resigned, they made up less than 1 percent. This change was due to Shawmut's decreased involvement in export-import transactions, though its Foreign Department continued a brisk business by placing new emphasis on extending sovereign-guaranteed loans within foreign countries, such as the loan to the Mitsui Bank.

It was also in this postrecession period that the Bank began to concentrate more on U.S. bonds and certificates, which had begun to offer significant returns. While they did not constitute a large part of total assets, the volume held by the Bank increased from a postwar low of $575,000 to a high of almost $11 million in December 1922, illustrating the administration's vigilance and effort to keep abreast of shifting opportunities.

5

Since Aiken's financial policies were largely dictated by rapidly changing external circumstances which occupied his attention, he had little time for long-range plans. Nevertheless, he oversaw the development of some very important bank structures. Not the least of these was the Foreign Department, which gained new dimension under his direction, and the founding of Shawmut Corporation. Other areas whose early growth must be credited to his administration were the Trust Department and the Business Extension Department.

Trust operations began under Gaston, when a change in federal law allowed commercial banks to pursue such business. It was not until August 1918, however, that a change in Shawmut's bylaws recognized that "there shall be a separate department known as the Trust Department." Its duties were carefully spelled out and subsequently modified in June 1920, when the bylaws were again revised.

Nineteen eighteen also saw the beginning of the Business Extension Department, also known as the Development Department. Originally called the New Business Department, it was designed by E. H. Moore, a Bank officer who had come to the Shawmut in 1902. Its function was to establish data outlining the relationship of customers and potential customers to the Bank and to pay personal calls on such persons. The department represented a pioneering effort on the part of Shawmut — it was apparently the first such department in New England, if not the nation. And while its full potential was not realized until the next administration, credit for its introduction belongs to Aiken.

Similar credit must also be accorded to Aiken for the introduction of a Time Sales Department. Organized in August 1923, Time Sales was designed to offer additional services and assist in auto purchases. In the next decade, it became one of Shawmut's major services.

An attitude — if not an innovation — that dates from the Aiken years concerns the remuneration of employees. The Shawmut always attempted to remain competitive in terms of compensation. It was not until after World War I, however, that the rapid fluctuations in the economy truly tested intention against performance. How the Bank responded to this test set a precedent for the future, and for this reason, a look at some of the salary changes during the period and the reasons for them will be valuable.

The start of the war in Europe introduced an inflationary trend, and the price of goods and services began to rise at the rate of 10 to 15 percent each year. Following the war these prices took an even sharper turn upward until, by June 1920, they were generally 25 percent above the wartime peak. The rise in the cost of living was accompanied by a demand for higher wages, and between 1915 and 1920 the average per capita income rose from somewhat above $300 to $800.

In response to these conditions, Aiken appointed a board committee, the Committee on Salaries, in the spring of 1918 to study salary increases. In July 1918, as a result of its findings, he introduced a new scale of clerical salaries ranging from $600 to $900. In deference to the committee's recommendations, the Bank also instituted a bonus plan according to which "during present abnormal conditions a bonus shall be paid in semi-annual installments amounting to 20 percent per annum on all salaries less than $2,000, and 10 percent on all others up to $3,000." The salaries of officers were also raised. In December these figures were further augmented with an additional bonus of 10 percent for all employees from the rank of clerk through cashier.

The following year prices were still rising, and still another raise was granted. At the time the Committee on Salaries, composed of Henry S. Howe, Louis K. Liggett, and J. Franklin McElwain, commented that the National Shawmut Bank employed about 450 men and women below the grade of assistant cashier, and that "the average wage is $1,100, although with the bonus this becomes $1,275." They went on to say that, although this scale was more or less in keeping with other banks in the area, they felt "the National Shawmut Bank should take the lead in paying its employees liberally and that by doing so direct and indirect advantages accrue to the bank." The committee then recommended that the bonuses should be discontinued and salaries generally raised, which was done.

It was also in 1919 that the idea of "profit sharing" was first introduced at the Bank. The suggestion gave rise to considerable discussion which focused on the idea that, although the scheme was "in vogue in some New York banks," it might not be appropriate for the Shawmut. The president was asked to investigate the plan; he did not, however, return his verdict until a year and half later, by which time the economy had already taken a downturn. How much this latter fact influenced his final conclusion — "profit sharing is not a good idea" — is difficult to say. But the length of time that he took to reach his conclusion suggests he would not have favored it under any circumstances.

In the meantime, periodic raises were granted at all levels, between June 1919 and December 1920. Then, as the cost of living as a whole was generally declining, no further raises were considered until January 1923.

Salary policy under Aiken adhered to the following principles: that the Bank should take the lead in paying its employees liberally; that remuneration should reflect larger economic conditions and take cost of living into account; and that particular merit or value to the Bank should also be recognized in salary. (This final policy provided a precedent for President Bucklin's later Executive Bonus Plan and for similar plans extant in the 1980s.)

The expansion of the Foreign and Trust departments and the founding of Shawmut Corporation of Boston, the Business Extension Department, and the Time Sales Department were part of the increased volume of business that Shawmut handled during the Aiken years. To aid in the efficient handling of this increased volume the Bank modernized some of its operations. The addressograph, the multigraph, and the photostat, all of which had profited from recent technological improvements, became important tools in Bank business. To oversee the purchase and operation of office machinery some central control was needed, so purchasing and supply activities, which had previously been conducted on a hand-to-mouth basis, were reorganized and formalized. It was also as a consequence of increased business that the Shawmut began to look for more spacious quarters.

In 1907, when the National Shawmut had moved into its new quarters at 40 Water Street, the directors were confident that they had provided room for years to come. Expansion, however, outstripped even the most generous predictions of need, and in May 1919 the board voted "that the purchase of the real estate on Devonshire St. and Congress Square adjoining real estate belonging to this bank, known as the Parker Building and Howe Estates, containing in all about 6,803.9 sq. ft. of land . . . be approved." The following year the minutes show "space considered an immediate need and the Building Committee authorized to proceed at once with the new building." During the course of the next several years, plans to convert the new property to Bank use and remodel the existing facility moved ahead rapidly.

Shortly before Aiken left the presidency, a new wing, forming a right angle with the vastly refurbished older portion of 40

Water Street, was opened to the public. Reflecting the latest in the growing art of bank design, the new wing housed those services directly related to public contact. An information booth was built for convenience, and the disposition of paying and receiving tellers was carefully calculated to provide easy access and reduce long lines during crowded hours. Here also was a great double stairway leading to new safe-deposit vaults, described as "having the delicacy of a chronometer and the strength of a battleship." Other customer facilities in this area included "retiring" or "coupon" rooms where safe-deposit boxes "adapted to the smallest or the largest need" could be opened in utmost privacy, and larger rooms for business meetings.

At the same time, the old building had been remodeled in such a way as to group together particular departments and give physical expression to their relationship. For example, the Foreign Department, previously relegated to a lower floor, was now placed near other specialized banking departments in recognition of the intimate connection that it had, or should have, with those specialized branches of the Bank.

Finally, to reflect the continuity of the whole, the facade of the new wing was designed in a classical Corinthian line that conformed with the architecture of the old building. To further conform with the Water Street portion, the interior walls were finished in Blanco marble, with great pilasters supporting decorated beams and a ceiling of recessed and elaborately bordered panels. Other sections boasted dark English-oak panels, terrazzo walls embellished with bas-reliefs in the designs of notable gold coins, and bays faced in marble and bronze. The overall impression of the new wing and renovated structures was of the opulence, order, and dignity that was so much a part of the banking atmosphere in the first quarter of the twentieth century.

6

In September 1923, just short of five years after he had assumed the presidency of the National Shawmut, Alfred Aiken resigned. His tenure coincided with a period of tumultuous upheavals not only in the financial world but also in the social and political world.

In Boston old wealth still lived in elegant Victorian mansions along Commonwealth Avenue and Marlborough and Beacon streets. Boston Brahmins, though they had long ago conceded their political domination of the city, remained its cultural mentors. Boston ladies were still "at home" on weekday afternoons unless they took their tea at the Chilton Club or the new Copley Plaza (built in 1912), or attended the symphony on Friday afternoons. Boston gentlemen still walked to work across the Public Garden and the Common, still knew that the greatest sin was to invade principal, that the greatest virtue was the prudent-man rule, and that the most dependable code was Holmes's axiom: "put not your trust in money but put your money in trust."

Nevertheless life was changing. Many a young Brahmin, returned from the war, was discovering new pleasures in fast cars, which could speed him to North Shore debutante parties where the sophisticated hostess provided jazz in lieu of waltzes. Married, he was finding the near suburbs as delightful as Beacon Street; confronted with career choices, he was beginning to wonder if Paris, or perhaps New York, might offer opportunities as challenging as those provided by the family business.

The young and the privileged, however, were not the only ones beginning to question old values and seek new horizons. In September 1919, in an unprecedented action, 1117 of 1544 Boston patrolmen walked off the job and did not return until the governor, Calvin Coolidge, placing the National Guard in control, declared, "There is no right to strike against the public safety by anybody, anywhere, anytime." In April 1920 two workmen, Sacco and Vanzetti, were accused of murdering a paymaster and guard at a South Braintree shoe factory, and the resultant trial focused a new kind of attention on the Athens of America.

In the meantime the country itself had begun to change. In 1919 the Communist Labor Party of America was founded. In January 1920 the Volstead Act forbade Americans their traditional drinking habits, and speakeasies promptly appeared. In November women voted for the first time in a national election under provision of the Nineteenth Amendment. In 1921 Warren

G. Harding won the presidential election on the slogan "back to normalcy," skirt lengths began to go up, and two years later, the House of Bishops of the United States Episcopal Church voted to delete the word *obey* from the marriage ceremony. Perhaps even more important, the population had begun to move. In 1919 railroad mileage reached an all-time peak of 253,000 miles. In 1920 the first municipal airport opened in Tucson, Arizona. In 1921, for the first time in American history, urban population (cities and towns) outstripped rural population 51 to 49 percent. In 1923 more cars were built than had been produced in the first fifteen years of the industry.

While few of these events directly affected the National Shawmut Bank (it did vote to subscribe $10,000 to the Funds for Defenders of Public Safety just before the end of the policemen's strike), they were symptomatic of a new attitude that was coming to dominate American thinking and mores. It was an attitude characterized by the sense that more was not enough, change was not to be resisted, and that "something" waited just around the corner.

Against this background, Aiken struggled to keep the National Shawmut responsive, introducing new structures that would capitalize on expanding foreign markets and answer new consumer demands. His opportunities to initiate policies, however, were curtailed by the need to react promptly to rapidly changing circumstances. As a consequence, the main thrust of his management was simply to keep the Bank on course and to hold it secure against the buffeting of economic change. But as the pace of life accelerated, there is some evidence that certain Shawmut directors grew restless with this prudential approach and yearned for a more adventurous leader, one who would not just keep things going but get them going.

Whether this restlessness actually existed and figured in Aiken's decision to step down from the Shawmut presidency is uncertain. In any case, Aiken gave his resignation to the Board of Directors in September 1923 and it was accepted. At the same time William Gaston, who had served as chairman of the board since 1917, also resigned, and Aiken assumed this basically emeritus position until April 1924, when he relinquished that also.

By this time, the administration of Walter S. Bucklin had begun. His predecessor had seen the end of one world, which came to a finish with the conclusion of the Great War, and stayed on through the beginning of what economic historians would call "The New Era." It was Bucklin, however, who charted the course of the National Shawmut in that era.

Chapter 9

The Twenties
The First Six Years of the
Administration of Walter Bucklin
(1923–1929)

IN September 1923, when Alfred Aiken tendered his resignation as president of the National Shawmut Bank and became chairman of the Board, Walter S. Bucklin was elected to succeed him. Six months later, when Aiken resigned as chairman, that title was temporarily abandoned, and Bucklin as president became the chief executive officer.

That Walter Bucklin assumed the central position of authority at the Bank less than a year after he had been elected to its Board of Directors suggests something of the personality and qualifications of the man. He was unquestionably a person with high ambitions and not in the least loathe to seize the reins and get things done when others of more cautious disposition might hesitate. That these characteristics appealed to the directors, eager to get the Shawmut moving after a year of postwar depression, seems certain. Indeed, in all likelihood, those who brought him onto the board in March 1923 anticipated Aiken's resignation and recognized in Bucklin, who was then president of Liberty Mutual Insurance Company, the kind of vitality that Shawmut needed to take advantage of the current resurgence in business activity.

1

Walter Stanley Bucklin was born on February 2, 1880, in New York City. His father was a successful shoe and leather merchant who retired while Walter was still a youngster and moved his family to a farm in New London, New Hampshire. There the future Shawmut president attended Colby Academy, graduating in 1898.

Even at the age of eighteen Walter Bucklin was strong-minded and determined. Despite family remonstrances, he decided to forgo college and try his fortunes in the working world of Boston. Answering a newspaper advertisement, he secured a position as an office boy at $5 a week in the Boston branch of the American Surety Company of New York. Impressed with the importance of law to the insurance business, he enrolled at the School of Law at Boston University on October 4, 1899, though he continued to work part-time. In 1902 he earned his law degree, graduating cum laude, was admitted to the Massachusetts Bar, and was promoted to assistant manager, in addition to counsel, of the American Surety office in Boston. Bucklin served in this capacity for seven years, until 1909, when he resigned to become an independent insurance broker.

Bucklin's success in his own office brought him to the attention of a group of businessmen who were in the process of forming a new company, the Massachusetts Employers Insurance Association, and young Bucklin was invited to join the organization. He accepted, serving as vice president and general manager from 1912 until 1914, when he was elected president. In this office one of his first acts would be to obtain permission for the company to assume risks nationally — previously it had been restricted to business in Massachusetts. He also petitioned for a change of company name, and on August 15, 1917, Massachusetts Employers Insurance Association became Liberty Mutual Insurance Company. Liberty Mutual grew into one of the nation's most prominent insurance companies, with Bucklin as its president until 1924 and its chairman of the board until 1954.

As vice president and general manager of Massachusetts Employers Issurance Association and later as president of Liberty

Mutual, Bucklin's administrative skills became clear to the general Boston business community. They were particularly clear to Louis Liggett, who was president of United Drug Company of Boston, a director of the Shawmut Bank, and a founding director of Massachusetts Employers. In addition, Liggett was president of United Drug Mutual Insurance Company, which in 1916–1917 became affiliated with Liberty Mutual. To bring about this affiliation Liggett and Bucklin worked together closely, and no doubt the former's favorable impression of his colleague was an important factor in Bucklin's invitation to join Shawmut's board. Walter Stanley Bucklin became a member of the Shawmut board on March 23, 1923, and six months later was elected president.

2

When Bucklin became president of the National Shawmut Bank, the 1920–1921 depression was two years in the past, and the mood of the country was one of confidence and optimism. Despite recent hard times, the immediate postwar faith in the limitless possibilities of business and industry had quickly revived. Factories geared up to full capacity. Industrial production rose, and the federal government cooperated by pursuing a laissez-faire policy, although at the behest of the business community, it did support certain restrictive tariffs to assure exports would remain higher than imports.

Ahead lay an era of "good times" that would extend from 1922 to 1929. One important factor of this was the growth in the United States population, which expanded approximately 12 percent during the twenties. Industrial production went up even faster: in 1922 the gross national product was $72 billion; at the end of 1928 it was $96 billion. Per capita income more than kept pace with this growth, rising some 30 percent between 1921 and 1929.

As the 1920s unfolded, confidence dominated the national mood — confidence that there was money to be made and money to be spent. The challenge for the banker was to assure that such transactions took place in his institution. It was a perfect challenge for Walter Bucklin, who was not a banker by training but a salesman and a promoter.

Shadows from the Past

When Bucklin took office as president, Shawmut's assets stood at $182 million, deposits had risen to $132 million, and momentum for new growth was established. One of his first tasks in taking advantage of the new conditions was to reevaluate certain past decisions. Those areas that came under particular scrutiny were: loans held over from the Aiken administration that had a poor record of recovery; the Shawmut Corporation of Boston, which had recently been reorganized and was at a crossroads in its development; and specific commitments to companies such as Caribbean Sugar and Cumberland Mountain Coal, both of which were ventures in which Shawmut had invested heavily and which had suffered reverses. Their nature, however, was such that their future was difficult to predict.

Past Loans. In order to clear the boards of past problems and open the way toward new growth, Bucklin began his administration with an extensive examination of both the Bank and Corporation's securities and loan portfolios. As a consequence of this examination, the next three years saw substantial write-offs. The process began on December 26, 1923, a mere three months and ten days into the new presidency. At this time Bucklin, on the recommendation of bank examiners, asked for and secured authority to write off $2,110,053. In 1924 he charged off $600,000; in 1925, $718,383, and in October 1926, $762,791, of which $600,000 was charged to the bond depreciation account.

Many of these bad loans represented investments carried by the Bank since the depression of 1920–1921, loans deliberately continued until such time as the economy rallied and their loss could be more easily absorbed. Nevertheless, Bucklin's statement of his stewardship to the Board of Directors in November 1926 suggests that he grudged these write-offs, not so much because they were losses but because they diminished the otherwise spectacular gains of his administration. Certainly he was not hesitant to cast blame or take credit.

Thus he declared that "over 95% of the loss of income from non-earning assets originated prior to the present management and under conditions over which the latter had no control." He went on to say that "the present management has been fortunate in keeping losses for which it is responsible below normal." And finally, after extolling the current "excellent earning power of the Bank and Corporation," he concluded that if his administration had not had to compensate for the past, "the average annual earnings for the period would have been at the rate of about 22%."

Significant in this report are also frequent mentions of the Shawmut Corporation of Boston, a problem that Bucklin inherited from his predecessor. He was quick to point out that, whereas previously it had been a source of loss, under his guidance it enjoyed new and profitable expansion. The accuracy of Bucklin's perception can be assessed by a brief review of this all-important investment organization.

The Shawmut Corporation of Boston. As mentioned in the previous chapter, the Shawmut Corporation of Boston was organized in 1919 to extend the Bank's involvement in international banking. After its difficult beginnings, the Corporation's focus was shifted in 1922 from international investments to the distribution of both foreign and domestic investment securities. By 1923 the Corporation had begun to rally.

One of the first steps Bucklin took to revive the Corporation was to expand its physical presence. In 1923 the headquarters were located at 40 Water Street, with a single branch office in New York. The new president opened a sales office in Philadelphia, which was designed to supplement the work of the New York branch. This was followed by another branch in Chicago that was equipped with trading, acceptance, and sales departments and that quickly grew to rival the New York office.

Between 1923 and 1929 the business of the Corporation surged ahead; it was particularly active in selling bonds of foreign countries and participating in the flotation of loans of both European and South American nations. By the end of 1925 the bonds of foreign governments, municipalities, and industrial companies amounted to 38 of 177 underwritings in the Corporation.

Throughout most of the 1920s, the Corporation did a large

acceptance business. Toward the end of the decade, however, the Board of Directors of the National Shawmut determined that it would be wiser to concentrate all foreign activities of the Bank in its own Foreign Department, so the Corporation began to concentrate on dealings with investment securities in the domestic market.

By the end of 1926 the affairs of Shawmut Corporation were in excellent order, and in May 1927, to allow for more activity, the Corporation issued 5000 new shares, which were subscribed to by the National Shawmut as the sole shareholder. National Shawmut investment in these new shares amounted to $854,000, bringing its total investment for the 15,000 shares of the Corporation to $2.5 million, or 10 percent of the Bank's newly authorized capital and surplus.

During the next eight months, Shawmut Corporation continued to grow, and on December 31, 1927, Bucklin proudly reported to the National Shawmut Bank stockholders:

> The Shawmut Corporation [of Boston], whose entire capital is owned by the Bank, each year becomes of greater importance in building up the business of the Bank. The increase in its business and earnings in 1927 was extremely encouraging. . . . Its entire volume of retail and wholesale security business increased 139% over the previous year. This is an indication of its increasing ability to distribute investment securities.

In December 1928 Shawmut Corporation reported to the Federal Reserve Board that its assets were $118,130,433 and net worth was $2,461,408. Among the assets was all the outstanding stock (1000 shares) of the Devonshire Financial Service Corporation, a service organization promoting installment sales for the Shawmut Bank with branches throughout New England. In summary, the Corporation did well in the first five years of Bucklin's administration, amply justifying the new president's decision to continue its expanding role, initiated under Aiken.

The year 1929 also began well for the Shawmut Corporation of Boston, although there were certain problems that had to be resolved. In 1927 Congress passed the McFadden Act, which spelled out conditions under which national banks could operate branches. Shawmut Bank's ownership of the Corporation, which in turn owned the Devonshire Financial Service Corporation and some shares of Shawmut Association, was considered subject to restrictions of the act. Moreover, the Corporation had made loans to certain officers of the Bank and Corporation, which the Bank was prohibited from making. As a consequence, by the spring of 1929 the Bank was required to revise its relationship with the Corporation in order to continue to realize the benefits of that relationship.

In May of 1929 Bucklin and the directors of the Bank decided to transfer the common shares of the Corporation that were held outright by the Bank to the Bank, as a trustee under a declaration of trust, for the ratable benefit of the shareholders of the Bank. In essence such a transfer was only a technical device, for it meant simply that instead of holding shares of the Corporation for itself the Bank would henceforth hold them as a trustee for its stockholders. Nevertheless the change satisfied regulatory requirements, and on June 15, 1929, the transfer was approved by the Shawmut Board of Directors, who then designated President Bucklin or the senior vice president of the Shawmut to represent the Bank as trustee.

Coincident with this transfer of stock ownership, although of quite different significance, was an increase in the amount of money that the Shawmut Bank was authorized to invest in the Corporation. That same June 15, the National Shawmut Board "authorized that sums not exceeding $5 million could be transferred by the Bank from time to time to the Corporation as an addition to its working funds" and voted to increase the Bank's own capital stock from $15 million to $20 million. Three weeks later, on July 9, 1929, the Bank transferred $1,850,000 of its new capital to the Corporation. This transfer was largely motivated by the Shawmut's knowledge that for the Corporation to increase its volume of sales it had to increase its inventory of bonds.

Such an extension of the Corporation's buying power suggests a certain faith in the future. However, that future was not so bright, for on October 29 the stock market crashed.

Unfortunately there are no available records of the Corporation's operation between the fall of 1929 and 1933. Some brief reports from the contemporary *Wigwam News* (the house organ founded under Bucklin) indicate, however, that the unsettled stock market did create some difficulties for Corporation salesmen confronted with the task of selling securities. It is also reasonable to assume that market values of both the domestic and foreign securities portfolios held by the Corporation declined drastically. Nevertheless, outlooks remained optimistic, and perhaps because the Bank, as trustee for the stockholders, held all the common stock of the Corporation, the public relations aspect of these losses could be handled as internal matters. Thus, if disaster occasionally seemed imminent, crises were weathered without undue publicity or trauma. But where the national economic situation could not scuttle the Corporation, the Banking Act of 1933 could and did.

In 1933, during the first frantic days of the Roosevelt administration and in response to national economic conditions, Congress passed the first of several banking acts. It was the death knell for Shawmut Corporation, and on October 14, 1933, after almost a decade and a half of activity, it ceased to do security business. Seven months later, on June 2, 1934, Bucklin issued an explanatory statement to the stockholders:

> Under the Banking Act of 1933 it is provided that no member Bank shall be affiliated in any manner with any Corporation engaged principally in the selling and distribution of securities. On October 14, 1933, shortly after the passage of this Banking Act, the Shawmut Corporation ceased to do a security business. . . .
>
> The Directors of The National Shawmut Bank of Boston have voted that all of the assets of the Corporation when liquidated, shall be turned over to the Bank for the benefit of the Stockholders of the Bank.

The liquidation took almost eleven years. During this time, between November 29, 1933, and October 3, 1944, at the end of which the name of the Corporation was changed to United Assets Corporation, the issued capital stock was reduced from $1.5 million to $24,000 in three separate transactions.

As part of the final capital-reduction transaction, the Bank received 88 percent of the Corporation's assets and sold the remaining 12 percent, in the form of $24,000 par value of stock, to Schirmer, Atherton and Company, which purchased United Assets Corporation on December 15, 1944. Five days later the Corporation was liquidated by its new owners. With these actions, the fluctuating fortunes of Shawmut Corporation of Boston came to an end. Although it had started poorly, it flourished in the mid- and late 1920s. By the 1930s, however, it was on the decline, and by the time of liquidation, Shawmut Corporation of Boston represented a substantial loss for the Bank.

Caribbean Sugar Company. Closely related to Shawmut Corporation of Boston, at least in the early years of that organization's operation, was the Bank and Shawmut Corporation's investment in a company called Caribbean Sugar Company. During the depression of 1920–1921, the company had experienced severe problems. By 1923, however, its fortunes were improving, although its ultimate profitability remained a question mark on the Bank's books: would it succeed or fail? It is indicative of Bucklin's approach that, confronted with such a dilemma, he exhibited exemplary patience. With a fifty-fifty chance that an investment might prove of value to the Bank, he took an optimistic view, biding his time — even though it might be years before the investment showed a profit. This does not mean that he did nothing. In the instance of Caribbean Sugar he did a great deal, including appointing to the Bank Walter Borden, who had direct experience with Caribbean Sugar, whose express charge was to oversee its development.

Caribbean Sugar stands as one example of President Bucklin's willingness to take a "long shot gamble" when circumstances dictated. Cumberland Mountain Coal Company represents another.

Cumberland Mountain Coal Company. Shawmut first began its long-term involvement with the Cumberland Mountain Coal Company in 1917, when it discounted a $30,000 note for the company. The company had been organized only two years earlier to exploit the potential of highly prized chestnut wood, growing abundantly on its Virginia and West Virginia properties. The land also contained coal, although no rail facilities reached the area until some twenty years later. Fred W. Estabrook, a Shawmut director since 1912, was one of the primary stockholders of this investment venture, and his personal endorsement was on the Cumberland Mountain note. Estabrook was also the owner of Estabrook-Anderson Shoe Company in Nashua, New Hampshire, a major customer of the Bank, and had interests in other investment properties, such as the Estabrook Gold Dredging Company.

Soon after this first note was discounted, the American chestnut blight hit with devastating effects. Despite its heavy toll on the trees, the magnitude of the blight was not recognized, and in late 1920 Cumberland Mountain Coal Company borrowed $80,000 directly from the Bank in expectation that the trees would recover. At this time Estabrook himself was running into difficulties, and soon afterwards, for the protection of creditors, all of his properties were consolidated into a single unit called Estabrook Properties, Inc.

Although the finances of Estabrook Properties, Inc., and Cumberland Mountain Coal Company were not in good shape in 1923, Bucklin apparently recognized potential, at least in the latter, and between 1923 and 1925 Shawmut increased its commitment to Estabrook Properties in a series of loans amounting to $78,285. Unfortunately, the financial conditions of Estabrook Properties did not improve; by 1926 it was in arrears in payment of both its debts and taxes and had made no payments on the principal of its Shawmut loans.

In May 1926 Estabrook Properties, Inc., declared its intention to sell Cumberland because of its unprofitable operations. In August Shawmut convened a special directors meeting to review the entire Estabrook situation but particularly Cumberland Mountain Coal. And in early 1927 the board declared its intention to keep the Cumberland properties alive either through investment of new money in the existing business or by purchase of the company at a receiver's auction. The Bank could then hold the coal properties for future development. Ultimately, receivership was the chosen course, although the Bank did invest an additional $25,000 in Cumberland in the meantime.

At the end of 1927 a financial summary of Shawmut loans to Cumberland and Estabrook showed that Cumberland owed $182,894 in direct loans and interest and Estabrook owed $314,747. Cumberland's debt to Shawmut was approximately half of its total obligations.

As 1928 began and Shawmut attorneys were preparing bankruptcy proceedings for Cumberland, the state of Virginia announced it would sell some Cumberland properties for taxes past due. Responding to the new situation, Shawmut authorized a Charleston law firm to purchase some of these properties for the Bank, which it did at an auction in November 1928.

The following year the Bank also bought Cumberland land in West Virginia.

By 1930 the Bank had purchased a total of 29,277.56 acres of contiguous coal lands in Virginia and West Virginia at a cost of $52,608 and thereby set the stage for recovery of its losses on loans to Cumberland Mountain Coal Company and Estabrook Properties, Inc. The transactions had required considerable time and effort — indicative of how far the Bucklin administration was prepared to go to protect the Bank's interests. But the depression intervened, and the full recovery of these losses remained for the future.

During the next decade, the National Shawmut focused its energies on trying to develop the coal resources by lease or sale. The coal industry, however, was depressed, and returns on the property were minimal. But in September 1939, war broke out in Europe, and suddenly demand for coal catapulted and exports expanded. Throughout the 1940s Shawmut derived income not only from coal but also from oil and gas royalties. The Bank also sold some of the Cumberland land and timber, while it acquired another nine hundred acres between 1943 and 1948.

Throughout this period, the bank examiner and the Comptroller of the Currency periodically questioned the propriety of Shawmut's holding the Cumberland property as an asset. The Bank consistently asserted that it intended to sell the land but insisted that the timing was inopportune to realize adequate recovery against its outstanding loans. Bucklin was particularly adamant on this point. At the end of his tenure at Shawmut in 1956, the Bank still retained interests in Cumberland. By then, however, the property began to be profitable, and by the end of 1956 the operating account of Cumberland Mountain Coal Company showed an overall gain of $26,872.

A good portion of Bucklin's time in the early 1920s was spent in clearing up past commitments to make room for future growth. His decisions to charge off certain loans, to develop Shawmut Corporation, and to retain the Bank's support of Caribbean Sugar and Cumberland Mountain Coal companies were all decisions that had long-term effects. In the long run, however, as Bucklin was well aware, the real challenge for his administration was not simply dealing with problems inherited from the past but generating new ideas and profitable actions to take advantage of the present.

New Business

During his administration, Bucklin was quick to point out, assets grew considerably. Whereas in September 1923 they stood at $182 million, by the end of 1926 they jumped to $227 million. During this same period, deposits rose by 30 percent from $132 million to $172 million. By late 1929 both assets and deposits were even greater. Bucklin's aggressive pursuit of new business was a primary factor in achieving this growth.

Business Extension Department. In 1918 Shawmut founded the Business Extension Department, the first such department in a Boston bank and one of the first in the nation. It provided a natural setting for Bucklin's promotional skills, and no sooner had he assumed office than he began to focus attention on it. A 1927 article in the *Wigwam News* sums up his actions: "When Bucklin arrived he threw the throttle wide open. A crew of promising young salesmen was hired, a training school was started, lectures on banking and salesmanship were given, territories were mapped out, contests in getting new business were arranged. Every month, and sometimes weekly, prizes were given to the salesmen bringing in the most accounts."

At the same time, the new president sought to imbue the officers, staff, and employees of the Bank with pride in their roles as a part of the Shawmut organization. Increased emphasis was put on the importance of the Bank to Boston, to New England, to the nation, but particularly to the employee himself. No small part of this emphasis was communicated through the *Wigwam News:* "Yes, every man at every Shawmut window, every man at every Shawmut desk is selling this bank to the public. It is our bank. Many of us own stock in it. The salaries of all of us depend on its growth and success. When we work for our customers, we work for Shawmut, we work for ourselves."

The tone and content here suggest boosterism. Indeed boosterism was very much the style of the day, and it was characteristic of Bucklin's administrative style. Apparently it was also effective. Between January 1927 and January 1, 1928, new business was added, including 455 new accounts brought in entirely by the clerical staff. Bucklin's own efforts also contributed to the growth in deposits, and under his prompting the Bank became a depository for the Philippine government.

New Loans. While deposits rose, new loan accounts were courted. The large volume of questionable loans incurred by the previous administration had impressed Bucklin with the wisdom of sound credit appraisals of all potential borrowers. As a result he became exceptionally cautious, involving himself directly in almost all discussions of loans and investments. Top officials generally leave such discussion to loan officers, except in the case of very large loans, which are automatically referred to the Executive Committee for approval.

To the extent that Bucklin's approach suggested a lack of confidence in these officers, it undermined morale. Nevertheless, throughout the 1920s loan activities continued to be vigorous. Every meeting of the Executive Committee was marked by long lists of loans and discounts to be approved, and amounts ranging from $300,000 to $1 million were extended to businesses operating nationwide.

Besides customary commercial loans to business and industry, a new loan area also opened up during this period — brokers' loans. As early as 1925 the Shawmut became actively involved in making brokers' loans to New York City Stock Exchange brokers, who were borrowing large amounts of money to underwrite their own customers' borrowings. On November 24, 1925, Bucklin reported to the Executive Committee on Shawmut's involvement, likening it to the similar practices of the Chase National Bank in New York:

> Our New York Stock Exchange Brokers' Time and Call Loans are supervised by the Collateral Loan Department and . . . were secured by an excellent class of securities. . . . All loans carry from 25% to 30% margins. The loans are reviewed daily and with special care at this time by the Bank.

Another kind of loan account also appeared during this time: acceptances and notes endorsed by major German banks, which later became known as the German Standstill Credits. The impact of these transactions was not felt until the 1930s, however, so a discussion of the particulars has been deferred.

The effect of Bucklin's efforts in the deposit and loan areas was a considerable increase in earnings. In appreciation of this fact and perhaps also to offset the ill feelings prompted by his peremptory style in monitoring loans, Bucklin proposed to the Executive Committee of the Board of Directors that the Bank institute a profit sharing plan that would benefit the executive management of the Shawmut.

The Additional Compensation Plan for Executive Management. The Additional Compensation Plan for Executive Management was introduced to the Board of Directors at the National Shawmut in 1925. This plan defined Executive Management as the president, the vice presidents, the cashier, the vice president of the Shawmut Corporation, and as the president might determine, Corporation branch managers. One or two junior officers might also benefit if in the president's "judgment any of them had rendered conspicuous services which deserve especial recognition."

Although the Additional Compensation Plan for Executive Management did not go into effect until the end of fiscal year 1926, as early as February of that year, the board made $75,000 available for distribution among Shawmut's officers, including Bucklin, and at the end of 1926, $141,817 was approved for the "Management Fund." In 1927 and 1928 benefits under the plan continued to rise in proportion to increased earnings. How much such incentive figured in the Bank's growth would be impossible to say, but grow it did.

New Shawmut Services

The development of loans and deposits was one way by which Bucklin sought to improve the Bank's earnings during the first six years of his administration. It was by no means the only way. The 1920s were characterized by rapid growth in industrial production, and contributing to this growth was a growing technological sophistication that brought new products to the market and vastly improved old methods of production. The coincidence of these factors, along with increased discretionary income, created new consumer demands. Bucklin, with a salesman's eye for what the public wanted, moved swiftly to assure Shawmut a role in satisfying these demands. The Bank introduced several services designed to capitalize both on the public's desire to purchase new products and on the speculative fever that accompanied rapid market expansion.

Devonshire Financial Service Corporation. The National Shawmut Bank had actively encouraged America's young automobile industry from its infancy. Long before Bucklin came to the Bank, Aiken and Gaston extended loans to auto manufacturers. During these prior administrations, Shawmut also expanded the auto distribution system by offering loans to car dealers. Still, the auto remained largely an expensive toy — only 1.4 million autos were registered in the entire country in 1914. Shawmut then focused attention on the individual consumer, and as early as 1916, it pioneered an installment plan that revolutionized the auto buying process. Loans to the auto dealers were secured by the inventory, the autos themselves. Why not, reasoned the Shawmut loan officers, extend loans to the actual consumer on the same basis, secured by the car itself? By facilitating the purchase of automobiles, this installment plan increased the sales of autos, the volume of Shawmut dealer loans, and the production of manufacturers.

Improved technology dramatically unleashed the American automobile industry after the end of World War I. Steady mechanical improvement made the car more reliable and acceptable to the general public, but prices remained high into the early 1920s. Then Henry Ford began adapting assembly line techniques to his auto production process, and by 1924 his plants were churning out uniformly black Model T Fords at a yearly rate of 1.6 million cars and at low prices. America took to wheels with gusto, and by 1929 a phenomenal 26.5 million vehicles were registered in the United States.

So much had the volume of Shawmut's installment-plan lending grown that in August 1923, just three months after Bucklin joined the Shawmut board, a separate Time Sales Department was created in the Bank. But Aiken was not aggressive in exploiting this area of new business. Bucklin, ever alert to the temper of his times, was.

Recognizing a great opportunity in the booming automobile industry, Bucklin courted it at every level. One month after he came to office, the Ford time-sales account for New England was successfully obtained and profited Shawmut handsomely. Furthermore, Bucklin's insurance background made him aware that even larger profit opportunities lay in installment plans, provided Shawmut could generate a sufficient volume of such business.

To tap this potential profit directly, Bucklin realized, Shawmut had to expand its consumer market beyond the metropolitan Boston area and cover all of New England. To do this effectively, Shawmut needed local outlets throughout the region, but federal law forbade the Bank to establish branch offices outside its Suffolk County base. This limitation did not thwart Bucklin; it only challenged his ingenuity. His novel solution was Devonshire Financial Service Corporation (DFSC), a wholly owned Shawmut subsidiary incorporated under the laws of Massachusetts on March 19, 1926.

Devonshire offices were not branches of the Bank. In fact they were not banks at all, because they did not accept deposits. They merely received the customer loan payments as these came due. Also, DFSC offices did not make any loans; they merely processed the installment loans and security agreements and performed any credit investigations needed by Shawmut to make an informed loan decision. In many cases, the formal loan was actually made by the dealer, who then sold the loan account to Shawmut through the local DFSC office. (DFSC did perform all the bookkeeping and collection services of these accounts. Hence, the "Financial Service" part of its name. "Devonshire" recognized the 82 Devonshire Street address of the side entrance to the National Shawmut Bank's 40 Water Street headquarters.)

Indicative of the close relationship between the Shawmut Bank and its new subsidiary were the stipulations of the contract between the two organizations. The contract specified that DFSC would act as a service organization solely for the Bank, which would reimburse it for all actual expenses, including salaries, wages, and rental costs. In addition to servicing the loan accounts, DFSC was also responsible for soliciting business from auto dealers and, if necessary in cases of default, for repossessing, repairing, warehousing, and reselling autos taken under terms of the security agreements.

DFSC went into operation almost immediately with its first office located in Boston. Other offices soon followed. By April 1926, it had facilities in Providence, Rhode Island, and New Haven, Connecticut. In the next few years, offices were opened in Augusta, Portland, and Bangor, Maine, and in Manchester and Portsmouth, New Hampshire; Connecticut operations were extended into Hartford and Norwich; additional Massachusetts offices were opened in Salem, Worcester, and Springfield. For a time DFSC even had an office in White River Junction, Vermont.

For the first year, Robert H. Hopkins served as the DFSC president, but Bucklin assumed that office on May 2, 1927. Throughout the remainder of the 1920s, the business of DFSC strongly justified its existence. Even during the depression it continued to do extensive business. Much of the credit for this success must be attributed to William W. McCarthy. In the late 1920s he was a sales manager in the Shawmut Time Sales Department and in 1930 became assistant treasurer of DFSC. Elected its vice president in 1931, McCarthy vigorously directed DFSC, which showed increasing profits. McCarthy was also elected a vice president of the Bank in 1937, another indication of just how closely interlaced the two organizations were. DFSC profits grew even more when the domestic economy rallied after World War II, and by the time of McCarthy's retirement in 1959, DFSC had extended its services to include loan accounts for mobile homes, appliances, and boats. DFSC also processed Shawmut Bank's machinery and equipment loans, and its home improvement loans under the Federal Housing Act.

Ironically, late in 1954 the Comptroller of the Currency raised objections to National Shawmut Bank's ownership and operation of DFSC on grounds that it violated branch banking laws. To satisfy the Comptroller's criticism, Shawmut sold all of its DFSC stock to Walter E. Borden, then president of the Bank, who agreed to sell it only to a purchaser approved and designated by the Bank. By such means the National Shawmut quelled the Comptroller's objection while managing to retain control over DFSC, which continued its services for the Bank until the mid-1960s, when circumstances warranted its dissolution.

Personal Loan Department. Just as the Shawmut was willing and
eager to help the consumer satisfy his need for cars, so also
was it eager to help him satisfy his need or desire for other
consumer products.

Between 1921 and 1928, the housing industry in America
constructed 3,500,000 new homes. Much of this boom can be
attributed to the formation of 2,300,000 new family units in
the country during the same period. Part of it can be attributed
to building that was postponed during World War I, and part
to a rise in automobile production, which within a decade created a new suburban, middle-class commuter family with new
consumer demands. Whatever the specific reason, within this
period new or improved products were enjoying new and vastly
accelerated demand.

Household appliances — refrigerators, washing machines,
vacuum cleaners — had been on the market for some time. During the 1920s they were redesigned and aggressively marketed
to appeal to housewives whose maids had left them for the
better wages and shorter hours on assembly lines, which produced the very items that replaced them in the home. Leisure-
time industries — sports, travel, entertainment — also enjoyed
new profitability. Radio and movies took a qualitative and quan-
titative leap forward, becoming major elements in American
life.

Although by the mid-1920s some financial pundits were already warning that the boom was no more substantial than
the shadows on the silver screen, few heard and fewer still
heeded. The spirit of the time was to buy and to buy now,
and to this spirit the Bank responded by creating the Personal
Loan Department. The idea of allowing the consumer to borrow
a small amount of money without collateral on the signature
of only one or two cosigners was not new, but traditionally,
commercial banks had not participated in such transactions,
preferring to focus attention on large borrowers. Growing consumer demand, however, made it clear that the sheer volume
of small-loan business could be translated into profits that
would easily offset the cost and inconvenience of handling small
individual accounts. At this time several banks in some of the
country's larger cities began to introduce personal loan plans.

Among these pioneers was the National Shawmut Bank of Boston. According to Shawmut's plan, any regularly employed customer could henceforth borrow from $100 to $1000 for a stipulated amount of time. Six percent of that sum was considered interest and immediately subtracted from the amount delivered to the customer. The entire amount was then divided into monthly payments, which the borrower repaid into a savings account that returned 3 percent. If the customer wished to make larger deposits than those required by his loan agreement, the normal 4 percent compound interest payable on a regular savings account was allowed.

The advantages of such a plan to the Bank are clear. Because the interest was collected at the outset, such loans yielded more than 6 percent against funds that actually left the Bank. Furthermore, even without collateral, the risk of loss was minimal not only because the amounts were small but also because the debt was consistently amortized over a period of months into an interest-paying account, providing funds to which the Bank had access. Finally, as long as the volume of loans remained high, the proportion and impact of defaults in relation to total repayments were small.

If Shawmut enjoyed advantages in the personal-loan business, so too did the customer. The Shawmut plan allowed him to buy what he wanted when he wanted it, which in the booming economy of the 1920s often meant stock purchases promising a considerably higher return than the small charges paid the Shawmut for use of its money. Thus the Personal Loan Department was ideally suited to the times.

Two other services introduced at this period that were also appropriate to contemporary economic conditions were the Shawmut Bank Investment Trust and the Shawmut Association.

Shawmut Bank Investment Trust. On February 23, 1927, the National Shawmut Bank created the Shawmut Bank Investment Trust (SBIT) and thereby, according to President Bucklin, became the first national bank in the country to organize its own investment trust. Such trusts were not new. One of the first and most successful in the United States was organized in Boston by Paul C. Cabot in 1923. They were, however, new to national banks, and it is indicative of the temper of the time —

the general faith that corporations would maintain their dividends and that their assets would appreciate — that these banks now seized upon the idea of investment trusts as a way to increase their own earnings and provide service to their customers.

SBIT was designed to provide the investor with an opportunity to enjoy the benefits of a large and diverse portfolio for only a limited contribution. The trustees reserved the right to choose the investments and thereby maintained complete control over the operation and management of the Trust. The investor collected a specified annual interest for a specified amount of time, at the end of which his capital investment was returned. The investor also received a warrant, which did not represent capital investment but rather a degree of participation in the Trust, and gave the holder a right to a proportion of the profits remaining after all obligations were met.

In 1927 the Shawmut Bank Investment Trust was established, with the National Shawmut Bank approved under the Declaration of Trust as its depository and registrar. Controlling the management of this money as trustees were senior officers of the National Shawmut: Walter S. Bucklin, president; Frank C. Nichols, vice president; Norman I. Adams, Vice President; Frederick P. Royce, a director since 1926 and vice president of Stone and Webster; and Paul C. Cabot, an officer of the State Street Investment Corporation and also a Bank director since 1926, when he was recruited to help the Bank set up the Trust. Cabot was also a partner of State Street Research and Management Corporation, an organization designed to provide advice on investment of trust funds, and with which the SBIT contracted.

As the SBIT began operations, confidence in its potential was high. The investment trust business as conducted in the 1920s, however, had serious flaws. Like many other trusts organized during the period, SBIT's capital structure was designed for prosperity with no real margin to accommodate trouble. The worldwide deflation in security values which occurred in the wake of the 1929 stock market crash thus doomed it to failure in a way that was not true for more conservatively capitalized investment trusts. By the early 1930s SBIT was in serious trouble and in 1933 liquidation proceedings began.

The proceedings went slowly. Although many felt that in the face of severe losses and with limited prospects for recovery, the Bank would have done well to cut its connection with the Trust quickly, it was Bucklin's hope that the security holdings would recover somewhat in value and that eventually the Bank and the stockholders would realize some return on their notes and debentures. Not until 1952, then, were final liquidation steps begun. On June 10, 1952, the name Shawmut Bank Investment Trust was changed to Mayflower Investment Trust by an amendment of the Declaration of Trust. The 75,000 common shares without par value were reduced to 7500 by issuing one new share for every ten original shares.

Simultaneous with the reorganization of SBIT was an offer by the Sheraton Corporation of America to buy from the National Shawmut its holdings in the original Trust. Negotiations went on for approximately one year between Sheraton and the Mayflower trustees. The trustees were: Walter S. Bucklin, now chairman and chief executive officer of the National Shawmut; Walter E. Borden, president of National Shawmut; Rohl C. Wiggin, vice president of National Shawmut; Jacob J. Kaplan, director of National Shawmut and partner in Nutter, McClennen and Fish; and Lee P. Stack, also a Shawmut director and a vice president of John Hancock Mutual Life Insurance Company. Finally, on September 16, 1953, the papers were completed, and the management of the Mayflower Trust was transferred to Sheraton Corporation of America from the National Shawmut Bank of Boston.

Shawmut Association. In 1928, when SBIT was still riding high and when stock market speculation was rising, the National Shawmut organized another investment trust, the Shawmut Association. This organization, however, differed substantially from SBIT in that its objective was to acquire substantial stockholdings in other banks. Its function was not simply to make investments but to pave the way for branching statewide, or even beyond state boundaries, if the opportunity for such expansion arose.

The distinction between the two trusts is important, for Shawmut Association demonstrates that Bucklin was not simply responding to the investment fever of the day but thinking ahead to a significant change in the structure of banking organizations; in this respect he was more progressive and farsighted than many of his contemporaries. Today's Shawmut Corporation —

the holding company, which (as of December 1982) has controlling interest in thirteen banks throughout Massachusetts as well as other subsidiaries — had its origin in this 1928 Shawmut Association.

Acquiring majority control of the stock in other banks outside Suffolk County, where the National Shawmut Bank could not expand directly, was a primary goal of the Shawmut Association, but it was only one of several. The new investment trust also invested in stocks, bonds, securities, and commercial paper. In fact, for almost twenty years, Shawmut Association invested only 25 percent of its funds in bank stocks. Of these banks in which it invested, Shawmut Association owned at least 50 percent of the outstanding shares, giving it majority control. This was a subject to which the Shawmut Association organizers were sensitive. In early drafts of association reports, the term "controlled by" was eliminated in favor of the more comforting "affiliated with" in describing the relationship with these banks. The name Shawmut Association itself was adopted because it expressed the "association" concept. However, control was undeniably the intent, rather than investment. One memorandum of the period states: "It is anticipated that the main holdings of the Association in stocks of the banks will represent dominant interests, the ideal case being 50% ownership in selected New England banks." As far as the public was concerned, however, all functions were to be given equal emphasis, for fear that to do otherwise would lead to a "great deal of controversy."

By May 1928 plans were complete for forming the new trust, and on May 21 the Declaration of Trust creating the Shawmut Association as a voluntary association, or Massachusetts Trust, was signed at Boston. The trustees were the same men who had been trustees of SBIT. They were given broad investment powers with extensive exculpatory clauses. They were also given full discretion to issue up to 1 million common shares of the Association and to do so for cash or in exchange for stock and securities of other companies. This provision was used advantageously in acquiring stock and ownership of other banks in subsequent years. The Association was created to benefit the National Shawmut Bank and its stockholders, but the Bank itself was not to own or hold any of its shares. The Association, however, was conducted and controlled by members of the management staff or directors of the Bank, and all trustee appointments were subject to approval of the Executive Committee of the Board of Directors of the National Shawmut Bank.

The first meeting of the Association trustees was held on May 23, 1928, at which time officers were elected. The following month, on June 8, 1928, the first set of investment policies were adopted: approximately 50 percent of funds was to be invested in the general manner the Shawmut Bank Investment Trust invested its funds; approximately 25 percent in other bank stocks and special underwritings; and approximately 25 percent in other commitments for reasonably quick return. (An additional policy, adopted on October 5, 1928, stated that the Association was not to hold more than a 50 percent interest in any other bank.)

At this same June 8 meeting, the first investments were also approved: $453,000 in stock of Merchant's National Bank of Salem; $120,000 in stock of Winchester National Bank; $336,000 in stock of various small banks located in Massachusetts, Connecticut, and Rhode Island; $42,000 in Bohemian Discount Bank stock to be acquired from International Acceptance Bank; $5,000,000 par value Dodge Brothers 6 percent bonds at a price of $99.08 each; $134,000 in $150,000 par value Province of Silesia 7 percent bonds. The Association was on its way.

In the course of the next several years additional bank stocks were acquired, and the Association continued to expand to eventually become what is known today as the Shawmut Corporation.

The diversity of new services — DFSC, the Personal Loan Department, SBIT, and the Association — added to the growth of the Shawmut Bank during the 1920s. But while Walter Bucklin was quick to see opportunities and germinate ideas, little could have been accomplished without the assistance of eager and capable personnel.

Shawmut Bank Officers and Important Bucklin Recruits

Upon taking over as president, Bucklin was able to draw on the experience of an established and knowledgeable staff, including eight vice presidents, two of whom had served with him on the Board of Directors. The two, Norman I. Adams and Robert S. Potter, were elected to the board at the 1920 annual meeting. Adams served the Bank from 1898 to 1949, when he retired at the age of eighty-five. Potter's tenure, however, lasted only until 1924.

The other six vice presidents in 1923 were W. A. Burnham, Jr., head of the Department of Banks and Business Extension; John Bolinger, in charge of the Foreign Department; Addison L. Winship, head of the Department of Publicity and Public Relations; Frank A. Newell, in charge of Collateral Loans and Loan Development; Frank C. Nichols, an associate in the Credit Department; and Edward A. Davis. James E. Ryder was the cashier and Bank manager, while Clarence E. Dunaven was the auditor. Ten assistant cashiers rounded out the complement of officers in the Shawmut Bank of September 1923.

In the course of the next few years, as part of his strategy for the future, Bucklin began to develop his ideas for new services. He also began actively to recruit officers from outside Shawmut, while keeping paths open for deserving staff members. During this early period, Bucklin attracted officers from other banks and from some of the leading investment houses in the East, as well as from his own territory at Liberty Mutual Insurance Company. Finally, the raw talent coming from the universities and graduate schools of the area presented attractive officer candidates.

Among the most significant officers recruited from other banks were William F. Augustine, Arthur W. Deibert, and George D. Grimm. Augustine came from the First and Merchants National Bank of Richmond, Virginia, in January 1927. He became a vice president upon his arrival and died in 1947, after twenty years of service. Deibert joined Shawmut in September 1928 from the Philadelphia National Bank. He became a Shawmut senior vice president and retired in 1963. George Grimm was recruited from the Valley Bank of Phoenix, Arizona, to serve as Shawmut's new auditor, a position he retained until his death in 1954. Other officers who came to Shawmut at this time from the world of banking but whose length of service was briefer were: John P. Dyer, George A. Macomber, William R. Cooper, and William S. Eaton. Dyer was appointed assistant cashier in Correspondent Banking in 1924, assistant vice president in 1927, and vice president in 1930, a role he retained until 1932, when he left the Bank. Macomber also entered Shawmut as an assistant cashier, and in 1926 served in Administration and Service. Another recruit to Administration and Service was William R. Cooper, who was appointed an acting comptroller in 1927 and the following year rose to the office of comptroller. William S. Eaton joined Shawmut in 1928 as an assistant vice president, working with Dyer in Correspondent Banking. These three men left the Bank in the early 1930s.

From investment banking, Bucklin recruited Rohl C. Wiggin in May 1927 from Merrill, Oldham and Company. By November Wiggin was an assistant vice president of the Shawmut Corporation and in charge of its Boston office. Later, he rose to some of the leading positions in the Bank and its various affiliated organizations.

Other investment-banking recruits had shorter longevity at Shawmut but were integrally involved in some of Bucklin's most important innovations. Especially notable in this regard was Frederick M. Thayer from the Philadelphia investment-banking house of Janney and Company. Thayer came to Shawmut Corporation in September 1925, and soon became vice president, general manager, and a director of the subsidiary, resigning in 1929 to return to Janney and Company. There was also Joseph Walker, who came directly from the Boston office of Brown Brothers but who had previously been associated with Rohl Wiggin at Merrill, Oldham and Company.

Liberty Mutual also proved a source for officers during Bucklin's early years. Three officers who proceeded to Shawmut through this route were Ray Ilg, Horace Schermerhorn, and Harold P. Janish. Ilg, a salesman who frequently handled special assignments for Bucklin, joined Shawmut in 1929, rose to vice president, and retired in 1958. Schermerhorn's specialty was bond investment analysis. He joined the Shawmut organization in July 1925 as a syndicate manager in the Shawmut Corporation. When the Corporation ceased these activities, Schermerhorn's talents were redeployed in the Bank's Trust Department, which he eventually ran as senior trust officer. In November 1956 he was appointed president of the Bank, and shortly afterwards, on Bucklin's retirement, he received the designation of chief executive officer. In 1960 he relinquished the presidency to Lawrence H. Martin, continuing as chief executive officer and chairman of the board of the Bank and Association until his own retirement in 1962. Janish's service at the Bank was briefer than those of his two colleagues. He came in as vice president and general manager in the Time Sales Division in 1928, but by October 1934 had left Shawmut.

Three other officers who came in during this early period but whose credentials do not lend themselves as easily to categories of banking, investment, and insurance, were Louis J. Hunter, Robert M. Tappan, and Frederick A. Carroll. The first two were initially retained as "Assistant to the President," the duties of which are not clear. Hunter went on to become important in establishing two Shawmut trusts and also became a vice president in the Corporation. Tappan's career with Shawmut, however, was brief. Carroll began as a vice president and trust officer in April 1924, and in the ensuing years guided the Trust Department with considerable success, until he died in October 1945 while on special assignment with the American Red Cross in postwar France.

Several recent graduates of the leading colleges and graduate schools in the area were also attracted to Shawmut Bank during this period. The standout among them was Lawrence H. Martin, who arrived in 1928 from Dartmouth College, where he had concentrated on the Amos Tuck School of Business Administration curriculum. Martin was only one of several Dartmouth graduates to launch a career at Shawmut. Others who joined the Bank in the 1920s included Benjamin H. Bowden, who became a leading figure in Shawmut Association's County Bank in Cambridge; Norman W. Stickland, who served several years in Shawmut's Trust Department; Loren Wright Taylor, who joined the Sales Department of the Shawmut Corporation; and Elpheage Kirouac, who joined Shawmut in June 1926 to serve the Arlington Street branch.

Another new arrival was William B. Schmink, a promising graduate of Ohio State University and Harvard Business School, who obtained a part-time Shawmut job while attending school from 1929 to 1931 and then took on a full-time assignment, eventually concentrating on correspondent banking services. Elected an officer in 1942, he retired in 1971 as a vice president.

Two others who rose to leading positions in the Bank and whom Bucklin attracted during this period were Henry J. Nicols and Walter E. Borden. Nichols joined the Bank as a vice president at the end of 1929. His service to the National Shawmut Bank included thirty-two years on the Board of Directors, from 1931 through 1962.

Walter E. Borden came to Shawmut Corporation from the presidency of a Rhode Island grocery chain in August 1928, although it was his previous experience as assistant manager of Caribbean Sugar Company, 1921–1925, and his current role as its treasurer that attracted Bucklin. Subsequently, he became an officer of the Bank and held a variety of senior positions, including the presidency.

Bucklin was also fortunate to find several good people already employed in the Shawmut ranks below vice president. In remarks addressed to this group, he emphasized that the policy of his new administration was one of building from the inside wherever and whenever possible. Within two years, Bucklin had promoted five staff members to the rank of vice president and nine others to assistant vice president or assistant cashier. These internal promotions included George E. Pierce, who became vice president in one of the earliest promotions under the Bucklin administration in 1924. Pierce became a director in 1927 and served twenty years as one of the five Shawmut Association trustees, until his death in 1951. Another leading figure in Shawmut's future was already at the Bank when Bucklin arrived: Joseph A. Erickson, a 1917 graduate of Harvard College and 1920 graduate of the Harvard Business School, joined Shawmut as a clerk in the Credit Department in 1920. An early assignment given to Erickson by Bucklin was to be branch manager of the new Park Square office at Arlington Street when it opened in 1924. Erickson rose through the Shawmut ranks, becoming an executive vice president before he was invited to become president of the Federal Reserve Bank of Boston at the end of 1948. Myron O. Wilkins also served many long years with Shawmut. One of Norman Adams's proteges in the Credit Department, Wilkins became the department manager in 1926. He later served a ten year stint in Shawmut Association's County Bank in Cambridge and then returned to the main banking floor of the National Shawmut headquarters. In conjunction with James Arrington, vice president, Wilkins trained many of the Bank's credit officers and was a vice president when he retired in the mid-1960s.

Physical Expansion

Keeping abreast of growth in the 1920s and also contributing
to it was the steady physical expansion of the Bank and the
Shawmut Corporation of Boston. Almost immediately upon assuming the presidency, Bucklin supported the opening of Corporation branch offices in Philadelphia and Chicago. More directly related to the development of the Bank itself, however,
was Bucklin's interest in increasing the size of the main facility,
to accommodate enlarged services, and in establishing Shawmut
branch offices to bring these services to the entire community.

The Purchase of the Monks Building. When Aiken left office in
1923, informal approval had already been given by the Shawmut
Board of Directors to square off the Bank's holdings on the
block north of Water Street, between Devonshire and Congress.
But it was not until the arrival of Bucklin and the stimulation
of Bank activities provided by the 1920s boom that formal action
was taken. On August 26, 1926, the Executive Committee of
the Board ratified the purchase of the lot and building on Congress Street (known as the Monks Building) adjacent to the
Shawmut headquarters. The purchase price was $1.3 million —
the cost of the building being put at $406,133, the land at
$893,867. Improvements over the years, however, brought the
final book value to $1,973,352.

The extension of the downtown Bank headquarters provided
Shawmut with the space to operate more efficiently; the parallel
development of branch offices throughout metropolitan Boston
added a new dimension to Shawmut's image and its capacity
to serve the community.

Branch Banking. When the 1920s began, the question whether
national banks should be allowed to open branch offices was
just becoming a major political issue. For years state-chartered
banks had been allowed branching privileges, but the National
Bank Act of 1863 had been interpreted to mean that national
banks could not enjoy the same advantage. Initially this had
caused few problems, but by World War I, this competitive
advantage was perceived as unfair.

Congress considered corrective legislation for several years
but took no action until 1921, when D. L. Crissinger was ap-

pointed Comptroller of the Currency. Sympathetic to the national banks' problems, Crissinger issued in 1922 a reinterpretation of previous rulings. According to his reading, national banks located in those states where state banks had the authority to operate branches might be allowed to have extensions to their main office. These extensions were not to be considered branches; they must be within the same city as the main bank, and their functions were limited to the acceptance of deposits and loan applications. The new policy did not resolve the legal problems, which were argued for many years; it did, however, effectively open the way toward their final resolution.

By 1923 Crissinger was already issuing to national banks permits for "uptown" offices, and Bucklin, perceiving the opportunity of growth for the Shawmut, promptly took advantage of the opportunity. In January 1924 the Shawmut opened its first uptown office in temporary quarters at the corner of St. James and Arlington Streets and moved it into permanent quarters in Boston's Park Square Building in June of the same year. The Shawmut's office was not the first "branch" of a national bank in the city. The First National Bank, through its acquisition of a trust company which did have branching privileges, was already operating several offices. Shawmut's Arlington Street office, however, was the first branch of a national bank opened in Boston under the reinterpretation of the law.

The location of Shawmut's first uptown office was particularly fortunate. Park Square was a growth area of the city; major enterprises — the Paine Furniture Company, the Park Square Building, the Statler Hotel — had recently located in the neighborhood; others — the Boston Gas Company Building, the Salada Tea Building, the Pettingill-Andrews Building, the new Boston police headquarters, the John Hancock and the Liberty Mutual buildings, as well as the Ritz Carlton Hotel — all soon were established there. Such placement gave the Shawmut a ready-made clientele of the thousands of employees who worked for the new businesses, and the branch, as the situation promised, proved immediately successful.

Further contributing to the Arlington Street branch's success was the intelligent planning of the office itself. State-of-the-art safe-deposit vaults, an area for the storage of bulk valuables, a ladies restroom, and more important, a new Women's Department, which was supervised by a Miss Anita Sturgis and especially designed to serve a constituency that had often been over-looked, were all provided.

The Arlington Street branch set the pace. Other uptown offices soon followed, and by the end of the 1920s Shawmut already had twelve branches within Suffolk County. (The 1927 law allowing national banks to branch in Massachusetts insisted that the extension be within the home county.) Between 1930 and 1933, it added five more, including three offices of the former Federal National Bank, which had failed in December 1931. During this period one branch was also consolidated with another. The Bank Holiday in 1933, however, so undermined faith in banking institutions that the practice of opening new offices was discontinued and not revived until 1941. Between 1941 and 1956, thirteen new branches and two special facilities were added. The latter were designed to accommodate the needs of service men and provided check-cashing and deposit services at hours convenient for them.

By the time Bucklin left office, the Shawmut had, in addition to its 40 Water Street headquarters, twenty-nine branches and two facilities. The idea of conveniently located offices where retail banking activities could be conducted had become a major element in Shawmut's community identity. It is a credit to Bucklin that he perceived the importance of this idea early and incorporated it into the Shawmut structure.

Bucklin's interest in branches, however, went beyond mere efficiency and convenience of locations. It was his dream to have the most beautiful branch banks in America. "This objective," he said in a memorandum, "is very close to my heart because I do not think it has been done in any other city in the way I think it is possible for us to do it." Under his direction Shawmut adopted a colonial style of architecture and a uniform color scheme for its branches, planned by one of America's leading contemporary design firms, McKim, Mead and White. Bucklin's passion for the colonial motif also extended to furnishings, which he supervised, insisting on ladder-back chairs, banjo clocks, colonial cupboards, murals of colonial scenes, and antique black-and-white or color prints of the same theme.

The main office building was also enhanced during his administration by a new library, which eventually became the current Shawmut Bank library. In a May 29, 1929, memorandum, Bucklin observed that "there are many business books of importance on accounting and other subjects that should be available to all of our officers . . . and I believe we should start now on plans for a general library of business books."

A Summary of Financial Developments in the 1920s

As the previous sections have amply demonstrated, the period between 1923 and 1929 was one of rapid expansion for the Shawmut. Much of Bucklin's attention in the first years of his administration was devoted to dealing with past problems and putting new structures into place, and by 1927 the fruits of these efforts were beginning to be realized. In the spring of that year, Shawmut increased its capital stock from $10 million to $15 million. At the same time the Shawmut Corporation of Boston issued 5000 new shares to the Bank, raising its book investment in the Corporation to $2,500,000, 10 percent of its own newly authorized capital and surplus.

Growth, of course, was not limited to capital increases of the Bank and Corporation. Although annual reports to stockholders were not common practice in the 1920s, in January 1928 Bucklin prevailed on the Board of Directors to authorize just such a "comprehensive statement of the Bank and Corporation's Financial Condition as of December 31, 1927."

The report notes that both the Bank and its subsidiary Corporation (not to be confused with the present-day Shawmut Corporation, which later developed out of Shawmut Association) were both in excellent condition. It goes on to note some specific areas. The Trust Department: "The funds held in personal trust gained 70%. In agency accounts the increase was 20%"; the Savings Department: "The Savings Department which is now a well established function of practically all national banks and trust companies, increased its deposits 35.5 percent, entirely apart from those accounts that were taken over with the business of the Citizens National Bank"; the Foreign Department: "The volume of business done by the Foreign Department was in excess of the previous year and the earnings show a pleasing gain. In December the acceptances made by the Bank reached a record peak for the year since the war."

The report also notes that net earnings reached a record $2,532,643 and that dividends "were maintained throughout the year at the same rate as formerly, 12%." Finally, after brief mention of some 1927 innovations — the Shawmut Bank Investment Trust, management participation in profits, the merger of the Citizens National Bank — the report concludes that "management believes that all of these developments coupled with the accomplishments of the past give promise for the future."

Although, no similar annual reports were issued in 1928 and 1929, evidence is clear that, at least through March 1929, such promise continued. By that date the total assets of the Bank had increased to approximately $256 million compared with $243 million in December 1927 and $182 million in September 1923.

But even as the Bank reached record assets in that March, a shiver was felt throughout the financial community. In November 1928, Hoover's election sparked a record rise on the stock market, with 6.6 million shares traded; stock prices dropped in December only to recover in January 1929, when loans to brokers increased by some $260 million. In February the Federal Reserve Bank issued a cautionary warning for member banks to stop extending speculative loans, but little heed was paid. On March 26 the stock market lost some thirty points, and the rate on call loans, which had risen to 12 percent at the end of 1928 and to 14 percent in February 1929, suddenly shot up to 20 percent. The *Wigwam News* duly reported the grim news: "March [1929] was the worst in several years for bank business." Nevertheless, the market rallied through the summer, dipped precariously in September, and then fluctuated more or less uncertainly until October 29, 1929, when a record 16.4 million shares were traded, and uncertainty began to look like the certainty of disaster.

Four months earlier, however, in May 1929, although confidence was not quite at the high level it had been a year and a half before, the Executive Committee of the Shawmut Board recommended another increase in capital, this time from $15 million to $20 million. In anticipation of the directors' approval, Bucklin entered into an agreement with Kidder, Peabody and Company to underwrite the issue of 200,000 shares at the new

$25 par value. It was a step forward and underscored the increased business of the Bank that had developed over the last six years.

Had Walter Bucklin's administration come to its conclusion in the summer of 1929 he would have been remembered as a president of promotional and salesmanship skills whose enthusiasm was instrumental in introducing new bank services, new branches, and keeping the Bank abreast of the 1920s. Bucklin's administration, of course, did not come to an end at this time but extended through almost another three decades. These years, ones of depression, war, and postwar readjustment, presented entirely new challenges, testing the mettle of the administration in ways that no one could have dreamed when Walter Bucklin was elected "to get things rolling."

Chapter 10

The Depression and World War II
The Bucklin Administration Continued
(1929–1945)

W ALTER Bucklin's energies had been well suited to a time of growth and expansion. History, however, does not tailor events to the man, and between 1929 and 1945, the country and the world were caught up in two events — the depression and the war — which called for a different kind of response from leaders. They were times that demanded determination rather than enthusiasm, faith rather than optimism, endurance rather than élan.

1

Between October 24 and November 13, 1929, the 1920s crashed to a close. During three weeks, the dizzying illusion that a few hundred dollars invested today would yield yachts and castles tomorrow, or even simple security, dissolved for thousands of Americans. Nevertheless, those caught in that first great tremor of the market — which began on October 24, peaked on October 29, when 16 million shares were dumped, and culminated November 13, by which time paper losses amounted to some $30 billion — were few compared with the millions trapped in the ensuing shambles.

The crash had not come without warning. The steadily rising price of money, the drop in the market that previous March, the frantic activity of the summer, the precipitous seesaw of stock prices throughout the fall provided sufficient warning that many left the investment field. On October 15, 1929, for example, Shawmut Corporation advised in a letter that "our clients accept their profits." Many, however, heeded no warning, and when the market fell, the inexperienced investor, the inveterate optimist, and the simply hopeful — anyone who had invested beyond his means on margin — went down together.

But despite headlines such as WALL STREET COLLAPSES, despite the image of respectable entrepreneurs leaping from tall buildings, despite a very real and abrupt closing of thousands of businesses that left lines of unemployed, the general sense of the business community in the weeks following October 29 was "Yes, there have been reverses. Yes, the economy is in trouble," but "No, it is not devastating. We will quickly rally."

Roughly, the effects of the crash on the Shawmut Bank can be divided into two periods: 1929 to 1933, when many, including astute business leaders, still saw the events of October 1929 as a necessary purgative, a way to cleanse the country of previous financial excesses, and 1933 to 1939, when the full impact of the disaster was finally admitted and the country struggled to right its balance and regain its economic health.

I. The First Phase: 1929–1933

Initially, Shawmut directors and administrators were among the group who believed that the collapse of October 29 and the following period of economic difficulty was no more than a time of adjustment that would end with a return to normalcy. The challenge for the present was to remain calm, to maintain morale, to ride out the storm. Not surprisingly, Bucklin shared this attitude. It was not his style to countenance disaster, and reasoning that the Bank had ample reserves and resources to withstand adverse business conditions and that even a substantial decline in its own earnings and assets would not be devastating, he maintained an upbeat tone. The *Wigwam News*, taking its cue from the administration, did not even mention the crash in its November 1929 edition, while Bucklin's Christmas address was a study in calculated optimism:

> This year of 1929 has been a most successful one for the Shaw-mut. We can afford to be proud of the progress which our institution has made. My message for 1930 is simple. Drive Shawmut ahead. As the Shawmut grows, you too will also grow. . . . We are looking forward to a great year. Working together we cannot fail to forge ahead.

Bucklin's statements, however, were not simply deliberate bravado. Nineteen twenty-nine had been a good year with assets remaining around $250 million. Even more substantial than such rhetoric in demonstrating the administration's continued faith that conditions would improve was the formation of two stock syndicates, one in 1929, another in 1930.

Stock Syndicates

On October 17, 1929, and again on April 16, 1930, the Board of Directors of the National Shawmut Bank organized stock syndicates for the purchase and acquisition, or later sale, of stock in the National Shawmut Bank of Boston. The first of these syndicates was put in place only two days after the Corporation had written its customers advising that "our clients accept their profits." The advice would seem to indicate that, while the administration was well aware of conditions in the market, it was confident of Shawmut's own secure position.

The October 17 syndicate went into effect with thirteen members — Walter Bucklin and twelve directors of the Bank and Shawmut Corporation of Boston. Together these men subscribed to 9000 shares of National Shawmut Bank stock at an average price of $101.76 per share. The funds required for purchase were obtained through the Corporation, which had negotiated a loan with an outside bank. Participants in the syndicate were to pay the interest on this loan.

Despite the optimism such activities suggested, National Shawmut shares did not rally. By April 1930 they stood at $72.50, and the first syndicate was dissolved. But the matter did not end there. Instead another syndicate was organized, this time with forty-three Directors and officers of the Bank and Corporation. Again National Shawmut stock was purchased and again prices did not rise but fell, until in October 1932 when the second syndicate was dissolved. The following excerpt from a letter of October 7, 1931, of Mr. Carl T. Keller to H. J. Nichols is suggestive of subscriber reaction:

> I have your thoroughly unwelcome note of October 5. I certainly do not want those cussed shares of our beloved bank and why trail in front of my eyes that I agreed to pay $72.50 for something that I thought I was going to make a profit on? You are extremely tactless, so please arrange with someone somehow to carry the stuff until these ratty times are improved.

Despite the failure of the syndicates to fulfill their promise, the National Shawmut Bank remained financially secure and enjoyed public confidence. Partially to maintain this confidence and partially because it was reasonable to do so, the Bank continued to pay its customary dividend of seventy-five cents per share each quarter up to and including January 1, 1932, although by this time shares were down to $23.10. This does not mean that the Shawmut did not encounter very serious problems; it did. As the 1930s unfolded, the growing volume of charge-offs and necessity to introduce new loan policies were clear indications that all was not well.

Charge-Offs and Loan Policy Changes

On October 6, 1930, loans in the amount of $306,099 and time-sales contracts in the amount of $70,439 were charged off. The loan losses were charged to Reserve for Depreciation of Securities and the time-sales contracts to Reserve for Bad Debts. These charge-offs were followed by additional charge-offs of loan losses and depreciation of securities amounting to $898,288 in 1930 alone.

Despite the poor business conditions, the Shawmut Bank continued to make loans to the business community and to individuals, both establishing new lines of credit and reaffirming old ones. The records at this time show substantial loans to local and national business concerns. However, the interest rates that could be charged to borrowers were declining steadily, thereby affecting the Bank's ability to pay interest on deposits. On March 10, 1931, the Executive Committee recognized this situation by authorizing the Savings Department to lower interest rates paid on accounts from 4 percent to a maximum of 3.5 percent, with rates on some accounts reduced to no more than 3 percent. Eventually these rates dropped to 1 percent on some accounts.

The growing impact of the depression on Shawmut's affairs is further revealed by the minutes of the Executive Committee of the Board of Directors on May 12, 1931. At this meeting Bucklin reviewed the statement of undivided profits, which showed a reduction of about $173,000 from December 31, 1929, to April 30, 1931. The reduction had occurred because earnings were not sufficient to cover both the dividends and the loan-loss reserve of $22,550 the Bank had been setting aside each month since October 1929. Bucklin described this practice as part of a conservative policy that he expected to continue for at least another year. He reassured the Executive Committee that the credit officers of the Bank were showing good judgment in rejecting "certain new credits and closing out existing credits." Finally, he asserted that "these decisions kept the Bank out of many heavy losses or frozen situations." Even so, loan losses remained substantial. New charge-offs were logged with dismaying regularity from December 29, 1931, through October 31, 1933, in accordance with recommendations by the bank examiner.

At this point Bucklin revealed that many of the charge-offs were made against a reserve "created a number of years ago to cover losses of any kind. Additions to this reserve have been made from excess earnings, and deductions have been made for loan losses and other purposes for a number of years past. The action, therefore, does not affect our surplus or undivided profits."

This statement undoubtedly heartened the directors, although today it might give rise to some questions. For instance, why had these excess earnings not been accounted for before? At the time no one asked. Bank accounting and auditing proce-

dures were not as strict or regulated then, and so-called "hidden
reserves" were accepted conservative management practice.

Reduction in Operating Expenses

While Shawmut was absorbing loan losses, it was also cutting
expenses. In April 1931 Bucklin reported to the board that
operating expenses had already been cut by some $292,434.
In January 1932 directors fees were reduced from $20 to $10
per full board meeting, and the 1926 Plan for Additional Compensation for Executive Management was discontinued. Then,
effective February 1, 1932, a general 10 percent pay cut was
imposed.

These internal measures were difficult but necessary to preserve the National Shawmut Bank. Reporting to the Board of
Directors in January 1932, Bucklin presented a strange amalgam
of hard facts and wistful optimism. On the one hand, he recognized losses of $506,000 for the first nine months of the year
and noted $1.5 million more than the bank examiner was listing
as doubtful loans and securities. On the other hand, he insisted
that "under present rates, earnings show an encouraging upward trend; that the condition of the Bank is extremely liquid
and shows no borrowing whatsoever." He went on to point
out that some of the doubtful loans cited by the examiner as
"slow" were simply advances to a local hospital.

Despite Bucklin's continued assertions that better times lay
ahead, he admitted that business conditions had worsened in
1931. Bucklin then proceeded to explain certain actions that
some of the stronger members of the Boston Clearing House,
including Shawmut, felt were necessary to maintain public confidence in Boston's financial community and to avert further bank
closings.

Assisting Other Banks through the Boston Clearing House Association

Leading bankers all understood that public confidence was the
fragile keystone of the entire banking structure and that even

the strongest banks would have difficulty surviving a panic run on deposits. For this reason, the Boston Clearing House took a leading role in coordinating the efforts of emergency federal organizations and in organizing several private rescue operations.

During Hoover's administration, the federal government did little to help troubled banks, but two steps it did take were authorizing the National Credit Corporation in 1931 and the Reconstruction Finance Corporation (RFC) in 1932. The first resulted from a plan "devised . . . to meet the cash requirements of banking institutions whose assets are of sound value, but, nevertheless, ineligible for rediscount under the provisions of the Federal Reserve Act." It was established in New York, and the Boston Clearing House Association voted to organize a local subsidiary to extend National Credit Corporation benefits to banking institutions in the Commonwealth of Massachusetts. In October 1931, the Executive Committee of the National Shawmut Bank authorized Bucklin and other Shawmut executive officers to subscribe for National Credit Corporation debentures, to become a member of the local subsidiary, and to carry out its purposes. Then, in January 1932, the Reconstruction Finance Corporation was created by an act of Congress to provide direct capital assistance to qualifying banks under stringent conditions. Capital restructurings usually resulted in the RFC purchasing large amounts of preferred shares to carry these banks through the emergency.

Without more federal intervention, the Boston Clearing House Association took on a much more significant role than observers in today's era of extensive government activity would expect. Several of the Boston Clearing House member banks needed some form of assistance, and the strongest took the lead in arranging it. The assistance took one of several forms.

The simplest was a secured loan by the stronger banks to shore up the deposits of a member experiencing heavy temporary withdrawals. Swift and sure action usually calmed the public mood. For instance, the clearing house arranged a $5 million loan to the United States Trust Company under just such circumstances, with the National Shawmut providing its share as a participant. Similar assistance was provided to the Bank of Commerce and Trust Company.

Some banks were beyond such assistance. In April 1932, the

Lee, Higginson Trust Company was unable to continue operating, but a $1,050,000 loan by Boston Clearing House members enabled it to pay off all deposits in full, without forcing a panic sale of its assets. The National Shawmut's share of this loan was 16⅔ percent.

A third form of clearing-house assistance involved merging a weak bank into one of the strong ones. This was how the Atlantic National Bank emergency was resolved. Then Boston's third largest bank, it began suffering large withdrawals and sustaining heavy loan losses, indicating the bank might be forced to close.

On February 15, 1932, Bucklin informed the Shawmut Executive Committee that the Boston Clearing House Association was arranging a $5 million loan by member banks to assist the Atlantic National Bank. Exacerbating the situation, according to Bucklin, were malicious rumors sparking even heavier withdrawals.

The danger was again the domino effect that one failed bank might have on all, especially one the size of Atlantic National. Shawmut agreed to an 18 percent participation ($910,000) in the loan. Then as of May 1, 1932, the Reconstruction Finance Corporation voted to lend Atlantic $10 million against $18 million worth of assets, but the situation continued to worsen. By late spring only three alternatives seemed plausible: to close Atlantic's doors, to authorize a takeover by the National Shawmut, or to authorize a takeover by the First National Bank.

The Executive Committee of the National Shawmut was opposed to closing the Atlantic National but also declined to take it over, claiming that Shawmut's proportion of frozen and slow assets to its total assets was larger than that of the First National and, further, that the risk of "transferring the odium of the Atlantic situation (whether or not deserved) to our institution was not in the self interest of Shawmut." Instead, the Bank recommended to the Boston Clearing House that the First National accept responsibility, with the support of other clearing-house bank members. Subsequently First National did assume the deposits and other liabilities of Atlantic, with the understanding that other clearing-house banks would assist in carrying some of the assets with a $5 million loan. For many years Shawmut insiders would argue whether that resulted in a pitfall avoided or an opportunity missed.

Even if Shawmut missed a growth opportunity in the Atlantic National Bank emergency, it was not standing idly by. Alert to similar opportunities on a smaller scale, the National Shawmut Bank did take over the business of the failed Charlestown Trust Company and opened a branch at that bank's former office in 1932. In early 1933 Shawmut opened branches at three former offices of the Federal National Bank, which had failed in December 1931. These were located at Mattapan, Fish Pier, and South Boston. Meanwhile, the National Shawmut also opened a branch serving Cleveland Circle on June 1, 1931, the last before the Bank Holiday.

Shawmut Association Activities: Aiding Affiliates and an Acquisition

As the Boston Clearing House members were experiencing their problems, so also were member banks of Shawmut Association outside Suffolk County. The financial pressures of the Great Depression seem to have had their first impact on the Hingham Trust Company. By June 1932 its weakened condition caught the attention of the Massachusetts commissioner of banking, and he demanded that remedial measures be taken. Shawmut Association and the Hingham Trust directors agreed to establish a $150,000 security fund, in proportion to their relative stock holdings. Outside stockholders were neither consulted on the emergency nor advised of the solution, because the participating majority felt further disclosures would be injurious to the bank. Shawmut Association contributed 84 percent of the fund, about $125,000, and Hingham Trust survived.

Soon after the 1933 Bank Holiday, the Association Trustees discovered that the Merchants National in Salem required similar special attention. In November 1933 the Merchants received a cash infusion of $450,000. Of this, $150,000 for second preferred stock was purchased by Shawmut Association, while $300,000 in first preferred stock was acquired by the Reconstruction Finance Corporation. The latter's investment meant that Shawmut Association did not have majority control of Merchants for several years. Unfortunately, Shawmut Association minutes do not indicate when Merchants finally retired the "A" preferred stock held by the RFC, but that occurred at least two years before Merchants retired "B" preferred stock through a new issue of common capital stock in 1943.

During 1933 the Shawmut Association stepped in to salvage some business of the Central Trust Company of Cambridge, which had closed on May 10, 1932. A new bank, the County Bank and Trust Company of Cambridge, was organized with one-tenth the former capital. The National Shawmut advised and supported the combined efforts of the reorganization committee of the Trust Company and the state commissioner of banking. When it opened on July 17, 1933, each stockholder of the reorganized bank received an offer from the Shawmut Association to exchange his new bank stock for stock of the Association with the proviso that Shawmut Association obtain at least a majority of the County Bank and Trust Company stock.

II. The Crisis: The Bank Holiday in 1933

The years between the crash of October 1929 and the spring of 1933 were some of the most somber in American economic history, although the anguish was somewhat relieved by the continuing belief that things would get better. Occasional spurts of business activity in 1931 and 1932 fueled this hope, but the cumulative effect of adverse conditions finally proved too much for the American psyche. In the winter of 1933 confidence collapsed, and a consequent run on the banks led to the Bank Holiday and new federal legislation that introduced the second phase of the Great Depression.

Exactly why the public's faith in the country's banking system faded when it did is a matter for speculation. Many banks had closed prior to the stock market crash and in the months immediately following, but somehow those closings had not resulted in widespread public distrust. The existence of the Federal Reserve System was regarded as a protection against a general breakdown in the banking system, while the presence of the Reconstruction Finance Corporation gave further reassurance.

But if the public did not question the banks, many of the officers and directors of these institutions were well aware of basic weaknesses and vulnerability. A report from the Boston Clearing House Association, published in 1956, shows that during the 1920 to 1933 period there were in Massachusetts alone thirty-six bank closings by failure or by merger with other banks; twenty of these closings or mergers took place in the period from 1925 to 1932. It is assumed that those banks which merged were in such financial condition that the interests of stockholders and depositors were best served by this action. This local situation was representative of a larger one that was becoming a national concern.

As the depression trailed on, 85,000 businesses failed, the gross national product dropped from $104 billion to $58 billion, and the national income fell from $81 billion to $41 billion. Banks were perceived as the symbol, if not the heart, of the weakness of the entire economic system.

Fueling misgivings was awareness of the federal government's problem in finding revenues to balance its budget while meeting financial demands of needy individuals, veterans, and businesses. From 1920 to 1930 the government's income exceeded expenditures, making it possible to reduce the public debt by more than $9 billion. Suddenly, deficit financing was the order of the day, and the fear was that the government might resort to issuing irredeemable treasury notes. This led to withdrawals of currency from banks, conversion of some of that currency into gold, and hoarding. In February 1933 the banking situation in Michigan deteriorated to the point that the governor of the state closed all of the banks. The pattern was repeated in approximately twenty states, and panic accelerated.

By March 2, 1933, a combined statement of Federal Reserve banks showed a shrinkage in one week of $226 million in gold holdings. On March 3 gold withdrawals in New York City banks were in excess of $100 million, while the transfer of balances from New York banks for the ten days through March 3 amounted to more than 15 percent of total deposits. To avoid further drains the governor of New York requested that all banks in the state be closed as of 4:30 A.M., Saturday, March 4, and proclaimed a bank holiday until Tuesday, March 7.

Awareness of the New York situation together with an awareness that the governor of Illinois had declared a similar holiday sparked financial leaders in Massachusetts — officials of the

Federal Reserve Bank in Boston, the acting governor, the Boston Clearing House Committee, officials of member banks of the Boston Clearing House Association — to declare that Massachusetts banks must also close at the end of the business day on March 3. The very next day President Roosevelt was inaugurated, and within twenty-four hours he declared a nationwide four-day bank holiday to meet the emergency.

For officials of the federal government and for the boards of directors of the various banks throughout the United States, the week of March 6 through March 13 was one not of "holiday" but of feverish activity: hastily summoned meetings, assessments and reassessments, the hammering out of regulations that would allow the country's financial institutions to open again.

Congress, gathering in special session, promptly passed an emergency banking bill validating President Roosevelt's action and establishing regulations for the resumption of business. It was also during this week that legislation was passed severely curtailing the export and transfer of gold and in effect removing the country from the gold standard.

In Boston, although banks were ostensibly closed, the directors of financial institutions, including the Shawmut, met in sessions that lasted well into the night. By Tuesday, March 7, the Boston Clearing House Association had determined that, in order to assure uniform procedures, all member banks should be guided by regulations and policies issued by the Boston Clearing House Association and based on federal regulations. In brief, these regulations authorized the continuation of specific bank transactions throughout the holiday. Access to safe-deposit boxes and the reception of valuables was allowed. Sharply curtailed or forbidden, however, were any transactions that involved redemption in gold or payment in currency of any funds "not absolutely necessary to meet the needs of the community for food, medicine, other necessities of life." The payment of usual salaries and wages was authorized, but checks could not be cashed. Normal trust actions were also permitted with the restriction that no coin or currency be paid out. Deposit withdrawals were to be made in counter receipts, although by March 9 this restriction had been relaxed to allow for $10 cash withdrawals, and on March 11, $25 cash withdrawals were authorized. In essence, for almost a week the country went off cash with the Boston Clearing House even preparing substitute "scrip certificates," although they were never used.

By Sunday evening, March 12, the situation was finally in hand, and at that point, President Roosevelt announced that all banks except those that were unsound would be permitted to open.

At the Shawmut the call came at 12:22 A.M., March 13, from Herbert Stone, manager of the Boston Clearing House, to Ray Ilg, vice president of the Bank, that Shawmut's license to reopen had been granted and would be forthcoming. The license, issued by the secretary of the Treasury and signed by Governor Joseph B. Ely, was received by Stanley Wyatt, Shawmut cashier, twenty-three minutes later, at 12:45 A.M. According to its provisions, the National Shawmut Bank of Boston, including its fifteen citywide offices, was permitted to resume usual functions as of March 13, 1933, except as these functions were prohibited by the executive order of the president of the United States issued March 10, 1933, and limited or prohibited by any executive order of the president or by regulations of the secretary of the Treasury.

III.   The Second Phase: 1933–1939

Hoover's essentially hands-off policy to the problems of the depression foundered in steadily worsening economic conditions that culminated in the run on banks in the winter of 1933. The challenge to the new Roosevelt administration was "to do something." The Bank Holiday was in a sense the first active response; the passage of emergency legislation, including the Banking Act of 1933, was the next step.

The Banking Act of 1933

The effect of the Banking Act, approved June 16, 1933, and subsequently amended in 1935, cannot be overestimated. To a large extent it revolutionized the American banking system, placing it under far greater regulation and accountability to the federal government than had ever existed. According to provisions of the new law, national banks and member banks could no longer deal in investment securities or stocks on their own account but only as such transactions were accomplished to the order of their customers. No association (bank) could underwrite any issue of security or stock. Furthermore, no investment banker could engage in commercial banking or even serve as a director of a commercial bank.

The Effect of the Banking Acts on the Shawmut Corporation of Boston. As a consequence of the provisions prohibiting affiliates of national banks from engaging in securities business, the National Shawmut Bank found itself faced with the need to divest itself of the Shawmut Corporation. On October 5, 1933, Bucklin announced to the Bank's directors the discontinuance and complete cessation of the activities of the Corporation. All banks having similar affiliates had to take similar action. At Shawmut this meant the liquidation of security holdings of the Corporation with probable losses. It also meant problems of staff dismissal or absorption by the Bank, and the loss of an operation that had given the Bank considerable visibility, as it had offices in New York City, Philadelphia, and Chicago, as well as Boston.

The Establishment of Federal Deposit Insurance. The Banking Act of 1933 provided for the establishment of the Federal Deposit Insurance Corporation, effective on January 1, 1934. Each member bank of the Federal Reserve System was required to become a member institution prior to January 1, 1934, and accordingly in December 1933 the Board of Directors voted Shawmut's participation.

The Effect of the Banking Act on Shawmut's Board of Directors. The Banking Act of 1933 made specific provisions regarding the composition of the membership of boards of directors of national banks and set the maximum number of directors at twenty-five. As recently as 1931, the Shawmut numbered forty-one directors on its board. This reduction requirement went into effect six months after the mid-1933 adoption of the act, so its toll was first apparent at the January 1934 meeting of the Shawmut stockholders.

In addition to the routine attrition of the board, at least ten directors did not stand for reelection, apparently because of the new federal law restricting the number of directors. The ten were the following: W. F. Augustine, a Shawmut vice president; W. A. Barron, Jr., of White Weld and Company; Elmer J. Bliss, chairman of the board at Regal Shoe Company; J. Gardner Bradley, coal operator; Chandler Hovey, of Kidder, Peabody and Company; W. Eugene McGregor, of Chase, Harris, Forbes Corporation; Francis Ward Paine, of Paine, Webber and Company; Frederick P. Royce, vice president at Stone and Webster; Edgar C. Rust, trustee; and Herbert L. Tinkham, president of W. L. Douglas Shoe Company.

Other Regulatory Measures

In the months following the reopening of those banks licensed to do business, there was still concern on the part of government officials, the Comptroller of the Currency, the Federal Reserve Board, regulatory authorities of state banking, the American Bankers Association, and bankers themselves about the financial soundness of banks, management practices, and how best to preserve and develop further a banking system in which the public at home and abroad would have confidence.

The Comptroller of the Currency raised questions to national bank officers and directors about dividend policies in relation to net earnings, salaries, expenses of operation, and the need for and further strengthening of surplus and reserve accounts. A letter addressed to the boards of directors of all national banks by the Acting Comptroller of the Currency, F. G. Awalt, dated April 29, 1933, was presented to the Executive Committee of the board on May 16 by Bucklin. The letter asserted that every reasonable effort should be put forth to build up and strengthen the capital structure of banking institutions, and that, in the interest of strengthening surplus and reserves, special consideration should be given "not only to the net earnings but also to the capital and surplus accounts of your institution, salaries, expenses of operation and to the advisability of reducing or deferring dividend payments to your stockholders for the time being."

Bucklin discussed this letter with the members of the Executive Committee, showing them a comparison of Shawmut surplus and undivided profit with those of selected large banks in the country from the close of 1930 to the close of 1932. He also showed them a comparison of total deposits, par value of stock, and market prices. The Shawmut Bank had been paying a quarterly dividend to its stockholders of fifty cents per share since January 1, 1932, and on July 1, 1933, this dividend was cut again to twenty-five cents per share.

Concern over regulation in the management of banks, however, was not limited to this single letter from the Acting Comptroller. In the spring of 1933, as emergency legislation was enacted to relieve the effects of the depression on both the economic and human level, President Roosevelt submitted to Congress a bill designed to put more of the unemployed back to work. Passed in June 1933 as the National Industrial Recovery Act, the bill not only appropriated large sums to finance public works but also very specifically regulated and recounted the rights of labor. In response to this bill, the American Bankers Association and the New York Clearing House Association formulated the Code of Fair Competition of the Bankers of the United States. The declared purpose of the code was "to effectuate the policy of Title 1 of the National Industrial Recovery Act." What the code did, in essence, was reiterate and spell out for American Bankers Association members the conditions of employment required under the new act. Points covered included the right to unionize, the restrictions against employment of persons under sixteen, the maximum number of hours that an employee could be required to work, and the minimum wages allowable.

The code was submitted and approved by the Executive Committee of the Shawmut Board of Directors on August 4, 1933. The interest to this history, however, is not the effect that it had on Shawmut employees but rather the lack of effect. There is no indication that any employment practices had to be altered to conform to the new rules. In fact, the ease with which the code was accepted by the board suggests that the Shawmut was perhaps ahead of some of its peer banks in general labor practices.

IV. The Great Depression: Its Overall Impact

The previous sections have distinguished two stages in the
Great Depression. The first, extending from October 1929 to
1933, was characterized by a sense of hope that conditions
would right themselves and was accompanied by a general laissez-faire attitude on the part of the government. The second,
extending from 1933 through 1939, was characterized by far
less confidence in the ability of the economy to regain its balance. As a consequence, the government took a far more active
role in shaping economic events. Marking the transition between these stages was — from the political point of view —
the election of Roosevelt; from the economic point of view,
it was the run on banks and subsequent Bank Holiday.

To compartmentalize history in such a fashion, however convenient, can be misleading, for in the long run the significance
of the Great Depression lies not in the distinctions between
its various stages but in the totality of the phenomenon itself.
It was a totality of extreme economic hardship extending over
a decade and ultimately touching all segments of American
society. That certain areas of the Bank's business were more
affected at one point than others is implicit in this. Time sales
and consumer credit business, for example, felt the impact immediately, and large write-offs and policy changes relevant to
credit were occurring by 1930. Shawmut Corporation of Boston
on the other hand, although profoundly affected by the drop
in the securities market and the general pressures levied against
banks, was not fundamentally altered until after the passage
of the Banking Act of 1933.

Other areas of Bank business, however, were shaped not so
much by specific conditions at a particular time as by the general
attrition of continuing bad times. Cumberland Mountain Coal
Company and credits endorsed by the German banks in 1925,
and which came to be known as the German Standstill Credits,
are examples of this kind of activity. Both were commitments
that the Shawmut undertook in good faith in the 1920s, and
both required continual reassessment throughout the 1930s
as the faltering economy took its toll.

Cumberland Mountain Coal Company

A speculative venture that Bucklin inherited (covered in Chapter 9), Cumberland Mountain Coal suffered when the price of coal plummeted in the 1930s. Nevertheless, it remained on Shawmut's books for several years, and is illustrative of Bucklin's approach to other depression-engendered problems. In cases where potential for profit did not change but only the timetable to realize those profits, Bucklin staunchly supported sticking the situation out. The story of the German Standstill Credits illustrates the same kind of approach. Although much of the "sticking it out" was initially regulated by the government, as Bucklin was the first to point out, when recovery of those credits became possible, Shawmut acted with patience and restraint.

The German Standstill Credits

Although Bucklin's approach to the German Standstill Credits demonstrated the same tenacity he had exhibited with the coal company, the problems with the investment were quite different. Problems over the credits arose not because of the financial difficulties of any single borrower but because of international lending policies. The German credits had been arranged in the mid-1920s by the allied powers, who imposed severe reparations on the German Republic following the outcome of World War I. These reparations payments placed a heavy burden on the domestic German economy, resulting in a drain of the very capital needed to restore Germany's economic health. Soon after they began, a bout of hyperinflation in the early 1920s devastated the German economy. To preserve the value of payments received as reparations, and to improve conditions in the domestic German economy, the allied powers arranged for postponements of the reparations payments and encouraged several banks and financial concerns to extend loans to German industrial companies, banks, and political subdivisions (states and cities), all with the intent of restoring confidence in the German currency and providing a solid foundation for the national economy. American funding represented two-thirds of the total amount advanced to Germany. Shawmut's initial participation in these extensions of credits began by February 1925 and peaked during 1929–1930 at a level of $26 million.

Shortly after 1930, however, the general international economic distress of the growing depression and the 1931 failure of Austria's Credit Anstalt Bank prompted bankers to reduce their exposure in Germany. Between the summers of 1930 and 1931, total credits available to German banks plummeted from $2.8 billion to $1.4 billion, with roughly half of them supplied by United States banks. Shawmut policy was to maintain its exposure in proportion to the commitments of the larger New York City banks. By June 9, 1931, Shawmut had already decreased its exposure in Germany to $12 million, less than half its peak figure. Of this amount $2 million was in time deposits in German banks and $10 million was in acceptances.

The precipitate withdrawal of these credits raised international concerns that the German economy would be further devastated. Bankers and statesmen from many industrial countries met at an emergency conference in London to stem the tide of canceled credits. As a consequence of the conference an agreement was adopted, which amounted to a moratorium on the withdrawal or cancellation of credits previously made available to the German debtor banks. Signed in mid-September 1931, it was the first of several agreements that came to be known as the German Standstill Credit Agreements and that affected the extension of credits over a period of years through and after World War II.

These developments obviously must have been of concern to Shawmut officials. Bucklin himself made a trip abroad in the summer of 1931, and upon his return at the end of August, he reported his observations to the directors. Though the minutes do not say, Germany was undoubtedly one of his primary destinations. Two weeks later, at the very time agreements were being signed in London, the Shawmut minutes confirm that Harold P. Janish, a Shawmut vice president, was in Berlin to discuss the Standstill Credit agreements.

The greater part of these outstanding credits were recovered by Shawmut before America entered World War II. From the $12 million of credits frozen by the 1931 agreement, Shawmut's exposure was reduced to $6,188,000 by December 1941. Originally Shawmut dealt with twenty-three debtors, but through consolidation and liquidation, this number was reduced to the nine leading banking institutions in Germany.

World War II caused an understandable hiatus in repayments on used credits or releases of unused credits, while the immediate postwar situation in which Germany was partitioned caused other problems. Nevertheless, repayment in some form or other resumed in 1950, and finally, on May 6, 1958, the Bank realized the recovery of $325,496.63, "representing payment in full of the remaining Standstill Credits." This payment culminated years of effort by Lawrence H. Martin, then vice president of Shawmut, to make full recovery on the twenty-eight-year-old credits.

A Financial Overview, 1929–1939

In spite of the popularly held view that the American economy came careening to a halt one dark day in October 1929, there was no such apocalyptic moment. At Shawmut, as at many other banks, assets actually rose in the two months following the crash, as businessmen sought loans to tide them over a brief time of straitened circumstances. As 1930 unfolded, however, the nation's banks began to falter, and it was not until June 1940 that they rallied again.

Within this "decade of despair" there were, of course, variations. In 1932 assets of many banks, including Shawmut, reached their lowest ebb. During the next three years, as the Roosevelt programs began to take hold, there were small but steady increases in overall figures, leading to an optimistic view that the depression was over. In 1936 the federal administration began to pull back and leave business to business. Unfortunately, the move was premature; 1937 was one of the darkest years of the decade, and bank assets, again including those of Shawmut, fell precipitously.

The fluctuation of Shawmut's assets during this period reflected the broadest trends of the larger economy. A closer examination of loans, deposits, and amounts invested in government securities reveals that there was also a change in the nature of the Bank's resources. During the decade of the Great Depression the proportion of deposits to total resources went from 66 percent to over 80 percent, suggesting, if nothing else, that the speculative trend of the 1920s was now well in the past. Even more informative is what happened in the loan area.

As the depression developed, as business began to realize that it could not afford to borrow, loan activity at the Bank slowed dramatically. Such a fact is not surprising. What is surprising is that as the Shawmut assets began to rise, and as deposits slowly grew from the 1932 low, maintaining the 80 percent proportion, loan activity did not show a corresponding expansion but continued downward. This condition reveals the reluctance, or inability, of business to restock inventory or invest in capital projects throughout the entire period. The source of Shawmut's expanding assets, then, was not increased business activity but increased investments in government securities and government paper, the proceeds of which went into financing recovery. For example, in December 1937 the Bank had $30 million in government securities alone; in December 1939 it had twice that amount.

As the depression dragged on, the patience of the country and its financial institutions was sorely taxed. In 1932 more than fourteen hundred banks had collapsed, but although new federal legislation, particularly the introduction of the Federal Deposit Insurance Corporation, slowed this particular phenomenon, the strain of remaining afloat continued.

Then in 1939 war broke out in Europe, and almost immediately conditions changed. The latter half of 1939 saw the Federal Reserve index of industrial production shoot from the 106 percent, which was the 1935–1939 average, to 125 percent. Commercial loans revived as business, shaking off the lethargy of the last decade, awoke to meet new market demands. At the Shawmut the change was recorded in the sudden jump in its own loan volume. The Great Depression had ended; nevertheless, it had left a legacy of government regulation and of caution, and the business of banking would never be quite the same.

2

With the outbreak of war in Europe in September 1939, the economic priorities of the United States began to shift away from priming the business pump to channeling and realizing the energy of new business and industrial productivity. Such a situation might have released Walter Bucklin's entrepreneurial energies, had not external circumstances intervened to dominate business decisions.

From late 1939 through 1945, the story of the Shawmut's development is largely a story of its response to the requirements of war financing. During this period investments rose rapidly, reflecting almost entirely the Bank's purchase of government securities. Deposits rose correspondingly, but loan growth was minimal. At the same time Bank services expanded, particularly those concerned with the distribution of government bonds and the cashing of government checks.

Government Securities and Obligations and Deposits

As the situation in Europe became increasingly tense in the spring and summer of 1939, more and more capital from foreign countries was shifted for safekeeping to the United States, becoming a major factor in gold imports. These imports were further augmented by British payments for war material. As a consequence, reserves began to expand rapidly, making it difficult for the Federal Reserve System to restrain inflation. To maintain orderly conditions in the capital markets and reduce the money available for loans, the Federal Reserve supported the sale of government securities in the open market. By the end of 1940, the System had sold $300 million in securities from its portfolio.

This restraint does not appear to have affected the resources of the Shawmut, which held roughly 15 to 20 percent of its resources in government securities throughout the depression and well into 1941. Directly after Pearl Harbor, however, government obligations began to reflect the cost of subsidizing the war effort. At this point Shawmut's purchase of obligations rose substantially.

In April 1942, government obligations represented 25 percent of the earning resources of the Shawmut bank; in June they represented 35 percent, and in December 1945 they stood at 62 percent of the Shawmut's total assets. Both the volume and the percentage show the degree to which the Shawmut was involved in the war effort. There were, in fact, few other investment alternatives available, but this does not diminish the importance of Shawmut's involvement. Instead the lack of alternative investment opportunities points out that during the war, the main earning asset of commercial banks, including the Shawmut, was not derived from traditional commercial loans but from government obligations.

During these years Shawmut's deposits also expanded exponentially, going from $212 million in December 1940 to $428 million in December, 1945. Such growth did not stem from an increased volume of loans, as might be expected in ordinary times, but rather directly reflected the purchase of government obligations and the increase in money in circulation, which was due primarily to an enlarged dollar volume of payrolls. While a large percentage of these deposits came from Shawmut's own customers, a good portion was also provided by correspondent banks, which were enjoying similar deposit expansion. Still another dimension of the deposit growth during the war was the increase from government accounts.

The Shawmut's financial experience during the war was quite different from that during peacetime. Certainly it was a time of growth: assets rose from $230 million in December 1939 to $462 million in December 1945, but it was a time of a unique kind of growth, the character of which reflected the impact of extraordinary conditions. This is not to diminish Bucklin's role during the war but only to point out that it was as much the times as the man that steered the Bank during these years.

Loans

If the story of the Shawmut's assets and deposits is a war story, the story of its loan commitments during this period is even more so. During the first year of hostilities overseas, Shawmut increased its commercial lending, reaching a peak in April 1941. From this point, the volume of commercial loans steadily declined, bottoming out in April 1944. In normal times such a decline would have indicated a disaster, but these were not normal times. The Bank was doing better than ever, with the slack being taken up by earnings from government obligations.

The decline in Shawmut loans reflected federal policy. The

government deliberately caused this drop by adopting measures to curtail the extension of credit for any purposes other than defense and encouraging the repayment of outstanding loans. The reasons for these actions were twofold: to stem inflation, which, aside from price controls, could best be achieved by diverting excess income into military expenditures; and to assure that available labor and material resources were directed to the war effort. As a consequence of these policies, which expressed themselves in rationing as well as price controls and in incentives for business and industry to develop their efforts for war production, regular commercial and industrial loans decreased by some $4 billion nationwide in 1942 alone. At the same time war-related loans to business and industry did increase some $1.7 billion, but this was not enough to offset the decline, and total loans fell by about $2 billion.

Cotton, woolen, and textile industries continued as an important segment of the Bank's portfolio as did the shoe and leather industry. A third traditional area of Shawmut interest was railroads and automobiles. By far the greatest volume of loans extended between 1942 and 1945, however, were guaranteed loans for war-production purposes, which were authorized on March 26, 1942, by Executive Order 9112.

According to this order, the War Department, the Navy Department, and the Maritime Commission could henceforth guarantee loans, discounts, or advances for the purpose of financing those engaged in any business or operation deemed by those agencies as necessary for the support of the war. Federal Reserve banks were authorized to act as fiscal agents operating under Regulation V (later Regulation VT), which prescribed rules and policies for handling such loans.

The purpose of the V or VT loans, as they came to be called, was to provide adequate financing for prime and subcontractors whose need for working capital had been increased beyond their borrowing capacity by war orders. The United States government established loan guarantees, providing protection that ranged from 65 to 90 percent of the total amount lent by private financial institutions. These amounts were not subject to peacetime legal lending limits. For example, on October 13, 1942, the Shawmut Bank considered participation of $12 million in a $1 billion line of credit to General Motors, the unguaranteed portion of $1.5 million being the only part that would apply against the Bank's lending limit. The size of this particular transaction was a notable exception. In general, amounts extended by the Shawmut ranged from $250,000 up to $3 million, usually as participation in a much larger loan.

War Loan Drives

As the country concentrated its attention on the production of war supplies, a constant and recurring threat was that of inflation. By 1942 the national income had reached $125 billion, but the value of available consumer goods stood at a mere $80 billion. Price controls and tightened consumer credit were both effective restraints on the impulse to bid up prices, but neither addressed itself directly to the problem of diverting excess income into the war effort. To achieve this end — that is, to stem inflationary forces and simultaneously derive the largest possible amount of war funds from current income — the government instituted the income tax withholding system in 1942. Even earlier, however, it introduced the first of seven massive war bond drives, which provided not only an alternative channel for excess income but had the added attraction of reducing government dependency on bank credit.

The first of these drives was initiated in April 1941, eight months before the United States entered the war; the last took place in the fall of 1945, several months after the war's conclusion. In all of them Shawmut participated vigorously, serving not simply as a passive agent in the dispersal of bonds, but becoming increasingly active in promoting their sale. Coordinating defense activities for all of New England was Albert Creighton, a director of the National Shawmut, who served much the same function as Colonel Gaston had during the First World War, and to whom some credit for Shawmut's active role in the drives can be attributed.

Other War Services and Branch Banking

In 1941, after a hiatus of almost eight years, the Shawmut again began to develop its branches with the addition of a drive-in facility in Dorchester. In 1942 four more branches and one temporary facility were added. The latter, located at the Boston Port of Embarkation was a limited facility which accepted checks and deposits, particularly for servicemen, and that, as a convenience for these persons, remained open at hours not customary for regular full-service branches.

Personnel Affairs

Even prior to the entry of the United States into the war, several of Shawmut's staff left the Bank to volunteer for service or to contribute their expertise to accelerating defense-oriented enterprises. As early as 1940 *The Indian Call* (the house organ which replaced the *Wigwam News,* disbanded in 1933) mentioned Shawmut members then in service. It was not until December 1941, however, when federal legislation was enacted requiring registration of all men between the ages of eighteen and sixty-four that staff attrition became substantial.

A survey conducted by William Augustine, Shawmut vice president, shows that on December 8, 1941, Shawmut had 477 male employees; one year later there were 328 male employees. The sudden drop was not accomplished by a decline in overall number of employees. In fact, in December 1942, 15 new positions were filled, but the number of men to women was now 328 to 462. An interesting by-product of this shift was the new opportunity it opened for women employees. In December 1941 there were only 5 women tellers, all of whom were in the Savings Department; in December 1943 there were 50 women out of a total of 82 tellers. Augustine's survey also showed that in addition to the increased employment of women, the bank had hired 43 men age forty-five or over to replace younger men who had gone into service.

Throughout the war the Shawmut supported its men and women in service. At a Christmas party held in the evening of December 17, 1942, attended by six hundred officers and employees on the main floor of the 40 Water Street headquarters building, a roll of honor plaque was unveiled. In dedicatory remarks, Frederick A. Carroll, vice president, noted, "There are those of our Shawmut family who are not here tonight —

one hundred and forty from the Bank and twenty-eight from Devonshire. Thirty-six of these men are officers. There is one WAVE — Miss Mildred Kilcoyne of the Bookkeeping Department." The Bank had not forgotten these people and kept in constant touch.

As the economy began to expand in response to war demands in 1940, wages also began to rise. Such a return to prosperity was not an unalloyed blessing, and the spectre of inflation haunted those charged with managing the nation's finances. In 1941 a wage and price freeze went into effect, but some price rises were inevitable. Competition for a shrinking labor pool put pressure on institutions to increase their pay scale. At the Shawmut these needs were met by board authorization of a supplemental pay increase during the last quarter of 1941. Called the Temporary Supplemental Compensation Plan, the program gave an increase of a specific percentage according to salary and remained in effect through March 1944, when the percentage was increased because of "prevailing conditions."

3

On February 2, 1945, only a few months before the end of the war, Bucklin reached age sixty-five, the accepted age for retirement. He had served the Bank for twenty-two years, ten of which were overshadowed by depression, five by war. During that last five years, Shawmut's assets jumped from $229,688,327 in December 1939 to $462,516,678 in December 1945. Although much of this increase was produced by the war economy, the rise was no less real. Perhaps in appreciation of this growth, the board voted that the president be invited to remain in the service of the Bank. When the war ended in 1945, Walter S. Bucklin was still firmly in control and tenaciously retained that control for the next decade.

Chapter 11

The End of an Era
Walter Bucklin and the Presidency of Walter Borden
(1945–1956)

T HE final decade of Walter Bucklin's administration was in some ways the most challenging of his long career at the Bank. In general it was a decade of prosperity. American industry flourished. Personal income rose, and with it consumer demand and inflation. The technology of war, unleashed for peace, sparked the production of new goods. Items as disparate as penicillin, air conditioning, and television created not only a new standard of living but also a new standard of expectations. At the same time the postwar emergence of the United States as a major Western power gave rise to new international responsibilities and tensions: it was a period of the Marshall Plan and the World Bank, of the cold war and police action in Korea. All of these circumstances in the larger world had their impact on the activities of the Bank and the kind of services it provided. Furthermore, it was during this period that a substantial reorganization took place attributable both to an attrition in the ranks of senior officers and to pressure for Bucklin to delegate more authority.

1

The activities of the Bank in the postwar era were shaped by rapid growth in the national economy, the changing character of the New England economy, the need to expand and extend traditional services, and the need to branch into new areas.

Loans and Discounts

The postwar reconversion of American industry to commercial production, as well as the public's demand for the durable goods that had been unaffordable during the Great Depression and unavailable during the war, created a demand for loans unprecedented since the 1920s. Between December 1945 and December 1956, the loan volume (including real estate and first-mortgage loans) expanded almost 200 percent.

Much of this expansion came in traditional areas with loans provided to long time customers of the Bank. For example, Shawmut continued to be a source of financing for many railroads, particularly those in New England, and served as an agent and participant in several large loans for the purchase of new diesel equipment. It also provided loans for shoe and leather manufacturing, although by the end of the 1950s this industry had begun to suffer sharp attrition, which was reflected at the Bank by a decrease in loans to this area.

Shawmut's loyalty to "old customers," however, was perhaps best attested to by its relationship with Sears Roebuck Company. On October 9, 1951, the Bank was offered a $2.5 million participation in a $200 million five-year loan to this firm. Although interest was described as "abnormally low," authority was given on grounds that "Sears Roebuck had been a valued customer of the Shawmut for 46 years."

But while service to traditional customers was an important aspect of Shawmut's early postwar loan portfolio the economy, particularly the New England economy, had begun to undergo a vast transformation. Specific industries that had been the staple of the region for years and which had turned to Shawmut for much of their support began, for a variety of reasons, to

lose their ascendancy. No better example of the change exists
than that which occurred in the textile industry.

Since its inception, New England had been deeply involved
in the trade of raw materials for textiles, and since the founding
of the Boston Manufacturing Company in 1813, had been
deeply involved in their manufacture. When Shawmut was
founded in 1836, it became a valued source of funds for this
industry and continued to supply financing for purchase of raw
materials, warehousing, and manufacturing throughout the
nineteenth and into the twentieth century. In the 1920s, however, the mills began to experience severe problems, which
were exacerbated by the depression. Although World War II
and the Korean War provided some respite for the industry
as orders for uniforms and blankets flooded in, by 1954 most
of the major cotton and woolen manufacturers were either
closed or moved south.

Such changes, of course, did not occur overnight, nor were
all aspects of a given industry decimated. For example, in March
1951 the Bank agreed to extend a $7.9 million letter of credit
to one company for importing cotton from Egypt to be purchased by the United States government through the Commodity Credit Corporation, itself a postwar phenomenon established in 1948. Importation of raw materials, in fact, continued
to be an important part of Bank financing, but no longer was
Shawmut called upon to provide loans to the vast mills in Lowell
and Lawrence. By the mid-1950s these had grown silent, and
it was not until the 1960s and 1970s that the Bank again became
an important resource of funds for a much smaller, but nonetheless significant, textile industry, one that focused on supplying
small lot, speciality goods such as fine woolens.

As the economy began to change, the Bank began to look
for and open new accounts in areas that previously were only
a small part of its portfolio. Following the war, energy needs,
particularly oil and gas for cars, increased dramatically, and
as early as 1947, Shawmut approved participation in an aggregate $102 million loan for Arabian American Oil to run for
ten years with a 75 percent guarantee by Standard Oil Company
of New Jersey and a 25 percent guarantee by Socony Vacuum
Oil. Other loans to other companies followed. Some were extended for the development and transportation of this resource;

others were for distribution. Another industry that experienced a massive postwar boom was the airlines, and Shawmut also began extending its portfolio here.

Despite the rise in volume of commercial loans, the charge has been brought that Bucklin was never as interested in developing them as in developing time sales and personal loans. The latter were, of course, more closely related to consumer financing and more familiar to him from his insurance experience. As a consequence, it is said that as early as the 1920s Bucklin placed a low priority on acquiring commercial accounts. The business stagnation of the 1930s further slowed their expansion, while the introduction of Regulation V, or government-guaranteed loans, during the war reduced the impetus to court and process transactions in the private industrial sector. The incentive and the structures that might have helped the Shawmut capitalize on postwar industrial activity were at best rusty. To counter this "rust" Bucklin appointed Lawrence H. Martin vice president of Credit in 1945, and probably much of the revitalization of viable commercial and industrial loans can be attributed to his efforts. Nevertheless, critics still assert that had Bucklin's priorities been different the Shawmut might have done even better in the postwar decade than it did.

In the meantime, government-guaranteed loans did continue, and the Bank also profited from VA or FHA guaranteed-housing and construction loans. In November 1948 the Federal Housing Administration reported that the Shawmut ranked third among all the banks in the country and eighth among all banks, financial companies, and other lending institutions combined in the volume of Title I FHA loans.

Thus, in the immediate postwar decade several changes occurred in Shawmut's loan portfolio. They included not only the acquisition of new accounts but a substantial increase in the total volume of loans. Interest rates on commercial loans also changed, going from a characteristic 1.75 percent rate in the late 1940s to 4 percent by 1956, although the potential profit from such increases was largely offset by inflation and the growing cost of money. Another change was in the size of individual loans. Where $3 million transactions (Shawmut's legal limit) were the exception in the late 1940s, they were commonplace by the 1950s.

Deposits in the Postwar Era

As loan volume increased so also did deposits. Reporting on deposit growth as of December 30, 1950, Bucklin noted that they now totaled $395,068,532, "the highest year-end figure since 1945 when the total was $428,461,000." But, as he pointed out, this 1945 figure had been inflated by $102,719,200 in United States deposits. The implication is clear that the Bank and by extension its president should be applauded for increasing deposits from the private sector.

A more informative review of deposit growth was provided in a report delivered to the Board of Directors in July 1955. This report showed the growth of yearly average deposits at the Shawmut for the fifteen-year span, 1939 through 1954, was 100.4 percent for total deposits and 144.8 percent for commercial deposits. In presenting this report, Bucklin went on to note that these figures "compared with growths of 94.7 percent in total deposits and 118.1 percent in commercial deposits for all Boston [Federal Reserve] member banks." At this point a slowing in the general economy as well as tight money began to exert influence, contributing to a drop in deposits during the final two years of Bucklin's administration.

Still another dimension of deposits that should be mentioned here was that of savings accounts. In 1950 these represented $60 million with interest of 1 percent on accounts up to $5000. Between 1950 and 1953 higher interest rates available at savings banks caused Shawmut's savings deposits to shrink and efforts began to court these accounts. Among these efforts was the Savings Certificate, introduced at Shawmut for the first time in August 1956. Although the event was not heralded with any particular emphasis, it was nevertheless significant. Traditionally, demand deposits had been the backbone of commercial banking. In the future, time deposits would become increasingly important, and 1956 was a pivotal year in Shawmut's recognition of this fact.

International Developments and the Foreign Department

During the 1920s the Foreign Department had grown in size and status. Particularly important for its growth was the decision to limit the Shawmut Corporation of Boston's activities to domestic investment securities. At that point the Bank's Foreign Department assumed most of the responsibility for affairs beyond the country's borders. Problems over the German Standstill Credits during the 1930s had dampened the Shawmut's appetite for business abroad, which even the advent of the postwar era, with its multiple international opportunities, did not revive.

Nevertheless, transactions with Western Europe and with Australia and New Zealand did continue to grow between 1945 and 1956, although on a somewhat more modest scale than might have been expected. In 1947 the International Bank for Reconstruction and Development (World Bank) was founded, and Shawmut participated in at least two major transactions arranged by this bank.

Furthermore, in January 1956 the board approved a $1 million line of credit to Banco Central de Venezuela, and in the meantime, the Bank also became a participant in loans to the Mexican Government for the development of oil.

The most dramatic international transaction during the period, however, at least from Shawmut's point of view, involved recovery of the German Standstill Credits. In December 1953 Bucklin reported to the Board, in tones that could hardly be described as modest, that "as a result of the judgment of the officers of this bank in retaining these [the German Standstill Credits] until this time, the Bank has recovered about 92 percent of the principal amount charged off. Many banks and other creditors who elected to settle their claims several years earlier realized a much lower percentage than Shawmut has recovered." Although the 92 percent figure is open to some question because of the changing value of the Deutsche mark, progress was being made, and by the following year the balance to be recovered had decreased even further. Despite this self-congratulation the German Standstill Credits left a residue of caution: Shawmut remained wary of international commitments, and enthusiastic development of this area had to wait for later administrations.

The Postwar Development of Other Earning Resources

In the postwar decade, lending resumed its proper role as the Bank's major activity. Government obligations, which had served such an important function during the depression and war years, shrank considerably. In December 1945 United States obligations made up $289 million of the Bank's total resources of $460 million. In December 1956 they constituted $90 million of $453 million in resources. Loans, however, were by no means the only source of income. Trust activities, new mergers, and even new branches contributed their share to overall growth, while the development of new personal services made Shawmut an increasingly attractive place to bank.

Trust Service Expansion. The postwar period was a time of major changes in Shawmut's Trust Department. In October 1945 Frederick A. Carroll had been killed in an accident while on special assignment for the American Red Cross in France. Horace Schermerhorn was appointed acting director in his place.

One of the new acting director's first moves was to create a trust service which went into operation in November 1947. Called the Common Trust Fund of the National Shawmut Bank, it was introduced to take advantage of new demands in this growing area. It was also in deference to this growth that, in November 1951, the entire department was reorganized on Schermerhorn's recommendation. According to the new design, which was based on a comparative study of competing trust departments, Shawmut henceforth had two trust committees instead of one. The first of these committees was made up of five directors and one officer and had policy-making and auditing powers. The second, called the Trust Investment Committee, had one director and five officers and was charged with carrying out operational details. The importance of trust activities to Bank earnings was attested by a note in the minutes that same November 1951. It declared that operating income had increased during the past year "due to increase in interest from loans and *Trust Department Commissions.*"

Mergers and Branching. In 1927 the Bank had added Citizens National, thereby augmenting its resources. Five and a half years later in 1932, it absorbed the defunct Charlestown Trust Company, but there were no further mergers until the postwar decade, when the Bank again began adding other banks. The first new addition was First Revere National in 1945. This was followed by Columbia Trust in January 1946, when the board approved an agreement dated December 29, 1945, between Walter S. Bucklin, representing National Shawmut, Andrew Porter, representing Columbia Trust, and Joseph P. Kennedy, representing two-thirds of Columbia Trust shares, whereby Shawmut agreed to purchase all the property and assets of the trust company. In 1947 the Chelsea Trust was also added, and two years later the Stabile Bank and Trust in Boston's North End was merged with Shawmut.

Still another way of increasing the Bank's business in the postwar decade was through further development of branches. Between 1945 and 1953, Shawmut added ten new offices, giving it a total of twenty-nine by the time Bucklin resigned in 1956. As earlier, Bucklin kept a watchful eye on the aesthetic development of these new offices. Memoranda of the decade are rife with examples of his concern that the facilities maintain the colonial motif established in the 1920s and that they be freshly painted and in all ways presentable to the public.

He was also concerned with the physical appearance and overall attractiveness of the 40 Water Street headquarters. Recognizing that color affects human responses to business, work, and play, the administration authorized the employment of color engineers to study the Bank's facilities and make recommendations on the shades that would be conducive to a cheerful and productive atmosphere. These scientific recommendations were then implemented in work and customer areas. One striking example was evident in the safe-deposit vaults. Here the previous closed-in effect created by steel-gray vaults was altered to a sense of spaciousness when the walls were painted medium blue and the ceiling pale yellow. Another change took place in the general banking area, where the high ornamental ceiling had created the sensation of a threatening canyon of business. Repainting the ceiling rose, blue, and off-white made it seem lower and the atmosphere less forbidding.

At the same time Bucklin authorized this modernization, he also authorized additions to the Bank's fine collection of colonial prints and the purchase of Oriental rugs. Frequently, and sometimes to their dismay, Bucklin invited senior officers to help make selections from samples exhibited in his office. Chosen items were relegated to the main floor, although when Shawmut moved to One Federal Street the rugs were put instead on the executive floor.

Personal Service Department. Earnings from the trust activities and expansion of business through mergers directly affected the income of the Bank. Convenient and attractive offices had a more indirect effect. Another "indirect" earner was the Personal Service Department introduced on March 19, 1951. Designed to attract new customers by providing them with new conveniences, the department offered one-stop banking service. Customers had a special checking account and could also make savings deposits and withdrawals. The department cashed payroll and government checks and provided facilities for personal loans, business installment loans, traveler's checks, the sale and redemption of U.S. savings bonds and installment-plan payments.

Publicity Developments

Walter Bucklin was not by training a banker but a salesman and a promoter. To some extent image making was his business and his particular talent. Throughout his long career at the Bank Bucklin was constantly concerned that the public be aware of what the Shawmut was, that the personnel and the physical makeup of the Bank present this image well, and that the media be tapped to the full extent of its potential to convey this image.

Under these circumstances, it is not surprising that the Bank introduced a house organ at his direction and that a constant theme of this newspaper was the need for the staff to be willing and cheerful in its contact with the public. Furthermore, it is not surprising that he devoted so much attention to the physical appearance of the Bank. Bucklin's major contribution in the public relations area, however, lay in the encouragement he gave to new and innovative forms of advertising.

During the 1920s ads were limited to conventional print media: newspapers, trade publications, national magazines, direct mail, billboards. Within these forms Shawmut did support certain imaginative campaigns of which the personal banker's ad —

"600 Bankers Serve You" — was one of the better known. Also, legends arising from the Indian logo were emphasized as indicative of the Bank's traditional American and Bostonian roots. (See Chapter 20.)

In the 1940s, however, Shawmut branched out, becoming one of the first banks in the New England area and among the first in the nation to explore the potential of radio advertising. Beginning in the fall of 1940 the Bank sponsored a thrice weekly newscast featuring commentator John J. Barry, a renowned *Boston Globe* reporter. By 1949 Shawmut newscasts were heard at 9 A.M., 1 P.M., and 7:45 P.M., on Monday, Wednesday, and Friday. In the meantime, Barry, who still took the evening news and who worked closely with Bucklin in developing Shawmut's sponsorship on six different stations, had become the Bank's first vice president for Advertising and Public Relations. Under his direction the Bank expanded the scope of its advertising, capitalizing particularly on the Indian bust as the Shawmut symbol. Also, and most significantly, it began to explore the possibilities of television advertising.

In 1939 television was introduced in New York. Though its commercial development was delayed by the war, by 1947 plans were already under way to introduce this new medium to Boston. It was not until May 14, 1948, however, that Bucklin announced to the Shawmut board that television would be available in Boston within the next few weeks and that he was of the opinion that the Bank should use it for advertising. The board was evidently predisposed in favor of the idea, for the following week vice presidents Erickson, Borden, and Barry went to New York to study the possibilities, and on June 9, 1948, less than a month after the subject had been introduced and when there were fewer than twenty-five hundred sets in Boston, the Bank became a sponsor of the "Shawmut Nightly Newsteller" on the city's first channel, WBZ-TV. Four months later, in October, the newsletter also appeared on the second channel, WNAC-TV.

In the next few years Shawmut extended its advertising to other channels and broadened the scope of the programs that it sponsored. Initially identified with news and with all of WNAC's weather forecasts, by the beginning of the next decade, Shawmut also sponsored the weekly "Shawmut Home The-

atre" which brought movies — mostly selected by Bucklin —
to the home viewer.

During these early years the budget allocated for television
was some 3 percent of the Bank's gross earnings and unlike
all other forms of advertising was charged to reserves rather
than operating expenses. Bucklin rationalized this anomaly on
grounds that television was still "experimental." The Comptroller of the Currency, however, was not convinced, and in 1952
pressure from this source caused some portion of television
expenses to be charged to the current operating budget. By
1955 the entire cost had been taken into operating expenses.
By this date, however, television advertising was also an accepted and extremely successful item in the Bank's presentation
of itself. No longer "experimental," it had come to replace
much of the effort poured earlier into more conventional forms.

Personnel Affairs

The major concern of the Bank in the postwar decade was to
expand its business to meet new demands and realize new earnings. To achieve these goals, it was important to ensure that
Shawmut remained competitive in terms of its staff — their efficiency, compensation, and working conditions. In 1947 the first
steps were taken in this direction when Walter Chase, vice president, at the behest of Lawrence Martin, then vice president
of administration, was asked to assume direction and supervision of all personnel functions. His appointment marked the
beginning of the modern Personnel Division.

Salary Increases. One of the primary issues of the postwar years
was that of fair compensation in an inflationary period, and
in April 1946 an across-the-board 12.5 percent raise was added
to the 10 percent supplemental compensation provided in the
last full year of the war.

In 1948 and 1950 clerical base wages were again increased,
and in 1955 the board recommended an "adjustment to salary
structure based on salary actions of New York banks." Henceforth, it asserted, "salary rates would be increased to a minimum
of $40 per week." At the same time, officers' salaries were also

increased to ensure that they were at least in keeping with the average of the local market.

Fringe Benefits. While periodic raises helped keep the Bank competitive in seeking and retaining good employees, no less important were the fringe benefits that it offered. Since 1911 the Bank had had the Retirement Annuity Program, which was periodically updated. In November 1929 it had also introduced, at Bucklin's recommendation, a group life insurance plan as part of its benefits. The plan allowed each employee to secure an amount of insurance equivalent to 1.5 percent of annual salary, figured to the nearest multiple of $500, but not to exceed $5000. In 1938 both these programs were revised in the interest of clarity and liberality, increasing the total amount of available insurance to $10,000.

In 1940 all employees of the Bank were brought under Social Security (the employees of Shawmut Corporation and Devonshire were already participants in this program). At this time the Retirement Annuity Plan was revised again. Its fees were changed so that the total cost to employees for retirement and Social Security would not be excessive and the aggregate value of benefits from both sources would remain the same.

In 1945 a further adjustment was made to the retirement plan. This change was tailored to the needs of those who had served during the war and was designed to ensure that there would be no reduction in the ultimate benefits that might accrue to "any member of our organization because of his absence in the service of our country." Other adjustments followed, and in general, the Shawmut remained competitive in terms of annuities and retirement benefits.

It was also during the early postwar years that the Bank increased its paid vacation time from two to three weeks for all clerical staff having five or more years of service. Perhaps even more appreciated was a shortening of the work week from six to five days. This was first introduced in May 1946, when the governor signed a law permitting all banking institutions in the Commonwealth to remain closed on Saturdays during June, July, August, and September. In February 1947 the law was extended to allow banks to be closed every Saturday of the year.

As hours improved, so also did physical working conditions.

In March 1949 the first floor of the main office and the Monks Building were extensively remodeled. Aided by postwar technology, the Bank changed from direct current to alternating current, which allowed for the use of more sophisticated banking equipment and for the introduction of air conditioning.

2

Throughout his long tenure at the Shawmut, Walter Bucklin consistently brought in new men and introduced new offices to expedite the handling of Bank matters. Although the charge has been brought that he was not always tactful in the handling of his officers or in the delegation of responsibilities, reserving too much power in his own hands, it is also true that he supported the careers of several persons who were instrumental in shaping the Bank. In the immediate postwar era, however, several of these senior officers either retired, moved on, or died: Norman Adams retired in 1949, Joseph A. Erickson left the Bank in 1948 to assume the presidency of the Federal Reserve Bank of Boston, while Frederick A. Carroll, William F. Augustine, and George E. Pierce died in 1945, 1947, and 1951 respectively. This attrition gave Bucklin an excuse — which he was not reluctant to use — to remain in power. He reasoned that there was no one on the staff with enough experience to replace him, that further changes would be disruptive, and that, in the interest of continuity, such change should be avoided.

In the junior ranks there were, of course, some very capable men who had come in under Bucklin. They included Horace Schermerhorn, Lawrence H. Martin, and D. Thomas Trigg, all of whom eventually acceded to the presidency. Although in 1951, their ages were fifty-five, forty-two, and thirty-four respectively, in the opinion of Bucklin, they were still too young for the top post. Nevertheless, as Bank activities increased and as Bucklin grew older, pressure increased on him to designate a successor. Finally in 1952, in a move that can only be seen as a compromise, he prevailed on the board to change the bylaws to allow it to "elect or appoint a Chairman of the Board who shall exercise such powers as the Board prescribes which may include being Chief Executive Officer." The directors quickly complied, and on September 11, 1952, Bucklin resigned the presidency to be appointed chairman and chief executive officer. It should be noted that the post of chairman had existed since 1907, when it was created for James Stearns as an emeritus position. It was not until 1952 that it became associated with chief executive status. With the reins then still securely in his own hands, Bucklin recommended Walter Borden to be elected president of the National Shawmut Bank, which was accomplished on September 11, 1952.

Walter E. Borden and his Shawmut Career

Walter Borden was a native of Goldsboro, North Carolina. He entered the United States Naval Academy in 1912, graduating in 1916. In 1920, following service in World War I as an ensign and lieutenant, SG, Borden resigned from the navy to work for United Drug Company as an industrial engineer. It was at just this time that Louis Liggett, United Drug's president and a Shawmut director, became interested in the Cuban sugar enterprise, the Caribbean Sugar Company. United's new young engineer was dispatched to Cuba to serve as assistant general manager of the sugar company. He remained in this position until 1925, when he returned to the states to take up other business commitments.

In 1928, when Shawmut was experiencing difficulties with its investment in the Caribbean Sugar Company, Borden was recommended to Bucklin as a man with hands-on knowledge of the company. And in September 1928, the Shawmut Corporation of Boston retained Borden to manage its interest in the sugar enterprise. From its inception, Walter Borden's career at Shawmut was largely focused on handling this particular investment.

When the fortunes of Shawmut Corporation of Boston declined in the early 1930s, Borden was transferred to the Bank. In the course of the next several years his titles changed, but his major concern remained the same. In 1932 Borden became an assistant vice president, in 1941 a vice president, in 1947 a director, in 1948 a senior vice president, and in 1950 the title general manager was added to this designation. But in the privacy of Shawmut's own corridors Walter Borden was generally known as "Sugar."

The title was not inapt, and it was largely due to his constant vigilance that Shawmut fared as well as it did in relation to the Caribbean Sugar Company investment. Over the years Borden negotiated a series of complex financial transactions designed to keep the company afloat and the Shawmut from suffering losses in a constantly declining sugar market. The success of his efforts finally began to pay off in 1946, by which time Caribbean Sugar Company had met enough of its obligations that the Bank began negotiations to sell its interest in the company to a certain Compania Azucarera Macareno in Havana, Cuba. Finally on December 17, 1947, National Shawmut Bank securities in Caribbean Sugar were fully transferred to the Havana company for a cash sale of $1.7 million.

Although ostensibly this was a happy conclusion to over two decades of problems, the story was not quite over. Records show that in 1947 Walter Borden actually held three titles: vice president of National Shawmut Bank, president of Caribbean Sugar Company, and president of the purchasing company, Compania Azucarera Macareno. How such a situation came about or its ethical implications were hard to assess. Probably part of the answer to the first question lies in the fact that, while the Bank had sold its interest, many of its directors were still personally involved in the Caribbean Sugar Company and more than interested in having Borden retain control until such time as the enterprise was dissolved. This finally began on October 22, 1952, with the first sale of 7 percent preferred stock and culminated in 1954 with the final distribution of stock.

There is little question that Walter Borden was an astute and courageous manager who represented well Shawmut's interests in relation to Caribbean Sugar Company. He also contributed to the management of Cumberland Mountain Coal Company. Both were problem areas, both survived the 1930s, and in both instances Shawmut finally recovered its initial investment. It should be noted, however, that although Bucklin gave a great deal of attention to these investments and used them as a rationale for the support of Borden as president, several senior officers felt the attention was disproportionate to their real value to the Bank. They were also concerned that

Borden's focus on these interests was not sufficient qualification for the presidency. Of course, as chief executive officer Bucklin retained his control of Bank activities, while Borden's own responsibilities remained very much as they had always been. The titles had changed, the responsibilities had not.

In May 1956, citing his wife's ill health, Borden resigned the presidency of National Shawmut. At this point Bucklin reminded the board that "it is common practice for an officer and chairman of the Board to serve as president." Bucklin was then appointed to this dual position, which he retained until October when Schermerhorn was elected President with Bucklin remaining on as chief executive officer.

That Bucklin was reluctant to surrender power is implicit in these maneuvers and further underscored by the fact that in October 1955 he prevailed on the Board to extend his own contract to January 1957. This occurred despite the fact that the board had the power to terminate on thirty days notice for any reason the employment of any officer. Having secured his extension, Bucklin then assured the directors that "he wished to be relieved of the responsibilities of Chief Executive Officer well in advance of January 1957." His intentions, however, apparently outstripped his expressed desires, for it was not until November 1956 that he actually submitted his resignation, and then at the specific request of a majority of the board. Even at the venerable age of seventy-six, he was dismayed to have it accepted.

3

Even in the 1980s the long administration of Walter S. Bucklin is a matter of controversy. His approach to the business of banking was pragmatic and eclectic. For those who sought a steady and consistent drive toward clearly defined objectives, the Bucklin management left much wanting, yet he accomplished a great deal. Part of Bucklin's approach was, of course, dictated by the times. He had been brought to the Bank in 1923 to "get it moving" after the 1920–1921 depression, and this he did with dispatch. To his credit at this time were the institution of new affiliates integral to National Shawmut's finan-

cial activities — Devonshire Financial Service Corporation, the
Shawmut Association, the Shawmut Bank Investment Trust.
He also introduced new departments, an outstanding example
being the Personal Loan Department. Furthermore, he supervised the expansion and development of the Shawmut Corporation of Boston and of existing service divisions such as the
Time Sales Department and the Foreign Department. All of
these flourished in the 1920s under his enthusiastic direction.
Shawmut's early branches must also be attributed to Bucklin's
energetic efforts. Many of these efforts were not strictly related
to banking services, but all were designed to capitalize — and
did capitalize — on the expansive economic spirit of the time.

With the depression, expansion collapsed; nevertheless, the
Shawmut weathered the storm, partially because its assets had
been built up in the 1920s. In the 1930s it cut costs, retrenched,
or as in the case of Cumberland Mountain Coal Company and
the German Standstill Credits, waited patiently to avoid losses.
When the war came, the Shawmut was ready to respond to
the opportunities it created, and when peace returned and circumstances changed, it was also ready, as Bucklin put his mind
to areas that would turn a profit. The postwar years saw the
conclusion of much old business, including the recoveries of
Cumberland Mountain Coal Company and the German Standstill Credits, the final liquidation of Shawmut Corporation of
Boston and Shawmut Bank Investment Trust. These years also
saw the development of the Trust Department, FHA loans,
branches, time-sales and personal loans, all areas that demonstrated again Bucklin's ability to perceive what the public
wanted and to augment earnings accordingly.

Nevertheless, in terms of raw figures, assets declined from
the immediate December 1945 postwar figure of $462 million
to $452 million in December 1956, and earnings did fluctuate.
In July 1954, for example, Bucklin admitted to the board that
earnings would be less in the next twelve months, adding
quickly that this was due "to the low rate of return on government securities and prevailing rate on prime business loans."
While this was undoubtedly a fact, in some instances low earnings were anticipated but did not materialize and there was
some question whether the president had not used reserves
in a highhanded fashion. Dividends, however, steadily climbed,
and it is doubtful that shareholders found fault with his manage-

ment. In October 1949 quarterly dividends rose to 30 cents per share in contrast to the 25 cents that had obtained since 1932. In December 1951 they went up again to 35 cents and in December 1952 to 40 cents. Finally in December 1953, it was voted that a dividend of 45 cents and an extra dividend of 20 cents should be paid to all the stockholders of record at the close of the business day December 15, 1953.

To Bucklin's credit was the high profile he created for the Bank through his pioneering efforts in radio and television, and the sense of Shawmut as a "friendly" and convenient institution, which was achieved by continued expansion of its offices.

Bucklin's thirty-three-year administration was the longest and one of the most colorful in Shawmut Bank history. It was a period which in retrospect still leaves a host of conflicting impressions. There are those still living who knew and worked with him and remember him as a man of strong convictions and opinions, and one whose attitude was often autocratic and authoritative in dealing with some subordinates and associates. Whether their appraisals were justified must largely depend on individual judgments. Under Bucklin's leadership the Bank did expand, and both it and the current Corporation are still beneficiaries of many of his actions and accomplishments.

Chapter 12

Years of Transition
Horace Schermerhorn (1956–1962)

O N October 18, 1956, Horace Schermerhorn became the twelfth president of the Shawmut Bank. During the next six weeks he served under Bucklin who had retained his position as chairman of the board and chief executive officer. On November 29, 1956, however, the board, convinced that in the interest of Shawmut's future growth Bucklin must relinguish control, asked for and received his resignation. The title chairman was temporarily set aside and Schermerhorn as president became chief executive officer.

1

Horace Schermerhorn was born on December 29, 1894, in Jersey City, New Jersey. During his youth his family moved north to Newton, Massachusetts, where young Schermerhorn was graduated from public school in 1914. Two years later he received a business and accounting degree from Bryant and Stratton in Boston and that same year was employed in the trust department of Spencer Trask and Company, a local investment firm. Here, except for a brief stint as a lieutenant in the United States Naval Air Service during the war, he continued until 1922, when he moved to the investment department of Liberty

Mutual Insurance Company. There the young trust officer came to the attention of Walter Bucklin, then president of Liberty Mutual. In 1925, when Bucklin was also president of the Shawmut Bank and looking for new personnel to help in the revitalization of the Shawmut Corporation of Boston, he invited Schermerhorn to join the Corporation staff as a security analyst.

Throughout the remainder of the 1920s, as the fortunes of the Corporation flourished so also did the career of Schermerhorn, and he ultimately became syndicate manager and sales manager of that organization. In October 1929, however, the stock market crash severely rocked the entire securities business; Schermerhorn, nevertheless, managed to rally his staff and maintain the morale of the Sales Division even in the face of rapidly disintegrating conditions. A note in the *Wigwam* for that period suggests the degree to which he was successful in that role:

> Fact is there is rather more than a bare possibility that somebody's going to sell some bonds from now on. The Corporation iron men are humming the old battle cry, "Onward Brave Shawmut Team — onto the fray," and it's our prediction that they're going to do some exceptional fraying in the coming bond market.

In 1933, however, the Banking Act dealt the Corporation the fatal blow that even the stock market crash had not been able to accomplish. Specifically, the law forbade all national banks and members of the Federal Reserve System and their affiliates from operating any security business or conducting any security trading activities for profit. Unfortunately the Shawmut Corporation of Boston, a wholly owned subsidiary of the Bank, had been performing exactly these now prohibited tasks. As a consequence there was no alternative but to liquidate its assets and holdings and dismantle the staff. In spite of these dire circumstances and the general cutbacks in personnel, Bucklin kept Schermerhorn on, and in 1933 the latter became a member of the Bank staff with particular responsibility for the Investment Research Department, which was designed to assist the Trust Department in its investment of funds.

During the course of the next two decades, Schermerhorn moved up rapidly through the Bank's hierarchy. In January 1934 he was nominated by Bucklin for election as assistant cashier of the National Shawmut and served in this capacity for the next two and a half years. His talents and experience, however, made him particularly valuable in trust operations and on June 23, 1936, he was elected assistant vice president and assistant trust officer, becoming vice president and assistant trust officer on January 14, 1941. In 1945 Frederick A. Carroll, who was then vice president and trust officer in charge of the Trust Department and who had taken a leave of absence from the Bank to serve as American Red Cross Commissioner for Great Britain and Western Europe, met with a fatal automobile accident near Paris; on November 16, 1946, Schermerhorn was elected to take over Carroll's tasks as vice president and acting trust officer. Two years later he became vice president and trust officer.

As the department grew, a new title, senior trust officer, was created to designate the officer in charge and allow for the election of additional Trust Department officers. Thus, on November 7, 1952, Schermerhorn was elected vice president and senior trust officer. His obvious talent and dedicated service in all of these roles, as well as his thorough knowledge of the Bank, led to his appointment as a director in 1955. For the same reasons, he was elected to the office of president in the following year, and six weeks later became chief executive officer of the National Shawmut Bank.

2

When Horace Schermerhorn became president of the National Shawmut he was already sixty-two years old, the oldest person elected to that office since the beginning of the Bank. Furthermore, it was now generally understood that the official retirement age should be sixty-five, although this understanding was not codified until 1959. Thus, unlike most of his predecessors, Schermerhorn did not contemplate a long career in office, and his policies reflect this awareness: he was not as concerned to initiate new actions as to bring to fruition some of those actions begun in the past. In addition — and this was perhaps his major contribution as president and chief executive officer — he was determined to see that the best men held the positions best suited for their talents and that the personnel policies and operating practices of the Bank be streamlined at all levels in anticipation of whatever new opportunities might present themselves in the final four decades of the twentieth century.

From almost the first day he took office, the new president's priorities, particularly in relation to "people policies," were evident. One of his first actions was to recommend that the titles of Lawrence H. Martin, first vice president, chief loan officer, and director of the Bank, be changed to executive vice president and director effective November 30, 1956.

It would be presumptuous, of course, to assume that at this point Schermerhorn was already anticipating his retirement and that Martin's promotion was motivated primarily by a desire to assure a successor whom the president respected and trusted. More simply, faced with the complexities of modern banking, Schermerhorn felt strongly that the team concept was a desirable business practice. In fact, the notion of bank staff, officers, and directors operating as a team might be understood as a cornerstone of his management approach. Certainly he worked with Martin much as a coach might with a captain, sharing knowledge and responsibilities for the good of the whole.

Under the new system Schermerhorn retained supervision and coordination of overall activities. Martin, in his turn, focused on what both he and Schermerhorn deemed to be the pressing internal problems of the Bank. Each of these problems was identified so that the new administration could take steps necessary to correct them and thereby strengthen the Bank internally and externally in relation to other banks and the community.

Specifically, Martin's tasks covered the supervision of the Bank's organization and staffing, the expansion of its services and customer relationships in all departments and divisions, and of course, the development of its financial assets, deposits, and foreign and domestic portfolios. As executive vice president, Martin was also appointed to the Executive Committee of the Board of Directors, where he frequently served as chairman in Schermerhorn's absence. In addition, on November 12, 1958, he was elected to the Trust Investment Committee of the board, a position that gave him direct access to major decisions in this area.

It was during Schermerhorn's administration that the composition of the board also began to broaden. Well-known community leaders who represented a variety of different concerns were actively recruited. New directors were drawn from the lumber, oil, and communications industries and the newly important, high tech electronics industry. In 1961, for the first time, the president of a major university was added to the board, indicating the rise in prominence of the university in the local financial scene. The Shawmut board had come a long way from that time when almost all its members were drawn exclusively from the ranks of the shipping, textile, and leather industries.

Schermerhorn's interest in the members of "the team" extended to the vice-presidential level and here he was instrumental in the appointment of three persons whose services proved invaluable to the Bank. They were Paul G. Black (later president of the National Shawmut); John S. Sullivan (later executive vice president of administration under Martin); and Robert C. Hussey (later president of the Merchants-Warren Bank of Salem and the Community National Bank — both of which were owned by the Shawmut Corporation — and executive vice president of the Shawmut Corporation in charge of all affiliated bank relationships).

One of the most significant personnel innovations under Schermerhorn was the appointment of women to officer ranks. In 1954, when he was still vice president and senior trust officer, he prevailed on Bucklin to promote Hilda Roberts and Ethel Monroe as assistant trust officers, making them the first women to attain officer rank in Boston's commercial banks. Then in 1959, Roberts was appointed assistant vice president.

It was also under Schermerhorn that a policy change affecting the appointment of other key personnel was implemented. Schermerhorn asked for and received authority from the Board of Directors for the chief executive officer or president to appoint branch managers and assistant managers, without that body's prior approval. The new method effectively streamlined a practice that had become increasingly cumbersome as the Shawmut expanded.

Horace Schermerhorn undeniably understood and respected the talents of a wide variety of people, and his appointments were based on such understanding. He also appreciated the dedication of the Shawmut team, and one evidence of this appreciation was manifest in the support he gave certain operational changes and expanded fringe and retirement benefits, though his interest was evident at all levels.

At the level of the Board of Directors, and in deference to the busy schedules of its members, Schermerhorn supported reducing the number of meetings of the Executive Committee to one rather than two a week and adjusting the fees accordingly. Furthermore, during his administration the annual meeting was changed from the second to the fourth Tuesday of January, although why this change was instituted is a matter of speculation. Possibly it sprang from an impulse of accommodation, a recognition that the earlier meeting placed undue pressure on participants at a time of year that was frequently inconvenient.

One of the most important innovations during the Schermerhorn years, and also evidence of his interest in the staff, was the modernization of Shawmut's retirement plans. Shortly after the new president took office, the Board of Directors, acting on Schermerhorn and Martin's recommendation, voted to change the method of funding these operations from a group annuity contract with John Hancock Mutual Life Insurance Company to a trusteed plan under the jurisdiction of the Bank, which would act as trustee. Unquestionably the shift saved on Massachusetts taxes and reduced investment expenses for the Bank, but the main reason for the new arrangement was to provide for greater investment flexibility, a fact which Schermerhorn, well schooled in trust investments, certainly appreciated.

If changes in the investment of retirement funds was one aspect of Schermerhorn's attempt to restyle Shawmut's retirement structure, regulations for the disbursement of these funds was another. To this end he formed the three-member Retirement Plan Committee of the Board of Directors and another committee of Bank officers to advise on the administrative aspects of recommendations and later to implement them.

As a consequence of the work of these men, a new retirement policy was instituted in the late 1950s. Interestingly enough, a major aspect of the new plan was a codification of the retirement age. Henceforth, officers and employees would automatically retire one month after reaching their sixty-fifth birthday (amended January 31, 1962, to the first of the following month).

Although some exceptions might be countenanced, in no instance could an officer or employee serve beyond sixty-eight. In light of the extended service of Bucklin, the revision suggests that the committee may have been particularly sensitive to the problems that could arise when the retirement age was not clearly specified. Other revisions simply modernized the policy to assure that Shawmut remained fully competitive with similar institutions.

These adjustments in personnel and personnel policies, many of which were worked out in concert with Martin, illustrate Schermerhorn's real concern for the welfare of his colleagues, and it is no coincidence that he was held in high regard and is still fondly and respectfully referred to by some who knew him then as "Skimmie." Schermerhorn's attention to internal operations and personnel areas, however, should not be interpreted to mean that he was disinterested in the financial dimensions of the Bank or its importance in the larger community.

3

In relation to the larger picture of the Bank's history, Horace Schermerhorn's administration must be understood as largely transitional. Nevertheless, it would be a serious mistake to underestimate his achievements in expanding the loan and trust operations of the Bank, in promoting the growth of the Association, and in developing the status of Shawmut as a Boston, state, and regional force.

Loan Development

Reviewing Schermerhorn's loan policies, one can see that they extended from the parochial to the international. He worked to develop activities that ranged from loans to Shawmut's own staff through loans to local citizens — including small businessmen, students, and consumers — to large corporate loans on both the national and international levels. Many of these borrowers had, of course, always been customers of the Bank, but

Schermerhorn's contribution was to broaden the base of such borrowers, particularly in the first two categories, while continuing to court the large borrowers as the Bank had always done.

From its inception the Bank always made loans available to its directors. Schermerhorn simplified and streamlined the procedure for extending these loans, which was appreciated by both those who borrowed and those who had to make judgments concerning whether to lend.

Employee loans was one aspect of small-loan operations that the Schermerhorn administration promoted. Personal and installment loans were another. The Shawmut Installment Plan, which had originated in 1916 and which allowed a consumer to borrow money for an automobile — the loan granted on the basis of salary or wages — was now extended to cover the purchase of pleasure boats and trailers.

Still another innovation in small loans was the introduction in September 1959 of the Shawmut Check Loan. A credit or cash reserve established by the applicant in amounts from $480 to $4800 enabled Shawmut Check Loan customers to make their own loans by writing checks up to the maximum in their credit reserves. Repayments, based on a twenty-four-month schedule, rebuilt the reserve for continuous use. The rate charged for this service was 1 percent per month on the average outstanding balance plus a charge of twenty-five cents for each check paid.

Of all the small loans, however, that were to have a profound effect on the operation of the Bank, those extended to individuals for educational purposes were among the most important. In October 1957 the Russians launched Sputnik, and the recognition that the United States could be bested in technology sent shock waves of disbelief through the national psyche. The country raced to educate its manpower. In 1958 Congress passed the National Defense Act with provision for undergraduate and graduate tuition loans. Individual states quickly fell in line, passing their own legislation for tuition supplements. In Massachusetts, the Higher Education Assistance Program was passed, and in January 1960 the National Shawmut began its participation in a program destined to become one of the major financial operations of the next decade.

In addition to participating in the state program, the Bank also responded to the educational crisis by instituting a Shawmut Insured Education Loan Plan, which went beyond the Higher Education Assistance Program. It was available to students at all levels, more extensive in its coverage, and an undeniable boon to the growing number of students and their families.

The extension of loan activities during the Schermerhorn years was not reserved to small loans. In November 1959 a change in the classification of the Bank's capital accounts allowed an increase in its maximum loans to any borrower from $3 million to $3.5 million. This was accomplished by the Board of Directors when it approved a transfer of $2 million from the Reserve for Depreciation of Securities, and $3 million from Undivided Profit Account to the Surplus Account of the Bank. The change increased the Surplus Account from $20 million to $25 million and combined capital and surplus to $35 million. According to stipulations of the Federal Reserve Board governing lending, 10 percent of this total might be extended to any one borrower.

Three years later, on December 20, 1962, by which time Lawrence H. Martin was already president of the National Shawmut and Schermerhorn the chairman of the board and chief executive officer, the Board of Directors approved another similar transfer. This time $5 million was recredited from the Undivided Profit Account to the Surplus Account, increasing that total to $30 million. The combined capital and surplus thus became $40 million, which permitted the Bank to make loans of $4 million. The beneficiaries were a variety of businesses and industries, such as automobile companies, airlines, and gas and oil companies, all of which were expanding rapidly in the postwar years.

In addition, the Bank financed or served as a lead bank in financing real estate construction, including FHA military projects at Portsmouth, New Hampshire, and Bangor, Maine. It also extended loans to government agencies and municipalities, including construction loans to colleges and universities and loans to students under the Massachusetts Higher Education Loan Plan. Lines of credit were extended to banks in Australia, New Zealand, Mexico, Colombia, and Japan. Further, the National Shawmut participated in foreign loans sponsored by other large U.S. banks and the International Bank for Reconstruction.

These were also the years in which some old accounts were settled. For example, on March 6, 1958, Schermerhorn was able to report to the Board of Directors the receipt of $325,496, representing the final recovery and liquidation of all German Standstill Credits.

Growth of the Shawmut Association

The overall expansion in loan activity was one in which the Shawmut directors and officers justly took satisfaction. So also they took satisfaction from the growing strength of the Shawmut Association. The most dramatic change in the status of the Association did not occur until 1965, when it became the Shawmut Association, Inc., a bank holding company having control of all the Association banks and the National Shawmut itself. Many of the events leading to this change, however, occurred earlier, during the Schermerhorn years.

During Bucklin's administration, Schermerhorn had been one of the Bank's representatives in dealing with the suburban banks in which the Shawmut Association had controlling interest. The details of these relations have been covered in a separate chapter. Suffice it to say here that, although the organization had been from its inception a bank holding company de facto, it was not until 1956 that a change in federal and state law allowed it to become one de jure. The most profound immediate impact of the new law on Shawmut Association was indirect: it encouraged new competition for purchase of bank shares.

President Schermerhorn as well as Executive Vice President Martin were both well aware of this competition. They were also aware that the future development of the entire Shawmut organization was in large part dependent on the future development of those banks in which the Association owned most or all of the shares.

Recognizing that were the trustees of the Association, several of whom were also directors of the National Shawmut Bank, to receive offers from outsiders to purchase shares of one or more of the Association banks they would be confronted with a conflict of interest, Schermerhorn proposed to the directors of the National Shawmut that the Bank itself purchase a twenty-year option on the shares of one or more of the suburban banks. The directors agreed and made it a matter of record that they wanted and expected a prior claim on shares. There is no evidence that such options were ever exercised.

It was also during Schermerhorn's administration that a rate of 0.5 of 1 percent of the net value of the Shawmut Association was established as the fee to be paid to the National Shawmut Bank for its services to the Association. The services were rendered in behalf of the total organization but most particularly in relation to the affiliated banks. The fee thus served both to underscore the relation between the two organizations and to defray some of the Bank's expenses in supervising the Association.

In 1960 specific moves began that set the path for the future transformation of the Association from an investment to a holding company. At this time the Association was already taking steps to obtain an IRS tax ruling on a proposed reorganization of the Shawmut Association. Jacob Kaplan, a director of the Bank and trustee of the Association since 1951, and Benjamin Trustman, of Nutter, McClennen and Fish, were authorized to seek this ruling.

In August 1960 Kaplan died, and in early 1961 Trustman was appointed to succeed him both as trustee and director. Trustman's role in promoting the new corporation was substantial. That same winter of 1961, it was determined to expand that board from five persons to seven, and John Wallace and Arthur W. Deibert were both elected. Then in May 1961 John K. Benson succeeded Rohl C. Wiggin. By the time Schermerhorn left the chief executive office of the Shawmut organization in 1962, the stage was already set and the key personnel in place to oversee the final metamorphosis of the Shawmut Association into Shawmut Association, Inc.

Creation of Warren Charitable Trust

During Schermerhorn's administration, the Bank renewed an interest in charitable giving to its local community. To facilitate

The Chronological Story of Shawmut

and orchestrate such contributions, the Board of Directors approved the creation of the Warren Charitable Trust on December 21, 1961. This new charitable foundation was designed to assist the Bank in making charitable contributions as permitted by relevant laws. Three Shawmut officials served as its first trustees: Horace Schermerhorn, Lawrence Martin, and John Wallace.

4

On December 29, 1959, Horace Schermerhorn turned sixty-five, the age of retirement according to regulations that he himself had instituted. The Board of Directors, however, asked him to stay on an additional three years until the end of the month following his sixty-eighth birthday. Schermerhorn consented, but by early March certain key changes in personnel indicated that he was seriously reconsidering his position. At this time D. Thomas Trigg and Arthur W. Deibert were both elected senior vice presidents, while John K. Benson became senior vice president as well as comptroller. Harold P. Trefethan soon succeeded Benson in this latter post and reported to him. All of these moves occurred on the recommendation of Schermerhorn, but there was little doubt in anyone's mind that they reflected the thinking of Lawrence H. Martin and were simply a prelude to the time when he would become president.

It came as no particular surprise when, on October 27, 1960, Schermerhorn asked to be relieved of the Shawmut Bank presidency and Martin was elected to that post. The new arrangement gave Martin full jurisdiction over Bank affairs. Schermerhorn, however, continued his authority over the aggregate Shawmut organization, an authority that was reinforced by his election as chairman of the Board of Directors. This title had not been used since Bucklin's resignation, and that the directors saw fit to revive it was a testament of their continuing faith that Schermerhorn could, and should, continue his work for development of the institution. Nor was their faith ill founded, for the next two and a half years were ones of considerable activity in several areas.

Organization Changes and the Development of the Trust and Municipal Bond Departments

In response to a growing volume of business, three new divisions were formed in the spring of 1961: the Real Estate Division, Branch Division, and Banking Division. The Banking Division represented a consolidation of three previous areas — the Loan, New England, and National divisions — and was designed to expedite and prevent overlapping in the work of all three.

Still another area which had grown under Schermerhorn's direction was the Trust Department. At the same time as the Bank was revising its own retirement policies in 1959, it also decided to provide increased investment and administrative services for the retirement funds of its corporate customers. In 1958 the Bank established a pension unit and hired its first officer, Frederick W. White, whose sole function was to develop and administer pension accounts. Soon thereafter, the Pooled Equity Fund and the Pooled Fixed Income Fund were developed to serve the investment needs of medium- and small-sized retirement accounts throughout the New England area. Shawmut's commercial offices welcomed the opportunity to increase the range of services the Bank could provide to their customers, and these products had a very satisfactory growth, eventually becoming among the most important product lines within the Trust Division.

In 1961 supervision of Trust Department activities by the Board of Directors was modified. Whereas the Trust Investment Committee had taken care of all aspects of the Trust Department's operations since 1917, the new Trust Acceptance Committee was formed in September 1961 to accept and retire trusts.

A second change, approved by the Board of Directors in December 1961, substantially improved one of the most important services provided by the Trust Department. This change split the Common Trust Fund into two separate funds, the Fixed Income Fund and the Equity Fund, each with a guiding investment policy. The new arrangement allowed the Bank to address the various needs of customers, permitting a variable blending of fixed-income and common-stock investments for their particular objectives.

Another development in the Trust Department occurred one year later when the Common Trust Municipal Bond Fund was created on November 2, 1962. This added a third investment option for Trust Department customers and was particularly helpful in meeting the needs of customers who benefit from tax-exempt income.

The National Shawmut Bank became a municipal bond dealer in 1961, and this gave rise to the development of the Municipal Bond Department, which went into operation October 1, 1961. Its duties included purchasing bonds for the Shawmut's own account and underwriting municipal bond issues, usually in collaboration with other dealers throughout the country. The project had been promoted by Schermerhorn, and he watched over it zealously. During the next several years, the department flourished, assisted by the fact that it had a ready-made market for the sale of bonds among the many banks — particularly in New England — that were correspondents of the Shawmut.

The first issues bought and sold by the new department were five-year bonds of Woodstock, New Hampshire, bearing 4.2 percent coupons, but it soon expanded to include a "street business," buying and selling bonds of municipalities throughout the United States. In short order National Shawmut became the leading dealer bank in New England, a position it retained for many years.

Bank Expansion

In the late 1950s, Boston began a citywide redevelopment program, and as always where community responsibility was involved, the Shawmut was both supportive and cooperative. Aware that redevelopment could mean demolition in some areas as well as construction in others, both Martin as president and Schermerhorn as chief executive officer encouraged foresight. Plans were submitted to relocate or expand branches in accordance with projected demographic shifts. Although no new branches were actually established or locations altered until 1963, the groundwork was done and authority solicited from the Comptroller of the Currency for new locations when circumstances warranted. Specifically, plans began for the improvement and development of the North Station branch and the Charlestown branch, and for a location in the new Government Center complex.

5

On December 20, 1962, at a meeting of the Board of Directors, Horace Schermerhorn, in anticipation of his official retirement, tendered his resignation as chairman of the board and chief executive officer effective December 28, 1962. At the same meeting Lawrence H. Martin was duly designated as chief executive officer. But though there were no reservations about Schermerhorn's successor, there was unquestionably sadness that "Skimmie" was stepping down.

Horace Schermerhorn had presided over the Shawmut during a period of transition for the nation as well as the institution. The traumas of World War II and the Korean conflict were in the past, the traumas of Vietnam and of civil dissension still lay in the future. It was a period of expansion remarkably free of national crises with perhaps the exception of Sputnik, which eventually proved a stimulus to growth rather than a deterrent.

In the decade of the 1950s the population expanded faster than during any decade in recent history, reaching 180,000,000 by 1960. At the same time, per capita income rose from $1501 to $2219, the highest in our history, while the gross national product reached a record $503,734,000,000. During the administration of Horace Schermerhorn, the Shawmut responded to this situation by broadening the base of those eligible for loans, and the services available to them, by increasing its lending capability to keep pace with growing business, developing its trust service, and branching into the bond business. The results of these actions were evident in such figures as the capital and surplus growth, which went from $30 million to $40 million between 1956 and 1962; in the steady increase in dividends paid shareholders, which rose from $2.20 per share in 1956 to $2.80 in 1962; and even in the increased interest payable on deposits, which the Shawmut now felt justified to increase from 2.5 to 3 percent.

But if the development of the Shawmut in financial terms

was an important aspect of the institution's history during the Schermerhorn years, for those inside the Bank it was Schermerhorn's care, concern, and interest in his colleagues that made his administration most memorable. Horace Schermerhorn was, in all senses of the word, a gentleman, and one of great good humor. These were traits recognized and appreciated by his colleagues who, in the *Shawmut News* of December 1962, noted:

> Often called the "Will Rogers of Banking," because of his humble manner and down-to-earth philosophy, the deeply loved and respected Chairman leaves a vacuum in Boston banking circles that only time can fill.

Horace Schermerhorn's contributions to his city and area, however, were not restricted to his efforts in banking circles. He also played an active role in civic and community affairs, roles that were duly recognized by an honorary degree from Amherst College "in appreciation of investment advice for endowments," and by his election as man of the year by the Boston University chapter of Beta Gamma Sigma, the national scholastic honorary society of undergraduate and graduate schools of business administration.

Chapter 13

Years of Expansion and the Establishment of Shawmut Association, Inc.

Lawrence H. Martin (1962–1972)

To a greater extent than any other Shawmut chief executive officer, Lawrence H. Martin is responsible for the emergence of the Shawmut organization that exists today. The Shawmut Corporation — originally designated Shawmut Association, Inc., in 1964 — and the new headquarters building at One Federal Street are only two examples of the achievements of the Martin administration, which reshaped the Shawmut's public image and continues to enhance its stature into the 1980s.

That Lawrence Martin had such a profound effect on the institution of which he became chief executive officer in 1962 is not surprising. He knew it thoroughly, having joined the National Shawmut Bank in 1928 and risen through its ranks in a variety of increasingly responsible positions. Martin ran the entire Shawmut organization as chief executive officer from 1962 through May 1972, a decade that offered unparalleled economic opportunities nationwide. Finally, he brought to this position his particular combination of business sense and humanitarian instinct, which allowed him to perceive opportunities and use them well to develop the Corporation into a solid financial entity and a responsible and respected corporate citizen.

1

Lawrence H. Martin was born in New York City on May 23, 1907. In 1928 he was graduated from the Amos Tuck School of Business Administration at Dartmouth and a few days later began what was to be a fifty-two-year career of dedicated service to Shawmut.

In the summer of 1928, of course, young Martin was not concerned with the next fifty years. At that time Shawmut had no training or orientation program, and although the new teller had worked for the Bank in the summer of 1927, his immediate concern was to perform well in his first full-time job; this he assuredly did. His superiors soon recognized that he was a young man of quickness and energy who seemed to enjoy thoroughly the challenge of any new task. In the course of the next ten years, he was asked to fill a host of positions that gave him not only first-hand experience of a variety of bank operations but also wide acquaintance among its officers and staff. These positions included assignments in the Savings, Statistical, Transit, Comptroller, Analysis, and Credit departments.

By 1938 it was clear that Lawrence Martin was officer material, and on January 11 of that year, he was elected assistant cashier. He continued to rise quickly, filling positions of increasing responsibility, and in 1945 he was elected to his first vice-presidential post, vice president of Credit. For the first time he had the opportunity to make a major contribution to the Shawmut operation, but this was only the beginning. In the course of the next several years Martin filled four vice-presidential positions, and in each instance he set that area on the path of new development, putting in place policies and structures that served to render the operations of the Bank more effective and prepare the way for new growth.

As vice president in charge of Credit, Martin recognized the department was in extreme need of reorganization and revitalization. Over the years its two major functions, credit analysis and approval, particularly of large commercial loans, had been neglected. Bucklin was more interested in retail lending than commercial and industrial loans and had placed heavy emphasis on time-sales and personal loans, methods of lending Shawmut had pioneered. As a consequence the commercial-loan function of the Credit Department began to erode.

During the 1930s, when commercial loans declined, this erosion continued, and it was not stemmed by the outbreak of World War II. At this time V loans to industry became a major part of the loan portfolio. But because they were guaranteed by federal government agencies, they required little in the way of analysis and approval by Shawmut's own Credit staff. By 1945 the future profitability of the Bank depended on rebuilding Shawmut's commercial and industrial lending to the private sector, and Martin initiated plans for the reorganization and restaffing of Shawmut's credit operation.

Among the first and most important of these plans was the appointment of a new manager of the Credit Department, and in the spring of 1946 Martin selected D. Thomas Trigg for this post. Trigg had been associated with Devonshire Financial Service Corporation and had been a credit analyst at the National Shawmut Bank prior to entering the U.S. Navy. Together the two men set about to put the department on the road to the future. Not only did they revive Time Sales to take advantage of the growing small-loan market but they gave new emphasis to commercial loans, which played an increasingly important part in the growth of the Bank in the postwar years.

Only two years after his appointment as vice president of Credit, Lawrence Martin earned a new position. By this time the affairs of Credit were securely in the capable hands of Trigg, and Martin's considerable talents and wide acquaintance with the Bank's staff and officers were now needed to help the Bank adjust its administrative practices to the demands of the postwar years. In 1947 Martin became vice president of Administration and Personnel Operations.

Shawmut did have employee benefits, including group life insurance and a retirement annuity program for officers and staff of the Bank and its affiliates. But such issues as recruitment, remuneration, sick leave, and retirement were still left largely to individual departments and officers. Martin felt strongly that these should be matters of bankwide policy. Consequently he set to work to formulate a new, more extensive retirement program and a comprehensive fringe benefit program, both of which would pertain to all employees of the Bank and its affiliated organizations. Working in close conjunction with John K. Benson, an officer of Shawmut who had joined the Bank from the Amos Tuck School of Business Administration in 1932 and would rise through the ranks to become Corporation president in 1968, Martin encouraged the development of new personnel practices. New measures included the institution of job descriptions, job evaluations, salary ranges, performance evaluations, and career-path plotting. Martin also supported the establishment of a centralized personnel department whose senior executive officer would become part of top management, and steps toward this end were taken almost immediately. Fulfillment of the concept did not occur until 1963, when the Personnel Division was formed, but the groundwork had already been laid by Martin earlier through the adoption of modern measures of personnel administration to which were soon added still other needed improvements such as new training methods, supervisory training, and a roster of promotable employees.

With these administrative developments well under way, Martin returned to the heart of commercial banking activities in 1951, when he was elected to his third vice-presidential post, vice president and chief loan officer. Two years later his title became first vice president and chief loan officer, and his standing in the senior management of Shawmut was clear.

On November 30, 1956, one day after the election of Horace Schermerhorn as president and chief executive officer, Martin was elected executive vice president of the National Shawmut Bank. Horace Schermerhorn was not a man jealous of position, and recognizing Martin's superior administrative knowledge and skills, the new president delegated to his executive vice president unlimited authority to pursue whatever course Martin felt would best ensure the continued growth and competitive status of the Bank.

As the Bank's principal internal operating officer, Martin gave priority to developing community relations and a strong internal management structure. In the interest of the first goal he encouraged officers and staff of the Bank to become involved in community affairs and in state, regional, and national banking associations. Setting an example himself, he assumed important directorial and committee positions in major banking organizations, such as the American Institute of Banking, the Boston Clearing House Association, the Massachusetts Bankers Association, the American Bankers Association, and the Association of Reserve City Bankers. He was also an active participant in numerous business and civic organizations, serving as a director of Liberty Mutual Insurance Company, Liberty Mutual Fire Insurance Company, American Biltrite Rubber Company, Massachusetts Business Development Corporation, World Trade Center in New England, and the United Fund of Boston. He was also treasurer and trustee of the Massachusetts Taxpayers Foundation, Inc., a member of the Regional Board of Directors of National Conference of Christians and Jews, the vice president and chairman of finance for the Boston Chamber of Commerce, and a member of the corporation and board of trustees of Northeastern University as well as its treasurer.

In the interest of the second goal, Martin recommended the election of three senior vice presidents in the spring of 1960. They were D. Thomas Trigg, who took charge of the new Banking Division that integrated the activities of the various lending divisions; John. K. Benson, responsible for Financial Control and Bank Investments; and Arthur W. Deibert, in charge of the Administrative Division. Eight months later Lawrence Martin became president, only the fourth person to have risen through the Shawmut ranks to this office.

2

Lawrence Martin's tenure as president (1960–1962), then as president and chief executive officer (1962–1968), and finally as chief executive officer and chairman of the board of the National Shawmut Bank and of Shawmut Association, Inc. (1968–1972), corresponded almost exactly with one of the most volatile periods in our nation's history.

When the decade opened John F. Kennedy had just assumed office and the Age of Camelot had begun. It was a time of optimism and innocence, when the man in the street had never heard of Vietnam, and when mind expansion meant four years in the Ivy League at $2,368 a year (room and board included) or a state university at less than half that. In Boston, in fact in all of New England, the tallest building was the twenty-six-story John Hancock, built in 1947 and topped with a flashing light that told the weather — and whether the Red Sox would play.

A dozen years later, Watergate superseded Camelot as the national theme, the country was still embroiled in the longest war in its history, and the carnage in Southeast Asia vied with burning cities at home for prime time attention. In the meantime a boom economy had come and gone; record-breaking business earnings were followed by a recession and record-breaking inflation, while Boston's skyline was transformed into a crenelated cutout of high-rises. For bankers and money managers, it was a time of considerable tensions and demands that shifted almost daily.

When Martin began as president of the Shawmut in the fall of 1960 under the direction of Schermerhorn as chief executive officer and chairman of the board, the future looked bright. Kennedy had promised "to get the country moving," and although 1961 and 1962 were relatively quiet, expectations ran high. The new Shawmut president continued his efforts to assure an efficient and well-controlled organization. On his recommendation, the restructuring of administrative responsibilities and appointment of new senior vice presidents had occurred just prior to his election. This arrangement remained the senior management organization of the Bank until Schermerhorn retired as chairman in late 1962. During these two years, efforts also continued to improve the welfare and training of the general staff. By the fall of 1962, a procedure for officer evaluation had been completed, salaries had been raised, particularly for the clerical staff, and the group life insurance plan had been revised to expand coverage. Equally significant to the long-term development of the Bank were an increase in automation and a new emphasis on certain products designed to increase deposits.

In the late 1950s a program of installing electronic equipment began under John S. Sullivan, vice president, and was proceeding ahead of schedule. By 1961, with the introduction of automated check collection procedures, the Bank handled seventy million deposit and check transactions, and Martin was eager to expand the operation. The expense of installing electronic data processing equipment initially struck many as exorbitant and risky. Later events, however, proved the decision to automate as many areas as possible to be a prudent policy, one that enabled the Bank to extend its services profitably to the community in a way that would have been impossible otherwise.

Another quite different kind of policy instituted in 1960–1962 that had far-reaching effects was the stress put on time and savings deposits. Recognizing that a growth in deposits was vital to meet the ever increasing need for commercial and mortgage loans in the New England economy, Shawmut management aggressively set out to increase its time and savings deposits. In 1961 it instituted a new plan to transfer savings from checking accounts, a new payroll savings deduction plan, and most important, it began to issue time certificates of deposit, which were destined to become a major instrument in money markets.

Commercial loans to manufacturers, wholesalers, retailers, and service industries, the bulk of such lending being located in New England, also showed growth during the first two years of Martin's presidency, as did consumer installment, real estate mortgage, and student loans. Altogether the loan policy of this time reflected Martin's concern that the Bank be a "truly productive servant of the community — a contributor to its growth, stability, and continuity." It was not until 1962, however, when the national economy really began to expand, that the full measure of Martin's administrative skills were felt.

3

On December 28, 1962, Horace Schermerhorn retired from all his Shawmut duties, and the Board of Directors appointed Martin as chief executive officer to succeed him. According to the Bank's bylaws, Martin also acted as chairman of the board, although the title itself was temporarily discontinued. Coincident with the change in Shawmut leadership was the beginning of a dramatic acceleration in the nation's fortunes and the beginning of an economic boom that would reach its peak in 1968.

The causes and effects of this boom were many, and the best that can be done here is to suggest some of its characteristics. These included a wider distribution of purchasing power. In 1960 one out of four families had incomes in excess of $10,000; by 1969 the proportion was one out of two. There was also a new emphasis on science, technology, and education.

In 1957 the Russians had launched Sputnik, and a stunned United States responded with almost fanatical zeal to catch up. Virtually overnight, education, particularly scientific and technological education, became the focus of frantic attention. By the mid-1960s educational activities, printed and electronic communications, and computer-related products had come to constitute one-fourth of the gross national product. The war in Southeast Asia — the economic impact of which is difficult to assess — sparked new productivity. The aircraft industry in particular profited from defense contracts, as did those industries involved with new high tech defense weapons. As discretionary income rose, new markets opened, and production expanded, so also did mergers and consolidations increase. These conglomerates comprised a variety of different enterprises and allowed their leaders to take advantage of new tax laws, counter seasonal swings in the market, and shift the energies of their organization away from old and mature markets to new and burgeoning ones without incurring losses. As a consequence, far fewer, but far larger, corporations came to control far more of the economy. And finally, American offshore investments grew tremendously. In 1950 they stood at $12 billion, by 1965, $49 billion, and by 1970, $78 billion.

The effect of these conditions on the economy, and particularly the New England economy, was profound. Massachusetts alone had 109 institutions of higher education, and education became a major growth industry. Furthermore, Massachusetts was providing a substantial portion of the nation's expanded electronics business. In addition, the new emphasis on defense meant even greater prosperity for the New England area, which commanded a tenth of the defense contracts. Employment catapulted to record heights. Engineers and others capable of working with high tech defense weapons were at a premium, and industrial parks around Route 128, Boston's circumferential highway, and adjacent white-collar suburbs and shopping areas expanded at a record rate.

Not all the news was good, however. Much of the source of the new wealth came from support of an unpopular war, which gave rise to deep social and political upheavals at home. Record prosperity was accompanied by record inflation. And although American investments overseas had never been so high, such expansion went on in the face of a growing national deficit that prompted the government to place more and more restrictions on the outflow of funds. To counter this turn of events, banks began to look for new and innovative ways both to provide needed services to their customers with international interests and stem the flow of American funds abroad.

The period from the end of 1962 through 1967 was, in short, volatile and contradictory. As Lawrence Martin later described it in the annual report of 1968, it was a period of "uneasy prosperity . . . a time of discontent and unparalleled opulence [when] business prospered mightily . . . [in tandem] with many grave problems unsolved for too long." To anticipate and keep abreast of these conditions was the challenge for the chief executive officer, and in these years Martin instituted a series of innovations that affected the Bank's administrative organization and the welfare of its personnel, the nature of its loans, deposits, and investments, and the quality and variety of its services. Perhaps most important of all, however, these years saw the reorganization of the Shawmut Association into Shawmut Association, Inc., which on May 6, 1965, acquired ownership of the National Shawmut Bank of Boston.

Internal Administrative and Organizational Changes, 1962–1967

With the election of Martin as chief executive officer of the National Shawmut Bank in December 1962, came a further reorganization of the management structure of the Bank. Three new divisions were added to the existing five. From the Administrative Division came two of these — Branch and Personnel — and a new Real Estate Division was spun off from the Banking Division. According to the new arrangement, two senior vice presidents, John K. Benson and D. Thomas Trigg, assumed bankwide administrative responsibilities that had previously been the purview of the president, and to them reported all division heads with the exception of John J. Barry, vice president of Public Relations, who would continue to report directly to Martin. The third senior vice president, Arthur W. Deibert, had announced his retirement plans effective January 31, 1963, after thirty-five years of notable service. His departure was taken into account in the new responsibility arrangements.

These administrative changes gave new responsibilities and authority not only to the senior vice presidents but also to the divisional vice presidents, who might now act autonomously in administrative and operational matters. The changes were symptomatic of a new management approach: they stemmed from Martin's belief that, in the face of rapidly expanding operations, it was necessary to delegate as much responsibility as possible to other senior officers. Such an approach freed him to attend to the increasingly complex task of coordinating the overall Shawmut operation and formulating new policies that would be more than simply a reaction to external forces.

The decision to form the new Branch, Personnel, and Real Estate divisions in 1963 was also motivated as much by anticipation of future needs as by response to current demands. The history of these divisions over the next few years shows the value of such foresight.

The Branch Division (Renamed the City Division, 1964). In 1961 Martin pledged "to match programs in urban redevelopment with appropriate recognition of the financial requirements of revitalized areas." The formation of the Branch Division with Thomas H. Ainslie as vice president was one way of signaling the Bank's intention to accept this responsibility. By placing more emphasis on its branches, Shawmut made clear that it intended to serve the public from convenient and appropriate locations, and from 1963 through 1967 the Bank opened or relocated five branches in key areas. (See Chapter 16.)

Real Estate Division. As was the City Division, the Real Estate Division was organized in 1963, and David L. Currier was appointed vice president in charge. The purpose of the reorganization was not simply to accommodate present needs for construction and mortgage loans but also to be ready for an increased volume of business when the Boston Redevelopment Program truly got under way and when the great number of office buildings, apartments, residences, shopping centers, and industrial parks, still in the planning stage, began to move from blueprint to steel and concrete. The role of the Real Estate Division in supporting urban renewal and private and commercial physical expansion will be discussed in more detail below. Nevertheless, it is important to note that by 1967 the division was handling almost $100 million in loans.

The Personnel Division. Anticipating a far larger staff and a growing diversity of Bank operations with greater need for coordinated personnel policies, Martin supported the formation of the new Personnel Division headed by Walter F. Chase, vice president. This division consolidated all personnel functions, and in the course of the next few years, its activities expanded continually. By 1963 Personnel had already begun to increase the employment of minority members, an action that demonstrated the Bank's sensitivity to social questions. The Bank's foresight in this regard reflected Martin's sense that it was the institution's obligation to serve its community, and when later in the decade federal legislation mandated Affirmative Action, the Shawmut had already implemented some of its policies ahead of its time.

Technology also affected the role of the new division. Increased automation meant some jobs were phased out; others dramatically changed their character. This situation, coupled with an overall expansion of Bank services and a concerted policy to recruit new and promising college graduates to assure appropriate management succession, put a new emphasis on job training. By 1966 training programs were a major interest of the Personnel Division. At the same time, new management tools were constantly introduced. One very important such tool was the Operating Standards Program. Begun in 1964 to encourage high levels of productivity, the program was not actually a Personnel Division responsibility, having been initiated by the Administrative Division under the direction of John S. Sullivan, executive vice president. It did, however, affect personnel concerns and contributed to operating efficiency in all areas of the Bank, not just those directly influenced by automation. Throughout the period Personnel was responsible for job-evaluation studies on all levels and for supporting salary increases that kept the Shawmut compensation and fringe benefits competitive with area institutions.

The aforementioned were the major organizational changes that took place immediately after Martin became chief executive officer, but others soon followed in response to both internal and external needs.

The Installment Loan Department and the Bank Investment Division. In late 1963, and largely as a result of the recognition that the customer of both Time Sales and Personal Loan departments was usually the same person — the general consumer — the two departments were consolidated. The consolidation allowed the Bank to provide swifter and more efficient service to this customer, who was becoming increasingly important as salaries and discretionary income rose.

That same year, Bank Investments, previously a department under Financial Control, became a separate division, and James G. Wilson was appointed vice president and division supervisor. The function of the division was to broaden services in portfolio management, municipal securities, municipal underwriting and trading, as well as related deposit-supporting services, all of which became increasingly significant as the economy continued to expand.

Public Relations Division. In 1965 the Public Relations Division, under the direction of John J. Barry, vice president, was reorganized into the Development and Public Affairs Division. Barry had been with the Shawmut since 1947 and had worked closely with four presidents — Bucklin, Borden, Schermerhorn, and Martin. Under his guidance the Bank had pioneered radio and television advertising, blazing a trail that allowed other banks and commercial institutions to use electronic media for promotional purposes. Barry had also developed print media advertising to new levels, and with his support, Shawmut's promotional literature had not only increased in volume but had become more tasteful and more imaginative. (See Chapter 17.)

It was Martin's intention to continue promotion in the direction established by Barry, but he also wanted to put a new and modern emphasis on marketing as an essential element of public relations. Sparking the need for a new approach was the formation of Shawmut Association, Inc., with all the concurrent problems and opportunities this development presented for conveying a unified institutional image. To help with these problems Martin brought into the bank as a vice president, Warren S. Berg, a nonbanker and former director of business development and consultant in public relations for Arthur D. Little, Inc., a Cambridge, Massachusetts, research and consulting firm. Berg's credentials also included chairmanship of Newsome and Company, Inc., New England's oldest and largest public relations firm. The first six months of Berg's appointment overlapped that of Barry, and the two men worked closely in developing new ideas. In early 1966 Barry retired, and Warren Berg assumed direction of the rapidly expanding operation. (See below for later developments in this area.)

The organizational changes that occurred between 1962 and 1968 anticipated and reflected an increased volume of business. Other developments reflected changing conditions in the business world and in the nature of commercial banking. One interesting innovation of the period, which had little to do with economics but a great deal to do with the climate of the times, was disaster planning. The catalytic event was the Cuban Missile Crisis of October 1962. In early 1963 the Board of Directors responded to this crisis by approving a contingency plan for maintaining operations in the event of damage caused by "war or other disasters." This plan defined the functions of the Board of Directors in the event of such a disaster. It created an emergency administrative committee consisting of officers of the Bank, defined the committee's powers, and designated a disaster organization officer and the location of the Bank's headquarters in the event that normal functions of the Bank could not be conducted at its 40 Water Street office. On November 19, 1970, the plan was updated and remains in effect in the 1980s. Other developments were more strictly related to economic affairs.

Financial Operations, 1962–1967

Between 1962 and 1967, broad upward trends in the economy spurred increased financial activities. Loans, deposits, and investments grew rapidly, although a rise in the cost of deposits introduced new problems.

Loans. Loans are the chief source of income for commercial banks. The business boom of the 1960s accelerated the demand,

and from late 1962 through 1967, the volume of loans extended by the National Shawmut grew from $296,996,000 to $432,-421,000. The largest portion of this increase was in the commercial and industrial category, but substantial gains were also made in mortgage and installment loans. Many of these loans were extended to traditional customers, others to new clients. Following World War II, New England suffered a steady erosion in its textile, leather, machine tool, and metal fabrication industries. In their place had risen science-based industries, and it was this customer that the Shawmut came increasingly to accommodate in the early 1960s, opening accounts for a host of high tech firms that clustered along Boston's "electronic belt," Route 128. High tech industry, however, was by no means the only new customer.

Real estate loans also reached higher levels. The reason was twofold: the availability of federal funds which made rehabilitation and redevelopment possible also created a need for massive private funding, and the increased dependence of banks on time deposits as a source of lendable funds made long-term investments more important. Construction loans became a major part of the Shawmut loan portfolio, with the Bank taking an active role in the Waterfront Redevelopment Program and the Central Business District Redevelopment Program.

A third type of loan developed at this period was the student loan. By 1968 the Bank's participation in the Massachusetts Higher Education Loan Plan, as well as the development of its own Tuition Aid Plan, had made the Shawmut a major source of funds for the area's 194,654 undergraduate and graduate students.

As the volume of loans increased, the average earning rate on the loan portfolio also went up, growing from 5.48 percent in 1962 to 6.45 percent in 1967. The total increase, however, was not entirely a blessing. If there was one problem that consistently confronted bankers during these years, it was acquiring sufficient funds to keep pace with the new demands while at the same time realizing appropriate return on capital, particularly as national financial policies became more restrictive and overall operating costs rose.

Deposits, 1962–1967. Until after World War II at least 77 percent of deposits were demand accounts, but between 1946 and 1962, demand deposits rose only some 27 percent, while time deposits, on which the Bank paid interest, rose approximately 172 percent. When negotiable time certificates of deposit were introduced at Shawmut in 1961, interest-bearing deposits grew even faster.

Between 1962 and 1967, the trend was modified, and growth in demand deposits revived. Nevertheless, in spite of their high cost, time deposits remained an important source of lendable funds. In addition, investment savings from estates, trusts, and large individual accounts grew steadily. Unfortunately the interest rate in these areas also rose in competition with the general market, diminishing the Bank's earnings. The situation sent bankers scurrying to develop new earning assets aside from loans.

Changes in the Investment Portfolio, 1962–1967. The investment portfolio offered a means of improving income, and between 1962 and 1967 important changes were made in its components. The shift in deposit structure made tax-exempt securities increasingly attractive, and Shawmut increased its holdings. There was also a growing sense of commitment to state and local governments throughout New England, and the Municipal Bond Department became active in underwriting securities operations in late 1961. Because of this activity, in 1963 the Bank began to sponsor the Municipal Finance Forum, which promoted an exchange of ideas among public officials involved in municipal finance. During this period, the Bank's investment department increased and diversified the scope of money market services that it performed for corporate and correspondent bank customers.

International Banking Development, 1962–1967

Essential to the overall evolution of the Bank in the mid-1960s was the development of innovations in traditional business areas that made them more profitable. At this time, the administration focused renewed attention on the international market.

The founding of the Common Market in 1958, involving closer economic integration of Western European countries, as well as the continuing imbalance of payments — the United

States first sustained a deficit in 1958 — had changed the character of world trade and aroused new interest in its development. This was further stimulated by a 1962 act of Congress eliminating the maximum allowable interest rate payable on funds deposited by foreign governments and foreign instrumentalities. In this environment, the activities of the Shawmut's International Banking Department expanded. The principal objective of the department was to assist domestic customers in extending their business abroad profitably. Toward this end it intensified its program of foreign-business travel and in 1964 added new officers for the specific task of helping develop correspondent bank and business connections in Latin America, the Far East, and Canada. The Bank also increased its financing of exports, operating in close conjunction with the Export-Import Bank in Washington and the Foreign Credit Assurance Association.

An important development in the growth of Shawmut's international activities occurred on December 15, 1965, when the Board of Directors of the National Shawmut approved the establishment of a subsidiary of the Bank, an Edge Act corporation, organized under provisions of Section 25(a) of the Federal Reserve Act, and to be known as the Shawmut International Corporation.

Shawmut International Corporation. With Federal Reserve Board approval, Shawmut International was incorporated on February 1, 1966. Twenty thousand shares of capital stock, each having a par value of $100, were issued, and the National Shawmut Bank purchased the full number at $125 per share, providing the new, wholly owned subsidiary with $2 million in capital and $5 million in surplus.

Initially, Shawmut International limited its investment to European Enterprises Development Company, a venture-capital organization located in Paris whose stockholders included thirty-five leading financial institutions in Europe. Later in the decade, Shawmut International added investments in two similar groups: Adela Investment Company, which operated in South America, and Private Investment Company of Asia (PICA), which had its headquarters in Singapore but operated throughout the Far East. In the course of time, European Enterprises dissolved, while Adela Investment Company encountered severe problems as a consequence of conditions in South America. Shawmut, however, continued active in PICA, which offered potential for long-term profits, even though as late as 1980 it was providing only a modest dividend of 5 percent on Shawmut International's investment of $200,000. In 1981 PICA was a key factor in Shawmut's Far East market strategy, providing contacts there when Shawmut and two partners activated Atlantic Capital, a Hong Kong depository institution.

Air Freight Cash Letter Service. Another innovative international banking service provided by Shawmut during this period was the Air Freight Cash Letter Service. In 1966 the Shawmut had approximately $5 million in foreign deposits from European banks. Air Freight Cash Letter Service was a collecting and clearance service for checks and cash. Checks drawn on United States banks and deposited in European banks left from Shannon Airport in Ireland in late afternoon and arrived that night in Boston, where they were then cleared through the Shawmut. It vastly expedited credit for these checks and was instrumental in building up Shawmut's foreign deposits. Approximately forty-five European banks used this service at its peak. The service continues even in the 1980s, but competition has reduced its volume, largely because the leading European banks have established New York City branches, which provide directly the same service for their parent institutions.

Other Bank-Related Developments

Still other areas developed by the Shawmut during this period and designed to increase income were the Trust Division and Electronic Data Processing. At the same time, the Shawmut, adjusting to the competitive situation, dismantled Devonshire Financial Service Corporation, which was no longer cost-effective.

Trust Division Development, 1962–1967. From 1962 through 1967, the book value of fiduciary assets managed by the National Shawmut Trust Division mounted steadily under the management of John Wallace, vice president. Steps were taken to strengthen the staff of the division, the most notable addition being F. Thayer Sanderson, an able trust officer recruited from the Lincoln-Rochester Trust Company of Rochester, New York. He ultimately assumed leadership of the division.

Although all categories of trust business increased, some of the greatest growth occurred in pension and profit sharing trusts managed by the Bank as a trustee or as agent for individual trustees. Between 1961 and 1966, the Bank's fee income for managing such services expanded by some 158 percent. During this period the Trust Division established two new pooled investment funds to provide specifically for the investment of the qualified retirement plans that were first permitted for self-employed individuals in 1962. Together with the previously established Pooled Equity Fund and Pooled Fixed Income Fund the Shawmut could now provide a complete spectrum of investments for both corporate pension funds and those of the self-employed.

Electronic Data Processing Services. By 1965 the process of converting conventional banking applications to the computer had almost been completed. This had a radical effect in increasing the efficiency of Bank operations, but it also allowed the Bank to offer new computer-based services to its corporate and professional customers, correspondent banks, and affiliates of the Shawmut Association, Inc. As a consequence, in 1965 fees earned from services doubled from the year before.

The Bank's Corporate Services Division, established in 1965 under the direction of John S. Sullivan, vice president, benefited particularly from automation, allowing Shawmut to increase its payroll accounting services to small and midsize businesses, and to increase its services to one of its most important users, the Fidelity Group of Mutual Funds, which experienced considerable activity during the stock market's lush years in the mid-1960s.

In 1966 a third-generation computer system was installed, and in 1967 two additional units were added to improve operating efficiency. Automation, which had begun slowly so many years before, had come into its own as an essential element in the Bank's operation, and although interest earned through loans remained the primary source of the Bank's income, the fees earned from the Bank's trust and general services had become, with Martin's support and encouragement, a meaningful addition to Bank resources with a potential yet to be fully realized. Ironically, it was also during this period of service expansion that the Bank terminated one of its oldest services, the Devonshire Financial Service Corporation.

Devonshire Financial Service Corporation. On August 18, 1966, it was announced to the Shawmut board that the Bank would discontinue Devonshire Financial's activities because of the decline in the profitability of the business. With increasing emphasis on personal loans and on service to consumer customers, Shawmut felt that it was more advantageous to focus on direct installment lending.

The demise of DFSC was scheduled, and on December 14, 1966, D. Thomas Trigg, executive vice president, announced to the Board of Directors the final discontinuance of floor plan loans to car dealers, thus ending the activities of the corporation.

Of all the changes initiated in these years, however, one that would have the greatest significance for the future was the formation of Shawmut Association, Inc., in 1964 and its subsequent purchase of the assets of Shawmut Association and acquisition of the National Shawmut Bank.

The Shawmut Association, Inc. (the Corporation)

The history of the organization that was destined to become Shawmut Association, Inc., will be covered further in Chapter 18. Suffice it to say here that it was originally instituted in 1928 as a business trust called Shawmut Association. Although de facto the Association was a bank holding company, contemporary laws dictated that, at least de jure, it be simply a subsidiary investment trust. In 1956 and 1957, however, federal and state laws regarding holding companies were amended, and the way was opened for reorganizing the Shawmut Association into a modern and legally recognized bank holding company. Although the advantages of creating such a corporation in terms of efficiency and expansion were clear, legal impediments still stood in the way until 1964. In that year the federal tax law was amended to allow reorganization of the type that Shawmut contemplated. Simultaneously, state law added the stock of bank holding companies to the list of authorized investments allowed to Massachusetts savings banks. The latter held 40 percent of the National Shawmut Bank stock, and before the amendment, this fact had stood as a major obstacle to reorganization.

Between 1957 and 1965, the Bank, but particularly Martin, who had become a trustee of the Association in 1956 and its president in 1961, worked to overcome these barriers, conceiving different organizational plans and supporting the changes in legislation. In 1962, when Martin became chief executive officer, the preparation for possible conversion intensified. During 1964 both amendments took effect, and plans came to a head with the incorporation of the Shawmut Association, Inc., on December 31, 1964. That day the six trustees of the Association were elected directors of the Corporation. The transformation culminated on May 6, 1965, when the Corporation acquired the National Shawmut Bank and assets of the Shawmut Association, thereby becoming one of the largest bank holding companies in the United States at that time.

On paper the change was little less than startling, for it suggested that the National Shawmut had surrendered its autonomy to become simply one of thirteen banks owned by another and larger company. Such a reading overlooks the important fact that the National Shawmut had dominated the Association from the outset, and despite the rearrangement, it continued to be the dominant factor in the new corporation.

Boards of Directors — the Corporation and the National Shawmut Bank

When Shawmut Association, Inc., took over ownership of the National Shawmut Bank on May 6, 1965, all the directors of the Bank joined the six original Corporation directors, who had been Association trustees. The Bank's domination of the Corporation was underscored by this fact. The new corporate responsibilities of the directors were simply added to their responsibilities as directors of the National Shawmut Bank. Not until 1967 would the Corporation begin to add directors who were not also directors of the Bank. However, in 1965 the Bank did have three new directors who were not on the Corporation board. As chief executive officer of both organizations, Martin had a strong influence on the type of individual elected to serve on their boards.

Central to his policy for these bodies was the belief that board members should be drawn from the leadership of businesses and industries. Such directors would enhance Shawmut's image as a community organization, and so the chief executive officers of major regional institutions were sought after. In instances where such persons were not available, subordinate officers who were likely to succeed to top posts in the near future were approached and invited to join the Board of Directors.

Martin's influence on the selection of the members had actually begun before he was officially in a position to make appointments, but his predecessor, Horace Schermerhorn, had welcomed the advice of his executive vice president. Thus, when Martin became chief executive officer, the Board already reflected the kind of leadership he desired, and later appointments merely served to enhance its general composition.

The assets of the new corporation were also principally the stock of the National Shawmut Bank, which accounted for more than two-thirds (68 percent) of the net asset value held. The remaining twelve banks of the former Shawmut Association accounted for approximately 18 percent of the assets, and marketable securities, other than bank stocks, accounted for the final 14 percent.

In terms of leadership and asset proportions, little had changed. In terms of the future development of the Shawmut organization, however, a great deal had changed. The Shawmut Association, Inc. — not the National Shawmut Bank — was now the umbrella or coordinating organization, and the focus of attention shifted to extending profitable banking services through the development of all the affiliated banks.

The Lighter Side

It would be misleading to suggest that during this period the business of the Bank was only business. In fact, some attribute the very prosperity of the institution not only to Martin's business sense but also to his spirited sense of fun. He was a leader who was accutely aware of the importance of morale to overall performance, and he gave hearty support to extracurricular activities, which are still fondly remembered by Shawmut personnel. Among these were three all-staff bank shows initiated by the Public Relations Department, which involved everyone from clerks to Martin himself and cheerfully spoofed the image of the dour banker. Abounding in such eloquent lyrics as "We have three men — each one is wise / Our Shawmut Bank they vitalize? When they hired us — these three inspired us / Trigg, Benson and Martin," the shows, the last of which was given in 1971, are often recalled as part of an earlier "funtime." Also contributing to the fun was the filming of *The Thomas Crown Affair*. With Martin's amused agreement, the Shawmut Bank was approved as a set, and for much of the summer of 1967, delighted Bank personnel and their somewhat disconcerted neighbors had the chance to rub shoulders with Steve McQueen and Faye Dunaway and to conduct business as usual in a forest of camera dollies, lights, and Hollywood glamour.

4

In December 1967, John K. Benson was elected president of Shawmut Association Inc., and Martin became chairman of the board and remained chief executive officer. Now he confronted two major challenges: the continuing development of the Association as a corporate entity comprising several disparate units, all of which must operate together harmoniously for the good of the whole, and the continuing development of each bank within the Association, but most particularly the National Shawmut Bank.

To carry out the first of these goals, it was necessary to develop an identity for the Corporation that expressed both the unity of the whole and the individuality of the parts and to put in place policies and structures that reinforced this identity. To carry out the second goal it was necessary to develop new ideas and services that took advantage of the relationship between the affiliated banks and allowed each to develop to capacity its particular possibilities.

A New Corporate Image

One of Martin's major contributions to the future of the Shawmut Association, Inc., was his introduction of the concept that the Corporation was "a family of banks." Commonplace as such an idea might appear on the surface, it would be difficult to overestimate its impact on the development of the organization — for to recognize the Corporation as a family was to recognize that all of the affiliated banks had a central loyalty and that they could and should be able to rely on one another. At the same time the family idea recognized the individuality of the members. Such a concept, viewed in the light of the Association's history, was important.

From the inception of the Association in 1928, the relationship between the National Shawmut and the suburban affiliates was an uncomfortable one. Unfortunately, certain administrative practices — particularly during the administration of Bucklin — did nothing to alleviate such discomfort and, indeed, exacerbated it. A suspicion existed among suburban bank officers that their positions were being usurped, that they were, in short, being taken over. As a consequence, an air of resentment, if not downright hostility, developed which did not begin to abate until the appointment in March 1960 of Leslie J. Scott, president of Winchester National Bank, as vice president of the Association, with particular responsibility to serve as a liaison between the Shawmut trustees and the twelve suburban banks.

Scott began his banking career at the National Shawmut in the 1920s and moved to Winchester National Bank, a Shawmut Association affiliate in January 1930. His thirty years' service there, including fifteen years as its president, made him a suburban banker who understood the operations of the local banks within the Shawmut Association structure. His appointment as vice president of the Association was both fortuitous and indicative of a new sensitivity to the needs of affiliate banks. This sensitivity was consistently demonstrated by Martin, and it can be justifiably asserted that only his careful handling of negotiations made the final incorporation possible.

To be a legal entity was one thing; to understand the dimensions and expectations that this entity involved was quite another. To speak of the corporate body as a family was the first step toward clarifying relationships; to impute to that family a recognizable character and role was another, and now Martin applied the National Shawmut Bank's traditional "service to the community" concept to the Corporation. During Bucklin's tenure, this tradition had fallen into disuse. Martin revived it, making clear that Shawmut Association, Inc., would be seen as a citizen of the entire area, willing to accept not only financial but social responsibility within that community. Toward fulfillment of this latter end, personnel of all the affiliated banks including, of course, the National Shawmut Bank of Boston were encouraged to become involved in community projects, ranging from serving on the boards of metropolitan-area colleges, universities, and businesses to playing support roles in youth, church, and charitable or philanthropic organizations.

Martin's sense of social obligation, however, went beyond support for individual activities and influenced many of the decisions made for the National Shawmut Bank and Shawmut Association, Inc. Thus it was at his insistence that the Bank began to recruit women and minority trainees long before federal legislation mandated such action, and he continued these policies in directing the affairs of the new Corporation. Their effect on personnel operations will be discussed later, but it is appropriate to note here that Martin's role in recognizing minorities in all institutions of the Shawmut Association, Inc., was acknowledged in 1971, when he was honored by the Boston Chapter of the NAACP. The citation presented to him reads:

> For your willingness to bring your own enterprise into the community by action not just words, your selfless leadership in the NAACP Positive Program for Boston has been and continues to be invaluable to us all, with deep gratitude for your devotion to the cause for which NAACP stands, Justice, Equality, and Dignity for all people.

He was also honored by the National Conference of Christians and Jews at its forty-second annual Northeast dinner and was presented with a citation for his "outstanding leadership in governmental affairs, welfare, health, educational and intergroup organizations dedicated to the finest ideals of understanding, civic operations and justice among men."

In addition to offering employment opportunities to minorities, the National Shawmut Bank also provided direct support to many minority enterprises. For example, Shawmut helped train some of the officers and arranged for some of the capital of the Unity Bank, a minority bank in Roxbury organized in 1968. Despite Shawmut's efforts Unity Bank faced difficulties in 1971, and a conservator was appointed. New capital amounting to $2 million was needed immediately, and Shawmut stepped in with its share.

Martin's philosophy of having Shawmut Association, Inc., serve as a model citizen of the community was further demonstrated in the support he gave to local redevelopment programs. Such programs sprang up in several communities, including Boston, and the affiliate banks as well as the National Shawmut played active roles in their respective areas.

Extending the Corporate Presence

As the image of the character and function of the corporate body began to expand and crystallize, so also did the corporate body itself. Implicit in Martin's notion that the Corporation was a family whose members were committed to community service was the sense that these members must grow in number and efficiency in order to fulfill their mission. As a consequence, there was a continued effort to streamline the organization in the interest of efficiency and simultaneously expand membership and branches in the interest of service.

To achieve these goals, Martin approved the consolidation of some banks. At the same time he worked with Benson, then a senior vice president and later president of Shawmut Association, Inc., to extend those banking facilities that would give citizens greater access to their community banks through more convenient neighborhood offices. As a consequence, nine affiliated banks in Middlesex County were reduced to six, but between 1965 and 1969, a total of fourteen new branches were added in communities not previously served by Shawmut Association, Inc. For example, in 1968 the Cambridge-based County

Bank expanded into Belmont. In 1969 the Lexington Trust began operations in Acton. In 1970 Needham National Bank opened a Bellingham branch, and the First County Bank added West Bridgewater to the communities it served.

Even more important to the welfare of the Shawmut Association, Inc., than consolidation and branching of the original affiliates was the addition of new banks, and Martin devoted a great deal of time and effort to approaching outside bankers. In 1970, as a result of these efforts, Shawmut acquired both the First Bank and Trust Company of Hampden County, with headquarters in Springfield, and the Framingham National Bank, which in 1971 merged with Waltham Citizens National Bank and Newton National Bank to become Community National Bank. These new acquisitions were in heavily populated industrial areas, and their earnings did much to increase corporate earnings and offset the impact of inflationary costs, the expense of new facilities, and increasing provisions for loan losses that were the legacy of the 1970s.

In 1971 the Corporation assisted in the opening of ten new branches for these banks, and at the end of 1971, Shawmut Association, Inc., could boast ten affiliates in key eastern areas of Massachusetts and a total of 114 banking facilities. It was by any measure an important and substantial growth for the Shawmut family.

Projecting the Corporate Image

As the Association began to expand and achieve identity as a corporate citizen the need to convey that image to the public became increasingly important. Insistence that officers and directors participate in the community, that the banks take a leadership role in community action, that they respond to the needs of that community through their services, was a way of conveying this idea, but Martin also recognized that it was essential to go beyond these actions and that only through intelligent advertising and promotion could the public be made fully aware of Shawmut. With the aid of Warren S. Berg, vice president of Development and Public Relations, a new emphasis was put on marketing, advertising and promotional literature.

The Personal Banker Program. One ongoing policy of the National Shawmut Bank that lent itself to projecting the image of the entire Corporation and all of its affiliated banks was the idea of a bank serving as a "personal banker at your side, on your side." The notion had actually been developed as long ago as the 1920s, serving as the basis for a popular advertising campaign which featured the slogan "600 people working for YOU."

The idea of a personal banker, however, was far more than an advertising ploy. It operated as an inspiration to the National Shawmut staff to develop comprehensive services and to create a banking organization that could meet all the financial needs of every customer, large or small. By the 1960s, these services had multiplied, and now a customer had access not only to deposit, checking, loan, trust, saving, and various financing services but also to advice on international markets and, with the advent of computerization, help in processing business accounts and sending out bills.

With the founding of the Corporation, the idea of the personal banker became even more significant. It was, in fact, an important point in convincing suburban bankers of the advantages of the organization. Now they too could be seen as personal bankers providing, through their access to the Boston facility, all those amenities usually available only in the cities, and affiliated banks were encouraged to develop and to advertise this approach.

Cooperative Advertising. Another promotional innovation that dates from the 1968 to 1971 period was the idea of cooperative advertising. According to this scheme, all of the affiliated banks co-sponsored certain events — for instance, the Red Sox baseball telecasts in 1969. The promotional copy used was relevant to all the banks — the Personal Banker Program was particularly effective here — and the approach underscored the concept of a family of banks, gave the suburban banks a chance for greatly increased publicity, and brought the Shawmut name before the public with far greater regularity than would have been possible had each unit been restricted to publicizing only itself.

It was also during this period, the early years of the Associa-

266   *The Chronological Story of Shawmut*

tion, that new emphasis began to be put on the Shawmut symbol. Martin himself encouraged research on the Shawmut name and on the sculpture of the Obbatinewat bust, commissioning reports on the etymology of the name and on the artist, Adelbert Ames, a Harvard graduate who went on to teach at Dartmouth. (See Chapter 17.) These efforts were not simply scholarly indulgence, rather they underscored a feeling that the Corporation could, and should, capitalize on Shawmut's past to present itself as part of a long regional tradition. But though it was not until 1975 that the modern blue image of the Indian, the renaming of all the Corporation banks to include the word *Shawmut,* and the standardization of type and graphics came about, it was Martin who laid the groundwork for the eventual change. It was his insistence on simplicity, consistency, and uniformity — not simply in purpose but in image — that set the standard for the presentation of the Association that still obtains in the 1980s.

Corporation Personnel Policies. With the establishment of the Corporation, benefits and opportunities of the Boston Bank employees were extended to the suburban banks as well.

The Profit Sharing and Savings Plan, begun in 1968, provided an incentive for improving earnings by giving full-time employees of all the banks a chance to share in a percentage of net operating earnings and to set aside automatically some of their income for investment. In July 1971, a similar bonus plan was introduced for the benefit of part-time staff. Other benefits included periodic salary increases and enhanced insurance coverage of all the Corporation employees.

During Martin's administration, the employment of minorities also grew steadily in all the banks. For example, in 1964 minorities made up 9.3 percent of the clerical staff at the National Shawmut Bank. By 1969 the figure had risen substantially. Affirmative Action had been so much a part of Shawmut personnel policies for so long that, unlike many of its peers, Shawmut suffered no dislocations or problems when new federal laws required institutions to make radical changes in their hiring practices.

Martin's view of the Shawmut Association, Inc., as a unified whole, the parts of which could be mutually beneficial, and his manner of implementing the idea proved effective in smoothing relations between the Corporation and its affiliate banks. At a meeting of the Corporation directors held on May 26, 1972, Robert A. Fairbairn, president of the Fairbairn Management Corporation and a director of Shawmut's Needham National Bank since 1955, clearly articulated the new mood:

> I cannot help but compare the way the Association is managed today and the conditions that existed in 1955. It certainly is a major achievement for Larry and his team to have accomplished all that has been done in such a relatively short period of time.

Martin's management of the relations between the Corporation and its affiliate banks is one example of his own foresighted approach. He was also an ardent advocate of long-range planning, which might be seen as a way to codify foresight. Further he encouraged the participation of twelve senior officers in a conference on long-term planning, which was conducted by the American Management Association in Hamilton, New York, on September 9, 1970.

As a consequence of this training, in April 1972 the Corporation adopted a five-year plan detailing many management objectives. Although, as with most such plans, this one provided less than a scientific guideline to the future, it did launch Shawmut management into long-range planning exercises.

5

If the notion of the Corporation as a family of banks with the responsibilities of citizenship was the cornerstone of Martin's general philosophy, it was a citizenship that had to be reaffirmed through responsible financial progress. Such was the character of the years between 1968 and 1972 that this responsibility was sorely tested.

Financial Developments, 1968–1969

Nineteen sixty-eight and 1969 were transition years between the prosperity of the early 1960s and the time of recession that shadowed the country in the early 1970s. Although business activity continued at a high rate, particularly in Massachusetts and the New England area which the Shawmut served, the drain on the economy caused by the war and by continuing inflation could not be ignored. National monetary policies were becoming increasingly restrictive, driving up the interest rate on short-term money market funds. As a corollary, time deposits, which banks had come to depend upon, declined as a source of lendable funds. With large business accounts clamoring for credit that might have taxed each bank's lending capacity under any circumstances, the Corporation board began to search for alternative financial resources that could satisfy their customers' demands.

By spring 1969, several plans were being discussed for obtaining funds. Included among these plans was the Loan Participation and Repurchase Agreement Plan, a complex economic strategy that allowed unit participation in larger repurchase agreements. The plan was approved by the board on June 6, 1969, with a $25 million maximum. By June 19, it had already exceeded its maximum by $8 million, and the ceiling was raised to $50 million. Still more funds were needed, and in July 1969, the board authorized the establishment of a subsidiary financial corporation to which the Bank could sell loans.

The Shawmut Financial Corporation. The function of the Shawmut Financial Corporation was to sell commercial paper. The ability to do this was unique to the holding company, and, in fact, the Financial Corporation was only the second such company to begin the sale of paper. Fifty million dollars of promissory notes were issued at the beginning of its operation, and the proceeds, which were held as short-term deposits in the Shawmut, increased the liquid funds of the Bank. The importance and rapid expansion of Shawmut Financial Corporation, headed by John K. Benson, is underscored by a comparison of marginal funds and rates for July 1969 with those of August 1969. Thus, in July additional funds employed by the Bank averaged $149 million. The average rate paid was 8.8 percent. By August marginal money sources were providing $192 million. At this point interest paid rose to 9.2 percent.

The cost of money hovered in this general area for the next

Benjamin T. Reed, President, 1836–1848

Exchange Coffee House

Top, left: John Gardner,
President, 1848–1853

Top, right: Albert Fearing,
President, 1853–1854

Opposite: William Bramhall,
President, 1854–1868

Shawmut bank notes

1

4

5

2

6

3

7

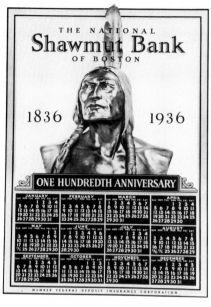

8

9

1. The Shawmut Indian as it appeared on bank notes in the 1850s and 1860s
2. The standing Indian used in the late 1800s
3. The Shawmut Indian as it appeared at the turn of the century
4. A brass engraved image placed on the marble floor at Water Street
5. The bust of Obbatinewat as we know him today, created by Adelbert Ames, Jr., in 1910
6. Contemporary logo, introduced in April 1975
7. A studio showing the production of Shawmut commercials for television, 1947
8. Calendar used during Shawmut's 100th anniversary year
9. National Shawmut Bank 1964 auto loan ad

John C. Cummings, Jr., President,
1868–1898

James P. Stearns, President, 1898–1907

Shawmut's 60 Congress Street
headquarters, rebuilt in 1874 after
the Great Boston Fire of 1872 and
occupied until 1907

Opposite: 40 Water Street,
Shawmut's headquarters from
1907 to 1975

William A. Gaston, President,
1907–1917

Alfred L. Aiken, President, 1918–1923
(courtesy of the American Antiquarian Society)

Opposite, top: Bank floor of 40 Water Street, 1907

Opposite, bottom: Main lobby of 40 Water Street, 1940s

Top, left: Walter S. Bucklin, President, 1923–1952; Chief Executive Officer and Chairman, 1952–1956

Top, right: Walter E. Borden, President, 1952–1956

Bottom: Horace Schermerhorn, President, 1956–1960; Chief Executive Officer, 1956–1962; Chairman, 1960–1962

THE NATIONAL SHAWMUT BANK

CAPITAL, SURPLUS AND PROFITS $19,000,000

BOSTON August 28, 1918.

TO OUR CUSTOMERS:

We are proud to say that more than one-third of our clerical force, upon whom we have depended to facilitate the daily routine of a great banking business, are now serving with the colors. Their places have been filled by an equal number of men and women who cannot serve at the front, most of whom came to us wholly inexperienced in the details of the positions they are called upon to fill.

As a customer of the bank, may we bespeak your consideration during the period of readjustment caused by these necessary changes in the personnel of our institution? We shall appreciate your assistance in promptly reporting to us any error or oversight that may occur.

Sincerely yours,

Alfred L. Aiken

President.

WITH THE COLORS

ROGER AMORY
JAMES ARRINGTON
GEORGE L. ASPINWALL
FRANK W. ASTON
FREDERICK C. BARRETT, JR.
JAMES F. BARRETT
JOHN O. BARROWS
JOSEPH P. BATEMAN
ALBERT BAXTER
ADAM BEAUMONT
RAYMOND R. BENSON
WILLIAM B. BLISS
F. J. BRADLEE, JR.
ROYDEN F. BROOKINGS
CHARLES G. BROWN
WALTER A. BURNHAM
ARTHUR W. BURTON
NORMAN L. BUTLER
JOHN R. CAMPBELL, JR.
WILLIAM A. CASH
EMIL W. CEDERBORG
ALEXANDER W. CHISHOLM
MEDVILLE L. CLARK
WILLIAM A. COLE
PAUL G. CURTICE
FRANK E. CURTIN
WILLIAM W. CURTIN
EVERETT D. DANFORTH
LLOYD E. DENT
ROBERT A. DONALDSON
WALTER S. DOWNING
HILARY A. DRISCOLL
HUBERT B. EAMES
JOHN E. FALVEY
EARL F. FILLMORE
RUSSELL P. FAULKNER
RALPH F. FOLSOM
ELPALET C. GARDNER
GEORGE H. GILBERT
HOWARD E. GILL
THOMAS M. GREENE
CHARLES E. GRIFFITHS
GEORGE R. GRIFFIN
GEORGE R. HALL
HAROLD A. HAM
RALPH A. HANSEN
EDWARD C. HARWOOD
GEORGE A. HENDERSON
CHARLES A. HOAR
ERNEST E. HOGQUIST
EHARD JOHNSON
BENJAMIN JOY
HERMAN P. KASPER

WITH THE COLORS

DAVID T. KEAY
JAMES KENNEDY
JOHN A. KENNEY
HORACE M. LEONARD
B. THEODORE LA FOLLEY
GEORGE H. LANGILL
CHARLES LEIGHR
CHARLES LUKE
CURTIS A. LUNDAHL
BRANDT S. LUPTON
FRANCIS A. MAHAN
GLEN H. MARTIN
CHESTER H. MATSON
DONALD McALLISTER
GEORGE A. McCUSKER
HAROLD E. MEYER
FREDERICK MITCHELL
THOMAS W. MORAN
JOHN T. MORRISSEY
CHESTER W. MORSE
ARTHUR L. MURPHY
ARO D. NELSON
HARRY T. NELSON
ALFRED K. NYMAN
A. HEATH ONTHANK
CLARK S. PAGE
ARTHUR H. PATTEN
FREDERICK PEARSON
LORING G. PEEDE
ERNEST W. PENNELL
ROBERT S. POTTER
EDMUND V. PUBLICOVER
ARCHIE D. ROSS
EDWARD C. SAUNDERS
DUANE R. SEABORN
JOHN A. SHERIDAN
FRANCIS E. SILVERWRIGHT
JOHN H. SKEHAN
ROBERT B. SNOW
MARCUS L. SORENSON
JOHN S. STOYLE
EVERETT H. SYLVESTER
RICHARD O. TEWKSBURY
JOHN V. TOLAND
LESTER A. TUCKER
ERNEST H. VEZINA
FRANCIS F. VOGEL
JOHN J. WALKINS
EDWARD A. WHEELER
C. BRYANT WIGGIN
VICTOR F. WILSON
ALEXANDER WINSOR
CHARLES C. WRIGLEY

Letter to bank personnel in the armed services, August 28, 1918

One Federal Street, headquarters of Shawmut Corporation and Shawmut Bank of Boston, N.A. The thirty-eight-story building is located in the heart of Boston's financial district. Construction began in 1972; the building was occupied in 1975.

Lawrence H. Martin, President, 1960–1968; Chief Executive Officer, 1962–1972; Chairman, 1968–1972

D. Thomas Trigg, President, 1968–1974; Chief Executive Officer, 1972–1980; Chairman, 1972–1980

John K. Benson, President of
Shawmut Association, Inc.,
and Shawmut Corporation,
1967–1975

Paul G. Black, President, 1974–1976

Logan Clarke, Jr., President, 1976–1978

Shawmut Corporation Officer/Directors, 1985: *(left to right)* Neal F.
Finnegan, Vice Chairman; William F. Craig, Vice Chairman; John P.
LaWare, Chairman and Chief Executive Officer; John P. Hamill,
President

John P. LaWare, President, 1978–1980; Chairman and Chief
Executive Officer, 1980–present

several months and did not begin to decline until March 1970. As national monetary policies relaxed and as more funds became available, the Shawmut Financial Corporation ceased issuing paper. It had helped to serve in the reallocation of short-term capital in the New England region during a particularly trying economic period and had fulfilled its primary purpose to retain loan customers for the Shawmut.

Master Charge. In the same year that the Shawmut Financial Corporation was founded to obtain more lendable funds, banks of the Shawmut Association, Inc., also began participation in a Master Charge system, which can be understood as a way to encourage small-loan borrowing. Although on the surface these coincidental moves might seem contradictory, Master Charge loans are in quite a different category from large commercial loans. The motive for initiating the scheme in 1969 was very much the same as that for establishing the Shawmut Financial Corporation — to meet competition, to provide additional services to Shawmut customers, and to bring in additional monies through transactions that could legitimately ask 12 percent, later 18 percent, on borrowed funds.

In 1969 the credit card system as a form of consumer credit was already well established. Its roots can be traced as far back as the 1930s, when certain stores and gasoline companies began to issue such cards to promote customer loyalty as well as the sale of their products. During the 1950s another form of card — Diners Club, Carte Blanche, and American Express — which was available for an annual fee and which gave their holders access to travel and entertainment, began to take hold. But it was not until the 1960s that bank cards came into being, and their emergence appropriately reflected the growth in consumer buying power.

By 1968 "plastic" had already become a way of life in many parts of the country. Holders saw the cards as a convenient substitute for immediate cash; bankers saw them as a new way to expand installment and personal loans as well as a source of new customers. At this point, it was only logical that Shawmut would begin to explore the system's possibilities as a new service for its clientele.

Accordingly, the banks of Shawmut Association, Inc., joined

with the First National Bank of Boston and the New England
Merchants Bank to conduct a study on the feasibility of entering
the bank charge-card field. The results were presented and approved by the Shawmut board in December 1968. The following
year all Shawmut Association banks became members of the
New England Bankcard Association (NEBA) and, consequently,
participants in the Master Charge Interbank Credit Card Program. The program was introduced in August 1969, with a
massive mailing to potential customers. James R. White, senior
vice president, and head of the City Division, carried the responsibility for the massive planning involved in Shawmut's participation in this charge-card system. An unusual feature of the
Shawmut Association's program was the opportunity for customers to have a photo identification appear on their cards,
which offered them additional protection.

Although it had been estimated in the 1968 study that profitability from the charge-card operation would be approximately
6 percent, during the first few years only losses were recorded.
Customer loan losses were heavy. Moreover, loans by the National Shawmut Bank to NEBA had to be written off in the
final quarter of 1972, although they were fully recovered in
1974.

Despite these problems, there is no indication that the Shawmut regretted its participation in the plan. Indeed, to have ignored such a service in the latter part of the twentieth century
would have been an abdication of responsibility to customers.

The Shawmut Financial Corporation and Master Charge were
two ways in which the Shawmut attempted to accommodate
to conditions in 1968 and 1969, when money was tight and
the demand for credit and purchasing power still high. Still a
third and very important development of these years came in
international activities.

International Developments, 1968–1972

The years between 1968 and 1972 saw an expansion in the
National Shawmut's international activities that was reflected
in the Association's earnings. The reason for the increase, which
took place in 1968 and 1969, was twofold: the tight money

policies at home which, combined with a growing need for available funds to meet the credit needs of the community, prompted the Corporation to increase its purchase of overnight funds and its participation in the Eurodollar market; and the continuing restrictions on amounts allowed to foreign borrowers, which had been determined under the 1968 Voluntary Foreign Credit Restraint Program. By 1969 the banks had almost reached the limit of the quotas, and thus, although foreign deposits at the National Shawmut had reached record highs in 1969, further expansion of international lending was threatened. As a consequence of these conditions, the National Shawmut initiated two new international services.

The Nassau Branch. Opened in 1969, the Nassau branch of the National Shawmut Bank in Boston was established as a "brass plate" operation. In short, it was an organization designed to accommodate offshore deposits and to allow the Shawmut to make short- and medium-term Eurodollar loans without being subject to the reserve requirements imposed by the Federal Reserve Bank. By the end of the year, the new branch had developed substantial Eurodollar deposits, which increased the following year. The loan activities of the branch were equally satisfying. In 1970 the branch extended about half of the year-to-year total loan increase of the Shawmut Bank, and in 1971 income from Nassau's loans contributed handsomely to the total earnings of the Bank.

Atlantic International Bank, Ltd. Still a second important factor in expanding the Shawmut's international business was the formation in London of the Atlantic International Bank, which was designed to make three- to ten-year loans in Eurodollars or other major currencies to American companies doing business in Europe, and to accept deposits and perform other functions of a conventional bank.

Although the organization did not begin operation until 1969, its roots can be traced to 1965, when the federal government, faced with a growing balance-of-payment deficit, froze U.S. bank loans overseas at a figure based on the amount of foreign loans extended by an institution as of December 31, 1965. At this point Shawmut was just beginning to build up its international business, having virtually retired from the area in the mid-1950s after the final recovery of the German Standstill Credits. Feeling that such circumstances imposed an artificially low ceiling on the Shawmut's international loans, Martin devised the idea of forming the Atlantic International Bank, which would allow participants to expand their business abroad without violating the limits imposed by the Voluntary Foreign Credit Restraint Program.

At this same time Charterhouse Japhet and Thomasson, Ltd., of London expressed an interest in extending its contact with the American financial market. Consequently, Martin advised them that four American partners could be obtained for such an enterprise if Charterhouse administrators would secure four European partners. Shortly afterwards, the United California Bank of Los Angeles, Manufacturers National Bank of Detroit, and First Pennsylvania Overseas Financial Corporation of Philadelphia joined Shawmut as the United States partners, while Charterhouse arranged to have Banco di Napoli of Naples, Banque de Neuflize Schlumberger, Mallet and Cie of Paris, and F. van Lanschot Bankiers of the Netherlands join as European partners. Each of these institutions was to hold 250,000 shares of the projected Atlantic International Bank with 50 percent paid in at the outset. The main burden of Shawmut's planning and negotiating on this project was carried by Paul G. Black, senior vice president, who was assisted by Nigel R. Godwin, vice president and head of the International Banking Department. D. Thomas Trigg, National Shawmut Bank president, was also an active participant.

On April 3, 1968, the idea was approved by the Shawmut Board of Directors. Six months later, on October 23, 1968, the arrangements for the new bank were completed, and the following summer, at its organization meeting, July 3, 1969, Martin was elected a director and deputy chairman of the bank with Hilton S. Clarke of Charterhouse becoming chairman (to be succeeded by Martin in 1970). Other Shawmut officers participating in the Atlantic's administration were Paul G. Black, elected a director as an alternate for Martin, and Nigel R. Godwin, elected a member of its executive committee. In the course of the next several years, Atlantic International, Ltd., proved an important factor in Shawmut's ability to extend overseas financial assistance, and its continued presence stands in the 1980s as a major accomplishment.

Further Financial Developments, 1970–1972

By the end of 1969, the golden age of opulence was over. Business growth began to slacken; companies which had been overconfident that expansion would justify the high rate on loans contracted in the mid-1960s now found themselves pressed to meet commitments; a drop in defense contracts exacted a heavy toll, particularly on high tech firms located along Boston's electronic belt; and some conglomerate marriages, consummated in the 1960s, were found to have been sorry mismatches and were subsequently dissolved through bankruptcy. At the same time inflation continued almost unabated, and attempts to control it brought extreme and disquieting shifts in the financial market.

As a major bank holding company none of these conditions left Shawmut Association, Inc., untouched. And quite naturally the effects were felt first and most significantly in the loan area.

Loans, 1970–1971. Although national monetary restrictions were relaxing in 1970 and lendable funds were again becoming more available, a recession in the economy meant that several large and small borrowers began to default, and more loans had to be written off. Among the small borrowers were many with Master Charge credit who, untrained and short of funds, began to use their cards as the equivalent of money rather than as promissory notes.

Most outstanding of the large borrowers was Penn Central Transportation, a company that had been formed from an ill-conceived merger between New York Central and Pennsylvania Railroad. The Bank's relationship with Penn Central had begun February 12, 1969, when the board approved a relatively large, unsecured five-year term loan to the company. The following month it approved a substantial participation in a revolving credit, with the outstanding balance to be converted to a five-year term loan on January 1, 1971, and in August the Bank approved an additional secured loan to New England Transportation Company, a Penn Central subsidiary.

From the vantage of hindsight, the degree of commitment to this organization seems ill advised, but in 1969 the future for Penn Central looked promising. Unfortunately, the picture quickly darkened.

On June 16, 1970, the Executive Committee reviewed the status of loans to the Penn Central Railroad and the Penn Central Company. The issue at this point was a new V loan in which Shawmut would take a $2 million participation. This was in addition to the existing credit secured by stock of the Penn Central Company, the unsecured term loan, and the loan to New England Transportation, the wholly owned subsidiary. The committee approved the new participation, which had a 100 percent guarantee from the U.S. Department of Defense. The approval of this new loan did not represent continued faith in the organization so much as an attempt to avert disaster with new, but guaranteed, funds.

That same day Atlantic International also paid $2 million in Swiss francs for Penn Central Company commercial paper, although they had been advised earlier to avoid financial involvement with the company. The advice might well have been heeded; for despite this transfusion of new money, on June 17, 1970, the Penn Central collapsed, and on July 1, 1970, the Shawmut board convened to hear a report on the corporate reorganization that had resulted in the merger of Pennsylvania Railroad and New York Central and ultimately the bankruptcy of the Penn Central Transportation Company.

Shawmut was certainly not alone in facing the loss. Seventy-three other banks had also been involved, although it is doubtful that the knowledge of being in good company did much to mitigate regrets. Shawmut's disillusion was particularly sharp, as in addition to its own losses, it had one-eighth equity in the Atlantic International Bank's loss. Furthermore, because of legal problems, Shawmut had no immediate recourse to collateral. In 1970 alone the Bank took a $2.1 million loss on Penn Central.

Although the impact of the loss cannot be minimized, it is indicative of how much the National Shawmut had grown that the consequences were not more severe. In July 1970 the Bank had $290 million in commercial loans, and Shawmut's loan portfolio touched on all areas of the American economy. So although 1970 and 1971 saw large loan write-offs, of $4.1 million and $2.8 million, these losses were cushioned by reserves derived from prior earnings.

Particularly important in offsetting loan losses was the continued good performance of certain Shawmut services. The international structures outlined above, particularly the Nassau branch, proved outstanding income earners. Other fee and agency services that continued to stand the Corporation in good stead and helped it weather the storms of 1970 and 1971 included the Money Market Center, trust and agency business, and new checking services. It was also at this time that Shawmut contracted for new outside auditing services.

Money Market Center. Established in 1969, the Money Market Center of the National Shawmut Bank became increasingly important in 1970 and 1971. Designed to assist correspondent banks throughout New England with management of their short-term money positions, this facility also served as a dealer in United States and municipal obligations. The Center supplemented the Shawmut's already existing services in this area, which included underwriting short-term notes and acting as a paying agent for many state and local governments.

Trust and Agency Business. Between 1968 and 1972, intensive effort was expended to develop additional trust business among clients in the suburban areas. As a consequence, the number of accounts managed by the Shawmut Bank began to increase dramatically, and despite a decline, particularly in 1969, of the market values upon which trust fees are based, the income from fees steadily grew. Assisting in making this growth possible was the 1970 conversion of personal trust records onto new computer equipment, a conversion that substantially enhanced the Bank's ability to serve its customers, and in 1971 fees from personal trust services reached a record high.

Additional trust activities in the Martin period included the establishment of programs through which trust representatives worked directly with Shawmut Association banks, and the establishment of the Trust Plus Program in February 1972, which provided that when directors, officers, or employees brought to the Trust Department new accounts involving management of $1 million or more, immediately or in the future, a contribution of $250 was to be paid to the charity designated by the person bringing the new account to the Bank. This person also received an award of a specially cast Shawmut medallion embedded in plastic in the form of a paperweight. It soon became a matter of prestige among Shawmut bankers to have the Trust Plus Award on their desks. In the 1980s the program still continues as a valuable business-development tool of the Trust Division.

Mutual fund services were also expanded, with fees from their management becoming an increasingly important source of income. Again the clue to this growth was increased volume, with much new business being directed to the Shawmut Bank of Boston through suburban bank contacts. In 1969 new accounts were added that effectively served to offset a decline in the volume of mutual fund activity, and in 1970 thirteen new funds were added.

Super Check and Courtesy Check Cashing. Still two other services put in place during this time, but designed not so much to increase immediate income as to attract new customers, were the Super Check and the Courtesy Check Cashing services. The first was established in 1971 as a checking account service. It combined the convenience of a regular checking account with a personal cash reserve. The cash reserve was actually a revolving credit that could be drawn upon whenever an individual wished. Moreover, a Super Check account holder could make his own loan by writing a check directly on the cash reserve.

The Courtesy Check Cashing Service permitted customers having checking accounts in any Shawmut Bank to cash checks up to a specific amount in any branch office of all the Shawmut Association, Inc., banks.

Altogether then, and in spite of fluctuating economic conditions, the earnings of Shawmut Association, Inc., showed a steady advance during the entire period of Martin's chairmanship. The clue to this advance during difficult times lay in the judgment of the administration, which worked to diversify the Shawmut's resources and services, and the sheer volume of business, the consequence of a closely knit organization in which the various members of the Corporation worked together cooperatively to assist and support one another.

New Auditors

In the early 1970s, the Securities and Exchange Commission (SEC) adopted some stringent asset-accounting regulations. In anticipation of these very regulations, Shawmut Association, Inc., entertained bids from the major accounting firms for a new auditing contract and accepted the Price Waterhouse proposal. Consequently, on March 20, 1971, this firm was appointed as outside auditor for the entire Corporation, beginning with the 1971 fiscal year.

A New Face

The development of the Shawmut Association, Inc., as a corporate family responsible through its members to the entire community it served, and the expansion of the financial services of the Corporation in terms of their variety, quality, and availability were major contributions to the evolution of Shawmut. Still another major contribution was the role Martin played in developing the Corporation's physical presence. During the period, the Corporation continued to support conveniently located and pleasingly styled branches of all the affiliates, but more important, it began to plan for a new Shawmut headquarters. It was also at this time that the Shawmut art collection was initiated.

A New Building. When Martin became president of the National Shawmut in 1960, the Bank's headquarters were still in the 40 Water Street building, to which it had moved in 1907. At that time its assets were $71 million, and business was conducted by a handful of staff, headed by President Stearns and six other officers. The Bank used only a portion of the building, leasing other space to tenants. Sixty-five years later, assets had increased to $1.3 billion, and operations at home and abroad required more than 2,300 employees. To accommodate this growth, the Bank leased space for itself in nearby buildings — Government Center, the Winthrop Building, the Rice Building, and the Woolworth Building. In 1963 the Water Street building was enlarged, but no one believed the final solution had been achieved. Planning began in 1964 for a new building, one that would bring together all Shawmut staff for the first time in many years. Such a move, it was reasoned, would lessen costs, improve efficiency, and increase employee morale.

The creation of a new headquarters building was, of course, a substantial undertaking. Planning for space needs, estimating financial costs and operating results, resolving legal issues, acquiring a site, and disposing of the 40 Water Street property and Monk's Building were only a few of the many issues to be confronted. The style in which this project was achieved, however, was typical of Martin's courage and foresight. The new building was a credit to him and the city, and it gave Shawmut a new image in the community.

The public's awareness of Shawmut's intentions began at a press conference on November 2, 1966, when Martin announced that in light of studies revealing that the population and personal income of the region would double in the years ahead, the Shawmut intended "to be equipped with facilities to meet this demand." For this reason, he went on, the Bank had acquired a city block bounded by Milk, Devonshire, Franklin, and Federal streets. This block contained a parcel of vacant land of 23,000 square feet, which had formerly been the site of the Stone and Webster Building, and the eleven story building of the First National Bank of Boston. First National was planning to erect its own new headquarters at 100 Federal Street, and hence the availability of its old property.

Originally Shawmut's plan was to adapt the vacated First National Bank Building to Shawmut's needs, to rent space to tenants, and to construct an adjacent high-rise office on the empty parcel of land. A careful examination of the old First National Bank headquarters, however, revealed that adaption of the existing structure would be costly and unsatisfactory, so plans were initiated for a completely new headquarters building that would occupy the entire city block, rise to thirty-eight stories, and have three floors below ground level. Construction was to proceed following the demolition of the old First National Bank Building, with occupancy slated for 1974. The decision was a milestone in the history of the National Shawmut Bank.

Financing a project of this scale, estimated to require $80 million, was a further reflection of Martin's ingenuity. Funds were provided by the Bank and the Prudential Insurance Company under a joint venture agreement. One of the members of this committee was Charles F. Avila, then president of the Boston Edison Company. As a professional engineer, he was particularly qualified to assess the quality of the plans for the building, and his contributions to the project, from planning to completion, were of immense value.

In 1966, at the time of the purchase of the site for the new headquarters building, a subcommittee of the Board of Directors was formed called the Directors' Committee on New Bank Quarters. The committee consisted of Martin, as chairman, and Charles F. Avila, Asa S. Knowles, Harold T. Marshall, John N. Philips, D. Thomas Trigg, Benjamin A. Trustman, and Vincent C. Ziegler. While the committee was charged with monitoring the general development of the building project, the responsibility for actually carrying it out was assigned to one of its members, David L. Currier, senior vice president and officer-in-charge of Shawmut's Real Estate Division. As project director, Currier served as the liaison between the directors, Bank management, and members of the project group, which consisted of architects, the builder, city authorities, the insurance carrier, and the joint venture partners.

Between the property acquisition in 1966 to occupancy in 1975, Currier, with the full cooperation of the project group members, accomplished the remarkable, bringing the project in on schedule and within the financial projections.

Dedicated in 1975, the new skyscraper, frequently referred to by its address, One Federal Street, but often called the Shawmut Bank Building, stands not only as a tribute to the growth of Shawmut but also as a testimony to the dedicated and cooperative efforts of all who contributed to its completion.

The Shawmut Art Program. While the Shawmut headquarters were still located at 40 Water Street, Martin, as chief executive officer of the Shawmut Bank, began the acquisition of paintings and art objects to enhance the appearance of public areas of the Bank as well as those areas used predominantly by the Bank's employees.

As he was always sensitive to the human needs of his organization, Martin's objective was to create an attractive environment for the Bank's customers, officers, and staff as well as to make a good corporate investment. He devoted innumerable lunch hours to visiting studios and galleries in Greater Boston to acquire appropriate paintings and art objects. Selected works were frequently brought to the Bank on consignment to determine their suitability before purchase approval was granted.

As a consequence of these efforts, approximately three hundred pieces of art were obtained for 40 Water Street. But this was only a beginning. Additional pieces in a more contemporary style were needed to enhance the modern decor of One Federal Street and to give attractiveness to the spacious lobby, banking floors, and reception areas. To help in selection of these pieces Lewis Cabot of Artcounsel, Inc. — a trustee of the Museum of Fine Arts and chairman of the Contemporary Art Committee — was retained as art consultant. Cabot worked in close conjunction with The Architect's Collaborative, the Shawmut architect for the new building, and the Shawmut's Directors' building committee to formulate a floor-by-floor assessment of art needs.

As the Bank's collection began, responsibility for its administration was placed with the Art Committee, consisting of Lawrence Martin as chairman, F. Thayer Sanderson, Lawrence J. Lynch, and Warren S. Berg, who became chairman on Martin's retirement. In 1977, when all acquired art previously owned by Shawmut had been installed in the One Federal Street building, the committee was disbanded and the services of Lewis Cabot, who had continued to play a major role in the acquisition and placement of art, came to an end.

The Shawmut Art Program, however, has continued. The basic functions of the program are to acquire approval of art for offices, meeting rooms, and public areas and to monitor and control the present inventory and new acquisitions for appropriateness, insurance, asset value, and security.

Among the major art items currently on view at One Federal Street are the corfam metallic sculpture array behind the tellers' counter, executed by Robert Goodnough of New York City, and the 57-by-14-foot oil on canvas in the main lobby, which was created by Freidel Dzubas of Ithaca, New York, and now of Boston. There is also a significant collection of Boston historical prints, eleven A. C. Goodwin paintings of Greater Boston scenes (1900–1921), and a modest collection of framed Shawmut memorabilia. The collection is among the best corporate collections, and it has elicited frequent and honored requests for viewing from art critics, students, and art groups.

6

Martin's final full year as chairman and chief executive officer of the Corporation and the Bank was 1971. Fittingly, it was a remarkable year for Shawmut. At its end the Corporation, including all of the affiliated banks and subsidiaries, listed assets of $1.9 billion, while the book value per share was $59.34. It was also during 1971 that the National Shawmut Bank became larger and more successful than it had ever been in its 135-year history.

Growth of the National Shawmut Bank, 1971

By the end of 1971, assets of the National Shawmut Bank alone had reached $1.37 billion, up 15 percent from 1970. Deposits were up 12 percent from the previous year, and loans stood at $660 million for an increase of 16 percent. Service fee income showed a similar and gratifying increase. Adding to this sanguine picture was the fact that, despite continuing inflation, expenses had been contained. Further, the National Shawmut Bank was one of the four major Boston banks to experience an increase in earnings in 1971, with operating earnings increasing 7 percent in the twelve-month period to reach $7.4 million.

In recognition of these accomplishments, on January 19, 1972, the Board of Directors of the National Shawmut Bank voted "an extension of gratitude to the management and staff of the bank for outstanding accomplishments in meeting challenging goals for the year 1971, acknowledging with pride the record of genuine excellence achieved by the bank during the year." It was a pride that was equally applicable to the "record of excellence" maintained by the Bank and the Corporation throughout Martin's administration.

Tribute to Martin's Leadership

Five months after his banner year, Martin retired as chairman and chief executive officer of the National Shawmut Bank and

the Shawmut Association, Inc. His had been a spectacular forty-
four-year career, and at the last annual meeting of the Corporation stockholders, Robert M. Jenney, president of Jenney Oil
Corporation and a director of the National Shawmut Bank since
1957, recognized Martin's contribution to both organizations.
Speaking on behalf of his fellow directors and stockholders
he said:

> I want to express our appreciation to you as the founder of
> the Shawmut Association on the occasion of your retiring as
> Chief Executive Officer for both the Association and the Bank.
> The leadership you have given the Bank and the strong support
> of the community have been outstanding; and your example
> has been stimulating to other officers and personnel. You not
> only leave the bank in the strongest position ever, but you have
> done a great deal for our state as well.

Two months later, on May 31, 1972, the directors of both
the Corporation and the Bank paid further tribute to Martin
at a dinner held at The Country Club in Brookline, Massachusetts. At that dinner, directors of the National Shawmut Bank
and the Shawmut Association, Inc., spoke of Martin's outstanding leadership and achievements on an individual and im-
promptu basis, expressing their affection and praising Martin's
long and dedicated service. Finally, at the conclusion of the
testimonial dinner, the officers and directors of the Bank presented the retiring chief executive officer with the paintings
that had hung in his office at the 40 Water Street headquarters
of the Bank and Corporation.

Still a further mark of respect and appreciation was registered
shortly after, when the Board of Directors voted to establish
the Lawrence H. Martin Scholarship Program. The program,
which began in the fall of 1972, provided scholarship awards
of $1000 per year — subsequently raised to $2000 — for four
years to children of employees of any of the banks or other
affiliated organizations of the Shawmut Association, Inc. (Shawmut Corporation as of 1975), who planned to enter a college
or postsecondary educational program following graduation
from a secondary school. A scholarship committee comprised
of directors of Shawmut Association, Inc., selects one winner
each year, chosen on the basis of high school achievement in

academic work and extracurricular activities. The scholarship program was a fitting tribute to Martin's service to the Bank and the Association and also recognized his intimate involvement in promoting social welfare through both his business and civic activities.

Even a decade after his retirement, Lawrence H. Martin is remembered by his colleagues as a man with an intimate knowledge of the commercial banking business, exceptional personal integrity, respect for fellow associates at all levels, and a deeply ingrained ethical consciousness. As one colleague recalled, "He was perceived by our clients and the public as a banker of great knowledge and an individual of great character."

Chapter 14

The Seventies
The Administration of D. Thomas Trigg
(1972–1980)

On June 1, 1972, D. Thomas Trigg became chief executive officer of the Shawmut Association, Inc., and the National Shawmut Bank. His appointment coincided with that moment in history when the country began to undergo radical economic changes that affected not only the Shawmut but all banks for the remainder of the decade.

Since the close of World War II, the national economy had experienced a time of accelerating expansion. Although there had been brief periods of decline, these were little more than cyclical pauses, rest stops preceding upward surges. The basic assumption influencing business decisions was that production would and could continue to expand, and events between 1948 and 1972 had generally proved the assumption correct. By the latter date, however, conditions were beginning to change. The idea that the globe was a finite place, that resources could be depleted, that markets could be sated, and that uncontrolled and automatic growth was not necessarily either a predestined or unalloyed good introduced a whole new set of problems for those charged with managing the economy. The Arab oil crisis of 1973 underscored and made concrete what many economists had already foreseen: the world's economy had changed and many countries, even the ostensibly richest, could be held hostage to the whim of a few.

For the nation's banks these changes meant that a host of activities undertaken in the past on the assumption of continued expansion suddenly became at best a luxury, at worst a drain. They also brought to the fore a long-unacknowledged, but very real, transformation in the nature of banking itself.

This transformation had been a long time in the making, and by the early 1970s, it was clearly evident. As certificates of deposit gained increasing popularity and other high-interest alternatives such as money market mutual funds appeared, demand deposits dwindled. Banks had to turn more and more to purchased funds as the basis for their loans. Suddenly "rate spread" became the key to earnings. Asset and liability management became the task of the day. Burgeoning electronic technology made it all possible.

The economic crunch of the mid-1970s gave all of these factors new importance; they became the foundation on which bank policies must be formulated. Previously, at least in the public's eye, banks were still primarily the repositories of other people's money, institutions apart from the hurly-burly of the market, places where conservatism, caution, and concern for security shaped decisions from investments to personnel. Confronted with economic crisis, however, most bankers realized their institutions could no longer afford the luxury of such an image. New stress was placed on marketing bank products and services.

This was the world to which D. Thomas Trigg became heir. It was a time of rapidly shifting conditions that to a large extent shaped what the new administration could and could not do. At the beginning of the period, inflation nibbled relentlessly at bank earnings; in mid-decade recession set in while inflation continued, and although by the end of the decade the economy had recovered, the continuous expansion of the past had come to an end, and yesterday's assumptions could no longer be counted on. It was a time of daily crises and constantly shifting priorities that demanded from those charged with managing the community's money an ability to define, analyze, and respond quickly to problems and at the same time show discipline and consistency of commitment. The Shawmut, however, was fortunate in its choice of a leader, for D. Thomas Trigg's natural style embodied all of these qualities.

1

D. Thomas Trigg's training for the tense times that would be
his lot as chairman and chief executive officer of Shawmut Association, Inc., can be traced to his early adulthood. Born June
30, 1915, in Eureka, Kansas, Trigg reached college age at just
that dark point in the country's history when many bright young
men were deciding that the sacrifices required for a higher
education were hardly worthwhile. Even as a young man, however, Trigg demonstrated the kind of unswerving commitment
to clearly defined goals that became the hallmark of his later
managerial skills. In the fall of 1933, determined to get an
education, he enrolled in the College of Emporia, where a term
scholarship helped defray the cost of tuition. In 1934 he transferred to Washburn College in expectation of a job. When this
was not forthcoming, he moved to the University of Kansas,
where he held three jobs in addition to being a student. By
this point, young Trigg was aware that his bent was for business,
and in the spring of 1936, encouraged by his family, he moved
East to enroll at Babson Institute in Wellesley, Massachusetts.

Although the times were hardly propitious for those considering careers in business, Trigg had no sooner graduated in March
1937 than he managed to secure a position as a credit investiga-
tor with Shawmut's affiliate, the Devonshire Financial Service
Corporation in Portland, Maine. Here the new man rapidly
proved himself, and in the next few years he held a series of
increasingly responsible positions within the Shawmut structure.

In 1938 Trigg moved to Hartford as assistant manager, there
to broaden his experience. The following year he returned to
Portland as assistant manager of that office and soon became
its manager. In 1942 the opportunity to join the Boston Bank
presented itself. Although the job, statement analyst, was not
as exalted as that of manager of DFSC's largest branch office,
the new position offered greater opportunity for advancement.
Trigg accepted the post and was quickly promoted to credit
analyst.

The new job was the beginning of a happy alliance inter-
rupted by only a brief two years: in 1944 Trigg served in the
U.S. Naval Reserve and was discharged as a lieutenant, jg, in

1946. He returned to the Shawmut, where Lawrence Martin, then vice president of Credit, appointed him manager of the Credit Department. Together the two men revived an operation that had been sorely eroded by both the Great Depression and the war.

Trigg's training — lending money — was the heart of banking, and he remained in that part of the business in positions of increasing responsibility that included assistant cashier, 1949, assistant vice president, 1950, vice president, 1954, senior vice president in charge of the Banking Division, 1960, and executive vice president, 1966. He was also appointed a director of the Bank in 1962, and that same year became a trustee of Shawmut Association. In 1964, when Shawmut Association, Inc., was created, Trigg served as an incorporator, becoming also a director, vice president, and member of the Executive Committee.

During these years D. Thomas Trigg was also establishing his visibility in the community. In the 1940s he was appointed an instructor at the American Institute of Banking. He served as governor of the Boston chapter from 1954 to 1956 and as a member of its advisory committee from 1972 to 1980. He also became a participant in Robert Morris Associates, a credit organization of which Shawmut's own vice president, Norman I. Adams, was a founder. Elected president of the New England chapter in 1956 and national director in 1966, Trigg received that national organization's highest honor in 1971 — the Distinguished Service Award, which is bestowed only on those whose contributions have been outstanding. He was also a member of the Association of Reserve City Bankers, where he served as a director and chairman of two major committees — the Committee on Membership and the Credit Policy Committee. Still two other financial organizations in which he played a role were the American Bankers Association and the International Monetary Conference, which he joined in 1972. Trigg's interests, however, were not limited to banking. His broad participation in community affairs touched most of the major aspects of life in Boston.

In 1966 Trigg became a member of the corporation of Northeastern University. Six years later he was appointed a Northeastern trustee and assumed a host of important committee assignments, becoming also treasurer of the corporation. (This title became vice chairman, finance, in 1979.) Trigg was also a direc-

tor and member of investment committees of Liberty Mutual
Insurance Company, Liberty Mutual Fire Insurance Company,
and Liberty Life Assurance Company of Boston and a director
of JOBs for Massachusetts. Additionally, he was an overseer
of the Boston Symphony Orchestra, a corporator of Babson
College and the Museum of Science, a vice president of the
Greater Boston Chamber of Commerce, a trustee of University
Hospital, and a director of the Greater Boston YMCA. It was
in recognition of his leadership in all these endeavors that the
Institute of Human Relations of the American Jewish Committee honored him with a testimonial dinner "to salute a leader
who has earned distinction for his achievements in professional
life and for his exemplary response to the educational, cultural
and humanitarian needs within the Boston community." He
was the first New Englander so honored, joining such luminaries
as Dwight D. Eisenhower and David Rockefeller.

All this, however, is to anticipate. In 1968, with a long record
of achievement already behind him, Trigg became president
of the National Shawmut Bank. By this time banking conditions
had already changed. Competition, volume, services, and development of time money — all underscored by profit-margin
squeeze — made it evident that a bank, as Trigg himself would
say, "is a business to be run as well as an intermediary for
attracting funds and investing them." His objectives as president were explicitly defined "to make management objectives
clear . . . to create a basic climate to bring the best out of
people." The success of these efforts and the accomplishments
of those years between 1968 and 1972 have been recorded in
the previous chapter. Among the highlights of the four-year
period were a rise in assets from $1 billion to $1.4 billion,
including a 50 percent increase in loans, participation in the
founding of Atlantic International Bank, Ltd., and establishment of a number of corporate-wide enterprises, including the
introduction of Master Charge. That the Bank had flourished
under Trigg's management was undeniable; in fact, 1971, Martin's banner year, must be seen as Trigg's as well. It came as
a surprise to no one, then, when Martin announced in January
1972 that, as of June, Trigg would assume the added responsibility of chief executive officer. Said Martin of Trigg, "His banking knowledge and long experience, and his participation in

senior management since 1957, equip him admirably to meet the requirements of leadership in the years to come."

2

The first eighteen months of Trigg's administration — summer 1972 through 1973 — were months of transition. Certainly it was a time of transition for the Shawmut as the administration changed from that of Lawrence H. Martin to that of D. Thomas Trigg. Even more important, it was a year of transition for the national economy.

At the Shawmut, the change was effected easily and without incident. In January 1972, at the same time that Martin announced the Board of Directors' approval of Trigg as his successor, he also announced approval of several organizational changes and new appointments. These included the promotion of Paul G. Black, Carroll Fossett, and John S. Sullivan to the executive vice-presidential level. Black was to direct a regrouping of line divisions, including Banking, International, Real Estate, City, and Trust. Fossett was to administer a group of central staff divisions including Fiscal Control, Market Research Development and Public Affairs, and Property Management. Sullivan took charge of the administrative area where two newly designed divisions — Mutual Funds Agency and Electronic Data Processing — had recently been formed.

To fill the vacancies created by these promotions still other officers were appointed. Philip H. See, Jr., became senior vice president, succeeding Black as officer in charge of the Banking Division; John T. Clifford became senior vice president, succeeding Fossett as officer in control of the Financial Control Division; and F. Thayer Sanderson, senior trust officer, was elected a senior vice president. Two final appointments were Edward E. Furash as senior vice president to head a new Market Research Division and Jozef van Vollenhoven as senior vice president in charge of the newly designated International Division.

These men worked in conjunction with vice chairman John K. Benson and senior vice presidents Warren S. Berg, Corporate Relations and Communications Division; Thomas J. Byrne, Mutual Funds Agency Division; Walter Chase, Personnel Division; David L. Currier, Real Estate Division, and Property Management; John J. Green, City Division; Clifford J. Kendall, Electronic Data Processing Division; and James G. Wilson, Bank Investment Division. Together they constituted a team of senior management that was already in place when Trigg took office. There was no need for the flurry of organizational changes that so often accompany the passing of power.

The transition between the two major officers at Shawmut was accomplished with ease, but no such ease accompanied the larger economic transition. From the vantage of hindsight, one can perceive that 1972–1973 was a watershed period, the apex of a quarter-century boom that culminated in the recovery of 1971 and the prelude to a time of contraction and new values that appeared with the recession of 1974–1975. To those living through the period, no such easy perception of conditions was available; in fact, economic signals were strangely mixed.

At the beginning of the period, January 1972, business was good and loan demand high. The economy continued at this pace into the summer of 1973, when business began to flag and loan demand to fall off. The fortunes of the nation's banks, however, did not closely mirror these conditions, as might have been expected. Instead, in spite of a rising GNP, bank earnings fell sharply during the first three quarters of 1972. This was the experience at Shawmut, where earnings fell slightly below those achieved during the first three quarters of 1971. To correct this an unusually low prime lending rate was increased, and earnings climbed to reach new heights by the end of 1972, allowing Shawmut directors to be optimistic for 1973. But despite their optimism, earnings were disappointing. Trigg commented in the annual report of 1973 that "for a considerable part of the year, the cost of marginal funds exceeded the average rates we were able to charge on commercial loans."

What he pointed out was that institution earnings were as closely tied to the fluctuations of money costs as they were to the fluctuations of business. Such costs, of course, had always been important, but it was not until the 1960s, when banks came to depend more and more on purchased funds, that this became a major factor in determining the profit to be derived from loans, and it was not until 1972–1973 that this dependency came into sharp focus.

Loans, 1972–1973

Initially Martin and (as of June 1972) Trigg responded to the high-demand, expensive-money conditions in a traditional manner. Thus both administrators put effort into expanding loans in the hope that volume would offset low yield.

Special energies went into the acquisition of commercial loans, and the effort was amply rewarded, as was attested in the annual report of 1972: "Our lending officers were successful in enlarging the volume of commercial loans. Much of this increase can be traced to new business relationships in the New England area."

Similar energies went into the development of international loans, and by the end of 1972, these had expanded some 67 percent over 1971. The growth was particularly significant in light of a drop in loans to Japanese banks from some $35 million to $22.5 million, which occurred as a consequence of a change in Japanese bank policies. The drop, however, was no reflection on Shawmut, which retained more of this business than did most peer banks.

Still another loan area that received new attention was Master Charge. Recognizing that increased volume was a requisite for better returns, the Shawmut aimed new marketing efforts at the special target group of young marrieds, the most active users of credit cards.

The growing volume of loans substantially contributed to Shawmut's good earning record in the last quarter of 1972, when the prime rate rose. The basic problem, however, remained: Bank business was increasingly dependent on purchased funds.

In November 1972 Trigg reported to the board that "borrowed funds as a percentage of total funds at the National Shawmut was only about 36 percent as contrasted with 38 percent for other Boston banks and 41 percent for New York banks." Nevertheless, the figure was high and left the Bank vulnerable. Shawmut was not quite as vulnerable as some others, for its policy was not to depend heavily on the national money market for federal funds. If this gave the Bank less latitude than some, the policy was still prudent and not without rewards, and as money became tighter, Shawmut continued to receive a good flow of funds from its established regional sources.

The vulnerability of banks to high money costs was brought to the fore in the summer of 1973, when loan demand began to drop. No longer could volume be relied on to offset low yield. At this point, Trigg, in conjunction with Paul G. Black, executive vice president, instituted a new policy of restraint, and on August 1 a program to control loan problems was introduced. The program included a restraint in offering long-term loans, and an attempt to hold maturity dates of new commercial loans to ninety days or fewer, while account profitability was carefully scrutinized with an eye to eliminating less profitable relationships. These latter two moves in particular can be seen as the first step toward a revised loan policy that Trigg had planned to initiate under any circumstances, but which conditions in 1973 made a top priority.

In the fall, as a part of this move to retrench, management further determined to place a limit on the expansion of assets relative to capital. Even before the recession struck in full force, Shawmut had begun to reef its sails.

Real Estate Investment Trusts

Before moving away from consideration of the loan picture as it began to emerge in 1972–1973, some attention should be paid to Real Estate Investment Trusts (REITs). A favorable change in the tax treatment of these trusts made them an attractive new investment opportunity, and by the summer of 1972, they had become quite popular. As potential borrowers, REITs made particularly interesting loan customers for banks, and some bank holding companies were even tempted to participate in their potential equity earnings by organizing and advising such trusts. However, Trigg and David L. Currier, senior vice president and head of the Shawmut Bank's Real Estate Division, were skeptical. Their skepticism was based in part on a reluc-

tance to participate through such a vehicle in a form of lending
that the Bank could do directly. They also recognized that the
trusts were established to pay out rather than retain earnings,
so debt would really be their source of funds. REITs had begun
to issue commercial paper backed by bank credit lines that they
claimed would not be used, always a questionable assertion.
In effect, REITs seemed to Trigg and Currier to be an unsound
device that would loose a horde of promoters with a new source
of money simply to make real estate investments in the hope
that the real estate would appreciate.

Not everyone agreed with their assessment, and conceding
to pressure, and in light of the fact that even a major New
York City bank had established its own REIT, Shawmut committed itself to a single $5 million loan in this area in September
1972. By 1974, when problems began to surface, it had a total
of some $14.1 million participation in five carefully selected
trusts. This commitment, however, was not nearly as large as
that made by other area banks, and the reservations Trigg expressed and implemented in regard to REITs must finally be
recognized as an important contribution to the stability of Shawmut. The significance of these reservations is further underscored when one recognizes that REIT-related losses incurred
by the nation's banks totaled over $15 billion dollars.

Deposits, 1972–1973

Closely related to the cost of money was the state of demand
deposits. In the 1960s, as business prospered and loan demand
increased, banks encountered increasing competition for deposits. Banks then developed certificates of deposit and other related interest-paying vehicles as competitive products to retain
old customers and attract new depositors. These certificates
were particularly appealing to commercial clients and affluent
individuals who had the thousands of dollars needed to participate and who looked to time savings as an investment more
appropriate to their needs than simple checking accounts. Such
deposits provided funds that a bank could lend, but the interest
paid on them lowered the profit margin. To the degree these
deposits could be maintained, they were usually less expensive

than funds purchased in the Money Market. In the 1960s Shawmut, as well as its peer banks, began to offer these deposit
alternatives. Consequently, demand deposits decreased as a
percentage of the overall deposit structure.

In the early 1970s, as the cost of money and loan demand
went up, competitive pressure again emerged. One source of
this pressure was the introduction of Negotiable Order of Withdrawal (NOW) accounts by savings banks in New England. A
new alternative to commercial-bank checking accounts, these
offered interest at passbook rates, appealed to small, retail customers, and threatened once again to siphon off demand deposits. Commercial banks soon began offering comparable NOW
accounts. Although many bankers throughout New England
would have much preferred to avoid any more interest-bearing
deposit accounts, they could not afford to lose what they had,
and the competition began.

In October 1972 Trigg remarked to the Shawmut board what
many of his banking colleagues were thinking: "It appears that
in the present rate climate the most important impact on earnings will be obtained by marketing programs to obtain increased
deposit balances from existing customers." Only by such an
increase could Shawmut reduce its reliance on more expensive
purchased funds. Trigg's statement was accepted as a challenge
for those with responsibility for obtaining new balances, among
whom, for example, was Warren Berg, senior vice president
and director of Shawmut's Public Relations and Development
Division.

While other banks confronted with a similar challenge to
increase balances were resorting to giveaways — a new account,
a new frying pan — both Berg and Trigg deplored such huck-
sterism. In its place, Berg, working with Lawrence J. Lynch,
advertising officer, conceived the idea of offering a six-month
family membership in one of three Boston museums — the Museum of Science, the New England Aquarium, or the Museum
of Fine Arts — for a $100 deposit to a new or existing savings
account. The theme, "For $100 you deserve more than just
interest — Shawmut gives you fascination," caught the public's
imagination. The number of new museum memberships generated by this campaign exceeded all expectations. The program
was a successful promotion for both the Bank and the museums

and won for Shawmut the Bank Marketing Association's most prestigious honor, the Golden Coin Award for Excellence in Marketing.

The Bank's sense of responsibility to the cultural life of its community, which was implicit in this program, was further augmented the following year, when Shawmut pioneered the Matching Contributions Program. Through the program the National Shawmut matched "dollar for dollar" contributions made by employees to some sixty member organizations of the Metropolitan Cultural Alliance, which included performing arts groups, museums, adult education centers, and historical societies. It was the first time an American corporation attempted a program of this kind, and it opened a whole new area in individual and corporate giving, while doing much to enhance Shawmut's community relationships.

Other Income Earners

The high cost of money — with the attendant problems it elicited in terms of loans, deposits, and money purchases — and the slackening of business in late 1973 were not the only issues of this transition period. Indeed, as net earnings from loans dropped, the need to develop other income-producing resources rose proportionately, and during Trigg's first year and a half, Shawmut became particularly active in these areas.

New Subsidiaries. At the time that Trigg became chief executive officer in June 1972, Shawmut Association, Inc., had only one wholly owned subsidiary in operation. This was Shawmut Financial Corporation, founded in 1969 to sell commercial paper, the proceeds of which were available to the Corporation and its subsidiaries. Recognizing that tight money mandated a new emphasis on such income sources, Trigg supported the addition of more subsidiaries that would diversify the Corporation's earning base. He began with Shawmut Securities Clearance Corporation, which was designed to handle all types of securities transactions for the National Shawmut Bank as well as its correspondent bank customers. It began operation in October 1972 with offices in New York City and Boston.

The policy of diversifying the corporate earnings base continued into 1973, and that year saw the introduction of still three additional subsidiaries. The first of these, the Shawmut Credit Corporation (SCC), began in July 1973 with offices at 82 Devonshire Street, Boston, and 25 Broad Street, New York City. Its function was to engage in commercial finance and related activities. In this role, SCC was closely related to the commercial lending activities of all Shawmut Association, Inc., banks. The second new bank-related activity in 1973 was Shawmut-Milberg Factors, a joint-venture company owned in equal portions by Shawmut Association, Inc., and Milberg Factors, Inc., New York, and designed to assist corporate clients in managing cash flows by purchasing their accounts receivable without recourse.

During this year, plans were also set in motion to establish American Cattle and Crop Services, Inc. The organization, which assisted in meeting the financial needs of agricultural industries, was owned in conjunction with Fort Worth National Corporation and came under the supervision of the National Shawmut Bank's International Division. Federal regulators had never before allowed two bank holding companies (as opposed to two banks) to form such a joint venture. Nevertheless, their approval was forthcoming, and in 1974 American Cattle and Crop Services (later renamed American AgCredit) went into operation. Ultimately it, as well as Shawmut Securities Clearance Corporation and Shawmut Credit Corporation, became well-established earners. Shawmut-Milberg Factors, however, remained active for only a brief time.

All of these nonbanking affiliates were Corporation rather than specifically National Shawmut Bank operations. Their effect on the latter, however, in terms of keeping business within the family, developing potential customers for the Bank, and broadening the scope of its available services should not be minimized. Similarly, the diversification and expansion of specific National Shawmut Bank activities served to broaden the financial services and geographic scope of the Corporation, with the result that two National Shawmut Bank operations, both of which were important in the area of international banking, also saw expansion during 1972–1973.

First, in 1972 Shawmut International Corporation, a wholly owned Bank subsidiary since being founded in 1966, expanded its interests, making a $200,000 equity investment in Private

Investment Company for Asia, a multinational investment company designed to promote Asian development. The amount involved was minimal, but to the extent the expansion helped Shawmut establish a foothold in the increasingly active Far East financial market, it is significant.

Even more important was National Shawmut's increased participation in Atlantic International Bank, Ltd. In 1969 Trigg had taken an active role in the development of Atlantic, and this venture provided access to European markets. (See Chapter 13.) He was well aware of the importance of the organization, and when opportunities to increase Shawmut's shares arose in 1973, Trigg supported the increased participation.

Investments Portfolio. As loan earnings highlighted the need for the development of subsidiaries, so also they highlighted the need for greater development of the Shawmut's investment portfolio. During 1972 the Bank's investment portfolio went up by some $20 million, but 1973 was not quite so productive. In November, as a result of a sale by the Japanese of U.S. Treasury bills to support the yen, the rates on Treasury bills rose, the bond market fell, and Shawmut experienced substantial depreciation of its investment portfolio.

Corporation Development, 1972–1973

Against the background of changing national economic conditions and the fluctuating earnings of the Corporation and Bank, the new chief executive officer moved to implement his plan for a more closely unified corporation. It was with this end in mind that he supported the first organizational change of his administration.

Organization Changes. In 1972 the Methods Department was redesigned as the General Systems Department with the officer in charge of that function reporting directly to the senior officer in charge of the Electronic Data Processing Division. This latter Division was also restructured to allow the senior Electronic Data Processing officer to concentrate his efforts on systems and related functions.

The reorganization allowed for the development and maintenance of reliable, responsive, and efficient systems throughout the Bank and its sister banks in the Shawmut Association. Under the new charter, the General Systems Department was responsible for developing systems concepts which considered the totality of banking and Association needs, including management and marketing information and efficiency of operations. Its staff was charged with taking the broadest and most professional view of systems projects, with full appreciation of the capabilities of not only computer-based systems but also organizational needs of the Shawmut Association. The Electronic Data Processing officer and his immediate staff focused on the development and maintenance of computer-based operations, control and information systems, while the entire Division was charged with developing, as part of the Association's long-range planning program, a supporting plan for maximum efficient computer service.

Without question the reorganization was an important step in tightening the entire corporate structure, although as a result of increased computerization, and much to the dismay of some older customers, the traditional savings bank passbooks were retired in favor of a single computerized monthly statement.

But the new method vastly improved operations and created still another tie between the affiliated banks and the National Shawmut, which provided the computer service. In the course of the following years these ties were further augmented as the National Shawmut extended the scope of its services to affiliated banks.

Officer Mobility

It was also during 1972–1973 that a corporate policy of extending the services of officers of the National Shawmut, the flagship bank, to the community banks began to gain momentum. One of the first officers to participate in this program of horizontal mobility was Robert Hussey, who in January 1972 resigned as vice president of the National Shawmut Bank to become president of Merchants-Warren National Bank of Salem; in 1975 he moved on to the presidency of Shawmut Community Bank in Framingham.

The precedent that this established continued throughout the Trigg years, with some officers moving outward from the

Boston headquarters into community banks, others coming
from the community banks into Boston, and still others moving
laterally within the community banks. It was a movement that
would increase as part of a policy to reinforce the relationship
between all of the banks in the Corporation. This interlock
was given further substance by Paul A. Miller, who made systematic visits to board of directors' meetings of the various community banks. As controller of Shawmut Association, Inc., and
Shawmut Bank of Boston, Miller was able to explain and clarify
the relationship between the National Shawmut and the community banks, and his visits did a great deal to promote understanding.

Personnel Developments

Still another area on which Trigg focused was personnel. During
1972 and 1973 training and Affirmative Action programs, which
had been initiated under Martin, were further expanded; medical and pension plans were improved; and provisions for early
retirement were liberalized. In addition to normal merit increases, salary range was also increased. Finally, convinced that
"socializing off the job stimulates cooperation and loyalty on
the job," the administration sponsored a family outing in September 1972. The outing, held in a nearby amusement park,
attracted some five thousand. It was the first of several such
affairs held during the Trigg years.

The first eighteen months of Trigg's administration made
clear that his priorities as chief executive officer of the entire
Association were substantially the same as those he had articulated on becoming president of National Shawmut. But as economic conditions deteriorated nationwide in the mid-1970s,
these priorities were increasingly tested.

3

Confronting the fluctuating economy of 1972 through mid-
1973, Trigg had maintained a restrained posture, attempting
to implement wherever possible policies that would strengthen

the Corporation and prepare all of the banks to meet an uncertain future. How very uncertain that future was, however, did not become clear until the fall of 1973, when the Arab oil crisis stunned the world. If inflation and rising money costs had been a constant worry, now the sudden jump in oil costs sent all prices rocketing and the interest-rate spread tightened again. At the December 20 meeting of the directors of the National Shawmut it was frankly asserted that there could be no forecast of earnings "because of the recent increase in rates arising since the outbreak of the energy crisis." As a consequence, 1973 ended on a note of wait and see. No one, however, was optimistic for the future.

"The performance of the United States economy during 1974 was extremely disappointing," reads the opening sentence of the Federal Reserve annual report of 1975, summarizing the previous twelve months. The statement was a masterpiece of restraint. The abandonment of wage and price controls in the spring, and an excess of demand in relation to supply brought inflation to a record peak. At the same time productivity and employment were down, and year-end figures showed a sharp decline in the GNP.

The situation was unusual — recession and inflation do not generally go hand in hand — but the gap between demand and production was all too explicable. At the top of the list of causes stood the oil embargo and the high cost of petroleum. A close second was a shortage of industrial material that, in its turn, could be attributed to a growth in export demands and devaluation of the dollar, and finally, there was the unfortunate tendency on the part of many to buy hastily before prices rose further.

In toto, 1974 was unquestionably a year of hardship, and 1975 was little better. It was not until 1976 that the Federal Reserve could report some upturn in an economy "that has only begun to recover from the deepest and longest recession since the 1930s." While this was generally true, the impact was even more severe in New England.

Problem Areas, 1974–1976

The Federal Reserve Board's summary of conditions was by its nature quite general and almost casual. It was simply another recounting of the cyclical trends that exist in the economy of any country. For the institutions and the persons whose experience contributed to such abstract assessment, however, and whose survival depended on responding to such conditions, the situation was anything but casual. For Shawmut this "deepest and longest recession" meant years of intense efforts to keep the institution on its course. Yet despite the problems, there was no break in continuity and no mere maintenance of the status quo.

Trigg's entire career had been with the Shawmut and this experience had given him not only a deep commitment to the institution but a clear image of its distinctive competencies and an understanding of what risks it was appropriate to take in light of Shawmut's history and future. As difficulties grew the administration focused its attention less on short-term results than on the long-term health of the Corporation, on the development of structures and policies that would in the long run enhance its corporate wealth — not only its financial assets but its human assets.

Loans 1974–1976. As 1974 opened, problems begun in 1973 gained momentum, with inflation and recession vying for center stage. Throughout the 1960s and early 1970s, inflation had taken its toll on business and industry; by 1974 the effects became devastating. The rise in oil prices meant a general increase in energy costs, quickly followed by new wage and price demands. Many firms that had borrowed in the 1960s and early 1970s in confident expectation of balanced growth, now found themselves faced with operating expenses that precluded any chance of profit. Businesses with long records of achievement as well as those with lesser credentials were equally vulnerable. Companies that managed to survive did so with little confidence in the future. Unfortunately it was a pessimism all too often substantiated. Again Shawmut had to resort to purchased funds, but the uncertainty of business conditions increased the risk factor. Responding to these conditions, Trigg reenforced his loan-review policy to keep the Bank abreast of problem areas, making reviews more frequent and intensive. Such reviews came to embody a strict classification system, which took into account a variety of factors and crystalized the Bank's understanding that many loans were long-term investments, providing debt capital rather than just working capital.

In addition to what these reviews revealed about the individual accounts, they made clear that, although Shawmut had not made the mistake of concentrating in any specific industrial group, it had an exceptionally high percentage of New England credits. A letter to the Corporation shareholders sent December 31, 1975, stated that approximately 75 percent of commercial loans were made to local companies. While this was an appropriate position for an organization traditionally dedicated to serving its community, it was an unfortunate position during the recession of 1974–1976, for nowhere were business failures more surely and bitterly felt than in oil-dependent New England. But if the situation was bad, Trigg insisted that it be boldly confronted and dealt with.

In the Corporation's 1974 annual report he articulated what he perceived, his response, and its effect: "Because of the uncertainties in the economy, management followed a policy in 1974 of restraining growth. At the end of 1974, total assets were $66 million less than the previous year-end, and loans increased less than 1 percent in spite of heavy credit demand." Of all the affiliated banks, National Shawmut experienced the most severe drop in assets. The following year the loan portfolio of all the banks controlled by the Corporation, including the National Shawmut Bank, was substantially reduced, with average commercial loans down by some $100 million. Foreign loans were also cut back, so that by the end of 1975 they represented less than 4 percent of gross outstanding loans. Consumer loans, however, did increase throughout the Corporation.

During this period, according to the 1974 annual report, the loans on the books were more carefully scrutinized: "Where collection possibilities were remote, particularly in light of existing uncertain circumstances . . . such loans were charged off as soon as they were identified." By January 1974, the ratio of classified loans (loans of questionable quality) to capital had climbed to 17.5 percent. According to Trigg this "did not represent just a diminution of the quality of loan accounts but was indicative also of a tightening up by examining authorities in the current economic climate."

The systematic write-off of loans required a correspondingly substantial increase in the reserves set aside for potential loan losses. Accounting rules regarding the treatment of loan-loss reserves had been revised in 1969. The revised rules required that such reserves could only be established through charges against current earnings. The recommended formula for determining appropriate loan-loss reserves was based on a five-year loan-loss average. Shawmut, like many other banks and bank holding companies, had experienced light losses in the late 1960s and early 1970s. Accordingly, Shawmut set aside the recommended provision, but it was not sufficient to cover the credit losses caused by the adverse economic conditions of the mid-1970s.

Shawmut Corporation realized this, and in late 1975 made a substantial addition to the loan-loss reserve. Coming all at once, this substantial increase had a drastic impact on earnings reported for 1975. Most of this provision was made in the fourth quarter alone, creating a $5,764,000 operating loss for that period. The loan-loss provision for the year was $22 million, compared to only $13 million in 1974. Write-offs for 1975 were $16 million, compared to $14.7 million in 1974. Both figures were unusually high due to the severity of the current recession. Other banks and bank holding companies faced similar difficulties but did not take the drastic step Trigg adopted for Shawmut. One result of the loan losses and the necessary increase in loan-loss reserves was a reduction in the dividend payable by Shawmut Bank of Boston to Shawmut Corporation, which in turn reduced its quarterly dividend to the shareholders from seventy-five cents to forty cents per share effective January 2, 1976.

Subsequent worsening credit conditions proved Shawmut's action in increasing the loan-loss reserve had been appropriate. Furthermore, the loan losses sustained by many banks and bank holding companies during this recession showed that the 1969 accounting rule, which established the five-year formula for determining the adequate level of loan-loss provisions, was not satisfactory, and it was eliminated in 1976.

One Federal Street. Still another problem was Shawmut's new home at One Federal Street. In June 1974 the building was "topped off," and the task of finishing up began. Although in the beginning construction had proceeded on or even ahead of schedule, a shortage of steel, a strike in the construction industry, and tests for glass strength contributed to increasing delays and rising costs. Equally worrisome was the task of filling the new building once it was completed. In the late 1960s and early 1970s, when real estate was booming, no one had anticipated a significant problem in finding tenants. A substantial drop in that market by 1974 left Shawmut officials anxiously seeking tenants to occupy space not filled by the Bank.

The One Federal Street cash flow took its toll on Shawmut's operating expenses. To finance the new building, the Bank had formed a joint venture company with Prudential Insurance Company. Initially both organizations operated through wholly owned subsidiary organizations: One Federal Street Corporation and Prudential Investment Company Realty. In the course of years, the joint venture was periodically reorganized in the interest of greater convenience and efficiency. These changes, however, are less relevant here than the losses that the Corporation had to sustain. Although many of these losses were anticipated and even budgeted for, Shawmut still had to bear a heavy financial burden as a consequence of its move, and its operating earnings suffered.

Countermeasures, 1974–1976

The strengthening of loan review procedures, the curtailment of commercial and foreign loans to reduce Shawmut's need for borrowing, and the building up of loan-loss reserves were three ways in which the management under Trigg attempted to stem earnings attrition. Other moves to increase the profitability included organizational changes, a new stress on marketing operations, completion of a corporate identification program, improved customer services, containment of operating expenses, and reorganization of the investment portfolio to the extent possible given the limits of the tax situation.

Changes in Personnel and Organization. To strengthen the organizational structure of the Corporation and provide Trigg with greater administrative assistance, the Board of Directors of the National Shawmut elected a new Bank president, Paul S. Black, in July 1974. At the same time Logan Clarke, Jr., was elected a director of the Corporation, and on January 13, 1975, with the retirement of John K. Benson, he became its president.

Black had been with Shawmut twenty-eight years. A graduate of Harvard College with an M.B.A. from Harvard's Graduate School of Business Administration, he came to Shawmut in 1945 as a loan and credit officer. He was elected assistant vice president in 1954 and vice president in 1957. In 1963 he became the officer in charge of Shawmut's Banking Division. In 1969 he was appointed a senior vice president and in 1972 executive vice president and director.

Black's extensive knowledge of the Bank and its affiliates, and particularly his reputation as an astute loan and credit officer, made him well suited to assume Shawmut's presidency at this time. His skill with loan and credit operations was most useful in helping him direct and implement new procedures. In early 1976, Black resigned as president and accepted appointment as vice chairman of the Bank's Board of Directors, a position he retained until January 1977 when he left the Shawmut. In the meantime, on February 5, 1976, Shawmut Corporation president Logan Clarke, Jr., assumed the additional duties of president of Shawmut Bank of Boston, N.A.

Logan Clarke, Jr., was a native of Atlanta, Georgia, and a graduate of the University of Pennsylvania. He had joined the National Shawmut in 1952, was named assistant vice president in 1955, and vice president in 1958. In 1970 he was transferred within the umbrella of the Shawmut Association, Inc., to County Bank, N.A. Here he was elected executive vice president and chief loan officer, becoming that bank's president in 1971.

Shortly after Clarke became the National Shawmut Bank president, William F. Craig was appointed executive vice president. Craig was a graduate of Villanova, B.S. in Economics 1953, and had received his M.B.A. from Drexel University in 1959. He came to Shawmut from a fifteen-year career at Irving Trust in New York, where he headed the Minerals and Energy Division and was deputy division head of Irving Trust's National Division. His appointment to Shawmut was fortuitous: his keen perceptions and fresh point of view were instrumental in helping the Bank recover from the effects of the recession.

New committees and new committee assignments also emerged during this crucial period. There was, for example, a change in the duties of the Executive Committee of the Board of Directors. Traditionally this Committee had reviewed all loans that were considered substantial. In June 1974, however, Trigg, responding to a recommendation from Black, who would shortly become president, instituted a system to rank loans in accordance with their viability. At the same time he recommended establishment of a credit committee composed of senior Bank officers who would help implement this procedure and who were specifically charged with the review and approval of all loans and lines of credit in excess of $2 million. The new Senior Credit Committee became operational in 1977. At this time, the responsibilities of the Executive Committee of the Board of Directors of the Shawmut Bank of Boston, N.A., were changed to make it a policy-making committee.

The following year, on December 21, 1978, still another new committee, the Committee on Compensation of the Board of Directors of the Bank, was also established, and the functions of the Bank board's Audit Committee were considerably broadened. The effect of both changes was to give the board more input into crucial financial operations.

Expansion of Marketing. During the 1960s, marketing became an increasingly important aspect of bank business. Institutions realized that they had to get out and sell their services to remain competitive and that such selling required more than business development, participation in community affairs, and advertising. All of these latter areas, which were part of Development and Public Relations at Shawmut, experienced a qualitative leap forward when Warren S. Berg, then vice president and later senior vice president, assumed their direction in 1965. In 1967 Edward Furash, who had worked with the Bank on an assignment for Arthur D. Little, Inc., in market research, joined Shawmut to implement new concepts of market research.

In January 1972, a new Market Research Division was established, and Furash was designated a senior vice president. Helping him in the development of this area was Kay Mazuy, who is credited with bringing state-of-the-art marketing to Shawmut, and who, in recognition of this contribution, became Shawmut's first woman senior vice president in 1973. Mazuy's efforts were largely responsible for shaping the Market Research Division's first major project, the Corporate Identification Program. Her influence did much to determine the particular form of the program, including the Shawmut graphics that are now so familiar. Marketing also played an important role in the pricing and packaging of NOW accounts and in the introduction of automated teller machines.

The Corporate Identification Program. In April 1975, a long and carefully planned program to give the Corporation a new and unified image was presented to the public. The object of the program was twofold: to increase the visibility of Shawmut's 121-office banking system and to increase cost efficiency through "standardization of both financial product lines offered to our customers and the operating procedures followed by the banks affiliated in the Corporation."

In effect, the program meant that from April 1975 on, the consumer could tell a Shawmut operation by the presence of a blue and white Indian image on all Shawmut forms, stationery, and advertising and by the inclusion of the Shawmut name as the prefix in the title of each affiliated bank and wholly owned subsidiary. At this time, National Shawmut Bank of Boston became Shawmut Bank of Boston, N.A. (See Chapter 19.) The eight other affiliated banks added the family name Shawmut in their new titles. They also adopted the new blue logo containing the familiar Shawmut Indian head and converted their signs accordingly.

Clarity, simplicity, and standardization were the essence of the new program. They were qualities that allowed Shawmut to realize a far better return on its advertising and communications investments. In short order the blue Obbatinewat became a regional landmark.

Improved Customer Service. Closely related to the desire to present a new unified corporate image, and thereby increase Shawmut's profitability and visibility, was the ongoing desire to improve all aspects of customer service. In a letter to all staff members dated December 4, 1975, Trigg announced a new goal, declaring that one way "to increase acceptable levels of profitability was by providing the best customer service attainable from any financial institution in this region." It was in the spirit of providing this service, and thus meeting competition, that the Corporation banks added the NOW accounts to the Shawmut Way Package in October 1974. In 1975 they also began to handle Individual Retirement Accounts, and by 1976 the Corporation began introducing automated teller machines, including three in the Shawmut Bank of Boston, N.A.

Expense Containment and Personnel Policies. Since the mid-1960s, when inflation first became a major issue nationwide, the problem of keeping overhead down and in reasonable relation to earnings was a prime concern of every business. The accelerating rise in wages and prices had been met by a variety of measures, including a federally imposed wage and price freeze that was eventually rescinded in the spring of 1973. Unfortunately, that same year the Arab oil crisis and subsequent rise in the price of petroleum helped to create an unusual situation in which low productivity and increased unemployment went hand in hand with a catapulting cost of living.

Within this framework the Corporation battled to keep a lid on costs. A stringent control program was stepped up in 1974, and for the first five months expenses rose only some 1 percent. Rising costs and the need for the Bank to remain competitive, however, made further cuts necessary. To achieve these, Shawmut adopted the Overhead Value Analysis Program (OVA) in 1975. This program provided a structured study of costs in relation to output and made recommendations of how these costs could be reduced.

In the fall of 1975 an outside team of advisors was called in to work with senior Bank officers in designing the overhead reduction program, and by early 1976, plans for such reductions were in place. In an organization such as the Corporation these plans focused almost exclusively on staff reductions, although the second phase included reduction of nonsalary expenses. Personnel cuts were to be based on a variety of factors, including level of performance and necessity of a particular job, with the actual decisions on who would be released to be made by division heads.

Although few questioned the need for overhead cuts or the

wisdom of a structured program to achieve such an end, the toll OVA took on personnel, even on those who stayed, should not be underestimated. Job security was traditionally an advantage of bank employment, and the OVA cutbacks undermined staff morale. Early in the year it was decided to make all the cuts within a single week. Even though this would mean higher severance costs, the immediate completion of OVA, it was felt, would minimize anxieties and return operations to normal as quickly as possible. Unfortunately the sheer number of layoffs within a restricted time span created a newsworthy item, which local papers picked up with avidity, if not accuracy. The headline of the *Boston Globe* of Friday, March 3, read 600 SAID TO FACE DISMISSAL BY BANK FIRM and the article went on to declare that major layoffs were unusual in banking, an industry which ranks employment security high among job benefits. Trigg's terse announcement that a more realistic figure was 350 did little to assuage fears.

As a consequence of OVA, 350 people were released by Shawmut Corporation in one week of March 1976. Of these, 160 were staff members of the Boston bank: 43 were officers, 47 were managerial staff, and 70 were clerical staff. The overall totals were far less than the 600 proclaimed by the *Globe,* but this did not reach the papers nor did any account of Shawmut's successful efforts to help relocate most of the officers and managerial personnel.

That OVA achieved its end by substantially reducing salary expenses is undeniable. In the 1976 financial review to Shawmut Corporation shareholders, Trigg commented on the final results of the program: "During the year a program to contain non-interest expense, including a reduction in staff levels was completed. Salaries decreased from 1975 by $2.1 million. This decrease, however, was partially offset by an increase in the pension expense of $.9 million."

While expense containment measures reduced and streamlined Shawmut's staff, it would be a serious mistake to think that such measures overshadowed or diminished the effectiveness of other personnel activities at this time. In fact it was during the recession years that Shawmut introduced flextime, an innovative concept that allowed employees a high degree of flexibility in determining their working hours. Installed in 1974 in three areas of the Bank, the plan was very much in keeping with Trigg's commitment to improving the spirit and enthusiasm with which employees undertook their daily tasks. Affirmative Action efforts were also refined with a three-person Affirmative Action Department established within the Personnel Division. Furthermore, while expense containment dictated some tightening of the belt, it by no means meant that the administration felt performance should go unrewarded. A new policy of merit raises was instituted which provided for a common review date, a predetermined Bank budget for merit increases, and a predetermined merit budget for divisions. Nineteen seventy-five also saw a comprehensive review of all compensation policies and practices, which served as a foundation for future salary and benefit changes.

One of the most valuable and highly regarded new personnel programs, however, was the in-house counseling service which was made available to all members of the Shawmut staff. Introduced in 1975, the program grew rapidly over the years, and under the direction of the Charles River Counseling Center and Community Care Systems, Inc., helped many Shawmut managers and supervisors with the interpersonal and psychological aspects of managerial responsibilities.

Investment Portfolio and Tax Issues. Still another measure that the Bank took to combat the effects of the recession was a revamping of its investment portfolio, a particularly necessary measure in light of new tax problems.

As Shawmut entered the recession, it held a relatively high proportion of state and municipal obligations. Some of the latter had been purchased with monies realized when Devonshire Financial Service Corporation was discontinued. At the time, the tax-exempt status of these obligations made them seem appropriate investments. As the years went by and the portfolio increased, some officers, including both Martin and Trigg, began to have reservations about their continued acquisition. In 1974 as the recession deepened, it became clear that these reservations had merit. By this time, particularly as the favorable tax attributes associated with the construction of the new One Federal Street headquarters building became available, investments generating taxable income had become preferable to tax-exempt state and municipal investments. Consequently,

Trigg began a deliberate policy to reduce such holdings. The effort culminated in a large sales program in the second quarter of 1975. Investments in municipal bonds were reduced by almost $31 million in 1975 and the proceeds from the sales were reinvested in assets generating taxable income.

During the entire recession the securities market remained weak, and in 1976, the Corporation further reviewed its holdings and sold off more state and municipal obligations in favor of U.S. Treasury obligations, which presented a more attractive investment alternative.

4

The years between 1973 and mid-1976 were among the most difficult that Shawmut had ever encountered. Speaking of them to a group of officers in 1980, Trigg said, "During the trying times of a few years ago what more than anything else kept the funds flowing to Shawmut was the Shawmut name and its reputation." He might well have added that it was also the determined effort on the part of staff and officers to continue developing certain traditionally successful policies and introducing new ideas that contributed to the Shawmut's recovery and expansion in the postrecession era.

Such recovery, of course, did not occur overnight, and much of late 1976, 1977, and early 1978 were devoted to resolving problems that had surfaced during the recession and to opening up areas that would be developed into the 1980s.

In general, as the national economy began to rally so did the fortunes of the Corporation and the Shawmut Bank of Boston. In 1976 Corporation earnings, before securities transactions, rose to $5.8 million, or $3.09 per share, compared to $1.5 million, or $0.81 per share, in 1975. By 1977 comparable figures were up to $7.7 million, or $4.12 per share, and in December 1978 income had reached $10.1 million, or $5.41 per share.

Contributing to this recovery were a variety of factors, both external and internal. Steady rises in employment and in the GNP, which had begun in 1976 and continued through 1979, were major elements in the expanding earnings of the entire Corporation. Even more important was the rise in interest rates, which dramatically improved loan yield. At the same time the institution of new administrative policies allowed the community banks and the Shawmut Bank of Boston to take advantage of improved conditions in the larger world. Top priorities of the postrecession years were expansion of the loan portfolio with high-quality credit relationships, improvement of the earning-assets mix to take advantage of higher rate opportunities, and refinement of the management structure to produce greater team effectiveness.

Loans and Deposits 1976–1978

In October 1976 William F. Craig reported to the Board of Directors on improvements to be made in loan business. They included moves to increase loan volume through national credits, initiation of a new loan officer training program, consideration of separating loan review functions from credit analysis, expansion of loan review functions to cover Commercial Finance, City Division and International Division, and formation of a clear and comprehensive lending policy. Further, marketing efforts resulted in the selection of certain industries as the focus for business development efforts. These included medical, broadcasting, fishing, finance, and utility companies. Within the Banking Division, the Equipment Financing and Leasing departments, disbanded in 1973 as part of recession cutbacks, were revived in 1977 to provide financing secured by equipment and machinery. Nineteen seventy-seven also saw the revival of brokers' loans, which had been allowed to decline through 1976 and which now rose again. In 1977 the Real Estate Division resumed first mortgage lending, which had been reduced during the recession.

By the end of 1976 these efforts had already begun to pay off. The second half of 1976 showed a year-end gain over 1975, and in 1977 average loans increased another $53 million over the 1976 average, to reach a total loan volume of $1.1 billion. By 1978 this figure stood at $1.3 billion. Simultaneously, the quality of loans improved, indicated by a decrease in the number and amount of nonaccrual loans and the decrease in the amount charged off. A great deal of credit for this improvement was attributable to the work of the Loan Review Committee under the direction of P. Clarke Dwyer.

As loan prospects grew brighter so also did the outlook for deposits. By the end of 1978, total Corporation deposits had reached $2 billion, compared with $1.9 billion in 1977 and $1.7 billion in 1976. While the figures suggest the degree to which the fortunes of the Corporation and the Bank were improving, it would be a mistake to assume that such improvement was simply an automatic response to the general upswing in the economy. The postrecession years of Trigg's administration were characterized by concerted efforts to improve performance at all levels. One dimension of the improvement was the restructuring of certain departments, the introduction of new ideas, and continued attempts to fill high-level positions with topflight personnel.

Reorganization

In 1976 the Bank Investment Division completed a major reorganization of investment and financial trading functions, and in the process "staffed up" a new department geared to the distribution of securities to New England area financial institutions and individuals.

This new Bond Dealer Department added capability in government and municipal securities trading personnel, and more important, several professional investment personnel who were knowledgeable in all fixed-income securities markets in which a bank is eligible to trade and underwrite. Correspondent and money market operations were also consolidated under a new person into the Money Management Department. In effect, all decisions — and their execution — concerning investment-oriented asset and liability management were now one area's responsibility, removing the separation that often existed between portfolio and liability management.

The Bank also created the Funds Management Committee, chaired by the manager of the Bank Investment Division. The committee was made up of key personnel whose responsibility

touched asset and liability decisions. Included were the chief
financial officer, the person in charge of wholesale banking (real
estate, commercial, and international), the officer in charge of
retail banking (branches and marketing), the president, and
the chairman of the board. The group was small enough to
be an effective decision-making force and included the two top
executives in order to ensure that its decisions were indeed
implemented. Meetings were held weekly to examine financial
results and projections and discuss current strategies as well
as long-term issues.

The following year, 1977, the Banking Division was also reorganized in the interest of better focusing its efforts; henceforth
that division consisted of five groups: National Northeast, National United States, New England Commercial, New England
Industries, and Correspondent Banking. A trainee program of
primarily M.B.A. holders was also stepped up.

Trust Operations

Throughout the recession Trust Division operations constituted
an important aspect of the Bank's business. Between 1972 and
the end of 1976 assets of the division increased 62 percent
and fee income increased by 43 percent. During this period
the executive management of the Bank consistently encouraged
a spirit of cooperation between the Banking and City divisions
and the Trust Division. The resultant flow of qualified referrals
from the officers of these divisions to the Trust Division contributed to the latter's growth rate, which more than matched
that of any other bank's comparable division in Boston during
these five years.

In November 1977 the Mutual Funds and Agency Division,
which had proved unprofitable, was merged into the Trust Division, and in 1979 a further reorganization consolidated all trust
functions of all the Corporation banks, except those of the
Shawmut First Bank and Trust Company, into the Trust Division of Shawmut Bank of Boston, under the direction of F.
Thayer Sanderson. This consolidation led to the ability to
establish business development offices in the growing suburban
banks to the north, west, and south of Boston. In the meantime,

the Mutual Fund Department was selected a custodian of the securities of a leading money market mutual fund, which added both to deposits and to service fee income.

An indication of the division's aggressive pursuit of business throughout the period and of its policies, which were based on the anticipation of business expansion rather than mere reaction, is suggested by the minutes for November 1977. At this time Sanderson noted that "the best stimulus for future growth is in the development of middle-market employee benefits." The division focused attention in this area and became a leading trustee of such programs in New England.

Electronic Data Processing Expansion

The immediate postrecession years also saw moves to further expand and update Electronic Data Processing, and at the same time the groundwork was laid for a new program, Customer Account Processing Services (CAPS).

Even before the recession was over, Trigg had recognized that the electronic data processing system, which since its introduction in the early 1960s had become increasingly important to banking, needed further expansion. So in 1975 the administration retained Arthur D. Little, Inc., to do an in-depth study of Shawmut's electronic data processing organization. One finding of this study was that its capability was "not sufficient to fully satisfy the needs of the Corporation." The study also revealed a substantial staffing problem. Ninety percent of the Electronic Data Processing Department's employees were concerned with maintenance, where 25 to 40 percent was a more normal figure. With these facts in mind Shawmut set about to improve its electronic services and several projects were initiated and came into operation in 1978. These included a mutual fund custody and shareholders systems and a new payroll and electronic funds transfer system.

In 1976 Trigg commissioned a separate, though related, study on automated teller machines, which resulted in the deployment of three prototypes at Shawmut Bank of Boston. Still a third study, of functional requirements, was conducted during 1977 to explore the possibility of developing a new customer account processing system. This system, popularly called CAPS (Customer Account Processing System), would represent state-of-the-art computer programming for banks and handle all deposit functions, consumer loans, mortgage loans, open-end credit, and central files information on all customer accounts and transactions. It would also feature a complex recall delivery, allowing the entry of transactions for execution at a later time, and have the ability to connect with all other systems currently in use. In place, CAPS would be the central brain of Shawmut's computer operations. Although CAPS would not be operative until the 1980s, its design at this time suggests that the world of the future had already begun.

Branching

Although the postrecession years were generally ones of expansion, there were certain cutbacks in the interest of greater streamlining and efficiency of operations. Realizing that the community banks in the suburbs were a better source of retail banking than city branches, Trigg supported a policy of rigorous evaluation of all branches. The idea of the study was that by focusing on returns rather than on the number of branches Shawmut could provide better service to customers. As a consequence five branches of the Shawmut Bank of Boston were closed between 1977 and 1980, and one was relocated. Meanwhile, four of the eighty-six branches in Shawmut's community banks were also closed in 1977 and 1978, although one new branch was opened in response to local need.

Other Postrecession Innovations

As the tempo of activities accelerated in the postrecession years, the Corporation responded with the introduction of several other new ideas and services designed to meet the demands of a new age. In 1976 Shawmut began an in-depth study of the burgeoning women's market, with a view to reexamining services and assessing new ways to advertise and deliver them. One innovative service introduced at the time was a job-posting program for nonofficer positions, designed to allow Bank personnel more mobility within the institution. Personnel also profited by the introduction of a new benefit plan: in May 1978 the Employees Thrift Plan was introduced as an alternative to the Profit Sharing and Savings Plan to which there had been no contribution for several years. Under the new plan the Bank matched 50 percent of employees' contributions up to 6 percent of salary. Money was then invested in four interest-bearing funds.

The period also saw concerted efforts to improve relationships between Shawmut and its general counsel. The introduction of new regulations with complex legal ramifications made such a move particularly significant.

While all of these moves in 1976, 1977, and early 1978 were instrumental in ensuring that, in Trigg's words, "Shawmut's light would glow ever more brightly," probably nothing was more important than the appointment of new personnel.

New Faces

In keeping with Trigg's ongoing concern to assure Shawmut had topflight management, three new appointments were made at the senior vice-presidential level in September 1977: Neal F. Finnegan, Banking Division, John J. LaCreta, International Division, and Paul A. Miller, Financial Control Division. Finally, in March 1978, Trigg reported to the Corporation and Shawmut Bank of Boston boards that, in light of his impending retirement, he had given considerable thought to the future of the organization. He concluded that the best interests of Shawmut required that a committee of directors be formed to determine his successor as chairman of the Corporation and the Shawmut Bank of Boston.

In June 1978, following the resignation of Logan Clarke, Jr., Trigg resumed the Shawmut Bank of Boston presidency temporarily, and in September the search committee returned their findings, unanimously recommending, with the full agreement of Trigg, that John P. LaWare become president of the Bank and Corporation. On September 28 LaWare was appointed a director on both boards, and on October 16 became the sixteenth president of the Shawmut Bank and the fourth president of the Shawmut Corporation.

5

John P. LaWare came to the Shawmut Bank of Boston, N.A., in 1978 with twenty-five years of broad-based major bank experience. In 1953 he launched this career when he enrolled in the management training program at Chemical Bank of New York. During the ensuing years he rose rapidly through a variety of positions to become senior vice president of both Chemical Bank and its parent holding company, Chemical New York Corporation. Under LaWare's leadership Chemical New York operated six banks in the state and six major nonbank subsidiaries, including a mortgage banking company and a consumer finance company, with offices in twenty-five states.

The depth of his experience made LaWare a particularly attractive candidate to become Trigg's successor, and for the next year and a half the two men worked together closely to assure Shawmut a bright future.

Planning

Essential to ensuring the future was a renewed emphasis on long-range planning. In the 1960s Martin introduced policies regarding long-range planning. When Trigg assumed office he continued and expanded them, pointing out at a meeting of officers in 1973 that "we must improve our planning . . . Because of our long range planning the individual will be able to see clearly the part that he or she can play in the success of the whole." During his administration he consistently placed emphasis on the need for such planning, and computer facilities were consequently employed toward this end. The recession, of course, had made it difficult either to project or achieve goals, but with the revival of the economy, with deregulation and uncertainties in the industry looming ahead, it became imperative to review Shawmut's position, where it hoped to go, and the means by which it would do so. Thus in November 1978, a task force for the entire Shawmut Corporation was established with a mission to set up a guide for the 1980s and articulate what Shawmut wanted to become five years hence.

Trigg and LaWare appointed members to this task force in November. Throughout December, it prepared background papers on five specific topics: corporate banking, retail banking, the regulatory environment, peer group banks, and the economic outlook for the five-year period, On January 8, 1979, the division heads of the Shawmut Bank of Boston and the presidents of the Corporation's banks convened on Goat Island, at Newport, Rhode Island, for the first in a series of discussions on long-range planning. The result of these initial efforts was a five-year plan, a synopsis of which was published in August 1979 for the directors and senior management. This synopsis alone was a comprehensive thirty-four-page document detailing the treatment and expectations of every division and department in the Shawmut Bank of Boston, and every subsidiary bank and organization. Called "Shawmut: Profit Planning for the Eighties," it came to be known as the "blue book" because of its Shawmut-blue cover.

The document was presented to the Board of Directors in September 1979, at which time Trigg reported that the plan had already had a tremendous impact in pulling the organization together. The new planning efforts indicated a faith in the future to which the growing business of the Corporation gave substance.

Loans, 1979–1980

Under LaWare's presidency, loan activities continued to expand. The consumer loan portfolio alone went up some 25 percent in 1979. This included a 30 percent rise in government guaranteed Higher Education Loan Plan (HELP) loans and a 25 percent rise in Master Charge balances. The latter expansion was effected by increasing credit limits for selected customers rather than by seeking out new customers. Auto loans also experienced substantial growth, as did home improvement loans.

In 1980 President Carter's anti-inflation policy asked that

banks keep their lending increases within 6 to 9 percent of the base achieved in December 1979. As a consequence projected goals for Shawmut's loan expansion that year had to be cut from 16 percent to 9 percent.

International Activities

The final year of the Trigg administration also saw continued expansion in the International Division. Traditionally the Bank was primarily interested in loans and bankers acceptances for financing international-trade transactions based in New England, as well as loans to foreign sovereignties and banks, rather than loans to private foreign corporations. Shawmut's policy in evaluating individual credits was based on amounts outstanding and commitments to borrowers in any given country, with a self-imposed ceiling on total exposure established from these data. Shawmut's investment policies abroad, in other words, were traditionally conservative. Although this conservative approach continued under LaWare, it was his feeling that loans to private corporations should not be disregarded, and in the minutes of September 1979 it was noted that the International Division "should have less dependence on sovereign risk lending."

Other postrecession expansion included plans for opening a branch of Atlantic International Bank in Hong Kong to increase business in the Far East. However, this did not happen. Instead, a distinct and separate entity was established called Atlantic Capital, Ltd., a Hong Kong deposit taking company. It was organized in March 1980 and opened for business in January of 1981. Shareholders were 40 percent Shawmut, 40 percent Manufacturers National Bank of Detroit, and 20 percent F. van Lanschot Bankiers, Holland. The facility functioned as a booking center for offshore loans approved in Boston, Detroit, and Holland. By June 1983 F. van Lanschot Bankiers had relinquished its holding, reducing the shareholders to Shawmut and Manufacturers National Bank of Detroit, each of which held 50 percent. The rationale behind Shawmut's participation was the recognition of its need for a presence in the Far East so that it might be close to China as that market developed. Still another plan for expansion during this period involved a major commitment by the Bank to increase its corporate business in foreign exchange. Thus in January 1979 it added substantially to its team of traders. As a consequence foreign exchange grew rapidly, and in the ensuing years showed greatly increased profit.

Compensation

Although the need to contain costs, particularly in light of inflation, remained a concern, 1978 through 1980 saw added compensation and benefits at all levels. In December 1978 the new Compensation Committee was appointed, and on the recommendation of management, it approved two incentive plans. The annual Senior Management Incentive Plan began in May 1979. The committee also started to develop a long-range executive incentive plan, which would be called the Performance Share Plan. The creation of these plans underscored how far Shawmut had moved from the constraints imposed by the recession. They expressed management's faith that business was picking up and that Shawmut could increase its share of the growing market.

New Directors. The final years of Trigg's administration were marked by a rapid recovery, not simply of the economy at large but the fortunes of the Shawmut. Such recovery was a credit to the administrative skills of the directors, officers, and staff of the Corporation and of the banks.

During the period, several new persons joined the ranks of directors. Following the policy of his predecessor, Trigg supported the appointment of strong community leaders who represented a wide variety of business expertise and interests. Between June 1, 1972 and July 1, 1980 fifteen persons were elected to the Corporation board and sixteen to the Shawmut Bank of Boston board.

6

On June 30, 1980, D. Thomas Trigg retired as chief executive officer and chairman of the Board of Directors of Shawmut

Corporation and Shawmut Bank of Boston, N.A. His retirement marked the completion of a forty-three-year career at Shawmut, the last eight as chairman. As has been amply demonstrated, these last years were not easy ones. The high cost of money, catapulting inflation, and uncertain conditions abroad were problems common to all financial institutions.

Compounding these general difficulties were other problems specific to Shawmut. These included too heavy a concentration in New England credits and an inefficient deployment of personnel. Furthermore, Shawmut's commitment to the One Federal Street building, which began during the boom years of the late 1960s and early 1970s became increasingly burdensome to manage as construction costs rose and the market for office rentals dropped in the mid-1970s.

Trigg confronted all of these problems with unflinching honesty, demonstrating a capacity for patience, prudence, and perseverence that ultimately guided the Corporation and the Bank farther along the path of growth. By 1979, the last full year of Trigg's administration, the momentum for future expansion was well established. Total Corporation assets reached a record $3.1 billion and would climb to $3.4 billion by the end of 1980. Earnings, which had bottomed out at $.81 per share in the dark year of 1975, were at $8.77 in 1979 and $9.30 in 1980 (pre-split shares).

Symbolic of Shawmut's solidity was One Federal Street. A triumph of modern architecture, soaring thirty-eight floors above Boston's financial district, by 1979 the building was 98 percent occupied and no longer a liability but a visible expression of Shawmut's triumph. Not the least of Trigg's accomplishments, however, was the formation of a strong senior management team. Thus when his term ended he was able to turn over to his successor an experienced and capable group of senior officers. At the executive vice-presidential level were William F. Craig, Paul A. Miller, and F. Thayer Sanderson. At the senior vice-presidential level were Neal F. Finnegan, Banking Division; John J. LaCreta, International Division; Richard A. Williams, Real Estate Division; John J. Green, City Division; Horace C. Sylvester, Bank Investment Division; Timothy J. Hansberry, Control and Services Division; Francis A. Smith, Information Systems and Bank Operations Division; Warren

S. Berg, Corporate Relations and Marketing Division; and Charles M. Bush, Personnel Division.

The presence of these talented men coupled with Trigg's recommendation that John P. LaWare succeed him in office and William F. Craig become president of Shawmut assured a strong future for Shawmut.

In 1972, when D. Thomas Trigg assumed chief executive status, he pledged to leave the Shawmut even stronger than he had found it. That he fulfilled this mission was warmly attested by the many who worked with him over the years. In April 1980 Asa S. Knowles, director, speaking for the Directors of Shawmut Corporation, extolled Trigg's leadership. The following month at the annual meeting of the Directors of the Shawmut Corporation banks, Leo M. Pistorino, Director, Shawmut County Bank, echoed this appreciation.

Then on June 12, 1980, on the occasion of Mr. Trigg's retirement as the chairman of the board and chief executive officer, directors Charles Avila and Sidney Stoneman, both of whom worked closely with Trigg for many years, expressed the sentiments of all the directors, stressing Trigg's leadership at Shawmut and in the community and the character that had made him a leader. Noting Trigg's long career at Shawmut, they spoke of "the many shining highlights" and of "his quiet courage and tenacity that have characterized his years in banking."

> In his forty-three years with Shawmut, Tom Trigg has earned the title of "banker" and is held in highest regard by his peers in the profession. We who are closer to him hold him in the highest esteem, not only for his banking ability, but for his notable personal qualities as a gentleman and a friend.
>
> Tom's retirement marks the end of a long era in the history of Shawmut, a period which began in the Depression years of the '30's and has encompassed three wars, continual financial excitement, and extraordinary changes in the life styles in these United States. He has met his challenges well; and he can view with great satisfaction his legacies to all of us, including a three billion dollar Shawmut, whose future is bright and promising.

That same month, and as a way of giving concrete expression to his colleagues' appreciation, LaWare announced that the then inactive Shawmut Library would be restored and revitalized to become a fully functioning operation. A special collection would be developed for inclusion in the library and dedicated in Trigg's honor. The appropriateness of this tribute was underscored by the final words of a commemorative plaque: "His example influenced others, as will this collection, to pursue professional excellence in banking."

Trigg's career at Shawmut, however, was not yet over, for the LaWare administration invited him to stay on as a consultant; he also continued as a director of both the Shawmut Bank of Boston, N.A., and Corporation and remained an active member of the Executive Committee of both boards.

Chapter 15

The Administration of John P. LaWare
(1980–Present)

To assess history in the making is a task that any historian dedicated to objectivity hastens to avoid. Today's incident too easily becomes tomorrow's trivia, while some seemingly small action too often becomes next year's headline. To end the story of Shawmut, then, at the beginning of the 1980s is a temptation. The 1980s however, are rapidly proving to be among the most exciting and important decades in the history of banking. Thus a dilemma looms. Should the story end with the close of the Trigg administration and the beginning of the LaWare, which would present a convenient break but a truncated tale, or should I attempt an assessment of the current administration, which would be an intriguing study but inevitably flawed by the closeness of perspective?

Seeking a solution to the problem, I recalled that in the introduction I had noted that "Shawmut's story is that of many dedicated persons working within the context of their particular time to assure the continued growth and development of a strong and responsive financial organization." What better way to at least begin to understand the present growth than through the perceptions of the person most responsible for shaping it? Thus I asked the current chairman and chief executive officer, John LaWare, if he would consent to jot down some of his observations: his own history, his impressions of Shawmut before he came, his thinking when he assumed the helm, his priorities. His response exceeded my happiest expectations, for the account he gave me not only encapsulated the present but also evoked a sense of the immediate past and hinted of the future.

For this reason, I have included the LaWare document here in its entirety as a fitting conclusion to our chronological section and as an introduction to our future.

The LaWare Story

My earliest memory of Shawmut dates to the days when I was an undergraduate at Harvard. It seemed then as though everywhere in Boston you saw the Shawmut Indian. Shawmut branches were all over the city, and they all had a very handsome bust of an Indian identified with the Bank in the window and in other places.

In those days the last thing that I was thinking about was a career in banking. My determination when I arrived at Harvard was to take all the premedical courses that I could manage and try to qualify for medical school when I graduated. It wasn't until two-thirds of the way through my college career that I realized medicine was not going to be my cup of tea, but I had to complete my major in biology in order to graduate on time. After abandoning medicine I took all the history, government, English, and literature courses I could fit into my schedule. I attended the University of Pennsylvania and earned a master's degree in political science with the full intention of teaching while working on a Ph.D. In fact, I was invited by the head of the Department of Political Science to be an instructor while I was getting my doctorate.

Meanwhile, the Korean War had heated up, and the draft board was getting rather impatient with my pursuit of higher learning, so I enlisted in the Air Force. I went to Officer Candidate School and was expecting to spend three more years in the Air Force after I had been commissioned, when the war suddenly ended in August of 1953. Those of us who were not in a critical assignment and who had twenty-four months of active duty were eligible for immediate release. I wrote to the head of the political science department at Pennsylvania, asking for the teaching assignment that had been offered to me. He responded that all assignments had been filled for the fall term, but that they'd be happy to see me in February.

Margery and I had been married in 1952. I had exactly $680 in separation pay from the Air Force and didn't know how we were going to get along on that money, so I wrote to people I knew back in New York, including my father, asking for advice. I had decided that I should look for a job as though I were embarking on a lifetime career. One of the industries highly recommended was banking. My father reasoned that no one had gone into banking in the 1930s because of the depression or in the 1940s because of the war. He reasoned there had to be a fairly sizable management gap, and if I got into the right bank in the right spot, I had a good chance to move ahead rapidly. I went around to see a number of banks in New York and was offered a job at Morgan starting in April. That wasn't satisfactory because it certainly didn't fit into the time frame I had in mind. Then someone said, "Try the Chemical Bank, they have a good training program." I did and I persuaded them that banking had been my lifetime aspiration. Typical of banks in that era, the starting salary of $3100 was about $800 less a year than I had been making as a second lieutenant in the Air Force.

After surviving the training program, I never really considered being in any other business. Banking, it seemed, was a business that touched every aspect of the economy — government, individuals, companies, other countries. It was the lifeblood of the economy. It was exciting and had all the elements I was looking for in a career.

At Chemical I had a chance to move ahead rapidly, largely because the management gap my father had perceived was really there and the bank was growing quickly. In 1956, I received my first assignment in the National Division: I was to travel in the northern part of New England, which my boss at the time referred to as "the cold country" and which included Maine, New Hampshire, and Vermont. My first trip was to Bangor, Maine, and for the next year or so, I traveled the three northern states. Later I was introduced to the business in the southern three states, and my new territory included Boston. One of the first calls I made there with my boss was on the National Shawmut Bank, one of Chemical's principal correspondents.

The talk in banking circles all over New England at that time was of the resignation of Walter Bucklin at Shawmut and the installation of Horace Schermerhorn and Larry Martin at the top. Those two gentlemen were very cordial to me on that first call. I can still remember "Skimmie" standing there with his jacket open and his vest draped with a heavy gold watch chain. He had a wonderfully warm and rather grandfatherly attitude toward the new young whippersnapper from New York who was trying to cover the territory. Larry was a little more aloof, tight and trim, and looked something like a Marine officer to me. Both of them inspired awe, particularly in the atmosphere of that magnificent banking room at Water Street and the executive suite which extended off on the Devonshire side.

Among the other people I met on that first call was Tom Trigg. His office was at the other end of the building, at the corner of Water and Congress streets, and I always thought it was the best office in the building. Tom was in charge of the Banking Department, and he received me graciously. I was introduced to the people in Correspondent Banking, including Rohl Wiggin, Bill Schmink, and Ansel Bucklin. We also went around the floor, where I met Bob Hussey and Ed Belden among others.

As the years went by, many of these people have become close friends and associates. I will always remember my great pleasure at the many courtesies that were extended to me, even as a competitor, by Bill Schmink. For example, the first time I attended a bankers' convention in one of the northern states — I don't recall whether it was in Maine or Vermont — the Shawmut was having a party, and I was invited as a matter of form. When I showed up, Bill Schmink caught sight of me and took me under his wing, making sure I was introduced to everybody in the room as the new representative of the Chemical for New England. He is that kind of gentleman. He was pretty sure of himself, because I never did succeed in getting any business away from the Shawmut. The correspondent bank business in New England was a tight, well-covered operation, with the Shawmut and the First National Bank having the dominant positions. Many times I called on banks to try to build up a relationship or establish a new one, and I'd know my work was cut out for me when I sat down across the desk from some banker and saw the Shawmut Indian souvenir bust sitting there staring at me.

In time, as my knowledge of Shawmut and the people associated with it grew, I came to be close to Ed Belden, Bob Hussey, and, to a lesser extent, Tom Trigg, who was several cuts above my level in the Bank. I remember one occasion when Ed Belden succeeded in getting all of the New York correspondents of Shawmut together for a lunch which Tom hosted. Years later when I came to Shawmut, someone dug out a picture taken at that lunch. It showed Ed at one end of the table and Tom at the other end, with all the New York bankers gathered around, and there I was, big as life, still with black hair, a clean plate, and only one chin.

In 1964 my career at Chemical took a new turn. For a brief time I had responsibility for nine states in the Middle West, centered on Chicago. Then I was given responsibility for starting the Marketing Division. At this time we started the credit card business, set up Master Charge, and a nationwide identification and common interchange and authorization system. This reintroduced me to Boston, because we worked with the New England Bankcard Association to get all the banks in Boston into the Master Charge–Inter-Bank arrangement. In the early 1970s I became involved with holding company affairs at Chemical and didn't have much contact with Boston again until early 1975, when I spent thirteen weeks participating in the Advanced Management Program at Harvard. Coming to the city after a four-year hiatus gave me a sharp awareness of the immense changes it was undergoing. There was the John Hancock tower, which was completed but unoccupied because the windows were still blowing out in high winds, and there was the redevelopment of downtown, including construction of several new bank buildings, one of which was Shawmut's headquarters at One Federal Street.

During my stay, a reception was held on the top floor of Faneuil Hall. The Quincy Market project was just beginning and the north and south market buildings were being gutted and rehabilitated. That whole area was still a wasteland, but one could see the pattern of the new Boston beginning to emerge. It was fascinating, particularly to one who had first

seen Boston in the late 1940s during Curley's last term as
Mayor. Later, I'd seen the changes brought about by Hynes
and Collins; now I was seeing the exuberant progress under
Kevin White.

After the thirteen weeks of the Advanced Management Program, I went back to New York and busied myself with holding
company affairs at Chemical. I really didn't have any further
contact with Boston until the Spring of 1978, when Tom Trigg
and I began to talk about his desire to find a new president
for Shawmut. We first met and talked about the possibility in
the old Bankers' Club at the top of the Equitable Building in
lower Manhattan. I guess we sat there for three or four hours.
I could see that Tom wasn't quite convinced that this person
whom he had always known as a junior correspondent banker
was really a viable candidate. But he was very patient, and I
can remember that the most challenging question he asked
me was, "Why do you want to come to Boston, and why do
you want to come to the Shawmut?"

I recall thinking hard about how to answer that question.
I'm sure I mentioned some of my respect and affection for
Shawmut and for the people I knew who were still there, but
I think the telling comment I made to Tom was that I felt I
was ready to manage something on a big scale. I had been
managing bits and pieces of the Chemical organization over
a number of years, but I never had the chance to get my arms
around a whole company. Yet I felt the diversity of experience
to which I had been exposed at Chemical gave me a good
background for just the kind of situation that Shawmut presented. Here was a company that owned a number of banks
and other kinds of subsidiaries. It was struggling to rebuild
its earnings record after the tough times of the mid-1970s,
and it was a bank looking for some of the new management
elements that had become increasingly important in the banking
industry, particularly in the area of long-range planning. In
any case, as a result of that first conversation with Tom and
one or two others, he invited me to meet with a search committee established by the Board of Directors.

I'll never forget that session with the committee. It was held
in a suite at the Parker House. They didn't want me to come
anywhere near the Bank, because they thought I might be recog-

nized, and word might get out that I was a candidate. Consequently we met with great secrecy, just after lunch. Before the meeting I had gone downstairs to have lunch by myself in the Grill Room. The waiter, who I suspected was a college boy earning some money on the side, managed to spill a whole glass of ice water down the front of my tie, shirt, and suit. Not only was that a rude shock to my system at a time when I was nervous anyway, but I certainly didn't want to walk into that session of very distinguished directors with a wet suit. I quickly finished lunch, went outside, and for an hour or so I walked up and down the sunny side of Washington Street to dry out. Fortunately, the sun was hot and the air was relatively dry, and by the time I went upstairs to meet with the directors, I had recovered. I looked a little rumpled, but at least I didn't look like I'd had an accident.

It was a fascinating meeting and the questions were probing. The directors involved were Ken Olsen, the president of Digital Equipment; Herb Jarvis, who at that time was with Emhart; John Pierce, partner of Gaston Snow; and Frank Staszesky, who was then executive vice president of Boston Edison. We met for about three hours. The burden of the conversation was really not so much on my experience, which I guess they had checked out, but rather on what I thought I would bring to Shawmut. We discussed long-range planning in great detail as that seemed to be a matter of great concern. I was told I was missing the chairman of the Search Committee, Ed Matz, who was president of the John Hancock. They asked if I would be willing to come back and have dinner with him. I jumped at the chance because by that time my appetite for winning the job was keen.

The meeting with the directors went fairly well, and about a week later I came back to Boston and had dinner with Ed Matz at the Ritz. He had just gotten off a plane from Europe and I know he was dead tired, but that session with him was probably as probing as any I've ever experienced. We discussed just about every aspect of the Shawmut situation, as well as the things that I thought I might be able to do. Still, I didn't know what sort of impression I'd made until two or three weeks later. I was on vacation with Margery in Jackson Hole, Wyoming. There I got a telephone message to call Boston, and when I did, I was offered the job as president of the Bank and the holding company. They mentioned a salary figure which I thought was too low, and I told them what I thought it should be. They called back and said that they were willing to split the difference. By that time I was so anxious to have a crack at it that I quickly agreed. When I told Margery that I had taken the job and we were going to be moving to Boston, she was in a state of shock for a couple of days — the idea of leaving Scarsdale and all our friends after twenty-five years was pretty tough. But, she quickly rallied and began to look forward to the move as much as I did.

The next step was the formal election. I remember waiting in Tom's office while the board was in session at the other end of the building. Pretty soon there was a knock on the door. Ed Matz came in, a big smile on his face, and said, "Well, welcome to the wigwam," and I knew I was in. A few minutes later I had to go across the hall and meet all of the division heads of the Boston Bank and the presidents of the subsidiary banks around the state. The atmosphere in that room was highly charged. They were getting their first look at the new boy, and I was trying very hard to make a good impression. Ed Matz made a graceful comment or two, as did Tom Trigg, and I went around the room and shook hands with each of the men there. I recall how glad I was to see Bob Hussey's smiling face. At that point he was the president of the Shawmut Community Bank in Framingham, and, of course, he remembered me. It was like seeing a friendly face in a crowd; it gave me moral support to know that there was somebody there who was familiar.

On the fifteenth of October I left Chemical, exactly twenty-five years to the day from the time I joined it. The following morning, Monday, October 16, I took up my responsibilities at Shawmut.

That first day, Tom Trigg and I went into his office and closed the door. We had a long chat about how we were going to operate. The thrust of his comments was that we ought to spend a lot of time with each other, and that all of the decisions about running the place should be joint ones so that I could learn as fast as possible and be ready to take over when he retired twenty months hence. It was an exciting conversation for me, and made clear the marvelous attitude Tom had about taking me under his wing and training me for the top job. When we finished, I remember saying to Tom, "Let's shake on all that, but at the same time we resolve to work closely together, let's also resolve to have some fun."

Tom and I never lost sight of the resolution that we made that day. We developed an unusually fine relationship. We worked extremely closely, and we did have fun. We accomplished a great deal, and we had a lot of laughs. It was the beginning of a friendship that has endured over the subsequent years.

One incident on my first day at Shawmut, I think, illustrates the charm of Boston and the graciousness of the relationships in the business community. I had been out of my office for a few minutes and as I came back down the hall, my secretary, Mrs. Storella, was waiting for me. She said that Mr. William Brown, the president of the First National Bank of Boston, was waiting for me in my office. I thought to myself, "I don't know Bill Brown very well; I think I've only met him once or twice in my life. I wonder what he wants to see me about." I walked into the office and there was Bill with his hand out and a big smile on his face. He said, "I just wanted to stop by, welcome you to Boston, and wish you the very best in the years to come." I guess I was really overwhelmed by the graciousness of that gesture. Bill and I, even while competing fiercely over the years, have been good friends. He's a fine gentlemen and a tough competitor.

My first assignment at Shawmut was to put in place as rapidly as possible some strategic planning for the company, taking a look at a more vast horizon than had been the planning practice at Shawmut in the past. We began in January of 1979, with our first planning retreat for senior management. About twelve of us went down to the Sheraton Islander on Goat Island in Newport, Rhode Island, for three days.

The first day we set about identifying the strengths and weaknesses of the Corporation. The second day we tried to analyze what those strengths and weaknesses meant, where they came from, and what ability we had as management to deal with each of them. The third day we set about trying to put together a set of goals and objectives for the Corporation which over a five-year period would bring us to full competitive status with our peer group and show the kinds of returns for shareholders that were our objectives. That's probably an oversimplification of dealing with the planning problems of a large and complex company, but it does describe the process in general terms.

From that beginning, we began to get Shawmut into gear to move forward. A major effort focused on improved communications. I found that communications moved up and down in the company fairly well, but lateral communication between division heads and peers at various levels of management was not as well developed. That became a major target of my effort. It was obvious that I had to make some decisions over a relatively short time about the quality of the management team and whether we were going to have to go outside to do a significant amount of recruiting.

I scheduled a series of breakfasts, luncheons, and dinners with the key members of senior management and their immediate associates in the various divisions. These were relaxed, give-and-take affairs, at which the purpose of the dialogue was to find out what was on their minds, what were their concerns, what they thought they could do with their parts of the Corporation. It gave me an opportunity to express my thoughts about Shawmut and to test the conclusions I had reached against their experience and their more intimate knowledge of the Corporation. It also gave me an opportunity to take a closer look at the individuals involved in the key jobs.

It was a significant and time consuming effort. But, as a result I felt the division heads at the Bank were excellent people of high quality and sound experience. While I was not satisfied that they were all in exactly the right assignments, I was convinced we didn't have to do a lot of recruiting outside in order to put together the kind of management team we needed.

That conclusion has held up over the intervening years. We have recruited at this writing only six senior officers from outside. The first was an economist, whom I felt we needed to do accurate planning and project an image of sophistication and detailed knowledge of the economy of New England. We were successful in recruiting Jack Kalchbrenner from the Federal Reserve Board in Washington. Jack's assistance to us in asset and liability management, in consulting with senior management on all kinds of management decisions, as well as in enhancing Shawmut's image through his own writing, teaching, and public speaking engagements has worked out exceptionally well. He's a very important member of the team.

The second move was to bring in John P. Hamill, who had been associated with me at Chemical in years past and had been president of Galbreath Mortgage Company, a mortgage-banking subsidiary of Chemical which reported to me. John is an exceptionally able manager, has excellent skills in dealing with people, and thinks and reacts in much the same way that I do on many issues. I was successful in recruiting him away from Bank One Trust Company in Columbus, Ohio, where he was president and chief executive officer. In the fall of 1980 he joined us as executive vice president and chief counsel. In December 1981 John was elected president of Shawmut Corporation and became my deputy in all matters relating to the management of the Corporation.

The third outside recruit was William C. Schrader. Bill had been for a number of years associated with the Underwood Company in the Boston area and then had gone to work for the Chemical Bank in New York. I really didn't know Bill at Chemical but John Hamill did, and when Bill indicated that he and his wife, Carolyn, would like to come back to Massachusetts, we were delighted to bring him in as executive vice president in charge of all of the back-office operations. Bill has consistently contributed to our increasing ability to handle the transactional business that has grown up over the years, and he keeps us on the cutting edge of technology. I don't think we would have been able to put in place automated teller machines and all the other electronic machinery of modern banking if we hadn't had him guiding that effort.

The fourth outsider to join the organization in 1981 was C. Keefe Hurley, Jr., general counsel for the Shawmut Bank of Boston and Shawmut Corporation. Con joined us from the Federal Reserve in Washington, D.C., where he was assistant general counsel. He has a broad knowledge of banking law and a fine ability to deal with all of the complex changes that have taken place or are being contemplated in banking. He is responsible for the Legal Department and reports to John Hamill. Con has lectured in the United States and abroad at banking conferences sponsored by groups including the American Bar Association and the American Bankers Association.

At the beginning of 1983 Frederick J. Knapp joined Shawmut as a senior vice president responsible for the Mutual Funds Shareholder Processing Department. Fred joined us from Boston Financial Data Services, Inc. Under Fred's direction the Shawmut Mutual Fund Servicing operation has turned around and made a contribution to the Bank's earnings.

The sixth senior officer from outside is Ann M. Moe, senior vice president and director of marketing, Shawmut Corporation. Ann is responsible for marketing across the entire Corporation, including providing marketing support to Shawmut divisions such as Financial Management and Capital Markets. Ann is a frequent speaker at national and regional seminars on bank marketing and management. She has strong management ability and a thorough knowledge of bank marketing. As Shawmut seeks to expand its activities in an ever changing environment, her experience and judgment will enable her to play an important role in our future.

Over these intervening years, we have accomplished much of what we set out to do in those first few weeks and months. The performance of the Corporation has greatly improved in terms of gross earnings, as well as in terms of returns earned on both assets and equity, and this performance has been reflected in the price of Shawmut stock. We've completely revamped the way the Corporation is managed. The community banks have been more tightly organized to make them an even closer part of one corporate management effort; we have established business lines that cross over legal-entity definitions and we manage the twelve banks that are now part of the Corporation as one institution. During the course of these six years, we have made two very significant bank acquisitions: the Worcester Bancorp and the Melville Bancorp, with its subsidiary the First National Bank of New Bedford. Worcester Bancorp, with $1 billion in assets, brought in four banks in addition to the Worcester County National Bank; and the First National Bank of New Bedford, with $150 million in assets, gives us a strong commercial presence in Bristol County. We have also been looking toward diversification in business lines and in interstate banking. We have explored a number of acquisitions in related activities, and we will aggressively pursue potential acquisitions when interstate banking becomes a reality.

There have been some disappointments and temporary setbacks from time to time, but by and large, we have reached the mid-1980s with a well-structured, highly competitive regional banking company that is well positioned to further diversify business lines as regulatory constraints are relaxed and opportunities for acquisitions present themselves. We are well prepared to expand into other states, but only where expansion gives us a presence in an attractive market and where we can operate profitably for our shareholders.

The senior-level management team is in place, and careful provision has been made for management succession. John Hamill is in every sense my deputy and alter ego, acting for me in my absence and serving as my principal assistant in every aspect of Shawmut's management. Neal Finnegan, who is vice chairman in charge of all of the retail and the Massachusetts middle market parts of the Company, has about 50 percent of the assets under his management. His ability to put us in a leading competitive position with regard to retail and middle market business accounts for a great deal of Shawmut's current success. Bill Craig, who has been with the Company since 1976, and who has brought excellent discipline to our lending and asset and liability functions, continues to be a strong fourth member of the top team.

From a personal point of view, these past years could not have been more satisfying. I am immensely proud of the Shawmut Corporation and all its people and am very confident of our ability to grow and prosper in the future to the benefit not only of our shareholders but our depositors and our employees as well.

We have strong boards of directors for all of the entities in the company. They are not only supportive but also bring to us the perspective of their own management experience and wisdom. They have given us the kind of authority that any management needs to do the job, and when we have sought their advice and counsel, they have been unselfish in providing it for us. The future is bright; it is challenging, and unquestionably, Shawmut is ready for it.

PART TWO

Identifying Features
of Shawmut

Chapter 16

Shawmut Locations

I N the fifteen decades since Shawmut was founded, several locations have been distinguished by its presence. Despite the variety of addresses, the Bank has always remained within two blocks of the Exchange Coffee House site where it was first organized by the founding directors.

Throughout Boston history, State Street has been synonymous with money and financial affairs, and it was home to Shawmut for its first thirty-three years. From colonial days, State Street has been a prominent commercial address in Boston, even though it has carried other names. At first the street was nothing more than an Indian path to the waters of Boston Harbor. When the earliest English settlers arrived, they adopted this route for their own needs. Soon it became popularly known as the broad street, but as other streets began to appear and the colonial outpost grew into a prominent seaport, Boston realized more formal designations for its streets were necessary. In 1708 they were all given names, and this most important one was named King Street to honor the English monarch.

After the Revolution, when patriotic spirit was celebrating the new republic, Boston citizens rechristened a number of their streets. King Street became State Street in 1784. Soon afterwards, Long Lane was renamed Federal Street, Dalton became Congress, and Marlborough gave way to Washington. Just one block away from Benjamin Franklin's boyhood Milk Street home, an impressive crescent-shaped residential development named Franklin Place was set out in 1792 on what is now Franklin Street. Of all the names assigned to Boston streets after the Revolution, only one was decidedly English: in 1784 Pudding Lane became Devonshire Street, named to commemorate the Bristol merchant who did so much to aid Boston after the devastating fire of October 2, 1711. With the exception of Washington Street, each of the above would eventually take on a special significance for the Shawmut Bank.

From the beginning, State Street served as a focal point, the market place where merchants, ship owners, and sea captains gathered to conduct their business. Boston's first town hall was established at the head of State Street, on the site of the present Old State House. The existing building was erected on this site in 1713, and served originally as the seat of the colonial government. Here the Massachusetts legislature regularly met until the Bulfinch State House was completed on Beacon Hill and opened in 1800. A merchants' exchange was incorporated into the street floor lobbies of the Old State House. As the congregating merchants became too numerous to meet comfortably within the walls of the building, they began the practice of conducting their affairs right on the street. This daily routine of merchants parading on State Street in their top hats, "going on 'Change," persisted until the 1840s, when the new Merchants' Exchange Building was erected on State Street between Congress and Kilby.

State Street was also the natural site for early insurance operations in Massachusetts. In fact, the first insurance office in America was established on State Street in 1724. Commercial banking in New England likewise began on State Street, when the Massachusetts Bank opened there in 1784. By the time Alexander Hamilton's First Bank of the United States opened a branch in Boston, locating on State Street was practically obligatory. The federal bank's directors selected the site just north of the east end of the Old State House, about where the present headquarters of the Bank of New England stand in 1982. When the state legislature removed to Beacon Hill in 1800, this only accentuated the financial orientation of State Street's prominence. At the time Shawmut Bank began its operations in 1836, two-thirds of all banks in Boston were located on State Street and most of the others were no farther than one block away.

Shawmut remained true to this tradition for thirty-four years, locating at various points along the original three block stretch of State Street from Washington Street to Merchants' Row. Temporary quarters at 16 State Street were the first home of the Shawmut Bank, then the Warren Bank. Within weeks of the Bank's opening, the president, Benjamin Tyler Reed, found an appropriate banking room at 72 State Street, where he also installed the Eastern Railroad office. This location was also convenient to the neighbor at 70 State, the Warren Insurance Company, to which so many Shawmut founders were connected. Shawmut remained at 72 State Street only about three years, for in 1840 the Bank is listed in an almanac at 92 State Street, though this change may have been caused by a renumbering of storefronts along State Street rather than an actual move by the Bank. Notably, Eastern Railroad is also found at 92 State in 1840.

In 1845 Reed moved the Bank again, this time to the south side of State Street at number 39, almost at the corner of Congress Street and just two doors away from the new Merchants' Exchange Building. Old pictures of State Street indicate 39 State was a modest two- or three-story building. Between it and the Merchants' Exchange Building was the Tremont Bank, which remained at 41 State throughout the period. Reed had an early interest in the Tremont Bank and probably eyed the new location from the very beginning.

The new Merchants' Exchange at 53 State Street was built in about 1842 or 1843. Almost immediately, two insurance companies took up offices in the Exchange, and by 1845 several had located there, including the Warren Insurance Company, which was still John L. Dimmock's personal bailiwick. Shawmut's location at 39 State Street was convenient to the personal offices of most all of the Bank directors at this time and it apparently agreed with Reed's successors, John Gardner and Albert Fearing, who made no attempts to move the Bank.

The location changed late in 1854 to 41 State Street just as William Bramhall assumed the Bank presidency. Perhaps a hole was opened through the wall to the neighboring building to allow use of the new address, but the choice may have been made because the Boston Marine Society held its meetings at this same address. Shawmut directors Bramhall, Dimmock, and

Jairus B. Lincoln were all active in this society. But Shawmut's residence at 41 State was also short-lived, lasting only three to four years. By 1859 Shawmut returned to the same block of its original, temporary quarters across from the Old State House, where it became one of the leading tenants in the new Globe Building, at 20 State Street. Bramhall must have been fond of the Globe Building for he kept the Bank there a full decade, the remainder of his time as Bank president and the longest period Shawmut had remained in one location up to then. One can only guess how he felt about his historic neighbor, the Old State House. After serving as City Hall for a decade in the 1830s, the stately elegance of this colonial landmark had been corrupted by a mishmash of commercial signs plastered on most of the available exterior wall space, proclaiming the variety of telegraph and travel offices, insurance companies, and shopkeepers tenanted inside.

The nomadic existence of the Shawmut Bank during its first three decades strikes the modern observer as surprising for a prominent bank. Perhaps the shifts indicate that the growing Bank required more appropriate quarters every so often, or that it was jockeying for position along the main avenue of commerce, or that it was simply trying to survive through a period of unusual ups and downs. Of all the Shawmut's early locations, the last has suffered most from the ravages of time. The Globe Building fell victim early to the city's plan extending Devonshire Street north from State Street to Dock Square. Later urban renewal obliterated this end of Devonshire Street altogether, and the present headquarters of the Bank of New England stands roughly behind the site the Shawmut Bank (and its contemporary neighbor the Merchants National Bank) occupied from 1859 to 1869, rising on land that formerly supported the Devonshire Street traffic.

While the Merchants' Exchange has served as the primary focal point in Boston, so too has the United States Post Office. In fact these two institutions were housed together for more than a generation, first at the Old State House when it served as City Hall, and then in the Merchants' Exchange Building at 53 State Street. The post office was set up in the rear of this building with direct access to Congress Street. While the location was ideal, increased postal volume rendered the facility obsolete. Pressure mounted and Congress finally appointed a commission in 1867 to select an appropriate new site for the post office. One year later the commission chose the full block surrounded by Congress, Water, Devonshire, and Milk streets. The tract was purchased and cleared, and in 1869 ground was broken for construction of the new facility.

These events happened just as John C. Cummings became president of the Shawmut National Bank. A man of remarkable courage and foresight, Cummings recognized the significance that would come to the new Post Office Square area, and one of his first acts was to relocate Shawmut to the building at the northeast corner of Congress and Water streets. Its address was 50 Congress Street, diagonally opposite the Post Office Building construction site. In so doing Cummings abandoned the tradition of a State Street address, but he led the vanguard that shifted Boston's financial district southward. At 50 Congress Street, Shawmut joined the National Hide and Leather Bank as the only national banks in the neighborhood when the Post Office cornerstone ceremonies were held on October 16, 1871. President Ulysses S. Grant and most of his cabinet were present, and one can imagine the Shawmut staff admiring the war hero from their exceptional vantage point across the way.

Shortly after Shawmut moved, the devastating fire of 1872 occurred, which gutted sixty-four acres in the heart of downtown Boston. The Post Office Building was almost ready for its roof raising, and it suffered $175,000 damage. Shawmut's offices were engulfed, and the fire even burned out the Merchants' Exchange Building and its existing postal facility. Shawmut found temporary quarters at 43 State Street while waiting for its Congress Street home to be rebuilt. The new building was redesignated 60 Congress Street, and there Shawmut resumed operations in 1874. This building still stands today, only slightly remodeled, in the shadows of grander structures, and it remained Shawmut's home until 1907, a period of thirty-three years.

By leveling such a vast tract of downtown Boston, the 1872 fire opened up the central city to significant redevelopment, which diffused the concentration of Boston's financial institutions along State Street. Already becoming prime locations, the blocks abutting the new Post Office Building were suddenly available for some of the most prominent banks and insurance companies in the city. Soon a dozen national banks and several savings banks joined Shawmut in the immediate vicinity, especially at Congress and Milk streets, which became known as Post Office Square.

Despite the physical relocation of the financial district to an area one to two blocks south of State Street, "State Street" retained its emblematic connotation of Bostonian financial affairs for decades to come. Immediately after the fire several major firms constructed majestic landmarks facing the new Post Office, including such leading insurance companies as Mutual Life of New York, Equitable Life Assurance, and New England Mutual Life, all of which were located on Milk Street. The Mutual Life of New York Building was particularly noteworthy for its tower and gilded balcony, which provided a dramatic view of Boston Harbor from the dizzying height of seven stories.

Among the several banks locating in the Post Office Square area, two selected sites on Water Street between Devonshire and Congress, directly across Congress Street from Shawmut's home — sites that together later became 40 Water Street, synonymous with the National Shawmut Bank. The leading Boston bank of the era, the Maverick National, selected quarters in the elegant Simmons Building at 50 Water Street, on the northwest corner at Congress Street. Miraculously unscathed by the fire, this building was flanked on the west by the National Bank of the Commonwealth Building at the corner of Devonshire and Water. By 1890 both the Provident Savings and Suffolk Savings banks had offices at 82 Devonshire, just around the corner. After the Maverick's dramatic failure in 1891, its site was taken over by the Traders National Bank. Eventually, these two banking offices were home to the Mercantile Trust Company and the State National Bank, occupants at the time Shawmut took title to the properties.

The investment banking firm of Kidder, Peabody and Company engineered a series of mergers in 1898 which consolidated eight of Boston's national banks into the newly formed National Shawmut Bank, the Shawmut National reincarnate. This dramatic expansion made Shawmut the largest bank in New England, resulting in an immediate need for larger banking quarters than Shawmut already had occupied since 1874 in the Howe Building at 60 Congress Street. The problem was obvious to the new Shawmut Board of Directors, which immediately procured a lease to the adjacent Codman property and made arrangements for alterations to both properties for an expanded banking floor. By December 31, 1898, the Bank arranged to take over all the leases of tenants in the Howe Building. Subject to existing leases, the longest of which expired in February 1902, this arrangement gave Shawmut leasehold rights to the entire building through the end of June 1907. In the meantime, a committee of Shawmut directors selected the 40 Water Street site for the new Shawmut Bank Building, which would be the first structure owned by the Bank after a career in leased offices. Shawmut gained an inside track on the Devonshire corner when the National Bank of the Commonwealth merged into National Shawmut in late 1901. Once again, Kidder, Peabody arranged the details of the merger. Two weeks prior to this November merger, Kidder, Peabody bought the bank property. Shawmut then purchased the Simmons Building. Both structures were razed to make room for the new Shawmut Building, destined to be the Bank's headquarters for almost seventy years.

The 40 Water Street site has an interesting history traceable all the way back to colonial times, when it was marsh land through which ran a stream, whence Water Street got its name. Fed by a major spring on nearby Spring Lane, this stream flowed down Water Street from the present Devonshire Street to Congress Street. At the corner of Congress and Water streets, the stream emptied into a cove of Boston Harbor, where Peter Oliver's dock once stood. When one of the earlier buildings at this corner was constructed in the mid-nineteenth century, excavations at the site revealed the long-forgotten timbers of this pier.

One of the earliest owners of the land by this stream was Elder Thomas Leverett, father of the colonial governor John Leverett. Congress Street was laid out originally as Leverett's Lane. An early property marker on this lane was the warehouse erected by Oliver on the corner of the present 40 Water Street lot. The cove itself was one of the earliest of the landfill projects that have continually transformed the geographic appearance of Boston. Once standing at wharf's edge, the 40 Water Street lot is now more than seven hundred yards from the nearest harbor shoreline.

A cluster of houses appear on Water Street in the earliest detailed cartographic representations of Boston, dating from the mid-1700s. The often quoted statement of an aged gentlemen, speaking at the end of the century, confirms both the former harbor site and the fact that some of these houses were actually shops. The gentleman recalled "that when the foundation of the Joy's Buildings was preparing, the remains of an old vessel with fragments of canvas, rope . . . were dug up. . . . On this spot now covered by the corner of the Joy's Buildings stood the shop of Kent, tanner . . . and in front was a wharf." The Joy's Buildings stood for some time into the 1800s, and here the Anthology Society established a reading room in 1806. The reading room was removed to the Scollay Building in the next year and became the Boston Athenaeum, one of the foremost private libraries in the nation.

The Water Street location of the National Shawmut Bank has an interesting connection to the fabled Mother Goose of nursery rhyme fame. In early colonial days, just a few steps down Devonshire Street, when it was called Pudding Lane, stood the print shop of Thomas Fleet. Long the publisher of the *Boston Evening Post* and a prolific printer, Fleet married the eldest surviving daughter of Isaac and Elizabeth Vergoose in 1715. A Boston legend almost as old as the Shawmut Bank itself identifies Mrs. Vergoose as "Mother Goose" and claims Fleet collected and first published the now familiar nursery rhymes she used to tell his children.

Although contemporary records do use the names Goose and Vergoose interchangeably for her family, few literary scholars accept the claim that there ever was a real Mother Goose. The rhymes are obviously derived from ancient English oral tradition, but only in the United States are they familiarly known as *Mother Goose Rhymes*. So Mother Goose and the Mrs. Vergoose legend have both entered the American cultural folklore, and whether the local tradition is based on fact or is just colorful myth, it adds a fascinating dimension to the history of the Shawmut's 40 Water Street neighborhood.

In an 1835 fire the buildings on that northeast corner at Water and Devonshire were devastated. In the early morning hours of October 1, the fire began in the fruit cellar of the large brick building on the corner. Before it subsided, Nathan Hale's book printing establishment and Mr. Lovejoy's carpenter shop were destroyed. Some fixtures and appointments of the Exchange Coffee House were damaged, although the building was saved.

After the fire in 1835, the 40 Water Street site remained commercial retail property over the next several years, even after the first bank arrived on the site in about 1864. That year the National Hide and Leather Bank is known to have been located at the northwest corner of Congress and Water streets in an office numbered 30 Water Street and referred to as 51 Congress Street in 1872, suggesting Congress Street was a preferable banking address. Banks have been associated with the site ever since. National Hide and Leather Bank remained only a few years, moving to High Street — even closer to the established shoe and leather district — after the 1872 fire. This district, south of Franklin and between Federal and Pearl streets, was undoubtedly home to the National Hide and Leather Bank's principal customers. The Maverick National Bank, Boston's largest bank at the time, moved into the offices vacated by this departure.

At the other corner of the block, Water and Devonshire, the National Bank of the Commonwealth purchased the existing building from the city in a tax sale in 1877 and remained there until merging with the Shawmut in 1901. Until 1891, when the Maverick collapsed in a spectacular failure, these two banks anchored the block, with Shawmut just across the way at its 60 Congress Street location. Throughout this period, banking did not require the space we are accustomed to today. Banking offices were little more than storefronts, having only recently come down to the street floor from upstairs offices. Retail merchants continued to operate from the other stores along the Water Street frontage. In 1864 these merchants included a brass finisher, cabinet maker, upholsterer, printer, and a variety of brokers. Similar tenants remained throughout the nineteenth century.

Shawmut directors became interested in the 40 Water Street site soon after the mergers of 1898 dramatically increased the size of its operations. As the new National Shawmut Bank, it soon outgrew the familiar surroundings at 60 Congress Street. Except for the leases to the Howe and Codman properties, the directors' minutes reflect nothing more regarding the location of the Bank until April 1904, when a new committee was appointed to consider the question of its future location at the expiration of the Howe lease. Other sources indicate that this decision had been made much earlier, at least by 1901.

Independent transactions by Robert Winsor, National Shawmut director and William A. Gaston, president, beginning in November 1901, reveal a well-conceived plan to obtain the prestigious block-long frontage of Water Street between Devonshire and Congress, directly across from the United States Post Office. The site became Shawmut's 40 Water Street home, where the Bank remained almost seven decades. In 1901 this Water Street frontage was held in two separate tracts. The National Bank of the Commonwealth had owned and occupied its building standing at the Devonshire corner of Water since 1877, and the Simmons Block Building standing on the corner of Congress was an income property belonging to the Simmons Female College which had inherited it in 1900, after the family beneficiaries had died.

The first evidence that Shawmut officials decided upon the 40 Water Street site came in November 1901. That month Kidder, Peabody arranged yet another merger with Shawmut, this time involving the National Bank of the Commonwealth. Two weeks before the merger was consummated, the four Kidder, Peabody partners, including Winsor and fellow Shawmut director Frank G. Webster, purchased the Commonwealth Bank's Water Street property. Negotiations must have been under way with the college, for within five months Gaston created the Simmons Building Trust to purchase, improve, hold, and manage the combined Simmons Block and Commonwealth Bank tracts. With Gaston and college official Horatio Lamb serving as trustees, the trust was funded by subscription pledge shares totaling $2 million. Simmons Female College subscribed for half this amount, Kidder, Peabody committed itself to 5 percent, and three others signed on for 5 percent each, representing 70 percent of the total. Twenty-three others subscribed for the remaining 30 percent in amounts ranging from $5000 to $50,000. The twenty-three included Gaston, his law partner

R. M. Saltonstall, eventual property manager Charles W. Whittier, Lamb, who was also the chairman of the Simmon's College Finance Committee, and even Estabrook and Company, perhaps headed by the same Estabrook who later became a Shawmut director and got the Bank so deeply involved in the Cumberland Mountain Coal Company.

On April 28, 1902, one month after the Simmons Building Trust was declared, Gaston and Lamb, as trustees, purchased both the former National Bank property from Kidder, Peabody and the Simmons Block property from the college. (In an interesting footnote to this purchase, the college treasurer who signed the deed was Charles K. Cobb. Five years later, while the new building was under construction, Cobb was elected a Shawmut Bank director.) The trust held the properties for three years, before selling them as a single tract to the Shawmut Bank on April 18, 1905. In the meantime, the Bank apparently purchased all of the shares in the trust, for Bank director Henry S. Howe reported to the Board of Directors on November 10, 1904, that "the committee have bought all the Capital Stock of the building and land owned by the Simmons Trust."

Plans for a new building to be erected by the National Shawmut on the site developed rapidly. The Board of Directors invited Professor William R. Ware of Milton to serve as an advisor and expert on architecture on December 1, 1904. He was to meet with Gaston, who appears to have taken the lead in preparations for the design and construction of the new Bank building.

The architects selected for the project were Winslow and Bigelow, an established firm headed by Walter T. Winslow (1843–1909) and Henry Forbes Bigelow (1867–1929). Several buildings designed by this firm stand to this day along Tremont Street overlooking the Boston Common. The design for 40 Water Street culminated Winslow's long career, and it is one of the few surviving examples of severely restrained neoclassic office architecture in Boston. The building features four doric columns and a granite facade.

The special attention given to the outward appearance of the building was also given to the interior. The directors wanted a building that would provide the most up-to-date facilities for banking and include the most secure arrangements available.

News accounts at the time the building was first opened for public inspection specifically mentioned that it would enable the National Shawmut Bank to make available the most recent banking methods that were available in the nation.

Even before it opened, the new Shawmut Bank Building at 40 Water Street was quickly recognized as a landmark in the business center of the city. One indication of its early acceptance was provided when the building was featured by the *Boston Post* in the very first week of its "Do You Know Boston?" photo-recognition contest series. Shawmut invited the public to inspect its new home on May 28 and 29, 1907, before opening the offices for banking. Contemporary newspaper accounts report that an immense throng toured the Bank the first day. Greeted with great fanfare from the start, the building remained the comfortable and distinctive Shawmut home for sixty-eight years.

The new building opened just weeks after Shawmut Bank President James P. Stearns retired. He assumed the newly created post of chairman of the board, and William A. Gaston took over day-to-day command as president. Under Gaston, Shawmut continued to grow, and within a decade it became evident more space would be needed than the original 40 Water Street frontage provided. Three neighboring tracts along Devonshire Street were purchased for expansion in 1919. The annex property included a part of the Exchange Coffee House site where the original Shawmut directors first met to create the Bank in 1836. Thus the expansion carried Shawmut back to its institutional birthplace. Three motley buildings stood on this property in 1919. They were removed and the Bank built a wing designed in harmony with the existing building. The new wing enabled Shawmut to add new safe-deposit vaults, an expanded banking floor offering more teller windows, and more support offices in the upper floors. Full access to the original structure was provided on each floor, making the new wing an integral part of the Shawmut Bank Building.

The wing opened at about the time Walter S. Bucklin was elected as president of the Shawmut in 1923. Bucklin took a personal interest in the decor of the Bank, wanting it to reflect the solid tradition that epitomized banking. For this reason he went to great trouble and effort to import English oak paneling for the Board of Directors room and other important offices in the Bank. The wing had a separate street address, 82 Devonshire Street, which was later adopted by Shawmut Association to distinguish it from the Shawmut Bank. The Association headquarters were set on the sixth floor next to the Bank's Board of Directors room.

With the marble floors and walls, bronze doors and grilles, and plush interior fixtures, the Bank matched the public's perception of what a bank should look like. This was implict years later in the decision to use the Bank as the set for the sophisticated movie *The Thomas Crown Affair*. During the spring of 1967, this movie was filmed in the Bank and on the street out front. Some staff members even appeared as extras in the movie, for when the script called for banking types, central casting could not improve upon Shawmut's actual bankers.

Despite the addition of approximately sixty thousand square feet of space when the wing was opened, prospects for future expansion were so pressing that Bank officers felt it necessary and prudent to purchase the adjacent Monks Building on Congress Street when it became available in 1926. Sitting at Quaker Lane, which was named for the Quaker meeting house that stood there for more than a century, the Monks Building site has an unusual background. The Quakers maintained it as a burial ground until 1826, when the remains of 111 bodies were removed to a graveyard in Lynn.

Over the years, the decision to buy the Monk's Building proved farsighted. It allowed the Bank plenty of room for expansion during the three decades after the purchase. But as the Bank entered the 1960s space pressures again began to mount. At this time the third and fourth floors of the Water Street front, originally part of the building setback, were extended out flush with the street facade. This expansion added four thousand square feet, providing room for computer operations, office space, and a new employee lounge. Despite the addition, several banking operations were forced out into other buildings. For example, the Bookkeeping Department, a vital function of the Bank, was moved into the new One Center Plaza building at Government Center in 1966. Moreover, for years the Consumer Loan Department was housed in offices above the Kenmore Square branch where the subsidiary Devonshire Financial long held sway.

Eventually, Shawmut Bank headquarters staff was scattered

among several buildings in the downtown area. This prompted the Bank officers to consider possible options for restoring all Bank functions into a single building. At first, the Bank officers considered the feasibility of purchasing more of the lots behind the existing structures, along Devonshire and Congress streets. This proposal was early rejected as too complex and prohibitively expensive, because of the variety of tracts and number of titleholders or leaseholders involved. Bank officers also considered purchasing properties across Devonshire Street, but this suggestion presented the disadvantage of maintaining the dispersal of operations over two or more locations, just the difficulty the Bank was trying to rectify.

During 1966 the First National Bank was concluding plans to erect a new office tower on Federal Street at Franklin and preparing to dispose of its premises at 67 Milk Street. The First National held title to the entire city block bounded by Federal, Milk, Devonshire, and Franklin, part of which was covered by its old headquarters and part of which was vacant land. This was an attractive package to Shawmut, just when space problems demanded a solution. Shawmut purchased the entire block in October 1966, and on it today stands One Federal Street, the thirty-eight-story office tower that houses the headquarters of both Shawmut Corporation and the Shawmut Bank of Boston.

As is true of so much of downtown Boston, this area was marsh and cow pasture during the earliest colonial period, and it actually touched upon an arm of the same cove that washed Water Street. In the eighteenth century, Shawmut's new site was part of the residential district where Benjamin Franklin was born and raised, his home being one block up Milk Street. Another figure of the Revolutionary era, Robert Treat Paine, a signatory of the Declaration of Independence, is even more closely identified to the One Federal Street location. From the end of the Revolution until his death in 1814, Paine lived on the northeast corner of the block, where Federal intersects Milk. During Paine's residence there, the Federal Street Theatre occupied the southern end of the block. It opened on February 3, 1794, was severely damaged by fire soon afterwards, and was remodeled by Charles Bulfinch, a Boston architect with national reputation. Lafayette visited this theater on the last night of his 1824 Boston tour. A quiet little lane running behind the theater from Franklin through to Milk Street was then known as Theatre Alley. In 1819 this land was all of ten feet wide at its Franklin Street mouth and narrowed down to a mere five feet by the time it reached Milk Street. In later years Theatre Alley was straightened and widened until Devonshire Street was extended over its course in 1859.

As the neighborhood changed from residential to commercial during the 1840s and 1850s, the One Federal Street site became predominantly a home for dry goods dealers and other retail merchants. A leading retailer on the site was Gardner Brewer, one of Shawmut's founding directors. Brewer's store and everything else on the block was burned out by the 1872 fire. In the aftermath of that disaster, the neighborhood character again changed dramatically. Financial offices took the place of retail stores, and the One Federal Street site enjoyed the same proximity to the new Post Office Building that made Shawmut's locations at Congress and Water streets so attractive. At the Milk Street end of the block, facing the Post Office and just a few steps away from Post Office Square, Equitable Life Assurance Society of New York erected an ornate structure of typically ostentatious Victorian-era architecture as its New England regional headquarters. In the years immediately after the fire, the John Hancock Mutual Life Insurance Company and a number of banks also chose to locate on the block.

As John Hancock outgrew its Devonshire Street office, the company purchased the tracts neighboring it to the south, including the parcel that belonged to the heirs of Gardner Brewer. On these tracts it added a ten-story annex with a new main entrance on Franklin Street. Together the two Hancock buildings covered more than the southern half of the block. Eventually, John Hancock departed the downtown area altogether for the Back Bay, and the firm Stone and Webster acquired the vacated premises for its own use. This building was demolished during the 1960s, shortly before Shawmut purchased the tract.

On the northern half, the Equitable Building remained the jewel of the One Federal Street site. For almost fifty years it stood proud, until the early 1920s, when it was leveled to make room for the First National Bank of Boston. Some smaller neighboring buildings, including the earlier of Hancock's two buildings, were also removed and in their place the First National erected a new ten-story Italianate bank building replete with dramatic cathedral vaulting on the main banking floor. Opened in 1924, the First National Bank Building covered 60 percent of the block and was the largest bank building in New England. It too remained almost fifty years on the site, before Shawmut decided to demolish it in 1971.

When Shawmut purchased the One Federal Street site from the First National Bank, one important provision was a lease-back arrangement allowing the First National to remain in its old building until construction was completed on its new 100 Federal Street offices. This period of construction allowed Shawmut almost four years to prepare its own final plans for utilization of One Federal Street. Originally, Shawmut intended to move into the old First National Bank Building and install an office tower on the vacant Stone and Webster lot for future expansion. However, though the existing building contained sufficient space to meet Shawmut's needs, the internal configuration was not suitable. Space considerations and expense projections convinced the Shawmut officers and directors that a better plan would be to raze the existing building and erect a new office tower on the full block. Senior Shawmut officers, including Lawrence H. Martin, chairman of the board, and David L. Currier, senior vice president, toured many bank facilities around the country in search of the best contemporary design features, construction techniques, and financing arrangements. The resulting One Federal Street building incorporated many of the lessons learned on these tours.

Once the decision to construct a new building was made, a special subcommittee of the Shawmut Corporation Board of Directors was assigned the task of monitoring all aspects of the new building program. This group was called the Directors' Committee on New Bank Quarters, and it established policy and approved a variety of recommendations for the building project, particularly those affecting the planning, architectural design, construction, and financing of the new main office. Martin personally supervised many of the developments during the planning stages of the project.

A similar committee was set up among officers of the Bank and this was chaired by Currier, whose extensive experience in real estate development and building construction proved invaluable to the Bank. He took on the role of project director and was the key coordinator of all dealings with the architect and the builder.

Shawmut selected The Architect's Collaborative of Cambridge, Massachusetts, to prepare the design and serve as architect for the new Shawmut Bank Building. World-renowned Walter Gropius was a senior partner of this firm and another principal, his protégé John C. Harkness, acted as the chief architect for the project. One of the lessons Martin and Currier learned was the necessity of creating a building designed to suit Shawmut's particular needs rather than some prior client's. The firm's willingness to work with the Bank in preparing an appropriate design was one of the reasons it was awarded the architect's contract. Several distinguished buildings throughout the world are credited to The Architect's Collaborative, including the John F. Kennedy Federal Building in Boston. Shawmut also selected the Turner Construction Company as general contractor for the whole project and retained C. W. Whittier and Brothers as rental agent and manager, continuing an affiliation dating back to 1906, when the 40 Water Street Building was being erected. Other groups Currier had to coordinate included the structural engineers, LeMessurier Associates, and the mechanical engineers, Jaros, Baum and Bolles, Inc.

Design plans called for a 520-foot-tall building (the height coincidentally matching National Shawmut's 5–20 Transit Number), including an eight-story base, covering the full extent of the site, surmounted by a tower of an additional thirty stories. The tower covers about half the lot surface area, flush with the sides of the base but set back from both ends. The eight-story base was designed to be compatible with the prevailing height lines of the neighboring buildings. Each base floor provides about fifty thousand square feet of floor space, while the tower floors have twenty-five thousand each.

Before plans for the building design were prepared, Currier devised a special questionnaire regarding the space requirements for each department of the Bank. His survey inquired into current and anticipated future space needs, as well as which departments ought to be placed near one another for efficient working conditions. Using the results of this survey, Currier, in coordination with the architect, was able to plan an optimum allocation and arrangement of space into the design from the outset.

Among the special or noteworthy features designed into the building is the novel placement of the vaults. Banks had traditionally positioned the vaults in the basement because there they were most secure and least expensive to install. But developments in construction and efficiency planning showed that the vaults could be placed above ground in locations more accessible to the people using them daily. The Shawmut Building is one of the first to stack four vaults, one over another, in the operating areas of the bank — in the case of the Shawmut on floors two through five. The building also includes many safety features designed to protect the occupants as well as the property, such as an advanced sprinkler system, providing the best in contemporary fire safety, and a smoke detection system. A safety and security monitoring system controlling the whole building is available to the Bank Security Department and allows the security staff to keep a watchful eye on conditions throughout the building at all times.

Some of the special features of the building were developed in response to other contemporary needs. For instance, the twenty-four-hour computer operations area required pure filtered air, special ventilation and cooling, heavy-duty circuitry for electrical power, a reliable back-up power source, and other special arrangements. Plans for the future expansion of the Bank and a concern for employee morale also dictated some care in the overall placement of individual departments. For example, the decision was made to put the employee cafeteria and kitchen on the eighth floor, instead of in the basement where large organizations often put such facilities. The decision was based on the recognition that the higher location was more convenient and more pleasant. It was also determined that the executive offices should be placed on the ninth floor rather than high in the tower, where they would seem less accessible and too far removed from day-to-day operations.

Financing a $75 million real estate project is a monumental endeavor, even for a major national bank. Shawmut was able to purchase the $6.6 million former First National Bank property with available funds, but had to arrange a mortgage loan package to cover the actual construction costs. The scope of the project really raised two separate issues. The first was the question of who the mortgage lender would be; the second was the questions of how title to the completed property would be held. The Bank was unwilling to take on the full commitment alone, and there were serious questions about whether the Comptroller of the Currency would allow it anyway, based on statutory limitations on the amount of real estate a Bank can own. Under the circumstances, Currier believed the bank should form a joint venture with a single corporate partner to assume the title and arrange the mortgage, preferably one in the financial field.

Just as Shawmut was contemplating the most appropriate financing arrangement for the construction project, insurance companies received new authorization to make equity investments in real estate joint ventures. They had long been a source for mortgage money, but the door was now open for them to participate in such a project both as lender and eventual part owner. Seeing this development as an attractive answer to its funding problem, Shawmut opened discussions with several insurance companies regarding the formation of a joint venture to take title to the One Federal Street property and construct the building planned for the site. Prudential submitted the most attractive package, so together Shawmut and Prudential embarked on one of the first such joint ventures in the country.

Because every transaction, agreement, and document had to be drawn up for the first time, the new joint venture became a learning experience for everyone involved. Similar ventures throughout the country have been modeled on this experience, often using the very documents developed for the One Federal Street joint venture.

From the time Shawmut purchased the One Federal Street property to the final completion of the building, one of the primary concerns was the tax planning involved. Remarkably, every tax objective Shawmut laid out for itself was achieved. The original leaseback arrangement of the First National Building provided some income-sheltering benefits to Shawmut, making the effective return on the purchase price somewhat higher than the actual rate of rental payment. Such later objectives as depreciating the property, recognizing loss caused by the demolition of the existing building, and even accomplishing the property transfer to the joint venture without producing a taxable sale were all skillfully and successfully accomplished. Surprisingly, the one significant tax disappointment to Shawmut was that the Bank did not enjoy sufficient taxable income in some of the pertinent years to take full advantage of the tax benefits produced.

One final remarkable aspect of the One Federal Street project is found in the long-term budget projections at the time construction commenced in November 1971. Ten years later, some of the predictions for cash flow and other financial returns on the project turned out to be surprisingly accurate, despite such notorious variables as the cost of construction, change orders, rental market conditions at the time of completion, and interest rate changes over the life of the project, which were more volatile than expected. Nevertheless, the 1971 prediction for the 1980 cash flow was off by less than 8 percent.

Actual work at the site began in November 1971, with the demolition of the old First National Bank Building; by mid-1972 the site was cleared and construction of the new One Federal Street building began. When the building was nearly finished, Shawmut rapidly moved its operations into the new facility. First to occupy space in One Federal Street was the Consumer Loan Department on June 23, 1975, ending a long exile outside bank headquarters. Each week thereafter, in a total of thirteen separate, well-coordinated moves, more functions were transferred to the new structure. This process was completed in October, culminating with the arrival of the executive offices, and marked the first time in forty years that all of Shawmut's operations were under the same roof. Together the Bank and Corporation filled almost 400,000 square feet of the building, about 40 percent of the available floor space, leaving 60 percent for outside tenants.

Firms that had a long association with the Shawmut Bank stand out among the most significant of the early tenants in One Federal Street. The law firm Gaston Snow and Ely Bartlett, once headed by Shawmut's seventh president, William A. Gaston, leased two full floors in the tower, and the building rental and management agent, C. W. Whittier and Brothers, also took space. The largest area assumed by an outside tenant was the five full floors leased by the Kendall Company, a major manufacturing subsidiary of Colgate, Palmolive, Peat.

At the end of 1982, the majority of the tenants illustrated One Federal Street's prominence as an address of distinction in the heart of Boston's financial district. Two of the Big Eight national accounting firms have their Boston offices in the building as do thirteen major brokerage houses, investment firms, and financial counselors. The presence of five of Boston's leading law firms enhances the professional atmosphere. Moreover, One Federal Street also houses the regional office of the Federal Home Loan Bank. Sitting atop the building is the fine dining facility of the downtown Harvard Club of Boston — a major attraction on the thirty-eighth floor with a panoramic view of the whole city. Formerly located in cramped and inconvenient quarters on Batterymarch, the Harvard Club has enjoyed renewed interest and a big boost in its membership since moving into its impressive new quarters. The Harvard Club's presence in One Federal Street has become a drawing card to prospective tenants of the building, which in turn enhances the prestige of the Bank. Shawmut reserved the use of the northeast corner of the thirty-eighth floor for special functions, catered by the Harvard Club, which have proven far more popular and successful than originally anticipated. After the Harvard Club met with such success upstairs, another Crimson venture was encouraged to share in the enthusiasm. The Harvard Coop decided to open a branch outlet downtown and selected retail space at the Milk Street end of the One Federal Street first floor.

Such an attractive list of tenants seemed to generate its own excitement, and by the summer of 1977, barely two years after occupancy began, Whittier was able to report that rental commitments had reached the break-even occupancy level for the entire building. Considering the size of the building and the conditions in the rental market at the time, this was a remarkable performance. By way of comparison, the experience of similar major office buildings demonstrates that two years is the shortest period any building of similar size has reached the break-even point, even in the dynamic western and southern cities of the United States. Rentals continued and the building was filled almost to capacity after only three years. Ironically, by 1981 the Bank found itself having to wait for rented space to be vacated in order to accommodate its own growth.

Today Shawmut Corporation can point with pride to its dis-

tinctive headquarters building. But it is merely the most prominent of many Shawmut buildings serving a large number of
geographical locations throughout the state. The leading corporate subsidiary, Shawmut Bank of Boston, currently enjoys a
widespread system of branches with offices located throughout
the city of Boston. These branch offices, however, did not always
exist.

Throughout the nineteenth century and well into the twentieth, Shawmut Bank of Boston had only one office at any given
time. National banks did not enjoy authorization to establish
branches, and many experts believed they could not do so.
Few even considered the possibility until branching became a
popular method adopted by some state banks to compete with
the more prominent national banks. In Massachusetts, state
trust companies began to establish branches as early as 1903.
Although Shawmut was a leader in the national-bank merger
movement of this period, its mergers did not involve state trust
companies until 1932. Before 1927, each time Shawmut merged
with a national bank, Shawmut scrupulously consolidated all
operations in its own office and closed down the home office
of the merged bank, thus adhering to the perceived policy of
restricting national banks to single offices. As the merger movement gained momentum in Massachusetts, some national banks
sidestepped the apparent restriction by absorbing trust companies that had existing branch systems. For instance, the First
National Bank of Boston acquired the International Trust Company and its seven branches in May 1923. Instead of closing
the trust company offices, the First National continued to operate them and effectively obtained a branch system. Although
legal questions regarding the authority of national banks to
establish branches were clouded in controversy in the early
1920s, competitive pressures together with rulings from a sympathetic Comptroller of the Currency encouraged Shawmut to
create a branch of its own.

Shawmut identified the Park Square district of Boston as the
site for its first branch. At the time, new development of this
area just southwest of the Boston Common and Public Garden
was in full swing, and several major insurance companies were
among the concerns planning to locate in the expanding neighborhood. Park Square presented an ideal location for a bank

branch because new businesses in that area found the downtown banking district just too distant to be convenient. Shawmut decided in 1923 to establish a branch on Arlington Street. Open for business on January 24, 1924, this branch was the first created by a national bank in New England. Originally housed in temporary quarters on St. James Avenue, the branch office moved into the east end of the new Park Square Building when that office was ready for occupancy on June 18, 1924. Located just one block away from the new Back Bay headquarters of John Hancock and Liberty Mutual insurance companies and near other major office buildings and hotels, it proved an immediate success, and remains in the Arlington Street end of the Park Square Building.

The success of the initial branch encouraged Shawmut to expand its branch concept. Dominant reasons for this decision included a new interest in retail banking and a desire to provide convenient banking locations to the customers. New branches soon appeared at Kenmore Square, Bowdoin Square, and the corner of Beacon and Charles streets. By the end of 1926, Shawmut could count nine branches in Boston, from Haymarket to Huntington Avenue. As similar systems sprang up around the country, Congress finally granted national banks express statutory authority to create such branches on February 26, 1927, when it adopted the McFadden Act. This act extended to each national bank the same branching privileges enjoyed by each state bank under the law of its home state. Furthermore, Massachusetts allowed branching only within the county of a bank's home office. This single-county restriction had two effects on Shawmut's future development. Branching inside the limits of Suffolk County continued, and the Bank took dramatic steps to arrange a network of affiliate banks in the neighboring counties.

Over the next seven years, a period marked by financial difficulties and the growing worldwide depression, Shawmut added eight more branch offices, while other banks were suffering. Three of these branches (Mattapan, Fish Pier, and South Boston) were opened in the early months of 1933 at offices that once belonged to the Federal National Bank, which failed December 14, 1931. Shawmut did close one branch in 1930, when it consolidated the Haymarket branch into the North Station office, which was then two years old. Thus the first major wave of branching by Shawmut resulted in a network of sixteen offices throughout the city of Boston, in addition to the main office at 40 Water Street.

Expansion came to an abrupt halt in March 1933, when the whole country was recovering from the Bank Holiday and confidence in the nation's banking structure was being restored. For eight years Shawmut did not add any new branches and sought to maintain the branches then in operation. Innovations in branching, particularly the drive-in facility, generated a new wave of branching in the early 1940s. Drive-in banking appeared in New England shortly before America was drawn into World War II, and Shawmut introduced this feature to its branch system on December 22, 1941, when the new Gallivan Boulevard office was opened in Dorchester. Within months, a drive-in window was installed at the existing Kenmore Square branch and four new branches were opened, all of which included drive-in facilities. Another special concept at the time was developed in response to the pressures of war preparations. In the fall of 1942, Shawmut opened a banking facility at the Port of Embarkation in South Boston for the benefit of departing servicemen and the work crews at the Navy Yard. This facility remained in use for the duration of the war, closing early in 1946.

A new wave of merger activity among Boston banks came with the end of the war. Shawmut absorbed four banks in various parts of Boston before the end of 1949, adding five more branches to the Suffolk County network. One of these mergers was with the Columbia Trust Company, run by Joseph P. Kennedy, father of the future U.S. president. This merger gave Shawmut the right to open a branch at Logan Airport, which it did at the end of 1946. Meanwhile, Shawmut created a new branch in Brighton, also late in 1946. The early 1950s saw the addition of four new offices, two of which were Navy Yard facilities at South Boston and Charlestown. Unlike the World War II facility, Shawmut retained these Navy Yard offices in service long after the Korean conflict subsided. The South Boston Navy Yard facility remained open until 1959, while the Charlestown Navy Yard office continued as a full service branch until the mid-1970s.

Another hiatus in branching followed 1953, and for a decade

Shawmut made no changes in the locations of its Suffolk County offices. Urban revitalization fomented by a dramatic Government Center design caused the next shift in Shawmut branching. The Bowdoin Square office was moved to a temporary building with a novel circular design in the spring of 1963. Three years later, the permanent Government Center branch was opened in One Center Plaza, a seven-story "skyscraper lying on its side." Across town, the Prudential Center was rising to completion over an old railroad switching yard, breathing new life into the western part of the Back Bay. Excitement and new activity in the area prompted Shawmut to build a new branch at the corner of Boylston and Fairfield Streets, a prime location directly across from the Prudential Building. A temporary facility was established nearby in the spring of 1964, and the branch itself opened on January 4, 1965. Three branches were opened in 1966, including the Government Center office. Nevertheless, demographic shifts in the Boston metropolitan area and a steady loss of population to the outlying suburbs made investments in an extensive branch office system within Suffolk County much less desirable than they had once been.

The changes of the 1970s saw a net decrease in the number of branch offices maintained by Shawmut Bank. One new branch was opened in Hyde Park for a period of about four years in mid-decade, raising the number of offices to thirty-four. Some offices were consolidated when neighborhood changes no longer supported two separate facilities. Such was the case of the Audubon Circle office, which was consolidated into the Kenmore Square office, three blocks away. In all, six branches were closed, primarily during a period of retrenchment in 1977.

In the 1980s, technological change has modified the strategy of branch offices. Automatic teller machines have reduced the need for full-service branches. By 1981, one office in Government Center had already been converted from a teller location to a service center — a better utilization of space and employees. Machines took over the role of tellers, allowing bank personnel to devote more time and energy to serving the more complicated transactions arising in banking. Automatic teller machines are also becoming available in places where the bank is unwilling to maintain a full branch for space or economic reasons. One such installation is the automatic teller machine at the North Market building in the Quincy Market complex, another can be found at Northeastern University.

One branch of the Shawmut Bank of Boston has a completely different purpose from the many serving Suffolk County. This is the Nassau branch in the Bahamas, through which Shawmut accepts Eurodollar deposits, which are not subject to the reserve requirements imposed on domestic deposits, and extends Eurodollar loans at a competitive rate. Loan customers include firms from forty countries worldwide. The Nassau office is little more than a "brass plate" mail drop maintained to meet legal technicalities: all the decisions are made and a distinct set of books is kept for this operation in Boston.

The second major change prompted by the 1927 McFadden Act had far greater significance to the Shawmut organization than promoting the growth of a network of branches within Suffolk County. As noted, the act applied the Massachusetts single-county banking restriction to national banks located in the state. But lawyers were quick to recognize a loophole in the act. While the law precluded any individual bank from branching across county lines, it placed no limit on the location or number of banks owned and operated by a nonbank entity.

Shawmut officials were among the first to take advantage of this loophole, creating the Shawmut Association as a business trust in 1928. A forerunner of the present Shawmut Corporation, the Association was designed as a common stock mutual fund on the model popularized just a few years earlier, long before the modern idea of a bank holding company came into vogue. Shawmut Association was one of the first business trusts in the country to adopt an investment policy concentrating half its assets in majority interests of the capital stock of selected banks. These investments gave the Association majority holdings in several banks located in the four counties immediately surrounding the Boston-based National Shawmut Bank, thereby creating a chain principally owned and operated by the Association trustees. In the event Massachusetts later relaxed its single-county rule, this chain could be easily converted into the branch system of one bank. Such a change in Massachusetts law never happened, and into the 1980s the hallmark of Shawmut banking operations in the state remains a chain of separate bank systems.

Almost immediately in 1928, the trustees of Shawmut Association obtained the desired foothold in Essex, Middlesex, Norfolk, and Plymouth counties, when they purchased controlling interests in the capital stock of Merchants National Bank of Salem, Winchester National Bank, Needham National Bank, and the Hingham Trust Company. Actually, the Needham National Bank was organized and opened by Shawmut interests because no existing Norfolk County bank had the features desired by the Association trustees. The Lexington Trust Company was added to the Association holdings in 1929, providing another entry in Middlesex County. Shawmut Association did not venture into another county until 1970, when, recast as the Shawmut Association, Inc., it acquired a controlling interest in the First Bank and Trust Company of Hampden County, obtaining its offices in Springfield and ten neighboring localities within Hampden County. In the intervening forty years, Shawmut solidified its entry in its first four counties by acquiring several additional banks.

First among the later additions was the County Bank and Trust Company, organized in 1933 by Shawmut Association as a successor to the failed Central Trust Company in Central Square, Cambridge. The Association next added the Melrose Trust Company in 1937. A spree of new acquisitions swiftly followed World War II, and before the end of 1947, Shawmut Association added five Middlesex County banks to the fold. They were the Everett National Bank and Newton National Bank, both obtained in 1945; the Wakefield Trust Company and the newly organized Waltham Citizens National Bank in 1946; and the Somerville National Bank in 1947. Almost a decade passed before Shawmut Association resumed its bank acquisition activities in the mid-1950s, when it purchased controlling interests in the Warren National Bank of Peabody in 1954 and the Brockton National Bank in 1955.

After entering Hampden County in 1970 through the acquisition of the First Bank and Trust Company, Shawmut Association, Inc., added the Framingham National Bank in 1971, extending its presence into southwestern Middlesex County.

In 1975 Shawmut Association, Inc., was renamed Shawmut Corporation, and its expansion of banking operations since then has taken the form of mergers with bank holding companies rather than the more simple acquisition of independent banks.

In 1981, Shawmut Corporation added Bristol County to the list of areas served by Shawmut Banks when it concluded a merger with the First Melville Corporation, bringing the First National Bank of New Bedford into the Shawmut family. This bank is now operated as the Shawmut Bank of Bristol County, N.A. Eight months later, Shawmut carried out a substantially more comprehensive merger, adding the five banks owned by Worcester Bancorp, Inc., to its organization on May 3, 1982. This merger gave Shawmut one more Middlesex County bank and extended Shawmut into four new counties where it previously had no banking offices: Worcester, Barnstable, Franklin, and Hampshire. The Worcester County National Bank, now called Shawmut Worcester County Bank, N.A., served the city of Worcester and seventeen other communities, while the other four banks of the merged holding company served sixteen communities in the four counties in which they were located. As a result of the merger, the First National Bank of Amherst became the Shawmut Bank of Hampshire County, N.A., the Franklin County Trust Company became the Shawmut Bank of Franklin County, and the First National Bank of Cape Cod became the Shawmut Bank of Cape Cod, N.A. The name of Peoples National Bank of Marlborough in Middlesex County was not changed. (In 1983 this bank merged into Shawmut Community Bank, N.A.)

In the 1980s Shawmut Corporation operates on a far wider scale than any of its component banks can. Present subsidiaries and joint ventures make Shawmut an active participant in the financial field throughout the world. Shawmut personnel are directly involved in banking offices of Atlantic International Bank, Ltd., and Atlantic Capital, Ltd., located in London and Hong Kong respectively. Another joint venture, one in which Shawmut has a 50 percent share, is American AgCredit, headquartered in Denver and serving the seasonal funding needs of growers and ranchers throughout the West. A wholly owned subsidiary of the Shawmut Bank of Boston, Shawmut Boston International Banking Corporation, is based in Miami to tap the burgeoning international banking business there. Shawmut Corporation also has a securities-clearance subsidiary operating both in Boston and New York City, while two other subsidiaries, Shawmut Credit Corporation and Shawmut Financial Corporation share the One Federal Street address. Shawmut Credit opened a new office in Atlanta, Georgia, in 1982 and another in New York in early 1983.

Historically, Shawmut has been active beyond the boundaries of Massachusetts for many years. The earliest subsidiaries of Shawmut Bank were created more than sixty years ago to operate in major financial markets across the United States and beyond. One, the old Shawmut Corporation of Boston, was created in 1919 to engage in the acceptance business and foreign banking transactions. Unrelated to the present bank holding company of similar name, its offices were established in New York City, Philadelphia, Chicago, Paris, and Berlin. Shortly after this Corporation was formed, its focus shifted to become primarily a bond and securities trading group, remaining active in this field until the banking acts of 1933 and 1935 forced it to cease such activities. Another early affiliate of the Bank was an installment-loan company named Devonshire Financial Service Corporation primarily serving automobile dealers and purchasers. Headquartered above the Kenmore Square branch of the Shawmut Bank, Devonshire had offices in most of the principal cities in New England.

Chapter 17

The Origins of the Shawmut Name
and the Shawmut Indian Logo

IN the 1980s there are probably few images better known to New Englanders than that of a stern-visaged Indian looking confidently out from an encircling blue background. The image is, in fact, familiar in many parts of the world. Although few may actually know his name — Obbatinewat — from Hong Kong to Miami, from London to Nassau, the features are readily identifiable as those of the Shawmut Indian, the logo of a Boston institution.

The existence of Obbatinewat, however, and the Shawmut which he represents, far antedate the logo that has brought them global recognition, nor has the institution always been represented by the now famous image. If the link seems inevitable and irrevocable today, it was by no means always so. The inevitable, as it turns out, was as much the result of accident and coincidence as of wise and deliberate choice.

It all began a hundred and fifty years ago when the directors of what was then the year-old Warren Bank petitioned the Massachusetts legislature for a change of name. The impetus for the petition was quite simply that the name Warren, which was the name of the insurance company with which eight of the Bank directors were associated, was also and confusingly the name of two other New England banks. To simplify the situation, Benjamin T. Reed, president of the Boston Warren Bank, requested a change in the designation of his institution, and on July 1, 1837, the Boston papers carried the following notice: "Warren Bank. This Corporation will hereafter, agreeable to an act passed at the last session of the legislature, be known as THE SHAWMUT BANK." An awkward matter had been brought to a satisfactory conclusion.

Unbeknownst to anyone at the time, however, the seed of a legend had also been planted. In the course of the hundred and fifty years this legend sprouted and flourished. It developed its own authority, its own scholarship, its own iconography, and most important, it gave to the Shawmut Bank that kind of singular identity that later sophisticated marketing agents of other institutions could regard only with wide-eyed envy.

1

In 1837 when the directors and stockholders of the Warren elected to rechristen the Bank the Shawmut, it is doubtful that they had anything more profound in mind than selecting a name that was distinctive and at the same time appropriate. The term "Shawmut" admirably fulfilled both criteria. Since 1630, when the word first appeared in Charlestown records as the designation of the peninsula directly to the south, it had been popularly accepted as the Indian name for the Boston area. Despite this acceptance, however, the term was apparently not much used in the naming of new enterprises. Coincidentally, it was not until the 1830s that it seems to have gained any currency, though only outside of Boston: in 1834 there is a record of a brig out of Salem called the Shawmut; in March 1837 a bill appeared before the legislature concerning the incorporation of mills in Andover, Massachusetts, to be called the Shawmut Mills; and in 1843 the Eastern Railroad named a massive new engine Shawmut.

This sudden resurgence of interest in the Shawmut name may have been sparked by contemporary arguments over its etymology. In 1817 a historian, Charles Shaw, in a work called *A Topographical and Historical Description of Boston,* introduced the idea that Shawmut was the Indian word for peninsula. A few years later his contention was countered by a Reverend

Samuel Deane of Scituate, who just as firmly asserted that it meant "living fountain." Then in 1834 George Bancroft published the first volume of his monumental history of the United States, which, if nothing else, spurred further interest in the whole issue of historical antecedents. Whatever inspired the Warren directors' choice, however, there is no question that the name Shawmut was to have profound implications for the Bank's future.

Unfortunately, the lack of early Bank records makes it impossible to know exactly when its officials began to realize some of these implications. But if the choice of name had been originally dictated by the simple fact that Shawmut was an accepted synonym for Boston, and thus provided the new institution with a "local habitation and a name," it soon became clear that the name had other advantages as well.

In the early days the purpose of any bank was simply to loan money through the medium of printed bank notes that served as currency and to redeem or discount the notes of other banks. Complex designs on these notes made counterfeiting more difficult, while pictures that also suggested the bank's name were an added bonus, easing the problem of identification.

The term "Shawmut" lent itself perfectly to both these purposes, and by 1854 Shawmut bank notes were displaying an Indian figure. (In all probability an Indian image also appeared on earlier notes, but there are none extant to prove it.) Whatever the specific date of the design, the mid-nineteenth-century figure bears little resemblance to the 1980s image. In contrast to the current, simple blue rendition, the 1854 Indian is a storybook illustration. Across the top of the note an Indian languidly reclines. Although he is elaborately portrayed with a feathered topknot, long shell earrings, and toga artfully arranged over one shoulder, there is no attempt to make him imposing or particularly individual. The features are undistinguished, the apparel is that associated in contemporary painting with almost every Indian — showing a distinct Greek-revival influence — while the pose is reminiscent of other mythological figures who draped themselves over the titles of nineteenth-century maps and official documents.

The Shawmut bank note, however, was not the only place

where early Bank officials found a use for their Indian figure. In May 1864 the Board of Directors unanimously approved a seal for use when the Shawmut changed its status from a state to national bank under provisions of the National Bank Act of 1864. The design of this seal again shows an Indian figure, but he is no languid sachem but rather a simple hunter who stands erect on a small plot of land, a bow in one hand and an arrow in the other. Although this figure bears little resemblance to his bank note cousin, he does bear a remarkable resemblance to the Indian on the seal of the Commonwealth of Massachusetts. Indeed, the similarity is so striking that it is difficult to believe it was not deliberate.

Again, and unfortunately, it is impossible to know exactly when the figure on the seal was designed. It may actually have been in use during the Shawmut state-bank period, and the May 1864 directors' vote may simply have authorized the continuance of the image with the new national bank name. Whenever the figure was designed, it is probably just to assume that the artist, unrestricted by any rigid notions of what a Shawmut Bank Indian must look like, was purposely capitalizing on the lucky coincidence that such a figure suggested both his own institution and the state within which it was located. Lending credence to this theory is the fact that many banks actually did incorporate a state symbol into their own seal.

Between 1837 and 1864, then, it is clear that the Shawmut was already beginning to use the Indian figure as a way to project its identity by a visual means, but significantly there was no attempt to standardize the image, to establish a trademark identity that would distinguish Shawmut Bank products from those of all other competing institutions. The figure was only used on the notes and seal, and any Indian would do.

Between 1864 and 1898, the Bank continued to grow and extend its operations. Oddly enough, however, the use of the Indian actually faded during this period. Official documents displayed the Indian seal (it is still in use in the 1980s, with the same image and only a change of name), but his presence on notes was far less evident, though the reason for the omission is hardly obscure.

With the passage of the Bank Act of 1863, national banks began to issue national notes, which used graphics of an appropriate national or regional rather than individual significance. The face of a Shawmut one-dollar note dated January 2, 1865, for example, showed two mythological women shaking hands before a pedestal bearing the national eagle and a perpetual flame. On the reverse was depicted the "Landing of the Pilgrims," flanked by the Massachusetts state seal and the eagle. Other denominations showed other national themes. An 1865 two-dollar note, "secured by Bonds of the United States Treasury at Washington," displayed another mythological woman with a halo of thirteen stars and holding a starred flag. The commemorative picture on the back was of Sir Walter Raleigh in 1585, apparently signing the first Colonial Royal Charter, and again flanked by the seal and eagle. Still a third note of the period, series 1882, signed 1884, had President Garfield on the face, the seals of the state and country on the back.

But if it is understandable that the Shawmut Indian disappeared from notes, it is somewhat surprising that he was not used on other material. During the early years of national banks, acceptance of deposits had begun to emerge as an important bank function, and demand deposit checks had come into wide circulation. (These checks are not to be confused with earlier checks, which the Shawmut had issued since 1837 and which were little more than written instructions to the Bank to loan the bearer a certain amount of money. They had no relation to demand deposits, which did not yet exist.) The newer checks were used as a form of currency, and in many instances they actually replaced the bank note. That the Shawmut did not see fit to embellish them with an illustration perhaps suggests that, after three decades of reliable service, the Bank felt its name alone was sufficient to convey its identity. In 1898, however, the situation changed dramatically, when an energetic attempt to capitalize on the meaning of Shawmut and the richness of its associations began.

The event triggering this was the merger of several Boston national banks, including the Shawmut National, into a completely new corporation, the National Shawmut Bank. In order to establish a spiritual, if not legal, continuity between the nine disparate units that made up the new organization, Shawmut officials began to emphasize Shawmut in quite a different way than they had in the past.

The first indication of this emphasis came in a resurgence

of interest in the Indian figure. Although he was no more evident on the National Shawmut bank notes than he had been on the Shawmut National bank notes, he began to appear with great regularity on the Shawmut checks. Here the figure served as a visual reminder to customers previously served by one of the merged banks that their accounts were now residing in the National Shawmut, and it also served to communicate a sense of the institution's roots.

Two images on two different checks issued shortly after the turn of the century demonstrate this point. On one the Indian stands on the edge of a cliff glowering down on what is apparently Boston. The legging costume is much more realistic than the toga of the 1854 figure, while the design — particularly if the town is intended to be Boston — is more historically and pictorially suggestive than the earlier mythological scene. The second image is even more interesting — here for the first time in the Bank's iconography, only the Indian head is shown. Furthermore, the precision with which the elegantly feathered headdress, the pendant earrings, the bear claw necklace were rendered, as well as the clarity of the features and very distinct expression of the face, suggest that this was meant to be a portrait of a particular Indian, perhaps the sachem of the tribe that supposedly inhabited the Boston peninsula before the arrival of the English.

If at this point the Bank made no explicit connection between their Indian and any specific person, the unknown artist may well have done so. In 1896 Charles Francis Adams published his massive *Three Episodes in Massachusetts History*. Herein Adams not only discussed the meaning of the term "Shawmut" but also retold William Bradford's early account of a 1621 meeting between Myles Standish and a local sachem called Obbatinewat, who had cooperatively signed an agreement with Standish, opening the Boston area to English development. What could be more appropriate to an artist, contracted to make an illustration suggestive of the Shawmut name and history, than to render this Indian who in a sense started it all. But whatever the intention of the particular design and whatever the Bank directors understood by it, at least it had now apparently become clear that a single head was more suitable for Bank purposes than a full figure.

From the early 1900s, then, dates the use of an Indian head

on Bank material, although there was still no particular consistency in its presentation. In 1907, for example, the invitation announcing the opening of the Bank's new quarters on Water Street employed a stylized rendition of the elegant Indian that appeared on National Shawmut Bank checks. Inside the new building, however, quite a different image, now cast in bronze, looked up at visitors from various locations on the marble floor. This rendition showed a coarse, rather than aristocratic, face, with braids, instead of shaved side locks, and a headdress of strangely common-looking feathers.

At this juncture all that can be said is that the Shawmut Bank Indian had evolved from being a general illustration into a kind of portrait that suggested a real person and, by extension, a real history of which the Bank was somehow also a part. Interestingly enough, it was during this same period that the National Shawmut began to promulgate what, for the lack of a better word, must be called "Shawmut lore."

The first printed evidence of this lore appeared in a pamphlet issued for the opening of the 40 Water Street building in 1907. On the first page under a heading, "The Bank," the text asserted that "the National Shawmut is the representative financial institution of New England. Since its incorporation seventy years ago it has always been identified with the best financial interests of Boston and the territory of which this city is the metropolis." The pamphlet then went on to state, under the subheading "Origin of Shawmut," that

> the very name Shawmut is old and honorable. Before the Puritans landed on these shores it was the name of the Indian village on the banks of the Charles. Early explorers transferred the name to the place of the three hills, later called Tri-mount or Tremont. All through Boston's venerable past we find it borne by established institutions, none perhaps so pre-eminent in its time as is the National Shawmut Bank today.

Although the intention of the text was to establish for the Bank a long and honorable connection, it was historically inaccurate. The Shawmut Bank, after all, not the National Shawmut had been founded seventy years ago, and the story of the Indian village was apocryphal. Nevertheless, despite the questionable facts, the idea of spreading word of the Bank through a history of the name was apparently effective, for shortly afterward another pamphlet appeared.

The second pamphlet, entitled "Origin of the Bank Name," could be considered the Shawmut's first publicity release, for it had no substantive function aside from publicity. Taking its information almost entirely from an 1845 book called *Shawmut, the Settlement of Boston by the Puritan-Pilgrims*, its text asserted that "the Indians had called it [Boston] 'Shawmut' which translated means 'Living Fountains' on account of the many good springs of water existing on a part of the peninsula."

Even in the first decade of the twentieth century this etymology would have seemed dubious. Many respected scholars, including Charles Shaw and Charles Francis Adams, had effectively argued for other meanings. The 1845 story, however, fitted the Bank's purposes nicely, for as the publicity pamphlet went on to explain, "Spring Lane and Water Street of today, separated by only a few feet, were named on account of these springs, and by coincidence the building of the National Shawmut Bank at 40 Water Street is directly over the course of perhaps one of the most important of the springs."

No self-respecting publicist could have allowed such a coincidence to pass, and this one did not. And if the effectiveness of an idea is to be measured by its longevity rather than its accuracy, he did well. As late as 1975, the Bank's publicists still asserted that the site of the National Shawmut Bank at 40 Water Street was "near the mouth of the spring which inspired the Indians to name the community in honor of 'its living fountain' as Shawmut." This, however, is to get ahead of our story. In the first decade of the twentieth century, prompted by an impulse to affirm the tradition of their institution as part of Boston's evolution and by the need to unify their disparate elements around a single image, Bank authorities gave their approval to a Shawmut story and to the image of an Indian as their identifying hallmark. It remained only for the latter to achieve final definition for legend to attain the status of fact.

2

Exactly why and when a young artist named Adelbert Ames, Jr., was retained to do the definitive portrait of the National Shawmut Bank Indian are unknown. We do know that young Ames, having been graduated from Harvard in 1903 and from Harvard Law in 1906, went into business with A. Henry Higginson, son of Shawmut director Henry Lee Higginson. In 1910, however, young Ames apparently decided that business was not his métier, and although he kept some business connections, he determined instead to become an artist.

Given these facts it is fun to imagine a scenario in which Colonel William Gaston, then president of the Shawmut, is invited to dinner one evening in 1910 by his friend and colleague, Major Higginson, now in his tenth year as a director of the Bank. In the candlelit dining room at 191 Commonwealth Avenue, with dinner over and the coffee and brandy set out, the two men begin discussing banking, perhaps commenting on how appropriate it would be to have a portrait of the Bank Indian in addition to the floor medallions in the lobby of the new building. At this point young Higginson, who is also present, thinks of the artistic ambitions of his partner and suggests his name. Higginson senior is, of course, a patron of the arts, having been instrumental in starting the Boston Symphony, while Colonel Gaston's humanitarian instincts are well known — as president of the Boston Elevated before coming to the Shawmut, he had established workers compensation long before it was adopted elsewhere. Thus both men are struck by the idea of helping a new and struggling young artist. Additionally, both Higginson and Gaston are businessmen, and the notion that a commission for an unknown might be less than that for a professional may also enter into their thinking.

This is apocryphal. What we do know for certain is that Adelbert Ames, Jr., began work on a Shawmut Indian portrait in 1910, that in the process he did a plaster bust, which was to serve as a model for the portrait, that he showed this to the Bank directors, who immediately canceled the portrait. The bust, they proclaimed, was exactly what they wanted; nothing could be better.

By 1912 the Adelbert Ames Indian had become *the* Shawmut Indian. A bronze casting of the bust was prominently displayed in the 40 Water Street lobby, a three-quarter-face engraving became the Bank's registered trademark, a line drawing of his profile appeared on the October 23, 1912, statement of condition, while a photograph of his profile decorated the lower left-hand corner of the 1913 calendar distributed in December 1912. Whatever the medium the message was the same — this is the Shawmut. That the figure bore no resemblance to a New England Indian was inconsequential. (Ames may, in fact, have been influenced by Cyrus E. Dallin whose bronze portrayal of a western native American was cast in 1910.) Much more important than accuracy or influence, however, was that the image conveyed all those qualities with which any institution would want to be associated.

What had appealed to the 1910 Board of Directors and what continued to appeal to the public through generations was the expression of Ames's statue. The figure looked outward to an unfathomable future, but the strength of the jaw made clear that no obstacle there would prove insurmountable. The mouth suggested strength without compromise, the lifted chin courage, the clear brow vision. Yet there was nothing fierce or arrogant about the visage. The very simplicity of the rendering, which now boasted only one feather that might be understood as emblematic of a single, but overwhelming, victory, gave the whole a concentrated focus that was difficult to forget.

With Ames's creation as the centerpiece, the story of Shawmut, and by extension the National Shawmut Bank, took on a new dimension. Paradoxically, however, the name of the young artist was almost obscured by the fame of his creation, and indeed Ames did not continue long in the art world. Although he would always paint for his own pleasure, the study of color led him into the career in which he eventually distinguished himself — research in the physiology of visual perception — and the Shawmut Indian remained his only sculpture.

3

In the course of the next seventy-plus years the reputation of
the Ames Indian and the stories that went with him grew steadily. Although it is not clear exactly when the bust was first
called Obbatinewat, that legendary sachem of the Shawmut Indians so glowingly described in Charles Francis Adams's history,
by 1923 it was clearly his name. Accompanying a small bronze
replica of the bust, a leaflet distributed much later claimed that
"because of its strength of character and historical association,
the likeness of Chief Obbatinewat was chosen by the National
Shawmut Bank to serve as a symbol and trademark." But this
seems to be a revisionist's view. There is no concrete evidence
that interest in a specific historical figure preceded the sculpture, and the first printed reference to an actual name does
not appear until the publication of a booklet "issued to commemorate the completion of the enlarged and remodeled Shawmut Bank building in 1923." This latter, however, does take
the name for granted: "One of the features of the main banking
room that remains unchanged is the bronze bust of 'Obbatinewat'." The text goes on to supply his past: "Obbatinewat was
the sachem of the Shawmut Indians when Miles Standish and
his party from Plymouth visited here in 1621 and he therefore,
as the first Indian governor of record for this territory, has
been taken to embody the significance of the name 'Shawmut',
which so many years ago was given to this bank." The facts
here, as later historians pointed out, were again dubious, but
no matter, the name like the image immediately fired the public's imagination. In 1929 Dartmouth's winter carnival, well
known for its snow sculpture, even featured a Shawmut Indian
carved of snow, which a subsequent, if somewhat disrespectful,
Bank article described as "our own Indian 'Obbatwhathave-
you'."

Other releases were not so disrespectful. The house organ
(significantly called *Wigwam* from its inception in 1926) devoted
a column and a half of its August 1929 edition to the explanation
of Shawmut and the Shawmut Indian. That living fountains,
Shawmut, and Boston were synonymous with one another was
again solemnly asserted, as was the notion that the main Bank

building lay over the course of one of the springs that fed the fountains. This time, however, the account went further than the 1907 one, making the importance of the connection explicit: "So it naturally followed that one of the oldest and strongest of Boston banks should carry the name Shawmut through its near century of highly significant banking." Finally, after stating that "the Shawmut Indian is without doubt the most famous trademark in the century of highly significant banking," the article concluded that "the Indian head which has gained international reputation as the mark of the National Shawmut Bank has been reproduced from its bronze bust of Obbatinewat, Sachem of Shawmut, by A. Ames, Jr."

Throughout the 1930s these "historical" items served as the basis of Bank publicity. But in 1944 Shawmut's Obbatinewat began to make history on his own. At that time the British destroyer HMS *Tyler* had put into Boston for repairs. The officers and crew, encountering the bust of the old brave and struck by his familiar features, appealed to the Shawmut president, Walter Bucklin, for a bust to be used as a mascot. Bucklin complied and the Shawmut Indian went to war where he saw action in the Atlantic and Mediterranean, participating in the sinking of forty-two U-boats. Such indeed were his accomplishments that he was awarded a Star for Service in Operational Waters, the Italian Star for Service in the Italian campaign, the France and Germany Star, and the Atlantic Star Clasp which entitled the chief to a Silver Rosette.

It was also during the 1940s that Obbatinewat was incarnated in human form when Bucklin and John J. Barry, then vice president in charge of Advertising and Publicity, authorized an advertising agency to bring him to life. An obliging Sioux Indian model was appropriately made up to serve in the first television bank commercial on the first telecasts of WBZ-TV in 1948. In this guise, Obbatinewat brought Bostonians and suburbanites the nightly "Shawmut Nightly Newsteller" and the prime time weekly "Shawmut Home Theatre," which featured full-length first-run movies. Perhaps inspired by this "live" image, Bucklin authorized Barry to paint the various busts, which by now appeared in the lobbies of the Bank's many branches. For the next several years Obbatinewat appeared with dusky skin, black braids and a red feather, a transformation that in 1949 elicited the comment from Ames, "That's not the way I dreamed him and made him. I loved the old white plaster model. Pretty or not, he was mine."

But painted or not, "Obie" continued to make his presence known and in a variety of places and forms. In 1950 his live counterpart showed up for a guest appearance with Shawmut newscaster Arch MacDonald on "Tucker Talk," a WBZ-TV disc jockey video venture. In 1958 a bronze replica accompanied Gerard E. Hayes, Shawmut assistant vice president, to Vatican City for the elevation of Archbishop Richard Cushing to the rank of cardinal by Pope John XXIII. It remained as gift with the papal secretary. In 1961 a savings bank Obbatinewat bust served as a centerpiece in a Viennese bank window devoted to a display of "Money Boxes from the United States." That same year a forty-seven-foot image, with a cut-out feather but no Shawmut-identifying signature appeared on a billboard adjacent to Boston's Central Artery. A later survey revealed that 88 percent of those who saw it immediately recognized "the Shawmut Indian." Finally, in 1963 Obbatinewat went to Hollywood when movie producer Otto Preminger, capitalizing on the fact that "the Shawmut Indian was the most popular banking trademark in the area," contacted the Bank's Public Relations Department for permission to reproduce him on 1916–1917 currency and coin banks for the Boston-based movie *The Cardinal.*

By 1970 the live Obbatinewat had all but disappeared, although he still showed up, generally accompanied by four Indian maidens, for occasional galas such as the opening of the Government Center branch in 1963. The new decade, however, was to see other and in some ways very radical changes in the manner of presenting Obbatinewat and in the substance of the stories surrounding him. During these years the painted bust was replaced by a bronze three-dimensional figure. Even more important, the current stylized blue version of the familiar features replaced the line drawings that had previously marked most Shawmut material. Keeping pace with these changes was a new scholarly interest in Obbatinewat's roots and the genesis of the word *Shawmut.*

The circumstances dictating the changes were various. They included the growing professionalism of marketing, which placed less emphasis on clever advertising gimmicks and more on trademark consistency and meaning; the changing character of the Shawmut organization and its affiliated banks, which demanded a new corporate image; and, on the simplest level, the increasing difficulties involved in reproducing a consistent four-color image. Of these, the change in organization was undoubtedly the most important.

In 1965 the Shawmut Association, begun as an investment trust company in 1928, had been converted into a modern bank holding corporation comprising thirteen banks, of which one was the National Shawmut itself. The birth of this new corporation sparked the need for a name and a logo that made clear the family relationship of all the affiliated members. It was not until the 1970s, however, that any real action was taken to satisfy this need. At this time, D. Thomas Trigg, chairman of the Corporation, authorized the development of a corporate identity system that would "unify the Shawmut family of banks in a contemporary manner, yet maintain a link with our past that directly reflects our character and heritage."

On April 1, 1975, the Shawmut Association, Inc., introduced the unifying plan to the public. The plan introduced two startling innovations. Henceforth all banks affiliated with Shawmut Corporation had the name Shawmut as the first word in their title. Such a rechristening was not accomplished without some reluctance on the part of suburban bankers, who were used to their "own" names, but the advantages of a clear corporate identification could not be denied. Thus the National Shawmut Bank of Boston became the Shawmut Bank of Boston, N.A. (the initials signify National Association); the Melrose-Wakefield Bank became the Shawmut Melrose-Wakefield Bank, N.A.; the Needham Bank became the Shawmut Needham Bank, N.A.; and so on.

As startling as the new names was the new and distinctive graphic treatment of Chief Obbatinewat, which replaced the "realistic" line drawings of the past with a stylized balance of positive and negative areas defining the facial features and feather, now projected against a blue circle. This fresh and modern interpretation of Ames's sculpture, of course, attracted public attention, but it was only one small part of a much larger and very comprehensive program that gave all the Shawmut Association banks a common identification, symbol, logotype, and name.

Nor were these the only innovations. A seventy-page manual issued by the Association carefully spelled out the elements of the system and provided rigid guidelines for their implementation. For example, the section on the corporate color, Shawmut blue, not only gave the formula for the shade but cautioned that "since variations in paper stock, printing techniques and ink formulation directly affect final appearance of a color, swatches must be used for visual matching." Other sections dealt with advertising, communications, and signatures, all three of which were referred to as the "culmination of the system" and which comprised three basic elements, "symbol, logotype, and bank name." How these elements were to be used in each specific instance and what variations were allowed was clearly outlined. Nothing was left to chance. From official correspondence to interoffice memoranda forms, from promotional literature to outdoor signs, the use of the word *Shawmut* and of the Indian symbol was carefully systemized and standardized. Obbatinewat, as perhaps best befitted the diverse organization he represented, had become "professionalized."

During this same period of the 1970s, the stories surrounding Shawmut and its chief were also subjected to a new scholarly scrutiny. Early in the decade Lawrence H. Martin, then president of the Corporation, and Warren Berg, a senior vice president, became interested in tracing the true roots of the Shawmut name and of Obbatinewat. Berg approached Dr. Irving Telling, a professor at Massachusetts Bay Community College, who had done work on the history of the area, with four key questions: What is the meaning of Shawmut? Was there a Shawmut tribe? What was Obbatinewat's tribe? What is the most learned opinion of the meaning of Massachusetts? If it (Massachusetts) was an Indian tribe, can something more be said about it? Dr. Telling accepted the challenge of finding answers to these questions and suggested that Dr. Dena Dincauze, assistant curator of North American Archeology at the Peabody Museum at Harvard and "the most knowledgeable person on the subject of Eastern Massachusetts Indians," might also help. With the Bank's blessing, as well as Professor Telling's warning that the facts might not conform to the myths, research began on a project that was indeed to change some of the Shawmut lore.

As a consequence of Dr. Telling's work the legend of the

living fountain quietly evaporated. *Shawmut,* it turned out, was not "a complete Indian word but rather a corrupted contraction, syllabified by English grammatical rules. The native form was close to *Machauwomuk,* a southern Algonquin word." The meaning of which, Dr. Telling went on to say, was elusive but in all likelihood referred to a broad low valley, "obviously the Charles estuary region, not specifically the Boston peninsula."

Dr. Dincauze, concentrating on the Obbatinewat story, added more information. Central to her findings was the fact that the Mushauwomeog Indians, who inhabited the country of Massachuseog (hence the name Massachusetts), had been decimated by plague and had disappeared from the peninsula that came to bear their name several years before the arrival of the English. Nevertheless, there appeared to have been a representative of the tribe living to the south of the Neponset River; he did go by the name of Obbatinewat; he did meet with Myles Standish in the Neponset area, where he may have fled to escape from the warring Tarrantines; and possibly for this reason, he signed a treaty of mutual aid with the English. Nothing more, however, is known of Obbatinewat. Was he a famous sachem? Did he change his name, as was the wont of Indians at significant junctures in their lives, and live on to accomplish great deeds? Or did he disappear from Massachusetts in 1620 as surely as he disappeared from any records?

In the 1980s whether a real Obbatinewat with any resemblance to his current form existed or not is immaterial. What is sure is that he exists today as the Shawmut Indian, looking out with ineffable dignity on the financial world — a symbol of strength and integrity.

PART THREE

The
Bank Holding Company

Shawmut Association and the 1965 Reorganization into the Shawmut Association, Inc. (1928–1965)

U P to this point, our Shawmut history has focused primarily on the Shawmut Bank of Boston, one of the leading financial institutions in New England. As important as the Bank may be, however, it is still only one part of a much larger organization, the Shawmut Corporation, which was incorporated in 1964 as successor to a Massachusetts trust established in 1928 by officials of National Shawmut Bank.

At the end of 1982, Shawmut Corporation, the second largest bank holding company in the region, controlled thirteen affiliated banks in eleven counties throughout Massachusetts. It had six wholly owned, nonbanking subsidiaries and a 50 percent joint venture engaged in bank-related activities. The consolidated assets amounted to over $5 billion of which the Shawmut Bank represented over half. The story of how this Corporation emerged from a small business trust controlled by the Shawmut Bank into a major bank holding company controlling the Bank is the subject of the following two chapters.

The story begins on May 21, 1928, when officials of the National Shawmut Bank created Shawmut Association as an investment trust. A year earlier the same officials had also created another investment trust, Shawmut Bank Investment Trust, but there was a significant difference between the two organizations.

Whereas the purpose of the first was to invest in shares of a variety of enterprises, the major investment objective of the second was to acquire controlling interest in particular bank stocks. The decision to create Shawmut Association and to implement this innovative investment policy represented efforts by Shawmut Bank officials to keep abreast of the rapidly changing financial environment that characterized the 1920s and that was to alter the face of commercial banking.

The Roots of Shawmut Association

Among the many factors contributing to this change in environment was the growth of the investment trusts and the rise of national bank branches, which began to develop shortly after the Comptroller of the Currency decided in 1922 to allow "uptown offices" and which received official sanction in 1927 when Congress adopted the McFadden Act.

Investment Trusts. In the early 1920s the investment trust concept was introduced in the United States after years of successful operation in the British Isles. Basically a mutual fund, the investment trust allowed many shareholders to pool their assets and carry a broader investment portfolio than any individual could obtain acting alone. After the McFadden Act and state regulations limited the ability of national banks in Massachusetts to expand through branching, the investment trust format presented a perfect vehicle for the National Shawmut Bank, through the Shawmut Association, to expand its market in the neighboring counties through stock ownership of local banks. This expansion was important to the National Shawmut Bank because it had decided to pursue another trend in the commercial banking field, the rise of retail banking and the attraction of the individual customer. Personal loans and deposits were viewed at the time as a major source of new growth for national banks willing to cater to these customers.

Shawmut's president, Walter S. Bucklin, coming as he did from the insurance industry, was keenly aware of the vast potential this market presented and was not constrained by the staid corporate conservatism influencing most commercial bankers. He energetically pushed Shawmut in this direction. Nevertheless, it was also clear that the coming years would see an inevitable shift of these very customers to the growing Boston suburbs outside Suffolk County, this because of the new mobility provided by the automobile. Thus, the National Shawmut needed some entry into the neighboring counties of Essex, Middlesex, Norfolk, and Plymouth without running afoul of the branching limitations. The investment trust concept, as carried out by the Shawmut Association, promised to provide just the flexibility needed for the National Shawmut Bank to obtain a network of affiliate banks in these neighboring counties. As it turned out, the concept was not really workable without significant changes in the law. The format of the Association, however, as laid out by Bucklin and the senior Shawmut officials formed the basis of what today is the Shawmut Corporation.

Branch Banking. As the 1920s began, branch banking by national banks was not allowed but was a leading topic of debate. While branch banking had a long history in the United States, language in the National Bank Act of 1863 had been interpreted from the beginning to mean that national banks had no authority to establish or operate branches. For almost sixty years, the validity of this interpretation was not questioned, and national banks each maintained only one banking office. Meanwhile, several states did permit their state banks to operate branches. For instance, trust companies in Massachusetts enjoyed countywide branching privileges as early as 1903, and several in Boston developed extensive branch systems. Thus, some state banks were able to gain a competitive advantage over the national banks serving the same areas. Further compounding their problems was the advent of Federal Reserve notes in 1913, which minimized the note issue advantage previously enjoyed by the national banks.

As more and more banks opted for state charters, the federal officials charged with supervising the vitality of the National Banking System sought to restore the attractiveness of national charters by providing at least comparable branching privileges to the national banks competing in states that allowed branching. During World War I and the years immediately following, the Federal Reserve Board and the Comptroller of the Currency recommended to Congress that some branching privileges be

granted to national banks, but Congress did not act on these
recommendations immediately. By 1922, the new Comptroller,
D. L. Crissinger, took a different approach to the problem.
He sidestepped the legal deadlock on this branching issue by
ruling that national banks in states allowing branches could
open limited purpose uptown offices within their home city.
These offices would be allowed to accept deposits and applications for loans. According to Crissinger's interpretation of the
law, so long as the loans emanated from and applications were
processed at the main banking house, the uptown offices would
not be branches. Immediately, he began issuing permits for
such additional offices.

The National Shawmut Bank was one of the national banks
to take advantage of this new policy, when Walter S. Bucklin
established an uptown office at Park Square early in 1924. Before the end of 1926, Shawmut had opened six offices throughout downtown Boston. Similar national bank "branch systems"
sprouted up in other states. It soon became evident that Congress would take some action on the issue of branch banking,
and rumors were rife that it would authorize full statewide
branching or even recognize another recent trend by allowing
interstate banking chains, such as existed in the Far West and
Deep South.

When Congress did act in February 1927, it adopted the
McFadden Act, endorsing a restrictive view of the branching
rights of national banks. Since the primary issue in the controversy had been the impact of branching on local competition,
the ingenious solution was simply to apply each state's branching law to the national banks operating in that state. Thus, in
each state the branching rights of state and national banks were
coextensive. Hindsight reveals that in Massachusetts, this was
the end of the branching issue, but at the time it seemed to
be just an intermediate step along a continuing path toward
more liberalized branching rights. In fact, the very language
of the McFadden Act seemed to open both the Congress and
the state legislature as forums to obtain provisions for more
widespread branching in the future. In this atmosphere the
Shawmut Association concept was perfectly suited to the National Shawmut Bank's plans for acquiring footholds for potential branching outside Suffolk County. In fact, the very success

of the Shawmut Association approach obviated the need for wider branching privileges in Massachusetts, although, surprisingly, the Shawmut officials did not recognize the full potential of their holding company operation for several decades. As late as 1956 President Bucklin himself still concentrated on the Shawmut Association banks as potential branches of the National Shawmut Bank, rather than as elements of a unified banking group serving the state.

Shawmut Bank Investment Trust. While the branching controversy was raging during the 1920s, Shawmut management was coming to recognize that the investment trust concept, if materially modified in respect to capital structure and control, provided an opportunity for profit, which might be large in relation to the amount of the Bank's capital that would be involved.

Shawmut officers had come to this recognition largely because of the customer relationship that was developing between the Bank and the pioneering investment trust firms of Paul Codman Cabot, the State Street Investment Corporation and the State Street Research and Management Corporation. One of the earliest and most skillful practitioners of the investment trust concept, Cabot had graduated from the Harvard Business School. While visiting Scotland, he had learned how the investment trust operated and, returning home, had adapted the idea to the American market. His success, manifest in the performance of his two firms, was striking, and in 1926, when Cabot was twenty-seven, he was invited to join the Board of Directors of the National Shawmut Bank. Certainly one of the reasons for the invitation was Shawmut management's growing interest in investment trusts and it is no coincidence that a year after Cabot joined the board the Shawmut Bank Investment Trust (SBIT) was established.

Although Cabot had a hand in designing SBIT, it differed significantly in its capital structure from the austere capital-stock-only design of Cabot's own State Street Investment Corporation. The major modification was an unusual three-tier capital structure. SBIT had senior debt (sold to the public), junior debt (largely bought by the Bank), and warrants for stock to be issued later at no cost to those who provided the funds. Five million dollars in capital was obtained from the 4.5 and

5 percent senior debentures, which were sold to the public
by Shawmut Bank's subsidiary, Shawmut Corporation, and $1
million came from direct sale, largely to the Bank, of 6 percent
subordinated debentures.

Managing these funds were five trustees selected by the Executive Committee of the National Shawmut Bank. They were
Walter Bucklin, Paul Cabot, Frederick P. Royce and Norman
I. Adams, all of whom were Bank directors, and Frank. C. Nichols, a vice president.

From its inception, and as was evident in its capital structure,
SBIT was designed to take advantage of prosperous times. Bonus warrants were attached to the debentures and could be
exchanged for common shares with no par value. Thus no capital contribution was represented by these shares. Their only
hope of value was that the earnings of SBIT plus an appreciation
of its assets would exceed its expenses, including interest on
its debentures. Payment of these were to come from paid-in
funds — net profits.

Unfortunately prosperous times were not forthcoming, and
in the worldwide deflation of the 1930s SBIT experienced severe losses. At this time Bucklin considered merging the Bank's
two investment trusts — SBIT and a second trust, Shawmut
Association. But whereas the former was based on debt instruments, the latter had issued no debt instruments and was exclusively an equity fund, with all its equity paid in the common
shares. This difference was too great a hurdle to be overcome;
merger plans were abandoned, and in spite of a few initial
good years, SBIT eventually had to be liquidated. In the meantime, however, Shawmut Association, which was to become
Shawmut Corporation had been founded.

Creation of Shawmut Association

In early 1928, after the Shawmut Bank Investment Trust had
been operating for about nine months and as a response to
the newly adopted McFadden Act, Bucklin began a series of
discussions with the other trustees about the prospects for initiating a similar trust for the purpose of obtaining control of
various banks. Vice presidents Louis J. Hunter and Frederick
M. Thayer did most of the brainstorming on this matter, laying

the groundwork for the eventual Shawmut Association. A series of memos during the month of March indicate the thinking behind the pending trust. The topics of these early discussions ranged from the investment policy to the manner of participation that would be reserved for the National Shawmut Bank. At one point they even considered the possibility of having the Shawmut Association take over control of the Bank through an exchange of stock with the Bank's stockholders. This idea was dropped on the realization that a group of more speculative investors than the Bank would like could gain control over the Bank itself by obtaining Association shares. National Shawmut Bank control over the affairs of the Shawmut Association was retained through the simple expedient of having the selection of successor trustees made subject to the approval of the Executive Committee of the Bank's Board of Directors.

Drafts of the trust instrument were drawn up by Shawmut Bank director Frederic E. Snow, who for almost thirty years had been the law partner of the retired Shawmut Bank president, William A. Gaston. After the plan was finally approved, the Declaration of Trust was signed on May 21, 1928, bringing Shawmut Association to life. The declaration named as trustees the same five men who then governed the Shawmut Bank Investment Trust — Bucklin, Adams, Nichols, Royce, and Cabot — and provided broad exculpatory clauses as well as broad investment powers.

In accordance with the declaration, assets for the Shawmut Association trust were to be obtained through the issuance of common shares. One million shares of no par value were authorized, but the original issue was limited to 400,000 shares. Subscription rights to these shares were divided among three groups of investors. Three hundred thousand shares were reserved for National Shawmut Bank shareholders, who could request two Association shares for each of the 150,000 Bank shares outstanding. Another block of 20,000 was set aside for management personnel of the Bank, and the final 80,000 were reserved for customers of the Bank. Original plans priced these shares at $50 each for Bank shareholders, $51.50 for management personnel, and $52.50 for Bank customers, but the actual call was discounted by $30 subject to later call, reducing the initial outlays to $20, $21.50, and $22.50 per share.

All the shares of the Association were distributed through

the auspices of the Shawmut Corporation of Boston, which acted as underwriter. The extra dollar per share charged to the Bank customers provided an $80,000 fee paid to Shawmut Corporation for its underwriting and distribution services. Assuming all shares were distributed at the rates shown, the asset pool available for investment by Shawmut Association amounted to $8,150,000.

Apparently the issue was not nearly as popular as the Association trustees hoped, for in November 1928, they deemed it necessary to cancel the $30 balance subject to call, leaving the shares fully paid at the $20, $21.50, and $22.50 prices. Even after this step, the express purpose of which was to make these shares more attractive and thus more easily marketable, 1929 figures show that Shawmut Corporation of Boston still held 100,000 of the Association shares, fully a quarter of the entire issue, which it had been unable to sell in the marketplace. Sales were so slow that Shawmut Corporation of Boston sponsored a contest among branches of the National Shawmut Bank to complete the distribution of Association shares during February and March of 1929. Issues of the *Wigwam News* for these two months report on the progress of the contest and congratulate everyone on the results. That being the situation in 1929, one can only guess how poorly the sales of Association shares had been faring before the $30 balance was canceled.

Despite the difficulties Shawmut Corporation experienced in trying to distribute the shares, Shawmut Association had its asset fund in hand from the beginning and initiated its investments just two weeks after the Declaration of Trust was signed. As they commenced making these investments on June 8, 1928, the trustees adopted a formal investment policy stating their goals. According to this policy, the trustees determined to invest 50 percent of the Association assets in the same general manner that the funds of Shawmut Bank Investment Trust were invested, 25 percent in other bank stocks and special underwritings, and the final 25 percent in other commitments for reasonably quick return. Originally, the trustees discussed in preliminary planning for the Association a policy that called for 50 percent of the assets to be invested in bank stocks. Presumably, the trustees believed that bank stocks were overpriced in 1928 and settled upon a lesser commitment of their assets for the time being. Of course, another motivation for the reduced concentration on bank stocks could have been efforts to disguise the Association's bank-holding purpose. Shawmut leaders also had to consider the impact the Association's acquisitions would have on the National Shawmut's own extensive business with correspondent banks in New England, who were sensitive to perceived encroachments by the Shawmut Bank.

As it turned out, almost twenty years passed before Shawmut Association's investments in bank stocks approached 50 percent of its total assets. On a cost basis, the 50 percent level was reached in 1947, but because the Association's other securities had appreciated so greatly, it was not until 1955 that the investments in banks equaled the market value of the portfolio of other securities. As late as the end of 1945, the net asset value of the affiliate bank stocks held by Shawmut Association amounted to less than 25 percent of the market value of all securities in its investment portfolio.

In line with the determined investment policy, the original investments made by the trustees were listed in the minutes of that June 8, 1928, meeting. Majority interests in both the Merchants National Bank of Salem and the Winchester National Bank were obtained in this first purchase, and together they totaled less than $600,000. Compared to the size of the National Shawmut Bank, both were modest surburban banks. At the beginning of 1928, the National Shawmut had $15 million in capital, and deposits totaling $189 million. By contrast, Merchants National Bank had $200,000 in capital, $200,000 in surplus, and deposits of almost $4,350,000. Winchester was even smaller in size, with capital of $100,000, a surplus of only $15,000, and deposits of barely $973,000. The Association trustees invested an additional $336,000 in several small blocks of stock of a variety of banks in Massachusetts, Connecticut, and Rhode Island. The total of the Association's original investments in bank stocks then amounted to under $1 million, less than half the 25 percent figure declared as the intent in the investment policy. The most significant investment made in the opening foray was a $5 million commitment to the Dodge Brothers bond issue, and the remainder of the Association's assets was held for the time being in cash and a small block of foreign bonds while further opportunities were studied.

Before the end of 1928 Shawmut Association added two more banks to its list of holdings. The trustees assisted in the organization of the new Needham National Bank for Savings and Loans, retaining a majority share of the stock issued. This bank opened for business on October 1, 1928, with a capital of $150,000 and several Shawmut-related names appeared in key positions. Horace A. Carter, an "old and valued customer of the National Shawmut Bank," was elected president of the Needham Bank. At the time he was treasurer of the William Carter Company in Needham and he remained head of the Needham Bank until 1957. Four of the original Needham directors had even closer ties to the National Shawmut Bank. They were Paul C. Cabot, a trustee of Shawmut Association and a director of the Shawmut Bank; Frederick M. Thayer, a vice president of both the Shawmut Corporation of Boston and the Shawmut Association; Robert M. Tappan, an assistant to the Shawmut president, Walter S. Bucklin; and Ralph E. Bailey, the National Shawmut Bank statistician. Finally, the new cashier of the Needham Bank was recruited from the National Shawmut branch at Bowdoin Square, where he had been assistant manager.

In December 1928, the Association announced the acquisition of a majority interest in the Hingham Trust Company, which had a $100,000 surplus, and $1,280,000 in deposits. Thus, before Christmas 1928, when the Association was barely seven months old, the trustees had obtained a foothold in each of the four counties immediately surrounding Suffolk — Essex, Middlesex, Norfolk, and Plymouth — and their total investment in bank stocks amounted to $1,254,000. During the next thirty-five years the Association continued to acquire banks in these counties, but it did not expand into additional counties until after adopting the corporate form of organization in 1965, when it became a full-fledged bank holding company.

At the end of 1928 Shawmut Association presented its first annual report, which indicated that 15.2 percent of its assets were invested in bank stocks. The remaining mix of investments is interesting for its comparison to the original investment policy. Thirty percent of the assets were invested in common stocks of American industrial companies, 10 percent in foreign common stocks and bonds, 5 percent in domestic industrial bonds and demand loans, and 39 percent in call money or cash. These figures emphasize the fact that Shawmut Association was much more than simply a bank holding company at this early stage of its development. While the acquisition of bank stocks was one of the prominent reasons for setting up the separate trust, focusing simply on the bank stocks overlooks the general investment nature of the Association.

Shawmut Association in the Great Depression

During its formative period, Paul C. Cabot, a trustee, was a dominating influence on the investment decisions made for Shawmut Association. His opinions were respected and proved valuable. The heavy concentration of fund assets in call money and cash at the end of 1928 was the result of Cabot's cautious approach to the overvalued status of the stock market at that point. During the ensuing year, he attempted to maintain the level of assets invested in common stock at no more than 25 percent of the fund's total asset value. In the rising market fueled by rampant speculation, Shawmut Association's overall asset value increased by some 12 percent, largely on the appreciation of the common stock holdings. Needless to say, when the market broke late in 1929, much as Cabot expected, the Association lost some of the $9 million market value of its assets, but the damage was held to a relative minimum. In the following few years, as the market continued to collapse, holdings of the Association sustained a much more limited decline than did the market as a whole. When the bottom was finally reached during 1932, Shawmut Association listed its assets at about $5.6 million, a decline of 45 percent from the peak. In contrast, the Dow Jones Industrial Average plummeted from 381.17 in 1929 to 41.22 on July 8, 1932, an 89 percent drop. Thus, the Association survived the market decline in much better shape than the typical investor, and this was due in large part to the advice, counsel, and accurate assessment of market conditions by Cabot and other trustees of the Association.

The course of action taken by Shawmut Association was not the product of just one man, however. As a group, the five trustees determined most of the policy decisions, and this group showed a remarkable continuity over the first twenty years of the Association's existence. Through the end of 1947, only three replacements occurred, two because of resignations and one the result of the death of Frederick P. Royce. The first change in the membership of the board came about when Frank C. Nichols resigned from the Bank on September 19, 1929. His resignation did not appear in the Association minutes, but presumably he curtailed all his Shawmut affiliations upon his departure from the Bank. His successor, George E. Pierce, was elected a trustee on February 7, 1931. At the time Pierce was a vice president and director of the National Shawmut Bank. Two years later, in late 1933, Royce died and was succeeded by George H. Clough, a Bank director who was elected a trustee of the Association on January 15, 1935. Both Clough and Pierce served until their deaths in 1948 and 1951, providing the board continuity, with the three remaining original trustees, over the entire course of the depression.

Despite the best efforts of these trustees, the difficulties of the market collapse and the ensuing depression had an undeniable impact on the balance sheet of the Shawmut Association. Still, this period also provided a unique opportunity for the Association to enhance its reputation as a paternal holding company concerned about the welfare of its affiliate banks. All of them were guided safely through the Great Depression. The Association was in a position that allowed it to draw upon the talents and resources of the National Shawmut Bank, to benefit from management guidance as well as capital infusions. Shawmut's success in endeavors to keep the affiliate banks afloat at a time when many banks across the country were failing proved to be a selling point later, when the Association resumed making bank acquisitions toward the end of World War II. It could then cite the assistance rendered to all its banks, especially the financial assistance provided in conjunction with the Reconstruction Finance Corporation in the 1930s to Merchants National and Hingham Trust.

While this assistance was allowing the banks to hold their own, Cabot became increasingly concerned that the Association was missing more valuable opportunities in other common stocks, which he viewed as more attractive than bank stocks. Despite Cabot's entreaties, the trustees, who were also Shawmut

Bank officers, persisted in holding on to the affiliate banks, because they were keenly intent on preserving the bank-holding character of Shawmut Association's existence. Through the years, the Association retained all the banks it ever held, adding several as the years progressed.

One of the early victims of the banking difficulties prevalent during 1932 and early 1933 was the Central Trust Company of Cambridge. Despite a capital and surplus of $3 million and deposits of almost $16.5 million, this bank collapsed and was reorganized under the supervision of the state banking commissioner. Shawmut Association took a leading role in this reorganization, which resulted in the formation of the new County Bank and Trust Company, capitalized at $300,000. County Bank issued 30,000 new shares of stock to the shareholders of the defunct Central Trust Company, and in June 1933 Shawmut Association obtained 20,000 of these new shares through a one-for-one exchange of its own shares. To accomplish this exchange, the Association issued 20,000 new shares of its own. This transaction relieved Central Trust Company shareholders of their stockholder liability in the old bank, bailing them out of a potentially large loss.

During this period, it was not at all clear the Association shares would be viewed as an attractive alternative. As early as August 1932, the Association was actively purchasing its own shares in the market, both to support the price and take advantage of the bargain value the market price then presented. This may have also been a strategy to preserve the Association from the clutches of some speculative buyer. Many of these shares were undoubtedly available to the Association after the exchange that enabled it to obtain the interest in the County Bank and Trust Company. In that transaction the Association authorized the issue of up to 40,000 new shares for the exchange. As noted above, only about 20,000 were actually issued. At the end of the year the Association had accumulated about 33,800 of its own shares through open-market purchases, and held them in the treasury. The trustees decided to retire these shares and cancel the certificates, resulting in a net decrease of some 13,800 outstanding Shawmut Association shares.

Even after retiring these shares, the Association continued to buy the undervalued shares in the open market, and the prices it paid for these shares indicate the ravages of the depression on the investors. Small-lot purchases by Shawmut Association of its own shares were reported to the trustees regularly throughout the rest of the 1930s. The severe drop in the market value of these shares must be compared to the original $20 to $22.50 investments and to the net asset value per share, which never dropped below $14. Even so, the market price for Shawmut Association shares in the midst of the 1933 banking crisis plummeted to just under $7 per share. Later in the year the shares fluctuated between $8 and $10, reflecting the true bargain the shares represented against their net asset value and the realization that the Association banks would survive the crisis intact. Doldrums still persisted though, and the market price again dipped in late winter 1934 to a low of $6.75 per share. Then the market price enjoyed a sustained rise, reaching $12 by late 1937, still a bargain compared to the net asset value, which was then hovering between $18 and $22 per share. Another break in the general stock market occurred in 1937, and the delayed reaction forced Shawmut Association shares down to $8.125 in early 1938. Before the end of the decade, the market price recovered to a level more consistent with the actual net asset value per share.

Potential merger or buyout talks surfaced at many stages during the decade. The sister trust, Shawmut Bank Investment Trust, fared quite poorly throughout the era, and after 1935 was unable to make the established interest payments on its outstanding notes. Shawmut Association, because of its nature as a bank holding company for the National Shawmut Bank, was more carefully protected by the trustees. This did not eliminate thoughts about liquidating or selling the two trusts. Approaches during the year 1934 were gently rebuffed, but the Association trustees and officers did indicate a willingness to consider reasonable offers from any source. One interesting proposal was made in 1938, suggesting a merger between Shawmut Association and Fidelity Fund, Inc., the financial investment group that has grown so substantially in the succeeding decades. This merger proposal came at the time Shawmut Association was considering a new issue of securities to increase the amount of funds in its assets. As it turned out, the Association trustees took no action on either suggestion and maintained the Association in its then current form and funding level. No decision on these proposals appears in the minutes, and whatever reasons dissuaded the trustees can only be surmised. It is safe to assume one major stumbling block in the proposed Fidelity Fund merger was the natural reluctance of the Association trustees to give up any control over the Shawmut Association assets, especially its seven affiliate banks. This network of affiliate banks, and their implicit ties to the National Shawmut, was one of the basic reasons for establishing the Association in the first place.

The trustees acquired control of a seventh bank, the Melrose Trust Company, in August 1937. This bank was capitalized at $100,000 and had a $100,000 surplus. Deposits held by the bank totaled almost $2.3 million. Shawmut Association obtained almost 8000 of the 10,000 outstanding shares, or an 80 percent interest, paying $30 per share. This $240,000 transaction appears to have provided a cash infusion to the National Shawmut Bank and the Webster and Atlas National Bank, the only two parties selling the 80 percent interest. Applying the $30 per share figure, National Shawmut received about $135,000 for the 4,483 shares it delivered, and the Webster and Atlas received about $105,000 for its 3516 shares. This transaction may have been necessitated by the unexpected dive of the domestic stock markets during 1937, wiping out much of the recovery experienced through the end of 1936. During the summer of 1937, the Association had decided to withdraw completely from the bond market, unloading all of its remaining bond holdings, with a par value of about $500,000. The market value of this transaction is not readily available, but presumably, the proceeds from the sale were applied to the Melrose Trust acquisition.

Shawmut Association in the Late 1930s and the 1940s

As the Shawmut Association entered its second decade of operations, political conditions in the world were rapidly deteriorating and the rising tide of World War II loomed ominously. Uncertainties of the day produced a steady decline in the American stock markets. The Standard and Poor's 90 Stock Index reflected this uncertainty from 1938 through the beginning of 1942 by dropping progressively lower until bottoming out at half the 1938 index value. In this same period, Shawmut Association suffered a similar but less marked decline in the value of its investment portfolio. Overall, according to published year-end figures, the market value of the Association's assets fell from $7,156,000 in 1938 to $5,791,000 in 1941, hitting an eight-year low. During this three-year period the net asset value of the seven affiliate banks actually rose $120,000, so the decline in the market value of the Association's other marketable securities amounted to $1.5 million. During this decline, Shawmut Association retained most of its holdings. Most of the loss in value was apparent only on paper, and the losses actually sustained by the Association were of modest proportions.

Market conditions improved during 1942, after the United States was drawn into the war as an active participant and the economy geared up for full-scale war production. Many young men were called into the nation's service in a variety of capacities. During the year Cabot resigned as a Shawmut Association trustee to assume an administrative position in the Office of Production Management in Washington, D.C. His resignation created a vacancy in the Association board, which remained unfilled until the end of 1946. During his absence, Shawmut Association still received the investment advice of his State Street Research and Management firm. During the war years, the markets enjoyed a sustained upward climb, culminating in 1946 when they surpassed the earlier 1936 crest and reached a fifteen-year high. Shawmut Association enjoyed a 73 percent increase in its overall asset value during the four years ending December 31, 1945, edging over the $10 million mark for the first time in its existence. The year 1943 was a particularly successful one for the Association. In that one year alone, its assets increased $1,250,000 in market value, almost a 20 percent rise. This was the greatest gross increase in asset value experienced until 1961, and marked the largest percentage increase the trust ever had in a single year. In the four years, Shawmut Association's marketable securities, other than bank stocks, appreciated by $3.5 million, more than restoring the values of the previous unrealized losses.

Expansion in the Postwar Years

The new strength of the market value of the Association's assets prompted the trustees to reconsider their investment policy with respect to suburban banks. Their intention of obtaining a group of such banks as a supplement to the Boston-based National Shawmut Bank remained a primary purpose of the Association, even though the trustees had committed only 25 percent of their assets to this end during the first sixteen years. As 1945 began the time seemed ripe for new dedication to this original purpose. The trustees determined to shift more assets into bank holdings, increasing them to 50 percent of the Association's total assets and taking advantage of the recent appreciation of the securities portfolio. This strategy involved a shift of $2 million from general common stocks into banking stocks. The actual sale of common stocks during 1945 and 1946 produced a capital gain of almost $1.2 million, which was due to the appreciation. The contemporary capital gains tax consumed 25 percent of this figure, leaving $900,000 of the gain for the new bank investments. Thus, almost half of the $2 million shifted into banking stocks came from appreciation of the earlier investments.

Acquisition of New Bank Shares. Within three years of the decision to increase its number of affiliate banks, by the end of 1947, the Association acquired substantial shares in five new banks, increasing the total number of affiliates to twelve. Although the trustees negotiated with banks in several of the counties surrounding Boston, by chance the five additional banks were all located in Middlesex County: the Everett National Bank, Newton National Bank, Waltham Citizens National Bank, Wakefield Trust Company, and the Somerville National Bank.

Shawmut Association's first bank acquisition since 1937 resulted from an option to buy 2,288 shares of the Everett National Bank, which was capitalized at $376,000, had a $74,000 surplus, and counted $7 million in deposits. The purchase price stipulated in the option agreement was $75 per share, but when Shawmut Association exercised the option, in a letter dated February 3, 1945, it offered $76 per share, a one-dollar premium. This offer was extended to all Everett shareholders, and resulted in the Association obtaining almost 5600 shares, a majority interest, in a $425,000 transaction.

Simultaneous negotiations with two other suburban banks failed to result in obtaining a majority position, so the Association was unable to gain entry into Medford or Norwood at the time. Soon after, the Association turned its attention to the Newton National, a bank with $200,000 in capital, $140,000 in surplus, and deposits totaling almost $5.3 million. Shawmut's offer to purchase a majority of the Newton shares at $52 per share was detailed in a letter dated August 13, 1945. The offer was conditioned, as were many others during the period, upon Shawmut Association receiving a 51 percent tender within two weeks of the offer. At the end of the year the Trust held 7771 shares, indicating the transaction cost just over $400,000.

Acquisition activities continued through 1945, with Shawmut Association assisting in the organizing and capitalizing of a new bank in Waltham. This organizing effort was authorized by vote of the trustees as early as October 1945, and resulted in the Association retaining 5157 shares of the bank, valued at $50 each. This $250,000 investment meant the Waltham Citizens National Bank was a Shawmut Association affiliate when it began operations in March 1946. By the end of that year its capital was $150,000, its surplus was also $150,000, and it had already attracted $1.5 million in deposits. Just as Waltham Citizens was beginning to function, Shawmut Association turned its attention to the Wakefield Trust Company, a bank whose capital of $225,000 was divided among three classes of stock and whose surplus was a mere $12,500. It did have $6.8 million in deposits, so the Association was willing to offer $30 per share for a minimum of 66.66 percent of the outstanding shares tendered by April 15, 1946. Shawmut acquired almost 4000 shares in a transaction valued at just under $120,000. Later in 1946 the Association minutes indicate Shawmut was unsuccessful in attempts to reach an agreement to acquire a Reading bank.

The final addition in this era of Shawmut Association bank acquisitions came during the summer of 1947, when the Association accepted an invitation from the Somerville National Bank to offer $38.60 per share for at least 51 percent of its outstanding shares. Somerville had $300,000 in capital, $400,000 in surplus, and $13 million in deposits. Shawmut's offer letter stated no deadline, but by September 17, 1947, it had acquired almost 23,000 shares, and was already applying to the Federal Reserve Board for permission to vote them, indicating the $888,000 purchase had been completed.

The Association minutes for these eventful years are quite stark and reveal little about the reasons why particular banks were selected for acquisition and why some negotiations succeeded where others failed. By all indications, there was no particular plan used to determine which banks Shawmut Association would seek to acquire. The more significant factors seem to have been practical ones, such as the availability of the bank, predisposition of its major stockholders, and attractiveness of the proposal. Specific purchases tended to be fortuitous rather than designed. One aspect of the acquisitions is apparent in the minutes: the competition Shawmut Association encountered from similar bank-holding entities, which were also preparing for the anticipated expansions in banking that postwar America might generate. Growth projections for the areas surrounding Boston must have been more promising than those for the city itself, making a solid, well-positioned group of banks, such as Shawmut Association then featured, a valuable asset.

Changes in Trustees. This flurry of acquisition activity was soon followed by a striking change in the personnel in the trustee positions. Three changes occurred in 1948 alone, after there had been only three changes in the prior twenty years. In addition, the Association learned that a former trustee, Paul C. Cabot, would not be returning after his stint in Washington because he was accepting an appointment as the treasurer of Harvard University. Accordingly, he and his advisory firm were severing some of their business ties. Shawmut Association lost his valuable counsel and the investment advice of State Street Research and Management, advice that had proved so valuable over the years.

The first trustee to depart during 1948 was attorney Robert G. Dodge, a director of the National Shawmut Bank. His resignation letter stated that the trustee meetings were inconvenient for him to attend, but other indications suggest he was concerned about the inherent conflict of interest a trustee endured while serving simultaneously as a director of the Bank. Dodge remained an active Bank director through 1962, and his vacant trustee position was given to Lee P. Stack, also a director of the Bank and vice president of John Hancock Mutual Life Insurance Company. Later in the year two more vacancies opened. George H. Clough, a director of the National Shawmut Bank since 1925 and a trustee of the Association since 1935, died late in 1948. In his place, Josiah B. Rutter joined the Board of Trustees at the December 14, 1948, meeting. At the same meeting, Rohl C. Wiggin was named to replace Norman I. Adams, an original trustee of the Association who was retiring after a fifty-year banking career. A vice president of the National Shawmut Bank since 1916, and a director since 1920, Adams had been an officer of the former Boston National Bank when the 1898 mergers brought him into the Shawmut ranks. His replacement as trustee, Rohl Wiggin, had been intimately involved in the affairs of the Association since being elected vice president on November 18, 1942.

Shawmut Association in the 1950s and Early 1960s

With the new trustees in office, joining Walter S. Bucklin and George E. Pierce, Shawmut Association was ready to ride the bull market of the next decade. An immediate postwar slump during the three years 1946–1948 reduced the value of the Association's assets to just under $9 million, putting the net asset value per share at $22.84 at the end of 1948. This short slump soon gave way, and over the next sixteen years, beginning in 1949, the Shawmut Association net asset value per share increased every year except 1953, when it slipped four cents. In some years the increase was dramatic. Most notable was the 1954 increase of 14 percent, bringing the total asset value to almost $13,750,000. Again in 1955 the Association assets appreciated by more than $1 million. In both years the Association added new banks: the Warren National Bank of Peabody in 1954, and the Brockton National Bank in 1955, thus enhancing Shawmut's position in the two counties of Essex and Plymouth.

New Acquisitions. Three factors undoubtedly influenced the decision to acquire these two banks. First, it was evident that the market value of the securities other than bank stocks in the

Association's investment portfolio were appreciating considerably faster than the net asset value of its various bank holdings. Thus the two acquisitions indicate an effort by the trustees to maintain the asset mix at 50 percent in bank stocks and 50 percent in other marketable securities by realizing some of the stock gains and shifting these proceeds into banking assets. Second, Shawmut Association undoubtedly felt compelled to find strong banks to buttress the once ailing Hingham Trust Company and Merchants National Bank of Salem through mergers. These two banks had both received Reconstruction Finance Corporation loans to carry them through the 1930s, and quite possibly they had never fully regained their fiscal strength. The Association did promptly arrange mergers between the earliest affiliates and their newly acquired neighbors. Finally, these two acquisitions occurred at a time when bank holding companies across the country were engaged in a rush to make final additions before enactment of a law concerning bank holding companies, which appeared imminent. The bill pending in Congress contained provisions that would render bank acquisitions more difficult in the future because it would require Federal Reserve Board approval of all such acquisitions.

Negotiations for the purchase of a two-thirds interest in the Warren National Bank of Peabody took place during much of 1954. The Warren was capitalized at $200,000, had a $200,000 surplus, and held $6.3 million in deposits. The sticking point in these negotiations seems to have been determining the appropriate price per share for the 1334 shares Shawmut Association wished to obtain. At first the Warren directors were asking $275 per share, an offer the Association trustees rejected as too high. In June the trustees approved an offer by the Association at $260 per share, including the right to the July dividend, but the Warren directors turned it down. The last offer mentioned in the Shawmut Association minutes, and presumably the one resulting in the acquisition of the bank, reduced the price to $257 per share, without making claim to the July dividend. This transaction amounted to about $350,000. Later in 1954 Shawmut Association purchased a few additional shares at $225, suggesting the negotiated price had been perhaps 10 percent higher than the prevailing market price.

Shawmut Association's final bank acquisition before the Bank

Holding Company Act became law involved the largest transaction value of any of the Association's bank acquisitions. The trustees paid more than $1,280,000 for almost 80 percent of the 30,000 outstanding Brockton National Bank shares. Brockton boasted $22.4 million in deposits, a capital of $600,000 and a surplus of $600,000. The transaction resulted from Shawmut's offer to pay $54.05 per share for at least two-thirds of the shares in the summer of 1955. At the August trustees meeting, vice president Horace Schermerhorn reported that considerably more than the minimum 20,000 shares had been tendered, requiring the Association to sell some common stocks from its general portfolio to raise the necessary cash. These general portfolio transactions, together with the other sales during 1955, allowed the Association to realize $665,000 of the appreciated value of its common stock holdings. Much of this gain undoubtedly funded the acquisition of the Brockton shares. When the year ended, Shawmut Association was the owner of 23,750 Brockton Bank shares and was well positioned for the imminent adoption of the Bank Holding Company Act.

Bank Holding Company Act. The ground rules governing bank holding companies changed markedly in 1956 when Congress adopted the Bank Holding Company Act. This act extended the supervisory authority of the Federal Reserve Board to cover bank holding companies as well as member banks. Proposals of this nature were nothing new. Bills on the subject had been introduced in every session of Congress since 1937. Efforts to regulate them dated back to the banking crisis in 1933, at the beginning of the Franklin D. Roosevelt administration. Year after year these bills died in Congress, often without coming to a vote. Several factors stood in the way of passage. But primarily, bank regulators and legislators could not agree on what legislation the situation required.

A preliminary step had been taken when the Banking Act of 1933 required companies to register with the Federal Reserve Board if they owned a majority interest in any Federal Reserve System member bank. It also required them to obtain a permit to vote majority share holdings. Aside from these two requirements, registered bank holding companies operated outside the purview of federal banking regulators.

During the depression and the banking crisis period, many bank holding companies proved beneficial in supporting their affiliate banks. Other bank holding companies sold off their holdings or disbanded, for banks struggling to survive the economic throes were no longer the attractive investments they had been in the 1920s. In the 1930s the unregulated power of bank holding companies was not as feared as it once was, nor did the companies generate the same level of animosity witnessed earlier. Just when the bills to regulate them began to appear in Congress, the urgency for action disappeared and the issue of regulation receded from center stage in the political arena. Not until after World War II did bank holding companies again become a focus of concern.

In the immediate postwar period Shawmut Association increased its holdings of banks significantly. This represented one major trend occurring generally among bank holding companies, and attracted the attention of those who supported regulations. By the early 1950s concern over the unchecked growth of these companies had crystallized in Congress, and some form of legislation became almost inevitable. Regulation and supervision by the Federal Reserve Board, which already had such powers over the vast majority of banks operating in the United States, became a recurring provision in proposed bills. Such a provision would authorize the board to review proposed acquisitions of banks by bank holding companies. In anticipation of change, then, a wave of late hour acquisitions began, including Shawmut Association's own acquisitions of the Warren National Bank of Peabody in 1954 and the Brockton National Bank in 1955.

No act could be adopted until Congress reached agreement on the appropriate definition of bank holding companies, determining which companies would be regulated under the act. The controversy centered around two separate aspects of bank ownership by holding companies: the extent of the interest owned and the number of banks so held. Proposals ranged from a majority interest to 25 percent, 15 percent, or even less for the interest owned and one or more than one for the number of banks. In 1956 Shawmut Association owned a majority interest in fourteen banks, so it was certain to be included regardless of the definition. Yet different combinations of the factors could change markedly the number of companies subjected to regulation. By the mid-1950s, there were some 163 bank holding companies operating in the United States that owned at least 25 percent of one bank. Of these, 116 companies owned 50 percent or more of one bank. If the definition required 25 percent ownership of at least two banks, then only 46 of the 163 companies would be regulated. The old registration requirement under the Banking Act of 1933 applied only to companies that held a majority interest in a Federal Reserve System member bank, and several companies counted in the group owning 25 percent or more of at least two banks did not own a majority of any member bank, so they were not registered.

Congress settled on the "25% of two banks" definition and adopted the Bank Holding Company Act in 1956. Thus, the number of companies subjected to federal regulation was relatively small. Some states also adopted measures to regulate bank holding companies, often with definitions differing from the federal law. When this happened, interesting anomalies arose. Some companies came under state regulation even though the federal law did not apply to them, while others fit within the federal definition but not the definition selected by the state. No such anomalies arose in Massachusetts when it enacted a bank holding company statute in 1957. The Massachusetts statute was closely modeled after the federal act and used an identical definition.

One major provision in the new federal Bank Holding Company Act restricted the extent of nonbanking activities a regulated bank holding company could engage in. Of the forty-six companies characterized as regulated bank holding companies in 1956, many had extensive nonbanking activities which were their principal lines of business, and the banks constituted just an interesting sideline. Rather than having all of their activities regulated by the federal authorities, these companies ceased being "Bank Holding Companies" under the Bank Holding Company Act by divesting themselves of their banks. About twenty companies did so shortly after the federal law came into effect, leaving about twenty-five regulated bank holding companies, of which Shawmut Association was one of the largest in the nation.

For several years after this decline, the number of bank holding companies remained stable, while banks and holding companies learned how the act would affect their operations. In the late 1960s, however, and largely because of the growth of single-bank holding companies, which were usually formed by the bank itself, a veritable explosion in the field began. And in the 1980s few, if any, major banks in the country were not part of a bank holding company.

Still Other Acquisitions. Shortly after Shawmut Association acquired its new affiliate banks in Brockton and Peabody — and after the Bank Holding Company Act of 1956 came into effect — Shawmut merged them with their respective neighbors in Hingham and Salem. This presented an interesting shift in the Association's policy regarding the independence and autonomy of each affiliate bank. Until 1956 Shawmut emphasized its practice of allowing each affiliate to retain its own identity and conduct its own affairs. The new mergers were the first break with that tradition and ended the viability of the claim.

The first merger combined the Hingham Trust Company with the Brockton National Bank. This transaction was reported to the trustees of the Association in September 1956, just before the shareholders of each bank met to approve the merger. Seeking shareholder approval was a pro forma matter, because the trustees held 79 percent of the Brockton shares and 75 percent of the Hingham shares. When 1956 began, Brockton had $600,000 in capital and $600,000 in surplus. Its deposits stood at $24.6 million. Hingham reported $100,000, $100,000 and $4 million in the same categories. The resulting bank retained all the offices of the two merged banks and operated under Brockton's charter as the National Bank of Plymouth County. It began 1957 with a capital of $750,000, surplus of $750,000 and deposits of just over $30 million.

In the second merger, Merchants National and Warren National were consolidated, effective October 18, 1957. Merchants, an affiliate bank of the Association from the very beginning, had grown considerably since the depression. It now had a capital of $250,000, a surplus of $550,000, and deposits of $14.6 million. Its Peabody neighbor, the Warren National Bank, entered 1957 with $200,000 capital, $250,000 surplus, and $7.7

million in deposits. After the merger, the resulting bank reported capital at $600,000, surplus of $700,000, and deposits at $20.5 million. It retained both historic names, operating for the next two decades as the Merchants-Warren National Bank.

Operations of the Association

Once these two mergers were completed, Shawmut Association stood in the form it maintained through the end of its existence as a trust on May 6, 1965, when it was reorganized and became Shawmut Association, Inc. This provides an opportunity to take stock of the Association, its activities, structure, officers, and relations with the various affiliate banks. Even though the Association had grown to twelve banks, which in 1957 amounted to more than half its total assets, its trustees still retained the original attitude that the bank holdings would not be generally publicized, and common ownership of the various banks was not introduced as a marketing development until the 1960s.

But even though there was no emphasis on coordination among the affiliate banks, Shawmut Association was nevertheless one of the major United States bank holding companies in the 1950s, both in terms of assets and deposits and in terms of number of banks controlled. In format, it was a model version of the bank holding company as an appendage to a major metropolitan bank. The links between the Association and the National Shawmut Bank of Boston remained as strong as ever. The trustees and officers of the Association continued invariably to be leading officials of the Shawmut Bank, and much of the specialized banking service provided by the Association to its affiliate banks was provided by the Shawmut Bank.

Trustees. If anything characterized the changes in trustees over the years between 1956 and 1963, it was the fact that the entire team of top managers of the National Shawmut Bank became trustees, reinforcing the Bank's domination of Association affairs and planning. The major change in personnel came at the end of 1956, when Walter S. Bucklin resigned. The president and a trustee of the Association since its inception in 1928, Bucklin had served twenty-eight years in its lead position, and his departure severed the final link between the 1956 board and the originators of the Association. In his place as president, the trustees elected Horace Schermerhorn, who had been elected president of the Shawmut Bank just three months earlier and stood as heir apparent under Bucklin during that period. Schermerhorn had also been elected to the Board of Trustees in June 1956, replacing Walter E. Borden, who retired that month after five years as an Association trustee and president of the Bank. The trustee vacancy caused by Bucklin's resignation was filled by Association vice president Lawrence H. Martin, who was then executive vice president of the Bank. Bucklin, Schermerhorn, and Martin each served at one time as the chief executive officer of the National Shawmut Bank and of the Shawmut Association. An appraisal of each man's significant contributions to the Shawmut Bank appears in the chronological segment of this history and need not be repeated here. In comparison to their duties and responsibilities at the Bank, their Association activities were relatively minor during this period. Eventually, the Corporation that grew out of the Association became the dominant force in Shawmut affairs, but during the 1950s the National Shawmut Bank was definitely the central force.

When the Bucklin administration came to a close late in December 1956, the National Shawmut Bank commanded assets amounting to more than $450 million. By contrast, the combined total assets of the thirteen Shawmut Association affiliate banks stood at just under $170 million, less than 38 percent the size of the National Shawmut alone. Of course, Shawmut Association was simply a stockholder of these affiliate banks, owning shares ranging from 55 to 79 percent, so that the total assets of the banks is a somewhat misleading figure for comparison. A more appropriate measure of the Association's bank holdings is its share of each bank's capital, surplus, and undivided profits. This net asset value of the Association's bank stocks amounted to just under $8 million of the $10.7 million combined total for the thirteen banks. Comparable capital, surplus, and undivided profits figures for the National Shawmut Bank put its 1956 net value at $35.75 million, more than four times the value of the Association's bank holdings. The Association also held other marketable securities, worth almost $7 million at market, and a small amount of cash, giving it almost $15 million in total assets. Thus the desire of the trustees to maintain an approximately equal balance between their bank holdings and their other assets was close to target, with the balance standing at 53 and 47 percent at the end of 1956.

The next major change in the composition of the Association's Board of Trustees occurred when Judge Jacob Kaplan died on August 8, 1960, after serving nine years as a trustee of the Association and a director of the National Shawmut Bank. An attorney in the prominent Boston law firm Nutter, McClennen and Fish, Kaplan was succeeded on February 10, 1961, by Benjamin A. Trustman, a senior partner of the same law firm. That same day the size of the board was increased from five to seven trustees, allowing the addition of Arthur W. Deibert and John Wallace, two senior officers of the Bank. Deibert had been recently elected to the new senior vice-presidential position of the Bank, along with John K. Benson and D. Thomas Trigg, who both soon followed him to the Association Board of Trustees. Wallace, a vice president and the senior trust officer of the Bank, brought his investment expertise to the trustees. The addition of Deibert and Wallace marked the first increase in the number of trustees above the original five. At the end of February, Rohl C. Wiggin, a Shawmut Bank vice president, resigned, ending his thirty-five-year Shawmut career, which included a thirteen-year stint as trustee of the Association. Benson was elected trustee to fill Wiggin's vacancy on May 25, 1961. During this same meeting, Schermerhorn was elevated to the new position of chairman of the board, and Martin was elected his successor as president of the Association, effective July 1, 1961. These changes replicated a similar shuffling of titles that took place in the National Shawmut Bank in October 1960, when Schermerhorn became chairman and Martin rose from executive vice president to president. Already sixty-six years of age, Schermerhorn was past the retirement age established after Bucklin's departure but given special leave to remain chairman until the month of his sixty-eighth birthday. Meetings of the Association Trustees were held quarterly, and President Martin, rather than Schermerhorn, presided over them during this period.

Effective December 7, 1962, Schermerhorn retired as chairman, ending his six-year administration at the top of both the Association and the National Shawmut Bank. In an orderly transition smoothed by the earlier selection of Martin as president, the resignation left Martin the senior officer of both institutions, with no new change in his titles. One week before Schermerhorn's retirement took effect, at the November 29, 1962 trustees meeting, D. Thomas Trigg was elected to take Schermerhorn's trustee position, effective December 10, 1962. Trigg, a senior vice president of the Bank, was the last of the four top management at the Shawmut Bank to become a trustee of the Association. The Board of Trustees at the end of 1962 included Martin, Benson, Deibert, Stack, Trigg, Trustman, and Wallace. Thus the board could draw upon the investment expertise of Stack, then a partner in the Paine, Webber firm, and the legal counsel of Trustman. The remaining trustees were the entire top tier of management at the Shawmut Bank. The final change in the membership of the trustees came in January 1963, when Deibert resigned upon his retirement from the Bank. No replacement was named to fill his vacancy, leaving the six remaining trustees to guide Shawmut Association through its final two years as a distinct entity. Only Stack and Wallace were not also serving as directors of the National Shawmut Bank, although previously Stack had been a director from 1947 to 1958, when he moved from the John Hancock Insurance Company to Paine, Webber and became ineligible to serve as a national bank director under federal law.

Officers. A look at the officers of the Shawmut Association is also revealing. Again the dominance of the National Shawmut Bank is evident, as most all Association officers had a link to the Bank. As 1962 ended Lawrence Martin was president of the Association. The three vice presidents were John K. Benson, Leslie J. Scott, and Frederick W. Swasey. Scott, the president of the Winchester National Bank, had been a dedicated Shawmut employee. He was a National Shawmut Bank branch manager at the time he was shifted to the Winchester bank in 1930. Mr. Swasey was a trust officer of the Bank and undoubtedly had responsibility for the investments of Association assets. He began reporting to the trustees as early as 1958, soon after he was elected an assistant trust officer of the Shawmut Bank.

Usually, his reports were made in the absence of Raymond N. Olsen, an assistant treasurer of the Association since June, 1947, and a vice president since 1951. Olsen remained an active officer of the Association until the middle of 1959, when health problems forced him to curtail his activities. During the late 1950s, Olsen was the one assistant vice president serving under John Wallace in the National Shawmut Bank Trust Division. At the end of 1957, because of Olsen's expertise in investments, he was named to head the new Investment Research Department within the Trust Division. As his health improved, Olsen took on new duties in the Bank's Investment Division, and beginning in the middle of 1961 he no longer held a title in the Shawmut Association. The only other man to serve as a vice president of the Association during this period was Arthur B. Tyler, the general counsel of the Shawmut Bank. He was elected vice president and general counsel of the Association on August 15, 1958, and served until his retirement in April 1962.

Relationship of Affiliated Banks. Despite the obviously dominant role National Shawmut Bank officials had in determining Association policies and affairs, the affiliate banks were able to exercise a remarkable degree of independence. Part of this independence stemmed from the Association's own policy of allowing the affiliate banks to operate autonomously, but even more of it came from the institutional reality of a suburban or small town bank. As majority shareholder, the Association theoretically could elect any individuals it wanted to the board of directors of each affiliate bank. But it was restrained from exercising this power by the fact that the banks depended on the deposits of local merchants and business customers, who were represented on the boards. Any effort to remove prominent local merchants and businessmen from the affiliate boards would probably have resulted in their withdrawing deposits, which could have had an adverse impact on the banks. Therefore each affiliate bank was largely free to choose its own directors, and each board was allowed to follow its own dictates, although the Association might frequently make suggestions.

Eventually, the identification of the affiliate banks as integral parts of the Shawmut Association's service to the greater Boston area became more important as a marketing strategy. And, after the Bank Holding Company Act of 1956 and the marked rise and acceptance of bank holding companies, it became more common to accentuate the ties that bound these banks to the Association and to the Shawmut Bank of Boston.

Forming the Present Shawmut Corporation

After 1956 the trustees and officers of the Association grappled with the new requirements of both the 1956 federal act and a similar 1957 Massachusetts act. Under these laws bank holding companies were regulated as they never had been before. As things stood in the late 1950s and early 1960s, both the Association and the National Shawmut Bank were treated as bank holding companies under provisions in the original 1928 trust agreement making Association trustee appointments subject to the approval of the Bank's Executive Committee. This meant that both organizations were forced to submit filings and respond to government questions relating to their activities. In time it became evident that Shawmut would have to do something to update the structure of the relationship between it and the Association, with its several banks in the surrounding counties, for the existing arrangement was antiquated and less attractive than it previously had been.

At some point soon after the federal and state acts became effective, the Shawmut officials began exploring potential restructuring of the relationship between National Shawmut Bank and Shawmut Association. The earliest tangible evidence that some reorganization was under consideration is the January 4, 1960, power of attorney given by the Association to three Nutter, McClennen and Fish attorneys for the purpose of obtaining from the Internal Revenue Service a tax ruling on a "proposed reorganization of Shawmut Association." The attorneys were Jacob J. Kaplan, Benjamin Trustman, and Earl Johnson. Kaplan was both a director of the Bank and a trustee of the Association, and after his death in 1960, Trustman succeeded him in both positions. The Association later added William Shelmerdine, Jr., in a new March 16, 1962, power of attorney granted for the purpose of "proposed transactions of

Shawmut Association." No details of either the proposed reorganization or transactions appear in Bank or Association minutes of that period, but presumably the reorganization plan adopted by the parties in 1964 was developed during the course of negotiations with the IRS.

One solution might have been to have the Association take over ownership of the National Shawmut Bank, but several impediments stood in the way of such a transaction. First, the existing formal relationship between the two organizations made this apparently simple transaction virtually unworkable. The trust agreement that originally established the Association gave the National Shawmut Bank formal powers over the Association that could not be exercised by a component part of the Association. Moreover, the Bank had a right to participate in the distribution of the Association's assets in the event the Association were dissolved, a process that would be unmanageable if the Bank turned out to be one of the assets to be distributed.

Still another principal difficulty was the disproportionate size of the Bank and the Trust. Shawmut Association had nowhere near the necessary assets to buy up the outstanding shares of the National Shawmut Bank, or even a majority interest in the Bank, without stripping the Association of most of its other assets. There was no point in disposing of all the other assets just to purchase the National Shawmut from its present shareholders. A similar proposal would have had the Association issue new shares instead of cash for the transaction, but this proposal was flawed because it did not address the principal difficulty of the relationships set forth in the original trust agreement. Finally, assuming the trust agreement could have been amended to remove this difficulty, there was still the problem inherent in the contemporary shareholders. A substantial percent of the National Shawmut Bank shares were held by state savings banks, which were limited by state law in the kind of investments they could make. Thus the savings banks, which could invest in national bank stocks but not in other types of holding companies such as the Association, were unable to participate in the suggested exchange of stock. The problem was a major one, for if the savings banks were unable to obtain cash for the shares, it would cause not only a disconcerting disruption in their investment plans but also, because of the massive quantity of shares involved, a shock to the market value of the Bank stock.

Strategists in the Shawmut senior management team, especially the attorneys Kaplan and Trustman, thus devised another plan of reorganization to accomplish the desired modernization and simplification. This plan called for the creation of a new corporation, which would take over the assets of Shawmut Association and then consolidate the National Shawmut Bank into a newly created, wholly owned subsidiary bank, issuing shares of the new corporation in exchange for shares of the National Shawmut Bank as part of the consolidation. Implementation of this complex plan required changes in two provisions of existing laws. For one thing, any reorganization of this sort would preferably be carried out in a tax-free manner, because it changed the legal relationships of the entities but not the underlying value of any of the interests held by the various shareholders. However, the federal tax code did not provide tax-free treatment for this type of reorganization. A special amendment to the tax code was adopted by Congress during 1964, correcting the problem just at the time Shawmut was devising the plans for the reorganization. However, this change alone was not sufficient to allow Shawmut to proceed. Massachusetts legislators still had to authorize the stock of bank holding companies as a legal investment for the state savings banks. Such an amendment was enacted on March 26, 1964. Once the two provisions were established, Shawmut could begin the arduous task of obtaining the necessary approval of the proposed plans from the various shareholders and the government regulators.

Shawmut's plans were sufficiently developed by July 30, 1964, for Martin and Benson to discuss their proposal with the Federal Reserve Board staff members and with the Comptroller of the Currency, whose approval was necessary for the formation of the new bank. Although used subsequently, the plan was notably the first successful one to employ an intervening subsidiary bank to effect bank consolidations. By early August the proposal had received preliminary approval and at this time the attorneys proceeded to sound out the Securities and Exchange Commission's reaction. The results of the early discussions prompted Shawmut Association to engage formally Nutter, McClennen and Fish on August 31, 1964, as legal counsel in "matters concerning the relationship between National Shawmut Bank and Shawmut Association." That same day First Boston Corporation was engaged as an expert advisor, primarily to provide an independent opinion on the relative value of shares in the Association and the Bank. The Association was committed to pay one-third of the fees for each engagement.

Nutter, McLennen and Fish drafted the Plan of Reorganization for Shawmut and submitted details of this plan to the SEC in a letter of September 18, 1964, requesting their opinion of the proposed transaction. The SEC responded on September 23 with a "no action" reply, indicating agreement that the transaction would not necessitate registration under the Securities Act of 1933. The next day the plan was presented to separate meetings of the Bank directors and the Association trustees, and each group approved the proposal.

The two basic features of this proposal provided that a new Massachusetts corporation created for this reorganization would assume all the Association's assets and liabilities, taking on its holding company status, and then absorb the National Shawmut Bank as a wholly owned subsidiary. Three reasons for this reorganization were presented with the proposal and may be summarized as follows: to adopt the more generally accepted corporate form for the holding company in place of the somewhat antiquated declaration of trust arrangement; to clarify the relationship between the Association and the Bank by eliminating the Bank's indirect control over the Association, and thereby placing ownership of both in the same hands, the stockholders of the new corporation; and to improve the business prospects and operating economies for the Shawmut Bank and the affiliated Association banks.

Two additional reasons undoubtedly supported the reorganization plan but they were not stated. One was minor — the desire to have just a single Shawmut entity registered as a bank holding company. This would reduce the need to report activities of both the Bank and the Association and eliminate any regulatory confusion generated by the interplay between them. The much more important unstated reason was a potential conflict of interest problem regarding the disposition of the affiliated banks owned by Shawmut Association.

Over the years the affiliated banks had been obtained by

the Association to provide National Shawmut with a network of affiliates that was available for quick transition into branches, should the day ever arrive when Massachusetts allowed branching across county lines. But, because the Shawmut Association trustees were so closely identified with National Shawmut, the potential transfer of Association banks to National Shawmut raised the possibility of conflict over price questions related to such transfers: Association trustees were responsible to Association shareholders to obtain the best possible price for these banks, but Bank executives would want to incur the minimum expense for such transfers. Martin was particularly concerned that an outside buyer might happen along, presenting an attractive tender offer for any affiliated bank, one the trustees could ignore only at their personal peril and a possible beneficiary's suit by Association shareholders. The trustees would then have to justify their refusal of the offer, perhaps by showing that National Shawmut was willing to match it. In the event county-line limitations were removed, the prospects of a bidding war made this conflict of interest problem particularly ominous, especially if the Bank were caught cash poor at the time such offers arose. The proposed reorganization was designed to eliminate these concerns.

Several carefully orchestrated steps were outlined in the plan of September 24, 1964, to preserve the tax-free nature of the reorganization. As originally presented the plan called for the Association trustees, acting in their individual capacities, to form and incorporate a shell for the new holding company, named Shawmut Association, Inc. The original Association would then organize a new national bank, which would become a subsidiary of the new holding company once the Association was absorbed by it. National Shawmut would then consolidate with this new bank, which was to be called Congress National Bank. National Shawmut stockholders would receive Shawmut Association, Inc., stock in exchange for their Bank stock. The result of this exchange of stock and bank consolidation would make National Shawmut a wholly owned subsidiary of the newly created holding company.

The IRS raised some technical objections regarding the tax implications of this plan on September 28 and suggested its tax-free status would be preserved by the expedient of organizing Congress National Bank as an independent entity rather than as a Shawmut Association subsidiary before the takeover by Shawmut Association, Inc. Shawmut attorneys replied that this change "seems not to be feasible under the governing corporate and banking laws and regulations and, indeed, is probably impossible under present circumstances." Within two weeks the impossible became the preferable, and the reorganization plans were modified to allow five trustees to organize the new Congress National Bank. When the proper moment came they were to issue a majority of the new bank's capital stock directly to Shawmut Association, Inc., so at no time would any part of Congress National Bank belong to the Association. Nutter, McClennen and Fish advised the SEC of this modification, and again the SEC indicated its approval of the reorganization in a November 2, 1964, "no action" letter. Then the IRS Reorganization Branch blessed the proposal with a ruling of December 22, 1964, confirming the tax-free status of the reorganization.

Having cleared these preliminary hurdles, Shawmut initiated the first official transactions to accomplish the reorganization on December 30, 1964. That morning Martin, Benson, Stack, Trigg, Trustman, and Wallace, the six trustees of Shawmut Association, acting in their individual capacities, formed Shawmut Association, Inc., and filed their corporate Articles of Organization at the State House. They elected themselves directors and then voted in a slate of officers duplicating the executive structure of the Association. An original issue of 7500 shares of common stock was authorized, but only five shares were issued (one to each director, with the exception of Stack). These five shares were issued April 29, 1965, the day of the stockholders' first meeting. The directors then committed Shawmut Association, Inc., to the proposed rearrangement by approving the Plan of Reorganization. The new corporation immediately filed applications with the Massachusetts Board of Bank Incorporation and the Federal Reserve Board for approval as a bank holding company. Also on December 30, the same five stockholders submitted to the Comptroller of the Currency, James Saxon, their applications to organize the Congress National Bank.

The significant developments of January 1965 pertained to the Congress National Bank organization process. The Comptroller granted preliminary approval of the application on January 13; the next day Martin, Benson, Trigg, Trustman, and Wallace began formally organizing the new bank by executing Articles of Association. The authorized capital of $200,000 was represented by 10,000 shares of $20 par value stock. The five organizers each subscribed for 50 shares of stock at $28 per share ($20 capital, $4 surplus, and $4 undivided profits) to provide the Congress Bank with an initial capital of $7000. The remaining 9750 shares were reserved for later transactions between the bank directors and Shawmut Association, Inc., as part of the process to make the Congress National Bank a subsidiary of the new corporation. In the initial shareholders meeting on January 14, Martin, Benson, Trigg, Trustman, and Wallace elected themselves directors of the Congress National Bank. A directors meeting immediately followed, when they received the Shawmut Plan of Reorganization and approved its general objective. The directors also voted to execute the agreement of consolidation with National Shawmut Bank and to issue to themselves an additional 700 shares of stock each. The consolidation agreement was signed that afternoon, while the additional lots of 700 shares were delivered on January 27 and immediately made the subject of option agreements between each Congress Bank director and Shawmut Association, Inc.

During the process of organizing Congress National Bank, Nutter, McClennen and Fish submitted an application on February 11, 1965, for Comptroller Saxon's approval of the proposed consolidation of Congress National and National Shawmut banks. The Comptroller returned supplementary forms and instructions the next day. Appropriate notices of the proposed consolidation were published during the month of March in compliance with the Bank Merger Act. Meanwhile, the Congress National Bank directors adopted several housekeeping measures on March 3 as part of the organization process, including the subscription for 144 shares of the Federal Reserve Bank of Boston required to represent 6 percent of Congress' authorized capital and surplus, as well as such mundane matters as authorizing Benson, as cashier, to obtain space, furniture, a bookkeeper, and a Banker's Blanket Bond for the bank. They also approved a petition to the New York attorney general for a written exemption from that state's Fraudulent Practices Act because residents of New York were shareholders of both Shawmut Association and National Shawmut Bank and would be affected by the proposed reorganization.

This process of organizing, operating, and consolidating a new national bank may sound unnecessarily complex, but it was purposely selected for its functional simplicity. The basic concept was designed to provide a clean method to make the National Shawmut Bank a wholly owned subsidiary of Shawmut Association, Inc. (not counting the qualifying shares held by directors). While being organized the new Congress National Bank sold its shares exclusively to its directors and to Shawmut Association, Inc., so it became a wholly owned subsidiary of the new holding company. By consolidating National Shawmut into this wholly owned subsidiary bank, Shawmut Association, Inc., could then control the stock transfer, providing, of course, that the necessary vote of Shawmut Bank stockholders was obtained. (This was the key, for it forced dissenters to ask for a valuation of shares — which one shareholder did.) This stock transfer ensured that National Shawmut itself became a wholly owned subsidiary as a result of the consolidation. Shares of the resulting consolidated bank were then delivered to the holding company in exchange for shares of the holding company being distributed to National Shawmut stockholders as their return on the consolidation.

If instead of following this plan Shawmut Association, Inc., had attempted as an alternative to obtain the outstanding National Shawmut shares through a direct exchange of stock, dissenting Bank stockholders would have ignored the offer, retained their Bank shares, and thereby prevented Shawmut Association, Inc., from obtaining full control of National Shawmut. A minority interest would then have remained outside the holding company (again not counting the qualifying shares held by bank directors). This very phenomenon occurred every time Shawmut Association obtained the various suburban affiliate banks through direct exchange of stock, and to this day such minority interests remain outstanding. Such a likely outcome from direct exchange made the clean result of the seemingly more complex consolidation process clearly preferable.

March 3 was also the date when Shawmut Association, Inc.,

directors authorized President Martin to sign various documents arranging the final transformation. These documents included the reorganization plan and agreement, the bill of sale of Association assets to the new corporation, and an assumption of liabilities agreement between the Association and Shawmut Association, Inc. Now all four separate entities, Shawmut Association, National Shawmut Bank, Congress National Bank, and Shawmut Association, Inc., adopted the final provisions of the reorganization by action of their boards of directors or trustees. All that remained before the transactions could be concluded was shareholder approval of these agreements.

Proxy statements pertaining to these agreements were sent to all shareholders of the National Shawmut Bank and Shawmut Association announcing special meetings in late April for the purpose of voting on the proposals. The proxy statements included a full description of the proposed stock transactions, which were an integral part of the whole reorganization plan. One basic intent of the plan was to place ownership and control of the new corporation in the hands of its stockholders, an improvement over the trust arrangement that gave shareholders only the power to vote on amendments to the Declaration of Trust (all other powers of Shawmut Association were granted exclusively to the trustees).

In 1965 Shawmut Association had about 390,000 outstanding shares in the hands of roughly 3700 shareholders, while National Shawmut Bank's 800,000 shares were held by 7300 shareholders. Neither organization held stock in the other and no substantial ownership existed by stockholders who held stock in both. According to the formula devised by the First Boston Corporation, Shawmut Association shareholders would receive one share of Shawmut Association, Inc., for each Association share held, while National Shawmut Bank stockholders would receive 1.4 shares of Shawmut Association, Inc., for each Bank share held. These two transactions required a total issue of 1,510,000 shares by the Shawmut Association, Inc.

Shareholders of the Bank and the Association were scattered throughout the United States, so to ensure that the proposed transactions complied with state disclosure requirements, Nutter, McClennen and Fish prepared a checklist of the Blue Sky provisions in all fifty states, the District of Columbia, and Puerto

Rico. Many had statutes obviating any registration requirement for the proposed transaction, but twenty-three states did not provide such an exclusion, and special exemptions had to be obtained from them between January and April. Most of these exemptions were pro forma, based on the SEC "no action" letter, but the better part of February and March was consumed by the correspondence clearing these Blue Sky hurdles.

On April 26, 1965, Shawmut Association shareholders gathered to consider the proposed Plan of Reorganization. Although their voting powers were limited to approving a proposed amendment to the Declaration of Trust that would allow the Association to carry out the transformation, shareholders were presented with the whole plan for their consideration. They cast 332,847 votes in favor of the amendment, representing 85.3 percent of the shares outstanding. Only 2,613 votes were cast in opposition. The next day National Shawmut Bank stockholders gave the plan even greater backing, with 88.9 percent of the outstanding shares, 710,850, cast in favor, compared to only 5473 cast against. These results allowed the Shawmut Association, Inc., directors to proceed through formalities of their own shareholder approval and final preparations. Shareholder approval by the Congress National Bank was also perfunctory, because the only shareholders were the five individuals from the Association board.

The Shawmut Association, Inc., meetings of April 29 are especially interesting as the last significant preparation for the May 6 closing date. First, the six directors — Martin, Benson, Stack, Trigg, Trustman, and Wallace — met and voted to issue the five shares reserved for this moment. These shares were sold by Shawmut Association, Inc., at $5 per share so that its first shareholders meeting could be held the same day. In a one-minute meeting immediately following, the shareholders voted to increase the number of authorized shares to 2,000,005. The new corporation then performed the necessary amendments to its corporate articles and filed them with the secretary of state. Soon after, the shareholders met again; they approved and ratified all votes of the directors, adopted technical modifications of the bylaws, and voted in two key provisions that would take effect only after 1 million shares of Shawmut Association, Inc., had been issued (in other words, when the reorganization became effective). These two provisions increased the number of directors to twenty-four and elected the eighteen other directors of National Shawmut Bank to the board of Shawmut Association, Inc. During this same meeting the stockholders surrendered their five shares and authorized Shawmut Association, Inc., to cancel these shares. They also voted to reduce the authorized capital to 2 million shares. When the meeting ended no stock was outstanding and the new corporation held all 2 million authorized but unissued shares. Then the six men reconvened in another directors meeting, performed the authorized reduction of capital, and concluded arrangements for the May 6 closing date. The directors approved details about the stock certificates, signatures, transfer agent, and registrar, and called a special meeting of the directors for May 6 to perform the reorganization.

Now that all the regulatory agencies had approved the proposed transactions, and the shareholders had voted favorably, everything was set for the closing. A summarized chronology of the events that day that fills four typed pages has been preserved, and the schedule and directions for document signings runs eleven pages. The first order of business May 6 was to convert the Association into the holding company. In the morning the Declaration of Trust was amended as previously discussed. Then the reorganization agreements were actually signed along with the bill of sale previously approved. Shawmut Association, Inc., then issued the 390,000 shares to the Association's distributing agent (Memo and Company, Shawmut Bank's nominee) at 2:43 P.M. and took title to all of the Association's assets.

The next order of business was the takeover of the new Congress Bank by Shawmut Association, Inc., with funds made available by Association assets. Shawmut Association, Inc., bought the 6250 unissued Congress National Bank shares for $175,000 and exercised its option to purchase 700 of the 750 shares held by each individual Congress National Bank shareholder leaving untouched for the moment their 50 qualifying shares. Each shareholding director of Congress Bank received $19,600 for his 700 shares. This transaction made Shawmut Association, Inc., the owner of 9750 of the 10,000 Congress shares. With all its stock issued and all capital fully paid in, Congress National

Bank was ready to commence operations and engage in the business of banking. Various forms were submitted to the Comptroller and at 2:57 P.M. his certificate to engage in banking business was issued and delivered to the Congress National Bank. During the rest of the afternoon Congress received deposits, made loans, and cashed checks until its business hours ended at 4:00 P.M.

The final business of the day was the consolidation of Congress National Bank and National Shawmut Bank, which automatically became effective when Congress National ended its business day. Congress shareholders then surrendered their certificates to the newly consolidated Bank in exchange for certificates of the new Bank so that they received 4000 shares each, while Shawmut Association, Inc., received 778,240 shares for its own account and 1760 shares to be distributed to the twenty-two directors of the Bank (80 qualifying shares to each). The five individuals then sold their 4000 Bank shares to Shawmut Association, Inc., so that the holding company ended up with 798,240 shares — all the outstanding shares other than the directors' qualifying shares. With these transfers completed, Shawmut Association, Inc., then issued 1,120,000 shares to the Bank's nominee transfer agent, Congress and Company, to be exchanged for outstanding old National Shawmut Bank shares at the 1.4-for-1 exchange ratio. These transactions were all performed perfunctorily within ten minutes, and before the afternoon ended the whole reorganization was completed. The Shawmut Association, Inc., stock was issued to the two transfer agents, concluding the legal formality of the exchange. All that remained was for these agents to complete the physical exchange of certificates with the thousands of shareholders scattered throughout the country.

Chapter 19

Shawmut

The Corporation (1965–Present)

T HE culmination of the 1965 Shawmut reorganization was a major event in the history of Shawmut's legal existence. The creation of a new corporation as a substantial bank holding company radically changed the formal relationship between the National Shawmut Bank and the former Shawmut Association, which ceased to exist on May 6, 1965, when its assets and liabilities were taken over by Shawmut Association, Inc. Shortly after the reorganization was completed, the June 30, 1965, midyear report was issued indicating the total assets of Shawmut Association, Inc., (parent company) at that point:

ASSETS OF SHAWMUT ASSOCIATION, INC., JUNE 30, 1965

Shares of National Shawmut Bank	$51,102,858	67.1%
Shares of other affiliate banks (12)	13,144,153	17.3
Portfolio of other marketable securities (at current market value)	10,731,613	14.1
Sundry assets (including cash, dividends, accounts receivable)	1,143,044	1.5
Total	$76,121,668	100.0%

These figures show that banking interests comprised 84.4 percent of the total assets of the new parent Corporation. They also indicate that the balance between the former Shawmut Association's bank shares and other marketable securities was approximately 55 percent to 45 percent, a balance appropriate to the type of organization that Shawmut Association had been, but not appropriate for the new bank holding company. Shawmut Association had been a pure investment trust, one that just happened to have 50 percent of its assets concentrated in banking stocks. (In fact, from the beginning, the Association had been intentionally a bank holding entity.) Shawmut Association, Inc., however, could realistically admit that it was first and foremost a bank holding company.

Between 1965 and 1970, the Corporation's investment in its subsidiaries, still almost exclusively the affiliate banks, ballooned from $64,247,000 to $106,915,000, increasing the concentration of its assets in affiliate banks from 84.4 percent of its total assets in 1965 to 92.6 percent in 1970. Much of this increased concentration of corporate assets in banking stocks was due to the issue of new corporate shares to acquire the First Bank and Trust Company and the Framingham National Bank, as well as the exchange of stock in 1968 to acquire the minority interests of the affiliate banks still outstanding at that time. Thus, Shawmut Association, Inc., became a genuine bank holding company, rather than the curious hybrid Shawmut Association had been.

Despite the change, and despite the apparent significance — at least on paper — of the 1965 reorganization, the day-to-day operations of the various affiliate banks were not initially much affected by the reorganization. Much as the Association had done before, the Corporation operated with a skeletal administrative staff. Even three years after the reorganization, Martin could still assert, "Your management has therefore drawn heavily upon the resources of the Boston bank in providing supportive effort and services to the management of the suburban banks. Aside from direct benefits to the group of banks, the availability of such resources makes it unnecessary to expand unduly a central holding company organization, with consequent economies." The Corporation's leading officials continued to be drawn principally from the National Shawmut Bank, and the Bank actually performed most corporate functions and continued to dominate all aspects of the holding company's affairs.

On the surface, then, relations between the various affiliate banks and the Corporation continued much the same as they had under the former Shawmut Association. The affiliate banks maintained a remarkable degree of independence from the dictates of the Corporation. This was largely due to the vitality of the local businessmen serving on each bank's board of directors, for even though the Corporation was a majority shareholder, it was limited in the power it could wield during the election of directors. At the same time, however, Martin's strategy of improving team spirit within the many banks, as carried out by the liaison efforts of Leslie Scott, vice president of the Corporation, was proving fruitful, and latent hostility had given way to a new attitude of joint effort that produced enhanced results.

Martin's strategy to weld the Corporation more tightly together also included a concerted effort to coordinate the banking activities and services of all the affiliate banks, and to make available to all Shawmut customers the capabilities of each affiliate bank. To achieve this end the National Shawmut Bank provided support services to all the banks through the auspices of the Corporation. Such support services allowed for the introduction of trust services at banks that could not support such an operation on their own, and for the introduction of the latest data processing techniques, which depended on state-of-the-art computers and electronic equipment available at the Shawmut Bank. Thus all banks had access to electronic check processing and clearing, investment counseling, credit analysis, and market analysis.

Even more significant to welding the Corporation closely together while reaffirming the dominance of the National Shawmut Bank was the composition of the Corporation's Board of Directors. As Shawmut Association, Inc., was initially organized on December 30, 1964, there were six directors, all of whom had been trustees of the former Shawmut Association. Of those six trustees, only Lee P. Stack and John Wallace were not also directors of the Bank at that time. Stack had previously been a director of the Bank but was required to resign in 1958 when he became a partner in the Paine, Webber investment brokerage house, thereby becoming ineligible to serve as a director of a national bank. On April 29, 1965, the new Corporation's board had been expanded to include the entire Board of Directors of the National Shawmut. With the former shareholders of the

National Shawmut Bank holding four-fifths of the Corporation stock and the Board of Directors comprised almost exclusively of the Bank's directors, the Shawmut Association, Inc., was clearly dominated by National Shawmut Bank interests. In fact almost three years passed before a person who was not already a National Shawmut Bank director was elected to the corporate board and seventeen years before the majority of the Corporation directors were not also directors of the Bank.

Also indicative of the key administrative role that the National Shawmut Bank played in the affairs of the Corporation is the roster of officers who were elected to corporate offices in December 1964. Seven of the eight people elected to the newly organized bank holding company were officers of the Shawmut Bank who had held similar positions in Shawmut Association. Their names and titles in the Corporation following the December 30, 1964, vote were as follows:

SHAWMUT ASSOCIATION, INC.

President	Lawrence H. Martin
Vice Presidents	John K. Benson
	Leslie J. Scott
	Frederick W. Swasey
	D. Thomas Trigg
Secretary, Treasurer and Clerk	William B. Wadland
Assistant Treasurers	Thomas J. Byrne
	Edward F. Gibbons

Martin, of course, was the top officer of both the Association and the National Shawmut Bank, as he had been ever since the 1962 retirement of Horace Schermerhorn. Over the coming years, Martin's titles in both the Boston Bank and the Corporation changed, but he remained the chief executive officer of both entities until his retirement from active management in 1972. Even after Martin retired from daily duties as chief executive officer, he continued to serve on both boards of directors for seven more years, and in that capacity he was an active participant in Shawmut affairs.

Of the four men elected vice presidents of the Corporation, Benson and Trigg were the two senior vice presidents of the Bank, ranked directly behind Martin. The third Corporation vice president, Frederick W. Swasey, who was responsible for the investment decisions pertaining to the Corporation's portfolio of other marketable securities, was also a National Shawmut officer, being the leading investment advisor in the Bank's Trust Department. Thus, three of the four corporate vice presidents held senior positions in the Bank. The fourth vice president, Leslie J. Scott, was not a National Shawmut Bank officer, although his ties to the Bank were almost as strong as those of the other three. Scott's primary responsibility in the new organization was to improve the relations between the Corporation and the several affiliate banks it acquired from the Shawmut Association in May 1965. His task was to instill a sense of common interest and purpose among the various banks and to help mold them into a viable, integrated system. Scott was admirably suited to this role and to Martin's plan to use a seasoned country banker to coordinate the affiliate banks. He had been with Shawmut Association's Winchester National Bank since 1930, serving as its president since 1945. Before taking up his position at Winchester, he had been a branch manager for the National Shawmut Bank.

While the functions of vice presidents Swasey and Scott were important to the well-being of the Corporation, real responsibility for the management of its affairs was in the hands of the president, Martin, and the two vice presidents, Benson and Trigg. Trigg guided the coordination of lending and banking practices of the several banks, and Benson was given responsibility for administering the overall operation and strategic planning of the Corporation. Benson also had the authority to act in the absence of Martin and stood as his heir apparent for the Corporation presidency.

In December 1967, Martin was elected chairman of the board of Shawmut Association, Inc., and Benson was elected president. One month later Martin also became chairman of the National Shawmut Bank, and Trigg was elected president of the Bank. As chairman, Martin remained the chief executive officer of both the Corporation and the Bank. However, he delegated much of the primary authority over the Corporation's affairs to Benson. For the next eight years, Benson held this functional authority, continuing to be the officer primarily responsible for corporate endeavors, even after Martin retired in 1972 and was succeeded as chief executive officer by Trigg.

Born on January 22, 1910, in Bridgewater, Massachusetts, John K. Benson graduated from Middleboro High School, then chose to attend Dartmouth, entering the class of 1931. Four years later, with his bachelor's degree in hand, Benson elected to remain in Hanover for an additional year, and in 1932 earned a master's degree in Commercial Science from the Amos Tuck School of Business Administration, concentrating on banking and finance courses. He then joined the National Shawmut Bank in June of that year.

His first two years at Shawmut were spent in a succession of short stints in nine of the principal departments that then composed the Bank. In these assignments, which lasted from two to five months, Benson gained valuable experience and exposure to the operations of the Transit, Bookkeeping, Analysis, Issue, Collection, Loan, Correspondent Banking Loan, Foreign, and Credit departments. Upon concluding his training, Benson was assigned to the Credit Department in September 1934. During the next eight years, he progressed through assignments in the Auditing, Investment Research, and Comptroller's departments. In 1943 Benson became an officer when he was elected assistant cashier, his first formal title in the Bank. The experience Benson had gathered through his various assignments made him eminently well qualified as a financial officer, even though he had had a somewhat limited exposure to the actual lending operations at the heart of Shawmut's activities.

As president of the Shawmut Association, Benson was delegated much authority over corporate affairs and was responsible for much of the strategy and conduct of corporate transactions. This was especially true of decisions pertaining to new acquisitions of banks.

One of the first acquisitions Benson identified as desirable for the new Corporation was a maximum possible number of the shares of stock for each of the several affiliate banks. It became apparent early in the corporate existence of Shawmut Association, Inc., that it could operate more efficiently if the outstanding minority interests were held to a minimum. When the various affiliate banks had been acquired by the former Association, different concerns were paramount, and the decision was made to obtain majority but not absolute control over affiliates. For this reason, when the Corporation obtained the bank shares from the Association, they were as small as 55 percent of the Needham Bank and no more than 79 percent of the Brockton Bank. The Corporation's average holding for the twelve "other banks" was only 71.9 percent of their outstanding shares.

As early as May 1966 plans were developed for the Corporation to reduce the outstanding minority interests in these banks to a minimum. As president of Shawmut Association, Inc., Benson announced an offer in 1968 to exchange Shawmut Association, Inc., shares for the shares of the several banks held by minority shareholders. To carry out the exchange offer the Corporation issued 129,000 new shares in 1968. The program was successful and as a result, Shawmut Association, Inc., reduced the outstanding minority interests to a bare minimum and increased its average holding in the twelve other banks to 96.2 percent, owning no less than 89 percent of any one bank. After the exchange offer, most of the shares that remained out of the Corporation's ownership were qualifying shares that federal law required all bank directors to hold in their own name. A recent change in this law allows bank directors to hold shares of a bank holding company as qualifying shares in lieu of shares of the bank. In the aftermath of this change, most of the Shawmut affiliate directors now own shares of the Corporation, allowing the Corporation to hold 100 percent of the shares of several of its banks. Nevertheless, to this day a small handful of shares in some of the banks remains in the possession of unrelated holdouts, but this percentage is minute. At the end of 1982, the Corporation owned no less than 97.7 percent of the shares of any Shawmut Bank.

During the same period that Shawmut Association, Inc., was executing the exchange offer, it was also pursuing a strategy to consolidate several of the banks it owned in Middlesex County. Beginning in 1967 and continuing well into the 1970s, Martin and Benson worked to simplify the nine affiliate banks in that county and thereby streamline the efficiency of banking operations. In each of the other four counties where Shawmut Association, Inc., owned banks — Suffolk, Essex, Norfolk, and Plymouth — it held only a single bank. At the outset of this consolidation process, Shawmut's nine Middlesex County banks presented a confusing array of minor institutions headquartered in Cambridge, Somerville, Everett, Lexington, Winchester, Waltham, Newton, Melrose, and Wakefield. Five of these were national banks, and the other four were state trust companies. The average size of their total assets was $17,150,000 and no one of them counted more than $30 million in assets. Shawmut Association, Inc.'s, equity share of their capital funds (that is, its net asset value) totaled barely more than $8.9 million for the nine banks combined, with no single bank counting for more than $2 million of this figure. The nine Middlesex County banks represented only 14 percent of the Corporation's total investment in the thirteen banking stocks it then held.

In an effort to improve operating economies and reduce the extent of duplicated effort in the filing of reports to the federal and state regulators, Martin and Benson concentrated on merging or consolidating these banks into a more manageable number. By the end of 1971, the number of banks had been reduced to five in Middlesex County. After Martin's 1972 retirement, the process continued so that three years later only three distinct institutions remained, with headquarters in Cambridge, Wakefield, and Framingham. Meanwhile, the Corporation increased the number of branches serving the communities where these banks were operating.

The consolidation movement was renewed in 1981, when steps were taken to obtain regulatory approval for the consolidation of the Shawmut Melrose-Wakefield Bank into Shawmut County Bank, N.A. The Massachusetts Board of Bank Incorporation approved this merger early in 1982, and at the close of business on Friday, July 30, the merger took effect.

Consolidations and New Acquisitions

In the meantime, Shawmut Association, Inc., was also pursuing a policy of expansion to further enhance the service it was providing to the various communities. This expansion took two forms. New acquisitions in 1970 and 1971 added two banks to the group. At the same time, in the most significant form of expansion during the first six years of the Corporation's existence, Shawmut Association, Inc., began also to open new branches of existing affiliates. Between 1965 and 1967, eight new branches were added to the network of the affiliate banks, including at least one new branch in each county served by a Shawmut Association bank. Another six new branches were established between 1967 and 1970, and ten new branches were added in 1971 alone, the greatest single year of branch expansion in the Corporation's history.

Throughout its corporate existence, Shawmut Association, Inc., was continually seeking out attractive bank acquisitions, even while the consolidations and branch expansion programs were under way. Through the 1960s no acquisition was concluded by the Corporation, but two occurred at the beginning of the 1970s. In 1970 the Corporation obtained more than 99 percent of the 275,000 outstanding shares of the First Bank and Trust Company of Hampden County through an exchange of stock. This acquisition plan was announced in 1969 and was consummated in March 1970, when Shawmut Association, Inc., issued .87 shares of its own stock for each share of First Bank stock tendered. In this way, Shawmut Association, Inc., obtained a substantial presence in the major Massachusetts banking market of the Connecticut River Valley, for First Bank and Trust Company had an established network of seventeen branches in that area. The acquisition marked Shawmut's first banking venture beyond the four counties of Boston's immediate metropolitan area in the forty-two years since Shawmut Association was formed. At the contemporary stock price for the 238,000 shares Shawmut issued to complete the exchange, the transaction was valued at about $11.9 million, assuming a $50 per share price. Actual 1970 prices ranged between $45 and $55 for Shawmut Association, Inc., shares.

Later in 1970, Shawmut Association, Inc., announced a similar acquisition plan involving an exchange of stock to obtain the Framingham National Bank and its eight banking offices in southwestern Middlesex County. The acquisition was consummated in early 1971, when the Corporation offered .52 shares of its own stock in exchange for each Framingham share tendered. It thereby obtained 97.75 percent of the 147,000 shares outstanding. (Both the First Bank and Trust Company and Framingham acquisitions were conditioned on the tender of at least 80 percent of the outstanding shares, which was obviously exceeded.) Framingham shares traded at $49 to $58 during this period, giving the transaction approximately a $4.4

million value, assuming the higher figure represented Shawmut's offer. The Framingham acquisition was coordinated with a plan to consolidate further operations of Shawmut Association banks in Middlesex County. Soon after the acquisition, Framingham absorbed the five Newton National branches and Waltham Citizens' single office, consolidating the three separate banks into a single entity. Renamed the Community National Bank, with headquarters in Framingham, it operated fifteen branches, including one newly opened during 1971.

The acquisition of the First Bank and Trust Company of Hampden County and of the Framingham National Bank proved to be the last simple single-bank acquisitions made by Shawmut Association, Inc. The Corporation's 1970 annual report, published just after the Framingham acquisition had been concluded, reiterated the policy of expansion: "Shawmut Association stands ready also to expand services through the addition of new banks to the present group of affiliates."

Despite this policy, however, economic conditions during the 1970s hampered expansion efforts by Shawmut. Tax provisions limited the attractiveness of any mergers other than those involving an exchange of stock, but during this decade Shawmut's own stock did not attract satisfactory merger agreements. Furthermore, the federal government imposed increasingly sharp antitrust criteria in determining whether or not to allow proposed mergers or acquisitions. These and other factors inhibited Shawmut's efforts to acquire new banks in Massachusetts.

It was not until the 1980s that the Corporation was able to add another bank to its group anywhere in the entire state. When acquisitions did resume, however, they took place in a different form than had previously obtained. Instead of acquiring the stock of independent banks, the Corporation now added affiliate banks by merging with other bank holding companies, a situation which arose from the new, attractive status of bank holding companies.

Nonbanking Financial Subsidiaries

Although Shawmut Association, Inc., was unable to expand through the acquisition of new banks during the 1970s, it did embark on a new strategy of creating financial subsidiaries for varying purposes. This strategy first surfaced during the severe pinch in the credit markets during 1969, when Shawmut Financial Corporation (SFC) was created as an expedient method of obtaining lendable funds that were otherwise difficult to attract. As a child of the tight money market of 1969, and in an effort to obtain funds at the current prime rate for commercial paper, SFC issued commercial paper backed by the guarantee of the parent Shawmut Association, Inc. It then used the proceeds of this commercial paper to buy loans from the affiliate banks and provide them with new funds to lend out at market rates, typically providing a slight spread over the prime rate cost of SFC funds. By increasing the volume of loans the affiliate banks were able to extend during this period of tight money, SFC allowed the whole Corporation to enjoy a better year than was otherwise possible. Money market conditions eased soon thereafter, so the urgency of SFC's mission declined.

During 1970 amendments to the federal Bank Holding Company Act of 1956 were adopted by Congress. The amendments allowed such companies to create or acquire subsidiaries providing services that the Federal Reserve Board determined to be closely related to the activities of banking. The amendments reaffirmed the rights of bank holding companies to engage in financial activities beyond the confines of traditional commercial banking. Although by that time Shawmut Association, Inc., had already established two nonbank subsidiaries, Shawmut International and Shawmut Financial corporations, it was reluctant to jump immediately into other fields now open to it. The major thrust of the period continued to be the selection of locations for new branches of the affiliate banks in outlying suburban areas, and on this note Martin concluded his Shawmut career.

Upon Martin's retirement in June 1972, D. Thomas Trigg succeeded him as chairman of both Shawmut Association, Inc., and the National Shawmut Bank. John K. Benson, whose own retirement was pending at the end of January 1975, remained president of the Corporation, and continued to have the primary responsibility for administering its day-to-day activities and planning its future development. Over the years, Benson and Trigg had worked well together, and their teamwork continued after Martin's departure from the executive floor at 40 Water Street.

Shortly after Trigg assumed the chairmanship of Shawmut

Association, Inc., new interest in the formation of subsidiaries was apparent. Four new subsidiaries were created between August 1972 and October 1973, with the intention of making the Corporation a provider of more diversified financial services. Although this shift away from being almost exclusively a holding company of banks was emphasized in the 1973 corporate annual report, the activity was less profound than the number of new ventures would make it appear. The new subsidiaries were rarely more than one-third the size of the Corporation's smallest banks.

The first of the new subsidiaries was created in August 1971, when the Corporation established Shawmut Securities Clearance Corporation to facilitate its own trading efforts on the exchanges in New York, and to provide similar services for Shawmut's many correspondent banks in New England, which were also actively trading securities. Shawmut Securities Clearance Corporation acted as the agent for these banks, holding their securities, making deliveries when transfers were required, and holding the new securities for safekeeping in offices convenient to the Wall Street exchanges. Organized in August 1972, this subsidiary began operations in November from offices in the financial district in New York City and the Shawmut Bank Building in Boston.

Ventures into other financial services followed rapidly during 1973, when Shawmut Association, Inc., organized three more subsidiaries to engage in activities related to banking. The first was Shawmut Credit Corporation, organized in March 1973 and unveiled at the holding company's annual meeting the next month. This subsidiary had an original capital of $1 million and was designed to compete in the commercial finance market, lending to borrowers who presented less satisfactory credit risks than the National Shawmut Bank was willing to take on for itself. This was a natural area for a bank holding company to add to its own panoply of financial services, without threatening the well-being of its several banks.

Even before Shawmut Credit began operating, the holding company announced another venture into the fringes of bank-related financial activities. In June Shawmut and an established New York factoring concern announced plans to form a jointly owned company. The new subsidiary was called Shawmut-Milberg Factors, Inc., but it was abandoned shortly after its inception.

Finally, on October 17, 1973, Shawmut Corporation became a joint venturer — through the National Shawmut Bank — with the Fort Worth National Bank in an agricultural lending institution called American Cattle and Crop Services. This joint venture combined Shawmut's experience with banker's acceptances and Fort Worth's experience with agricultural borrowers to provide a consistent treatment of the agricultural industry during periods of fluctuating loan demand. Originally headquartered at Guymon, Oklahoma, this joint venture now operates under the name American AgCredit, and is headquartered in Denver, Colorado. Through the end of 1982, Shawmut Bank's interests in this venture were supervised in the International Department of the Boston office, which handles most Shawmut banker's acceptances.

These new corporate activities did much to give Shawmut Association, Inc., a broader, more diversified posture in the financial services field. They were developed while the new One Federal Street headquarters building was being erected. These several events encouraged Shawmut to consider a whole new image for itself.

As Shawmut Association, Inc., entered 1975, it was poised on the verge of an eventful year, one that severely tested the strength and resiliency of the whole enterprise. The new building under construction at One Federal Street was scheduled for completion during the summer and would be ready for occupancy before the end of June, marking a new chapter in the history of the Shawmut presence in Boston. The dramatic move by Shawmut from its sixty-eight-year-old home at 40 Water Street, just one block away, called for some equally dramatic change to heighten the event, one that was timed to occur shortly before the move was initiated: thus the adoption of a new name by the Corporation and each of the affiliate banks, designed as part of a new marketing approach to take advantage of the economies of common identification.

The first event of the year, however, was the retirement of John K. Benson, bringing to a close his forty-three-year career at Shawmut Bank. For many of his later years in the Bank, Benson held administrative authority over the affairs of the

Shawmut Association and its successor, Shawmut Association, Inc. Since 1967 he had been president of the Corporation and was an important contributor to the shaping of its current features. Trigg, as chairman of the board, recommended Logan Clarke, Jr., as the new president of Shawmut Association, Inc. Since 1973 Clarke had been serving as president of Shawmut's affiliate bank in Cambridge, the County Bank, N.A., and before that he had been a National Shawmut Bank vice president.

One of the first actions Logan Clarke took as president involved renaming the Corporation and introducing the name Shawmut into the titles of all the affiliate banks. This program was designed to allow all the affiliate banks to benefit from the advertising and reputation built up around the National Shawmut Bank. The Bank had used the Obbatinewat logo to good effect for almost sixty-five years, had a worldwide reputation, and was well positioned in the Boston banking market. So successful was the Indian head as an identifying logo that the National Shawmut Bank used it on a billboard together with the phrase "Where Boston Banks," but with no mention of the name Shawmut. When Shawmut Association, Inc., was established in 1964, it obtained a license from the National Shawmut Bank to use the Indian head, but it was of much less value to the Corporation until the various banks became identifiably Shawmut Banks.

During this period, the Marketing Department of the National Shawmut Bank developed a new concept, with the help of the Cabot Agency, which tied each of the Corporation's affiliate banks together more directly in the public mind. Called the Shawmut Identification Program, one of its key points was the insertion of the name Shawmut as the first word in the title of all affiliate banks. Convincing the suburban bankers of the advantages of clear corporate identification was one of the first problems for those charged with implementing the program, but by March 31, 1975, agreement had been reached and the names changed as follows:

National Shawmut Bank	Shawmut Bank of Boston, N.A.
County Bank, N.A.	Shawmut County Bank, N.A.
First County National Bank	Shawmut First County Bank, N.A.
Needham National Bank	Shawmut Needham Bank, N.A.

First Bank and Trust Company	Shawmut First Bank and Trust
Community National Bank	Shawmut Community Bank, N.A.
Melrose-Wakefield Trust	Shawmut Melrose-Wakefield Trust
Merchants National Bank	Shawmut Merchants Bank, N.A.
Winchester National Bank	Shawmut Winchester Bank, N.A.

At the same time the Shawmut Indian was redesigned and the now familiar blue logo with the word *Shawmut* printed in bold graphics just to the right of the circle was introduced. This new logo would be used by every bank in the Shawmut organization, and its appearance served to indicate the mutual relation of all the banks.

With the new names and distinctive logo, the various banks were easily identified by the public as members of the Shawmut organization in a way that was not possible when each had a separate name and symbol. The basic thrust of this marketing strategy was devised by Kay Mazuy, the Corporation's senior vice president in charge of Marketing.

As part of this whole corporate identity program, Shawmut Association, Inc., was rechristened with the more succinct title Shawmut Corporation, effective April 25, 1975. For the first time since 1928, the word *Association* was no longer a principal feature in the Shawmut organization. Just in case the Corporation ever wished to revive the name Shawmut Association, Inc., one of the minor, virtually inactive subsidiaries of Shawmut Corporation was given the name Shawmut Association, Inc., thus reserving the use of the name that had served the Corporation so well for almost a full decade.

With a new face set before the world, Shawmut Corporation and its principal subsidiary, the Shawmut Bank of Boston, N.A., were both ready to move into the stately One Federal Street building. The move was both a boon to Shawmut morale and a burden to the economic vitality of the organization, in the early years. For the first time in decades, all the operations of the Shawmut Bank of Boston and the holding company could be gathered conveniently under one roof, instead of being scattered in several buildings throughout the downtown area. A side effect produced by moving all operations into a new building, however, was to increase dramatically the apparent operating expenses — attributed to high rents based on the floor space they used — of several of them. Of course, these rental expenses benefited the Bank eventually through its interest in the joint venture that owns the One Federal Street property.

Opening a new downtown office structure has its inherent problems, and the Bank's internal rental accounting points this up. Shawmut wanted desirable tenants to add stature and prestige to the address, but in the tight market of the mid-1970s, large areas of the building remained vacant for as long as two years. New England was suffering a severe local recession during 1975–1976, and although it was only a short recession, it dampened the ability and enthusiasm of many prospective tenants. The operating expenses that could not be recouped during this initial renting period were foreseen and budgeted for, but they still caused some difficulty to the Bank.

Short as the local recession actually was, it had a severe impact on Shawmut Corporation's own fiscal health. Several good loans by the Corporation's banks turned sour as the borrowers fell victim to the hard times, forcing the Shawmut banks to write off loan losses and set aside unusual levels of loan-loss reserves. These reserves were provided from current earnings of the banks. Shawmut Corporation derived the bulk of its earnings from these banks, so it also suffered. Corporate earnings per share fell to a level previously unknown, and an operating loss was actually recorded in the fourth quarter of 1975. Sufficient reserves enabled Shawmut Corporation to carry on without unnecessary difficulty, but several drastic steps were considered to ease the jolt.

Review and Closing of Branches

Among the steps taken to reduce operating expenses was a full review of the many branches of Shawmut Corporation banks. This review resulted in the recognition that technological advances, the changing character of specific neighborhoods, and the proximity of certain facilities made it practical to close or consolidate specific branches. In 1975 Shawmut Bank of Boston closed its Navy Yard and Roslindale branches, and between June and November 1977 it closed five more branches, including the Audubon, Charlestown, Dudley, Hyde Park, and

Airport offices. Meanwhile, between 1974 and 1977, the Corporation also closed three branches of Shawmut Community Bank, three branches of Shawmut First County Bank, and one branch of Shawmut Melrose-Wakefield. After 1974, until confidence in expansion was restored in 1979, only two new branches were opened in the whole Shawmut system, the Marblehead branch of Shawmut Merchants and the Nagog Square branch of Shawmut County.

Changes in Administration

In 1978 Logan Clarke, Jr., resigned as president of Shawmut Bank of Boston and the Corporation, and Trigg resumed the presidency of both until an appropriate successor could be found. Pressure to find one was exacerbated by the fact that Trigg's retirement was scheduled for mid-1980. A joint search committee of Corporation and Bank directors recommended John P. LaWare in September 1978 for the two presidencies.

Shortly after taking on his responsibilities as President of Shawmut Corporation in October 1978, LaWare introduced a "matrix" management concept, which more fully coordinated the activities of the Shawmut Bank of Boston with the Corporation and its other subsidiary banks and better integrated the leading officers of the Bank into the Corporation. As a result, the Corporation officer corps, which numbered only ten at the end of 1978, was increased almost immediately. The rank of executive vice president was reintroduced between the president and the senior vice presidents. The three incumbent senior vice presidents — Robert C. Hussey, Paul A. Miller, and William F. Craig — were then elevated to executive vice president, and several new officers were designated senior vice presidents, granting them titles in the Corporation comparable to the titles they held in the Boston Bank. By the end of 1981, the number of corporate officers doubled to twenty, including the chairman, vice chairman, president, five executive vice presidents, six senior vice presidents, and five vice presidents. This trend continues as LaWare has engaged in a significant recruitment drive of his own, seeking experienced executives and technical advisors of many skills and fields. At the end of 1982, the following new officers who had joined Shawmut since LaWare arrived as president included:

John P. Hamill, 1981	Former Chief Executive Officer of Bank One Trust Co., N.A. and prior president of a mortgage subsidiary of Chemical New York. LaWare's successor as President, Shawmut Corporation
John Kalchbrenner, 1980	Director, Division of Research and Statistics for Board of Governors, Federal Reserve System
C. Keefe Hurley, 1981	Assistant General Counsel for the Board of Governors, Federal Reserve System
William Schrader, 1982	Senior Vice President and Systems Operations Planner at Chemical Bank in New York

By the end of 1982, the new sense of energy emanating from the top had led to a number of significant moves by Shawmut Corporation. Most clearly evident was the new surge in Shawmut's acquisition activities through mergers with other bank holding companies in Massachusetts. Throughout the 1970s the Corporation reviewed opportunities for expansion into areas where Shawmut did not yet serve the Massachusetts populace. However, conditions were not conducive to the completion of merger or acquisition negotiations until the 1980s. In 1981 and 1982 Shawmut Corporation renewed negotiations with two holding companies, which resulted in agreements providing for mergers with the First Melville Bancorp and Worcester Bancorp, Inc.

The First Melville Bancorp merger was accomplished for an exchange of stock, and it brought the First National Bank of New Bedford into the Shawmut organization. Renamed the Shawmut Bank of Bristol County, N.A., it marked the first entry into Bristol County by Shawmut Corporation. Two shares of Shawmut Corporation stock were offered for each share of First Melville tendered. This transaction involved the issue of 527,000 new shares of Shawmut stock, valued at approximately $2.5 million at the prevailing market price on September 20, 1981.

A merger of far greater size and geographic scope was announced by Shawmut Corporation shortly before this First Melville merger was consummated. In June 1981 the Corporation disclosed that it had signed an agreement to merge with the Worcester Bancorp, Inc., itself a billion-dollar holding company, which owned five banks in separate counties in the state. The Shawmut-Worcester merger involved an exchange of stock valued at over $47 million, based on the offer of $30.30 per share for each of the 1,558,081 shares of Worcester outstanding. Based on 1981 year-end figures, Worcester Bancorp's $1033 million in total assets increased the size of Shawmut Corporation by almost 25 percent, to more than $5 billion in total assets.

The principal bank in the Worcester Bancorp system was the Worcester County National Bank, renamed upon the date of the merger, May 3, 1982, as Shawmut Worcester County Bank, N.A. It accounted for 80 percent of the total assets of the former Worcester Bancorp, with the other four banks — the First National Bank of Cape Cod, First National Bank of Amherst, Franklin County Trust Company, and the Peoples National Bank of Marlborough — making up the remaining 20 percent. Except for the last of these banks, each was renamed that same May 3, becoming respectively Shawmut Bank of Cape Cod, N.A., Shawmut Bank of Hampshire County, N.A., and Shawmut Bank of Franklin County.

Some Details of the Shawmut-Worcester Merger

In the newly composed Shawmut Corporation, the Shawmut Bank of Boston remained the single most dominant bank, but its share of the total assets declined from 69 to 55 percent. The share of the other eight banks that were in the Corporation prior to this merger declined from 31 to 24.4 percent of the postmerger corporate assets. By far the second largest bank in the new group was Shawmut Worcester County Bank, N.A., which comprised 16.5 percent of the combined total assets, over three times the size of the third largest of Shawmut Corporation's thirteen banks. The four other banks that formerly composed Worcester Bancorp represented only 4.1 percent of the postmerger total assets.

A significant effect of the Shawmut-Worcester merger was

the impact it had on the composition of the Shawmut Corporation Board of Directors. Prior to the merger, a core group of twelve men served simultaneously on the twenty-four-member Shawmut Bank of Boston Board of Directors and on the nineteen-member Corporation board. While the merger was pending approval, Shawmut Bank added a twenty-fifth director to its board, and that same month a twentieth director was elected to the Shawmut Corporation board at its annual meeting. These additions diminished the dominance of the twelve core directors, but it was not until the Shawmut-Worcester merger on May 3, 1982, that the Bank finally lost its majority position on the Corporation board. At that time, in accordance with the merger agreement, five new directors were elected to the Shawmut Corporation board, increasing its size to twenty-five. The five new directors had all been directors of Worcester Bancorp. Their seats on the Corporation board closely matched the share of assets Worcester represented in the postmerger Corporation, and henceforth, the core group no longer comprised a majority of the Corporation board.

Although these changes indicated a reduction in the influence of the Bank directors as a whole in the Corporation board affairs, the influence of the senior management continued. In May 1982 at the time of the Worcester merger seven of the nine Executive Committee members of the Corporation board were directors of the Bank. The seven were Melvin B. Bradshaw, William F. Craig, John P. Hamill, John P. LaWare, J. Edwin Matz, Francis M. Staszesky, and D. Thomas Trigg. The two members who were not Shawmut Bank directors were Graves D. Hewitt and Kenneth H. Olsen. A year later the committee was expanded to eleven with the addition of Bronson H. Fargo and Neal F. Finnegan, neither of whom were Bank directors. Thus the proportion of Bank directors on the Corporation board was reduced, although they remained in the majority.

After the mergers with First Melville and Worcester Bancorps had taken place and Shawmut operations began to adapt to the new scope of their banking system, which had expanded from six counties to eleven in less than eight months, the Shawmut senior management began seriously considering more distant vistas. The prospects for new authorization to conduct interstate banking became more encouraging in the early 1980s than at any time since the late 1920s, and although at the end of 1982 federal law still forbade bank holding companies to own national banks in more than one state (with limited exceptions), the Federal Reserve Board had indicated a willingness to allow bank holding companies to acquire troubled thrifts in other states. At the 1982 annual stockholders meeting La-Ware announced that Shawmut Corporation was seriously studying opportunities for prospective expansion outside the state of Massachusetts.

As 1982 came to a close, the prospect of interstate banking on a major scale loomed just over the horizon. Such an occurrence had been discussed in several forums, and predictions were that if the interstate barriers were removed, a major overhaul of the banking system could result. Shawmut Corporation stood ready to take advantage of new developments in the banking industry.

Chapter 20

The Board of Directors
and Professional Management

ALL powers that the Shawmut Corporation and Shawmut Bank of Boston have reside in their boards of directors. An appreciation of how these boards function, what limits are imposed on them, and how they have changed is essential to appreciation of the organizations which they govern.

Composition of the Boards

Over the years a body of both state and federal laws has been enacted establishing the qualifications required for bank board membership and dictating the size of bank boards. Included among the qualifications for individual service is the stipulation that a director of a national bank must own a prescribed amount of qualifying shares so that he or she will have an established interest in the affairs of the bank. For many years the requirement was ownership of $1000 worth of shares in the bank itself. Recently this rule has been relaxed and a director now need only own $1000 worth of shares of the bank holding company, if the bank is owned by one.

Directors of national banks must also be citizens of the United States, and a majority must also be residents of the state in which the bank is located. Before the advent of the National Bank System in 1864, an analogous law in Massachusetts required that directors of state banks be residents of the state. Residency requirements have presented no problem for Shawmut directors, who from the Bank's inception in 1836 have been — with very few exceptions — Massachusetts residents.

On the other hand, laws disqualifying certain persons from a place on a national bank board have presented Shawmut with some problems. Among these restrictions were those imposed by the Clayton Antitrust Act and subsequent Kerr Amendment, both of which emerged as a consequence of the Federal Reserve Act of 1913, and both of which attempted to prevent an interlocking of major financial organizations by forbidding investment bankers, securities brokers, and trust company officers and directors from serving on boards of national banks. As a result of these laws, ten Shawmut directors were forced to resign between 1914 and 1917.

Still other federal or state restrictions that have affected the composition of Shawmut's Board of Directors are those pertaining to the size of the board. In 1836, when Shawmut Bank was first established, state law declared that a bank could set its own board at between five and twelve directors. Then called the Warren Bank, it commenced with a full complement of twelve. Tight control by the early directors and general conditions in the banking world made being a director unattractive during the ensuing two decades, and the size of the Shawmut board declined through attrition to only six members. Not until 1861 did it regain the nine-member level. The nine-member board must have been a convenient and effective size, for it was the size specified by the directors themselves in the Articles of Organization when Shawmut obtained its national bank charter in 1864 — the National Bank Act required a minimum of five directors. The Shawmut National Bank operated from 1865 through the last week of November 1898, and during this time the authorized size of the board was changed only twice, both times in the decade of the 1890s. These were minor housekeeping changes. In January 1896 one provided for a minimum of seven directors, with no change in the actual number of directors from the current nine. The second change, on January 12, 1897, reduced the minimum number of directors to five and imposed a maximum of fifteen. At the same time the actual number of directors was increased to eleven.

Much more significant in determining the size of the Shawmut's board, however, were the changes that occurred as a consequence of the mergers of 1898. For a short time during November of that year, after the National Shawmut was chartered and before Shawmut National was disbanded, two separate boards existed: the Shawmut National board with fifteen members, and the National Shawmut board, which was authorized to have between five and twenty-five members but was actually established with seventeen.

The seventeen men selected make clear the nature of the 1898 mergers and the dominant role Shawmut played among the banks being merged. Bankers as a group made up a majority of this new board, but they were for the most part beholden to Kidder, Peabody and other investment banking firms, who were also represented heavily on the board. Among the nine bankers on the seventeen-member National Shawmut board, five were carryovers from the Shawmut National and four were presidents of other merged banks. Subsequent mergers introduced more directors to the National Shawmut board. On January 14, 1902, eight new directors were added, which brought the board to the established limit of twenty-five. On January 15, 1908, the Articles of Association were amended to provide a new maximum of thirty, and twenty-nine directors were elected at that annual meeting. Three more were added at the following annual meeting, when the maximum was increased to thirty-two. A third increase in the authorized size of the board was voted by the shareholders of the Bank on January 9, 1912, when the maximum size was pushed to forty, and thirty-five directors were elected. By 1931 the number had grown again and Shawmut had forty-one directors.

Shortly thereafter, the passage of the National Bank Act of 1933 put into effect a law which prohibited national banks from having more than twenty-five directors. At the annual meeting of the Shawmut in January 1934 ten directors did not stand for reelection. Their numbers, in conjunction with those of the directors who did not stand for reelection for other reasons, brought the board within the proscribed limits. (Interestingly enough, while the qualifications for membership on the board of a national bank are equally pertinent for membership on a board of a bank holding company, federal law imposes no limit on the size of a bank holding company board, although Shawmut Corporation's own bylaws set a maximum of thirty-five directors.)

Committees of the Board

The fluctuating size of the Shawmut Bank board and the affiliations of its members were to a large extent dictated by changing laws and other external circumstances. In contrast, the way in which the board operated was more closely affected by the expansion of banking responsibilities.

As the Bank grew, a more structured approach to business became a necessity. As a result committees became more evident and more powerful, and their meetings became more frequent. By 1864, when the Shawmut National Bank was established (and probably even earlier), the Bank had two formal committees: the Exchange Committee and the Examining Committee. They were the forerunners of the current Executive Committee and Auditing Committee respectively.

Exchange Committee. The 1864 bylaws of the Shawmut National Bank assigned to this committee the president, the cashier, and one other director to be appointed by the board every three months. The committee took up the day-to-day business of the Bank's exchange and lending activities and reported its transactions at each regular meeting of the board, which then occurred each Monday. Soon after John C. Cummings, Jr., became president of the Shawmut National Bank in 1868, the committee was increased to four members so that two directors could serve on it in addition to the president and the cashier. As the Bank began to rely more on loans and investments than on exchange charges for its income, the committee was renamed the Finance Committee. Eventually, it was replaced completely by the Executive Committee.

Examining Committee. The other committee provided for in the Shawmut National Bank bylaws in 1864 was the Examining Committee. This was not then a standing committee of the board but was appointed every six months to examine the condition of the Bank and report to the directors at the next weekly meeting of the board. The examination was conducted in conjunction with a federal law requiring the cashier of a national bank to file a biannual report of the condition of that bank signed by three directors. After reporting to the board and signing the cashier's report, the Examining Committee of Shawmut had completed its work and was discharged. Six months later a new committee was appointed, which frequently had new members. In that earlier day, the examination amounted to a simple inventory of the discount and loan documents, bond holdings, and cash on hand and was meant to ensure that all figures recorded in the books of the Bank corresponded to the actual holdings. Deposit balances and circulation figures were also checked. This examination was usually carried out in a single sitting of the committee.

Much later, the Examining Committee became a standing committee serving for the entire year, and an entire Auditing Department developed within the Bank to carry out its supervisory functions. Still, there is no indication that the formal duties of the committee became substantially more rigorous until the 1970s.

The new impulse for formal auditing stems primarily from Securities and Exchange Commission regulations effective in 1971, which required more extensive financial disclosures by banks and bank holding companies. From its inception Shawmut Corporation (first as Shawmut Association, Inc.) had had a board examining committee of directors similar to that of the National Shawmut Bank. In 1971 the Corporation engaged Price Waterhouse as its independent auditor, which, to this day reports its findings and recommendations directly to the committee.

Audit Committees. Both the Shawmut Corporation and the Shawmut Bank of Boston boards of directors amended their bylaws during the winter of 1977, changing the name of each Examining Committee to that of Audit Committee. The variety of new responsibilities, some decided upon by the directors and some imposed from the outside, gave both committees extensive new powers within the Shawmut organization.

The Audit committees are appointed by the Corporation and Bank boards at their annual meetings. Only "outside" directors, those not in the employ of the Corporation or the Bank (or any of their respective subsidiaries), may be named to these committees. In addition to engaging the outside auditors, each committee approves the scope and timing of the audits. Much of the auditing work is performed by a large staff of auditors who are responsible to the boards and who conduct audits of the Shawmut Bank of Boston, most of the other affiliate banks, and the corporate subsidiaries.

The Bank also has a permanent staff of internal auditors. The work of this group, as well as its policies and procedures, is reviewed by Price Waterhouse and directors on the Audit committees. Price Waterhouse also advises the Audit committees on internal-accounting controls and accounting procedures. Moreover, it reports to the Audit committees on the extent of cooperation it receives from the internal auditing staff and the rest of the Corporation's employees. The Audit committees also receive the audit reports of the federal and state regulatory agencies. In 1980 the Audit Committee of the Shawmut Bank of Boston Board of Directors assumed responsibility for auditing the Trust Department. This task had previously been performed by the now disbanded Trust Audit Committee.

Compensation Committees. Shawmut Corporation and the Shawmut Bank of Boston each have a Compensation Committee of the Board of Directors. Like the Audit committees, the Compensation Committees are composed entirely of outside directors. At the end of 1982 the Corporation Compensation Committee had three members, J. Edwin Matz, Melvin B. Bradshaw, and Herbert W. Jarvis, who also served on the five-member Bank Compensation Committee together with Stephen J. Griffin and John P. Pierce, Jr. Matz was the chairman of both Compensation committees. The two committees work together, meeting in joint sessions about six times each year.

While the name Compensation Committee is relatively new — the committees were so designated in 1978 — most of their responsibilities are not new, having been carried out in the past by other entities. These include the Employees Retirement Income Security Act (ERISA) Compliance Committee and the Thrift Plan Revision Committee, which assigned their responsibilities to the new Corporation Compensation Committee, and the Salary and Succession committees of the Bank's Board of Directors.

The mandate of the Compensation committees has been broad. Tasks include determining the compensation for directors, senior management officers of the Corporation, and senior management officers of the Boston Bank and several of the leading Corporation subsidiaries. The committees also review the performances of the presidents of the affiliate banks (other than Shawmut Bank of Boston) and are responsible for the variety of employee benefits, including the pension, insurance, thrift, and medical plans and the early retirement program. In addition, the Compensation committees review and supervise several incentive plans designed to increase profit and productivity. Three primary plans of this type extant at the end of 1982 were the Senior Management Incentive Plan, Key Manager Incentive Plan, and Performance Share Bonus Plan. The Compensation committees develop and review these various employee benefits and compensation packages with a view to maintaining a balance between competitive needs, employee morale, and the Corporation's ability to pay.

Other Committees. The boards of directors of the Shawmut Corporation and the Shawmut Bank of Boston have a number of other committees. Most significant among these are the Directors' Policy Committee, the Trust Committee, and Nominating Committee, and for the Bank alone, the Community Affairs Committee and the Lawrence H. Martin Scholarship Committee. In the past the directors have had many other special-purpose and ad hoc committees. Among the most significant of these were the Trust Audit Committee, whose functions have since been assigned to the Audit Committee, and the Directors' Building Committee, which was established at the time of the decision to build One Federal Street corporate headquarters.

Officials of the Shawmut Bank Board

Through the first seventy-one years of the history of the Shawmut Bank of Boston, in its various names and legal forms, the chief official of the Board of Directors was the president, and no other director held any special title within the board. On occasion, one of the directors would act as the president pro tem, when the president was unavailable to serve.

In 1907, however, when James P. Stearns decided to retire from the day-to-day responsibilities that went with the presidency, he was not ready to retire from the board. The directors then saw fit to create the office chairman of the board for him as something of an emeritus position. The practice of having a president and an emeritus chairman continued until the end of Alfred Aiken's administration. When Walter S. Bucklin became president in September 23, 1923, it was clear that Aiken was not retiring from business but was considering a move to other ventures at the New York Life Insurance Company. Until he left the Shawmut Board altogether in April 1924, Aiken served as chairman of the board. At this point, the chairmanship was vacated and remained so for almost thirty years.

In 1952 Bucklin revived the title of chairman but gave it the status and authority of chief executive officer. As chairman, Bucklin retained full power over the Board of Directors and over the man who succeeded him as president, Walter E. Borden. When Borden retired in early 1956, Bucklin resumed the office of president himself for a short time until he saw Horace Schermerhorn elected to the post on October 8, 1956. Bucklin, however, continued as chairman of the board and continued to exercise the powers of chief executive officer for another couple of months, until his retirement was requested and accepted by the Board of Directors in November 1956. Schermerhorn did not chose to assume the chairmanship, and it remained vacant for some four years while he exercised the chief executive powers through the presidency. In 1960 Schermerhorn did become chairman, and Lawrence H. Martin was elected president, and at this time the chairman of the board was again granted full chief executive power. Upon Schermerhorn's retirement at the end of 1962, Martin remained president and the chief executive powers devolved once more upon that office, with the chairman position remaining vacant.

In late 1967 changes in the Corporation and National Shawmut Bank made it fitting for Martin to become chairman of each organization, and this he did in December 1967 and January 1968. Since that time, the chairman of the board has been the chief executive officer of the Corporation and of the Bank, and to this date both offices have been held simultaneously by the same individual. Also at that time the bylaws of the National Shawmut Bank were also amended to clarify the powers and duties of the top officers. In the old bylaws the President was designated the chief executive officer whether or not there was a chairman. If a separate chairman was designated, he presided at board meetings but did not take the chief executive officer title, although he might assume those powers de facto. In 1968 an amendment shifted the chief executive officer title to the chairman of the board.

Professional Management

Another natural outgrowth of the increase in banking activities and the size of the Bank has been the rise of the bank officer as a professional manager. Before the National Shawmut Bank came into existence in 1898, the Shawmut National at its largest counted no more than two-dozen employees on the entire payroll, including part-time help. Assuming that the tellers, then an important position in the Bank, were officers because their appointment was approved by the board, five of the employees could be considered officers. In fact, the number of officers was so small that the Shawmut National Bank did not even see fit to elect a vice president until late in Cummings's presidency. At this time the cashier, James P. Stearns, was elevated to the post. The timing of this appointment is interesting in view of the fact that the Bank's bylaws had authorized the election of a vice president from the time Shawmut became a national bank in 1864. The thirty-year delay suggests, if nothing else, that there was nothing imperative about filling the post. Even when the National Shawmut Bank came into existence in 1898, two full years passed before a vice president was elected. This was E. Hayward Ferry, a chief officer of one of the banks brought into Shawmut after the first round of mergers. A year later, and within weeks of the merger of the National Bank of the Commonwealth, the number of vice presidents of the National Shawmut increased to three, with Francis B. Sears and Abram T. Collier being elected to that office at the annual meeting on January 14, 1902. Collier was the first man in Shawmut history to be elected to the post of vice president without serving simultaneously as a director of the Bank.

Prior to the early twentieth-century focus on the vice-presidential office, the cashier had been demonstrably the leading professional officer of a bank. Although the bank president was his superior in rank, it was understood that the president should be free to attend to his private business affairs, leaving the cashier to manage the day-to-day operations of the bank. Significantly the cashier's was the only position for which state law in 1836 required the posting of a bond; it was also generally the most highly paid position. At Shawmut, for almost fifty years the cashier's salary was a great deal more — sometimes four times more — than the president's. From 1836 to 1846 Thomas Drown, Shawmut's first cashier, earned more than twice the salary of Benjamin T. Reed, the president. Similarly, Stephen G. Davis, the Shawmut cashier from 1846 to 1876, earned more than any of the four presidents under whom he served, and when Davis retired at seventy-three to be replaced by the thirty-six-year-old James P. Stearns, the latter was more highly paid than the sixty-four-year-old Shawmut president, John C. Cummings, Jr. In 1884, however, the president's salary was increased above the cashier's, and from that time on the president's position in the bank became clearly more important than the cashier's.

In the late nineteenth and early twentieth centuries, the power and prominence associated with the title of cashier eroded as new officer ranks were established. Among the first of these new ranks was the vice presidency created for Stearns in 1894. By 1902, when Shawmut had three vice presidents, the importance of this rank was clearly established. In the course of the next several decades still other titles and ranks were introduced between the president and the cashier. These included the office of executive vice president, senior vice president, controller, and auditor. Despite the eroding power of the cashier, the title assistant cashier remained the first title an officer at the Shawmut could earn, even though the designation bore little relation to the job that such an officer performed. In 1968, however, Martin moved to have this vestigal practice abandoned, and from that point onward more descriptive and functional titles were adopted.

Another development in the past thirty years has been the

rise of employees who have no officer title but are deemed important enough to the operations of the Bank to receive special treatment regarding salaries. Thus, a complex system of point ratings has been developed to indicate the level of importance a given job has to the Bank regardless of the title that goes with it. This development is also a reflection of the inflation in officer titles that has occurred recently. For instance, it used to be a mark of high achievement to rise to the position of assistant cashier after years of service to the Bank. Even the best talent in the Bank did not attain a vice-presidency until serving ten to fifteen years in banking. More recently, vice-presidencies have been granted within three years, which is one reason for the preponderance of them today. But this is to be expected, as the Bank has grown from fifty employees in 1900 to almost three thousand in 1982.

Rise of the Bank Holding Company and Boards of Subsidiary Organizations

As Shawmut Corporation has grown since its establishment in 1964, its Board of Directors has had a significant impact on the boards of many subsidiary organizations, including the many affiliate banks that make up the bulk of its interests.

One of the most obvious signs of the growth of the Corporation over the past fifteen years has been the declining overlap between the boards of the Bank and the Corporation. Shawmut Bank officers and directors, however, do serve in large numbers on the boards of several of Shawmut Corporation's subsidiary organizations.

The affiliate banks themselves present an interesting example of Shawmut practices. In years past the forerunner of the present Shawmut Corporation, Shawmut Association, often elected one or two officers of the National Shawmut Bank of Boston to the boards of the affiliate banks. More recently, the Corporation has determined that local business leaders are more appropriate as directors of these local institutions. Proposed directors are selected by the local bank management, subject to review and approval of corporate management.

Appendices
Index

APPENDIX ONE

Presidents and Chairmen, Shawmut Bank of Boston, N.A. (1836–1982)

Warren Bank, organized May 6, 1836
Shawmut Bank, 1837

Dates	President	Chairman
1836–1848	Benjamin Tyler Reed	
1848–1853	John Gardner	
1853–1854	Albert Fearing	
1854–1868	William Bramhall	

Shawmut National Bank, January 2, 1865

1868–1898	John C. Cummings, Jr.	

National Shawmut Bank, November 26, 1898

1898–1907	James P. Stearns	
1907–1917	William A. Gaston*	James P. Stearns
1918–1923	Alfred L. Aiken*	William A. Gaston
1923–1924	Walter S. Bucklin*	Alfred L. Aiken
1924–1952	Walter S. Bucklin*	
1952–1956	Walter E. Borden	Walter S. Bucklin*
1956 (May–Sept.)	Walter S. Bucklin	Walter S. Bucklin*
1956 (Sept.–Nov.)	Horace Schermerhorn	Walter S. Bucklin*
1956–1960	Horace Schermerhorn*	
1960–1962	Lawrence H. Martin	Horace Schermerhorn*
1962–1968	Lawrence H. Martin*	
1968–1972	D. Thomas Trigg	Lawrence H. Martin*
1972–1974	D. Thomas Trigg	D. Thomas Trigg*
1974–1976	Paul G. Black	D. Thomas Trigg*

Shawmut Bank of Boston, N.A., 1975

1976–1978	Logan Clarke, Jr.	D. Thomas Trigg*
1978 (June–Oct.)	D. Thomas Trigg	D. Thomas Trigg*
1978–1980	John P. LaWare	D. Thomas Trigg*
1980–	William F. Craig	John P. LaWare*

*Chief Executive Officer

Directors of the Shawmut Bank (1836–1982)*

Original Directors — Shawmut Bank — May 6, 1836

Reed, Benjamin T.	(1st President)	1836–1874
Bramhall, William	Bramhall & Howe	1836–1871
Brewer, Gardner	Gardner Brewer & Company	1836–1843
Bridge, John D.	Bridge & Stevens	1836
Dana, Nathaniel	Dana, Greely & Company	1836–1845
Dimmock, John L.	President, Warren Insurance Company	1836–1855
Fearing, Albert	Fearing, Thacher & Company	1836–1854
Gardner, John	Treasurer, Hamilton Woolen Company	1836–1863
Lincoln, Jairus B.	N. Lincoln & Company	1836–1866
Reed, Josiah	Stanley, Reed & Company	1836–1840
Rice, Aaron	Fisk & Rice	1836–1856
Scudder, Horace	Horace Scudder & Company	1836–1843

Elected under Benjamin Tyler Reed

Whitney, William	1843–1849

No New Directors under John Gardner.
Elected under Albert Fearing

Davis, Barnabas	Horace Scudder & Company	1854–1885

Elected under William Bramhall

Crocker, Henry H.		1856–1858
Abbott, John C.	President, Shoe & Leather Dealers Fire & Marine Insurance Company	1858–1878
Johnson, George		1858–1860
Salisbury, D. Waldo		1861–1890
Scudder, Prentiss W.	Danforth, Scudder & Company	1861–1898
Wyman, Edward		1861–1868
Whiton, David	Fearing, Thacher & Company	1863–1874(?)
Cummings, John C., Jr.	John Cummings, Jr. & Company	1867–1898

*Titles of directors pertain to the time of appointment

Elected under John C. Cummings, Jr.

Harrington, Leonard B.		1869–1889
Potter, Silas	Silas Potter & Company	1871–1892
Gilbert, Horatio J.	Dodge, Gilbert & Company	1874–1882
Allen, William Henry	Allen, Field & Lawrence	1875–1878
Bills, Charles C.	Stowe, Bills & Hawley	1879–1889
Hayden, Edward D.	Vice President, Boston & Albany Railroad	1879–1902
Bassett, William	Brester, Bassett & Company	1883–1898
Stearns, James P.	President, National Shawmut Bank	1886–1922
Arnold, Moses N.	President, M. N. Arnold & Company	1889–1898
Coburn, George M.		1889–1903
Clough, Micajah P.	C. A. Coffin & Company	1892–1933
Spaulding, William S.	Nash, Spaulding & Company	1892–1925
Rice, Nehemiah W.	N. W. Rice & Company	1896–1898
Russell, William E.	Attorney, former Governor of Massachusetts	1896

Directors of the National Shawmut Bank Elected under James P. Stearns

Higginson, Henry Lee	Partner, Lee, Higginson & Company	1898–1914
Newhall, Horatio	(served continually as Secretary, intermittently as Director)	1898–1912(?)
Winsor, Robert	Partner, Kidder, Peabody & Company	1898–1914
Howe, Henry S.	Lawrence & Company	1898–1930
Moseley, Frederick S.	Partner, F. S. Moseley & Company	1898–1914
Woodworth, Alfred S.	Robinson & Woodworth	1898–1911
Gaston, William A.	President, National Shawmut Bank	1898–1924
Hallett, Daniel B.		1898–1908
Webster, Frank G.	Partner, Kidder, Peabody & Company	1898–1914
Codman, Edmund D.	Attorney at Law	1898–1904
Williams, Jeremiah	Jeremiah Williams & Company	1898–1916
Draper, Eben S.	The Draper Company	1898–1914
Ferry, E. Hayward	Vice President, National Shawmut Bank	1900–1907
Ames, Oliver	Treasurer, Oliver Ames & Son Corporation	1902–1916

Endicott, Henry B.	President, Endicott-Johnson	
	Company	1902–1904
Foster, Francis A.	Francis A. Foster & Company	1902–1921
Russell, Joseph B.	Treasurer, Boston Wharf	
	Company	1902–1926
Sears, Francis B.	Vice President, National	
	Shawmut Bank	1902–1914
Tower, William A.	Tower, Diggins & Company	1902–1904
Williams, Moses	President, State Street Trust	
	Company	1902–1916
Crane, W. Murray	Governor of Massachusetts,	
	1900–1902; Crane &	
	Company; appointed	
	U.S. Senator, 1904	1903–1904
Bacon, Robert		1905
		1912–1913
Beebe, E. Pierson		1905–1906
Choate, Charles F., Jr.	Attorney, Choate & Hall	1905–1914
Bemis, Frank B.	Estabrook & Company	1905–1914
Cobb, Charles K.	Attorney at Law	1907–1931
Locke, Charles A.	Locke, Tolman & Company —	
	Leather Manufacturers	1907–1914
Murdock, Harold	Vice President, National	
	Shawmut Bank	1907–1925
Swan, Walter S.	President, Charles River	
	National Bank	1907
Wells, George W.	President, American Optical	
	Company	1907–1911
Coolidge, Harold J.	Loring, Coolidge & Noble	1907–1934

Elected under William A. Gaston

Byrnes, Timothy E.	Vice President, N.Y., N.H.	
	& H. R.R.	1908–1913
Greene, Edwin F.	Treasurer, Pacific Mills; also	
	Lockwood, Greene &	
	Company	1908–1928
Weld, C. Minot	President, New England	
	Cotton Yarn (1914 Amory,	
	Browne & Company)	1908–1918
Vialle, Charles A.	Vice President, National	
	Shawmut Bank	1908–1923
Hayden, Charles	Partner, Hayden, Stone &	
	Company	1909–1916
Brown, Jacob F.	Brown & Adams	1909–1929
Stone, Albert		1909–1922
Wellington, William H.	Wellington, Sears & Company	1909–1925

Wadsworth, Eliot	Stone & Webster	1911–1914
Homans, Robert	Hill, Barlow & Homans	1912–1917
Lyman, Ronald T.	Treasurer, The Boston Manufacturing Company	1912–1924
Sias, Charles D.	Chase & Sanborn	1912–1913
Atkins, Edwin F.	E. Atkins & Company	1913–1916
Burrage, Harry L.	Treasurer, Connecticut Cottons Company	1913–1914
Estabrook, Fred W.	President, Second National Bank, Nashua, New Hampshire	1913–1920
Sprague, Henry B.	Treasurer, Boston Woven Hose & Rubber Company	1913–1930
Vail, Theodore N.	President, American Telephone & Telegraph Company	1913–1920
Dumaine, Frederic C.	Treasurer, Amoskeag Manufacturing Company	1914–1916
Draper, B. H. Bristow	Draper Corporation	1914–1923
Sears, Edmund H.	Willet, Sears & Company	1914–1918
Lockwood, H. De F.	Treasurer, The Bates Manufacturing Company	1914–1942
Joyce, John	Vice President, Gillette Safety Razor Company	1915–1917
McElwain, J. Franklin	President, W. H. McElwain & Company	1915–1922
Liggett, Louis K.	President, United Drug Company	1916–1935
Joy, Benjamin	Vice President, National Shawmut Bank	1917
Tuckerman, Bayard, Jr.	O'Brion, Russell & Company	1917–1924
Coolidge, T. J., III		1917–1920
Curran, Maurice, Jr.	Vice President, Gillette Safety Razor Company	1917–1934
Aiken, Alfred L.	President, National Shawmut Bank	1917–1924

Elected under Alfred L. Aiken

Borden, Spencer	President, Fall River Gas Company	1918–1957
Adams, Norman I.	Vice President, National Shawmut Bank	1920–1948
Ayer, Nathaniel F.	Treasurer, Nyanza Mills	1920–1940
Edwards, Harold S.	Treasurer, Francis Wiley & Company	1920–1925

Hunt, Thomas	Attorney, Gaston, Snow, Saltonstall & Hunt	1923–1926
Potter, Robert S.	Vice President, National Shawmut Bank	1920–1924
Thayer, John E.		1920–1924
Gifford, W. S.	Vice President, American Telephone & Telegraph Company	1921–1922
Rich, William T.	Chase & Sanborn	1922–1931
Saltonstall, Leverett	Attorney & Trustee, Gaston, Snow, Saltonstall & Hunt	1922–1935
Bucklin, Walter S.	President, National Shawmut Bank	1923–1956

Elected under Walter S. Bucklin

Creighton, Albert M.	Albert M. Creighton Shoe Manufacturers	1923–1941
Blair-Smith, H.	Treasurer, American Telephone & Telegraph Company	1925–1932
Shearer, William L., Jr.	Treasurer, Paine Furniture Company	1925–1930
Keller, Carl T.	Lybrand, Ross Brothers & Montgomery	1925–1936
Bailey, Harry L.	Trustee (Wellington Sears)	1925–1952
Bradley, J. Gardner	Coal Operator	1925–1933
Clough, George H.	President, Russell Company	1925–1948
Cabot, Paul C.	State Street Investment Company	1926–1942
Carroll, Frederick A.	Vice President, National Shawmut Bank	1926–1929
James, Ellery S.	Brown Brothers & Company	1926–1931
Newell, Frank A.	Vice President, National Shawmut Bank	1926–1929
Ryder, James E.	Vice President & Cashier, National Shawmut Bank	1926–1927
Tinkham, Herbert L.	President, W. L. Douglas Shoe Company	1926–1933
Trumbull, Walter H., Jr.	Kidder, Peabody & Company	1926–1930
Royce, Frederick P.	Vice President, Stone & Webster	1926–1933
Davis, Edward A.	Vice President, National Shawmut Bank	1927–1929
Paine, William	Paine, Webber & Company	1927–1929
Pierce, George E.	Senior Vice President, National Shawmut Bank	1927–1951

Spencer, Carl M.	President, Home Savings Bank	1927–1962 (Hon. 1962)
McGregor, W. Eugene	Chase Harris Forbes Corporation	1927–1933
Rust, Edgar G.	Trustee	1928–1933
Snow, Frederic E.	Attorney, Gaston, Snow, Saltonstall & Hunt	1928–1934
Leach, Robert M.	Chairman of the Board, Glenwood Range Company	1929–1952
Bliss, Elmer J.	Chairman of the Board, Regal Shoe Company	1930–1933
Paine, Francis W.	Paine, Webber & Company	1930–1933
Proctor, Redfield	Vermont Marble Company	1930–1935
Barron, William A.	White Weld & Company	1930–1933
Augustine, William F.	Vice President, National Shawmut Bank	1931–1933
Dodge, Robert G.	Partner, Palmer, Dodge, Gardner, Bickford & Bradford	1931–1964 (Hon. 1962)
Janisch, Harold P.	Vice President, National Shawmut Bank	1931–1934
Nichols, Henry J.	Vice President, National Shawmut Bank	1931–1962
O'Connell, P. A.	President, E. T. Slattery Company	1931–1958
Hovey, Chandler	Kidder, Peabody & Company	1932–1933
Maddison, Arthur V.	George L. DeBlois & A. N. Maddison	1936–1945
Sprague, Oliver M. W.	Professor of Banking, Harvard Business School	1936–1953
Coolidge, Lawrence	Gaston, Snow, Rice & Boyd	1937–1949
Flanders, Ralph E.	President, Jones & Lamson Machine Company	1938–1941
Erickson, Joseph A.	Executive Vice President, National Shawmut Bank	1943–1948
Dinsmoor, Daniel S.	Vice President, Monsanto Chemical Company	1944–1946
Kenny, Norman W.	C. W. Whittier & Bro.	1945–1963
Stack, Lee P.	Vice President, John Hancock Mutual Life Insurance Company	1947–1958
Borden, Walter E.	Senior Vice President, Shawmut Bank	1947–1956

472   APPENDIX TWO

Rutter, Josiah B.	Monsanto Chemical Company	1948–1951
Smith, J. Newton	President, Boston Woven	
	Hose & Rubber Company	1949
Morss, Everett	President, Simplex Wire &	
	Cable Company	1949–1956
Ilg, Ray A.	Vice President, National	
	Shawmut Bank	1950–1959
Wellman, Arthur O.	President, Nichols &	
	Company, Inc.	1950–1965
Kaplan, Jacob J.	Nutter, McClennen & Fish	1951–1960
Bird, E. H.	Executive Vice President,	
	Eastern Gas & Fuel	
	Corporation	1952–1960
Doriot, Georges F.	President, American Research	
	& Development Corporation	1952–1975
		(Advis. 1970)
White, Francis M.	President, American Woolen	
	Company	1952–1975
Martin, Lawrence H.	President, National Shawmut	
	Bank	1953–1980
Sprague, Robert C.	Chairman of the Board,	
	Sprague Electric Company	1953–1955
Bolton, J. Hugh	President, Whitin Machine	
	Works	1954–1964
Schermerhorn, Horace	President, National Shawmut	
	Bank	1955–1962

Elected under Horace Schermerhorn

Carey, Charles C.	President, General Radio	
	Company	1957–1963
Hobson, John L.	President, St. Croix Paper	
	Company	1957–1963
Jenney, Robert M.	President, Jenney Oil	
	Company	1957–1983
Jones, Robert V.	Vice President & Comptroller,	
	N.E.T. & T. Company	1957–1969
McHugh, Thomas J.	President, The Atlantic	
	Lumber Company	1957–1964
Stocker, Crawford H., Jr.	President, Lynn Five Cents	
	Savings Bank	1957–1975
Young, Richard B.	President, Acushnet Process	
	Company	1957–1984
Volpe, John A.	President, John A. Volpe	
	Construction Company	1958
Avila, Charles F.	Vice President, Boston Edison	
	Company	1958–1979

Blackall, Frederick S., Jr.	President, Taft-Pierce Manufacturing Company	1958–1963
Geneen, Harold S.	President, ITT	1959–1973
Marshall, Harold T.	Executive Vice President, The Kendall Company	1960–1969
Collier, Abram T.	Senior Vice President & General Counsel, John Hancock	1961–1966
Knowles, Asa S.	President, Northeastern University	1961–1978
Loring, Caleb, Jr.	Partner, Gaston, Snow, Motley & Holt	1961–1964
Trustman, Benjamin A.	Nutter, McClennen & Fish	1961–1975
Benson, John K.	Senior Vice President, National Shawmut Bank	1962–1975
Gordon, Elliott M.	President, Towle Manufacturing Company	1962–1977
Smith, Bryan E.	Chairman, Liberty Mutual Insurance Companies	1962–1968
Trigg, D. Thomas	Senior Vice President, National Shawmut Bank	1962–*
Ziegler, Vincent C.	President, Gillette Safety Razor Company	1962–1979

Elected under Lawrence H. Martin

Philips, John N.	Senior Vice President, Eastern Gas & Fuel Associates	1963–1974
Sinclair, Donald B.	President, General Radio Company	1963–1975
Bartlett, Charles W.	Partner, Ely, Bartlett, Brown & Proctor	1964–1978
Garrett, Norman F.	President, Whitin Machine Works	1964–1965
Hammond, Franklin T., Jr.	Partner, Gaston, Snow, Motley & Holt	1964–1974
Cole, Alton P.	President, Home Savings Bank	1965–1969
Hewitt, Colby, Jr.	President, Boit, Dalton & Church, Incorporated	1965–*
Phillips, Thomas L.	President, Raytheon Company	1965–1979
Matz, J. Edwin	Executive Vice President, John Hancock Mutual Life Insurance Company	1967–1983

*Indicates directors of Shawmut Bank of Boston, N.A., on April 30, 1985.

Mergott, Winston	Senior Vice President, Liberty Mutual Insurance Companies	1968–1973
Kendall, John	Vice President, The Kendall Company	1969–*
Gray, Paul Edwards	Chancellor, Massachusetts Institute of Technology	1971–*
Black, Paul G.	Executive Vice President, National Shawmut Bank	1972–1976

Elected under D. Thomas Trigg

Stoneman, Sidney	Vice Chairman, General Cinema Corporation	1972–1984
Bradshaw, Melvin B.	Executive Vice President, Liberty Mutual Insurance Companies	1973–*
Jarvis, Herbert W.	President, USM Corporation	1973–*
Snowden, Muriel S.	Co-Director, Freedom House	1973–*
Pruyn, William J.	President, Boston Gas Company	1974–*
Pierce, John B., Jr.	Of Counsel, Gaston Snow & Ely Bartlett	1975–*
Staszesky, Francis M.	Executive Vice President, Boston Edison Company	1975–*
Clarke, Logan, Jr.	President, Shawmut Bank of Boston, N.A.	1976–1978
Bartlett, Joseph W.	Partner, Gaston Snow & Ely Bartlett	1978–*
LaWare, John P.	President, Shawmut Bank of Boston, N.A.	1978–*
Ryder, Kenneth G.	President, Northeastern University	1978–*
Griffin, Stephen J.	President & Chief Operating Officer, The Gillette Company	1979–*
Saltonstall, William L.	Partner, Saltonstall & Company	1979–*
Craig, William F.	Executive Vice President, Shawmut Bank of Boston, N.A.	1980–*
Short, Winthrop A.	President & Director, Knapp King-Size Corporation	1980–*
North, John S.	Executive Vice President, N.E.T. & T.	1980–*

*Indicates directors of Shawmut Bank of Boston, N.A., on April 30, 1985.

Elected under John P. LaWare

Hamill, John P.	Executive Vice President & General Counsel, Shawmut Bank of Boston, N.A.	1980-*
Segall, Maurice	President & Chief Executive Officer, Zayre Corporation	1981–1983
James, Howard P.	Chairman, President, & Chief Executive Officer, The Sheraton Corporation	1982–1985
Snider, Eliot I.	President and Treasurer, Massachusetts Lumber Company	1983-*
Finnegan, Neal F.	Executive Vice President, Shawmut Bank of Boston, N.A.	1984-*
Boyan, William L., Jr.	Executive Vice President, John Hancock Mutual Life Insurance Company	1985-*
Lydon, James M.	Executive Vice President, Boston Edison Company	1985-*

*Indicates directors of Shawmut Bank of Boston, N.A., on April 30, 1985.

Presidents and Chairmen of Shawmut Corporation and Its Predecessor Organizations, Shawmut Association and Shawmut Association, Inc.

Shawmut Association, Formed May 21, 1928

Dates	President	Chairman
1928–1956	Walter S. Bucklin*	
1956–1961	Horace Schermerhorn*	
1961–1962	Lawrence H. Martin*	Horace Schermerhorn
1962–1965	Lawrence H. Martin*	

In 1964, Shawmut Association, Inc., Formed under Massachusetts Law. It Acquired the Assets and Liabilities of Shawmut Association on May 6, 1965

1964–1967	Lawrence H. Martin*	
1967–1972	John K. Benson	Lawrence H. Martin*
1972–1975	John K. Benson	D. Thomas Trigg*
1975–1978	Logan Clarke	D. Thomas Trigg*

In 1975, the Name of Shawmut Association, Inc., Changed to Shawmut Corporation

1978 (June–Oct.)	D. Thomas Trigg	D. Thomas Trigg*
1978–1980	John P. LaWare	D. Thomas Trigg*
1980–1981	John P. LaWare	John P. LaWare*
1981–present	John P. Hamill	John P. LaWare*

*Chief Executive Officer

| *Benson, John K. | Vice President, National Shawmut Bank | 1961–1965 |
| *Trigg, D. Thomas | Vice President, National Shawmut Bank | 1962–1965 |

Directors of Shawmut Corporation
(Incorporated on December 30, 1964, as Shawmut Association, Inc.)

Martin, Lawrence H.	President, National Shawmut Bank	1964–1980
Benson, John K.	Senior Vice President, National Shawmut Bank	1964–1975
Stack, Lee P.	Limited Partner, Paine, Webber, Jackson & Curtis	1964–1968
†Trigg, D. Thomas	Senior Vice President, National Shawmut Bank	1964–
Trustman, Benjamin A.	Partner, Nutter, McClennen & Fish	1964–1975
Wallace, John	Vice President & Senior Trust Officer, National Shawmut Bank	1964–1975
Avila, Charles F.	President, Boston Edison Company	1965–1979
Bartlett, Charles W.	Partner, Ely, Bartlett, Brown & Proctor (later Gaston Snow & Ely Bartlett)	1965–1978
Collier, Abram T.	Vice Chairman, John Hancock Mutual Life Insurance Company; later President, New England Mutual Life Insurance Company on retirement	1965–1966
Doriot, Georges F.	President, American Research & Development	1965–1970
Garrett, Norman F.	President, Whitin Machine Works	1965
Geneen, Harold S.	President, ITT	1965–1973
Gordon, Elliott M.	President, Towle Manufacturing Company	1965–1977
Hammond, Franklin T., Jr.	Partner, Gaston, Snow, Motley & Holt	1965–1974
†Jenney, Robert M.	President, Jenney Manufacturing Company	1965–

*Indicates trustee who also served as an original director of Shawmut Association, Inc.

†Indicates directors of Shawmut Corporation on April 30, 1985.

Jones, Robert V.	Vice President for Finance; Comptroller, New England Telephone & Telegraph Company	1965–1969
Knowles, Asa S.	President, Northeastern University	1965–1981
Marshall, Harold T.	President, The Kendall Company	1965–1978
Philips, John N.	Senior Vice President, Eastern Gas & Fuel Associates	1965–1978
Sinclair, Donald B.	President, General Radio Company	1965–1975
Smith, Bryan E.	Chairman, Liberty Mutual Insurance Companies	1965–1968
Stocker, Crawford, H., Jr.	President, Lynn Five Cents Savings Bank	1965–1976
Young, Richard B.	President, Acushnet Process Company	1965–1984
Ziegler, Vincent C.	President, The Gillette Company	1965–1979
†Brooking, G. Edward, Jr.	President, Fanny Farmer Candy Shops, Inc.	1967–
†Olsen, Kenneth H.	President, Digital Equipment Corporation	1967–
Mergott, Winston	Senior Vice President, Liberty Mutual Insurance Companies	1968–1973
†Staszesky, Francis, M.	Executive Vice President, Boston Edison Company	1969–
Almgren, Herbert P.	President, First Bank & Trust Company of Hampden County (a Shawmut Bank)	1969–1983
Atwater, Victor P.	Chairman & Chief Executive Officer, The County Bank, N.A. (a Shawmut Bank)	1969–1972
Fossett, Carroll A.	Executive Vice President, National Shawmut Bank	1972–1976
†Hewitt, Graves D.	President and Director, Cameron & Colby Company	1972–
†Bradshaw, Melvin B.	Executive Vice President, Liberty Mutual Insurance Companies (in 1975 Executive Vice President, United Brands Corporation)	1973–
Gelsthorpe, Edward	President, The Gillette Company	1973–1975

†Indicates directors of Shawmut Corporation on April 30, 1985.

Clarke, Logan, Jr.	President, Shawmut Association, Inc. (Corp.)	1974–1978
Black, Paul G.	President, National Shawmut Bank	1975–1976
Matz, J. Edwin	President, John Hancock Mutual Life Insurance Company	1975–1983
†Newhall, John B.	Partner, Nutter, McClennen & Fish	1975–
†Putnam, Roger L., Jr.	Chairman, Package Machinery Corporation	1975–
Tanenbaum, Morris	Executive Vice President, Bell Laboratories, Inc.	1975–1979
†Pruyn, William J.	President and Chief Executive Officer, Eastern Gas & Fuel Associates	1978–
Bartlett, Joseph W.	Partner, Gaston, Snow & Ely Bartlett	1978–1983
†LaWare, John P.	President, Shawmut Corporation	1978–
†Jarvis, Herbert W.	Former President, USM Corporation (a subsidiary of Emhart Corporation)	1979–
†Page, Robert G.	President and Chief Executive Officer, Leesona Corporation	1979–
†Craig, William F.	Executive Vice President, Shawmut Corporation (later President, Shawmut Bank of Boston)	1980–
†Hamill, John P.	Executive Vice President, Shawmut Corporation (later President, Shawmut Corporation)	1981–
Steele, Richard C.	President and Chief Executive Officer, Worcester Telegram & Gazette, Inc.	1982–1983
Adam, John, Jr.	President Emeritus, The Hanover Insurance Companies	1982–1984
†Fargo, Bronson H.	President, SURE Oil & Chemical Corporation	1982–
†Finnegan, Neal F.	Senior Executive Vice President, Shawmut Corporation (later Vice Chairman, Shawmut Corporation)	1982–

†Indicates directors of Shawmut Corporation on April 30, 1985.

Hosmer, Walker J.	Chairman of the Board, Millers Falls Paper Company	1982–1984
†Jacobson, M. Howard	President and Treasurer, Idle Wild Foods, Inc.	1982–
†Colloredo-Mansfeld, Ferdinand	President and Chief Executive Officer, Cabot, Cabot & Forbes Company	1983–
†James, Howard P.	Former Chairman and Chief Executive Officer, The Sheraton Corporation	1983–
†Pierce, John B., Jr.	Of Counsel to Gaston Snow & Ely Bartlett, Attorneys	1983–
†Segall, Maurice	President and Chief Executive Officer, Zayre Corporation	1983–
†Spaulding, Helen B.	Consultant to the Board of Directors, Spaulding Rehabilitation Hospital	1983–
†Bell, W. Douglas	Chairman of the Board and Chief Executive Officer, State Mutual Life Assurance Company of America	1984–
†Lee, Bertram M.	President, New England Television Corporation	1984–
†Tsongas, Paul E.	Partner, Foley, Hoag & Eliot, Attorneys	1985–

†Indicates directors of Shawmut Corporation on April 30, 1985.

APPENDIX FIVE

Quarter Century Club of Shawmut Bank of Boston, N.A., 1984*

1938
Robert F. Perkins

1939
Catharine L.
O'Connor

1940
Donald Armitage
John W. Constantine

1941
Frederick J. Grant
Ethel P. Laracy

1942
Eileen M. Chapman
Marguerite S. Parker

1943
Helen Gregerias
Emmy R. Nelmes

1944
Mary M. Flaherty

1945
Louise D. Downey

1946
William R. Dewey, III
Winthrop L. Glazier
Donald B. Hitchcock
Anne M. Kelly
Lawrence Mulrey
Robert H. Peterson
Stephen J. Sotakos
Earl J. Sweeney
George Waal

1947
Richard E. Fischer
Raymond F. Garon
Anna R. Mann
Francis McCarthy

Marie H. Monahan
Henry T. Roche
John T. Shea, Jr.
Richard A. Williams

1948
James J. Anastas
John F. Cawley, Jr.
Donald F. Geary
Edward W. Gillespie
Anne N. Hubbard
Charles J. Hurley
Donald R. Johnston
Marion M. O'Brien
Irving Olick
Andrew A. Orrock
Roland A. Prid-
ham, Jr.
Erwin Schmuck, Jr.
Francis A. Smith
Bruce A. Stevens, Jr.
Loring E. Trott

1949
Jean M. Celley
Charles S. Hopkins
Charles E. McArdle
Robert Philbrick
Powell Robinson, Jr.

1950
Edmund O. Burke
Bennett S. Ferguson
Douglas R. Muise
Clarence W. Peter-
son, Jr.
William G. Stevenson
Gustavus T. Tolman
Gerald K. Vogel

1951
Shirley M. Carlson
Ann M. Deluca

Patricia A. Doyle
Rose M. Fahey
Frederick Hersey
Marie A. Liotine
Joan R. Lynch
Carol D. Marshall
George F. Morgan
Michael C. Odess
Rose M. Pantaleo
Marie V. Powell
Catherine A. Reilly
Elizabeth A. Sweeney
Angela G.
Szymanowska
James K. White

1952
Raymond Abdella
Dolores Capotosto
Helen B. Foti
Anne M. Howley
Francis X. Masterson
Donald W. Murray
Mary Frances O'Hare
Olympia
Panagiotakopoulos
John A. Rein, Jr.
John J. Ryan
Jean M. Williams

1953
G. Ronald Armbruster
Kathleen A.
Armstrong
Jean F. Bedard
Nancy L. Carroll
John J. Green
Sarah H. Hary
Marjorie L. Isnor
Marie R. Logiudice
Mary R. McCarthy

Dolores M. Milano
George E. O'Neil
William J. Polcari
Robert S. Rogers
A. June Sahagian

1954
Gladys H. Adamczyk
Charles S. Brown
Walter Butterworth
Katina Caramanis
Edward S. Cayon
Joan M. Corkery
Freeman L.
  Coville, Jr.
Janet M. Drummey
Brewster J. Gifford
James P. Hayes
Francis E. Howe
Priscilla S. Legault
Dorothy H. Peterson
Anthony C. Polcari
Robert E. Schaejbe
Joseph P. Sullivan
Irene H. Turner

1955
Marie T. Brown
Robert C. Burr
Alice F. Byrne
P. Clarke Dwyer
Thomas F. Finn
Claire M. Finnegan
John F. Gill
Robert W. Herig
Marie Brown Hurley
Kenneth Karlberg

Stanley J. Kowalczyk
Donald J. Lunney
Raymond J.
  McCarthy, Jr.
Maureen P. O'Connell
Daniel J. Shields
Lawrence J. Sullivan
Julie C. Vaiani

1956
Robert E. Alden
John T. Chambers
Mary A. Corzo
Mary M. Donovan
Frederick J. Fox
Stephen R. George
Peter B. Hathaway
Alice Hovenanian
Jean M. Lewandowski
Barbara C. Looser
Ellen A. Mastrangelo
Irene B. McCarthy
Barbara M. Melanson
Gladys M. Pothier
Geraldine B. Storella
William M. Wads-
  worth
Nancy Webb
John J. Wright

1957
Susan Chase
Catherine P.
  Cunningham
Esther R. Donovan
Neal F. Finnegan
Cecile D. Gleason

Paul M. Maniff
Donald M. Milbury
Anesti Nasson
Elaine M. Ruff
Pauline M. Rush

1958
George Biagiotti
George Carlson
John C. Gardiner
Carter H. Harrison
Stamatia P. Mavrellis
Francis E. Rodrigues
Mary F. Souza
Frederick W. White

1959
Robert A. Berger
Madeline Blodgett
Robert J. Campbell
Mary F. Clogher
Diane E. Corey
Donalee Cotter
Ronald J. Foster
Eileen M. Grieshaber
Albert F. Haddad
Rosemarie R.
  Karavidas
Eliza W. Kerr
Vincent G. Marchese
Rita M. Moglia
John D. Mullen
Helen C. Schroth
John G. Spanks
Claire J. Tierney
John J. Wilson

Retired Members

Arsine P. Aharonian
Thomas M. Ainslie
Dorothy K. Allen
Edward H. Allen
Eric Anderson
John F. Andrews
Edgar C. Bailey
Albert J. Baillargeon

Robert G. Bain
Robert S. Baker
Lincoln E. Barber, Jr.
David A. Barr
William A. Barrett
John A. Bartholomew
Eugene O. Bata-
  stini, Jr.

Stanley G. Bennett, Jr.
John K. Benson
C. Kenneth Bentley
Paul G. Black
Janet Bradlee
Lawrence E. Brennan
Herbert G. Bridges
Emma W. Brooke

Harold P. Brown
Eileen G. Bryan
William R. Buckingham
William H. Burtt, Jr.
Walter M. Bush
Thomas J. Byrne
Francis G. Carmichael
Clinton W. Cashman
Harold C. Cashman
Roy F. Cederholm
James T. Chamberlain
Marjorie L. Chapin
John G. Clinch
Howard C. Cobb
Dorothy Rooney
   Copelas
Charles L. Crampe, Jr.
Alfred H. Crump
David L. Currier
Arlene E. Dadley
Walter M. Davis
Vincent DeFilippo
James W. Degnan
George P. Devlin
Arthur W. Deibert
Benoit A. d'Eon
Edwin B. Dexter
Alba DiGiannantonio
Eleanor R. Donahue
Anna R. Donovan
James H. Donovan
Evelyn B. Ducie
Charles O. Duff
Melvin F. Dwyer
Leo V. Egidio
Beatus Faeh
Olive Whiting Farmer
Harry W. Fay
Robert D. Fields
Leo T. Finn
Lamoine B. Fogg
Margaret F. Fox
Edward N. Franklin
Robert G. Fraser
Elizabeth D. Fuller
Margaret M. Gaich

Clarice M. Gamache
William E. Garrity
Marion S. Genovese
Dorothy J. Gillis
Frances G. Giuffrida
George H. Goodwin, Jr.
Arthur P. Gorham
Francis A. Grenier, Jr.
Francis F. Griffith
Wendell S. Grover
Grace M. Hager
Davis K. Hamer
Mabel E. Hamilton
Richard E. Harris
Wendell K. Hasey
Mary E. Heffernan
Walter C. Hellmann
Katherine A. Hichens
Francis Hines, Jr.
Albro L. Hodgdon
William A. Holmes
Paul H. Hopkins
Elizabeth Howard
Leslie J. Howlett
Robert C. Hussey
Carl A. Johnson
Robert A. Johnson
Edna W. Joseph
Henry J. Jwanowski
Clifford P. Keay
James P. Kelly
Frederick R. Kennedy
Therese J. Keonane
Charles W. Kespert, Jr.
Alma E. Kihlgren
Thomas J. Killeen
Ralph B. King
Floyd B. Kyle
Maria D. Lane
Rene V. Laurian
Sylvia G. MacLaren
Leslie F. MacNeil
Kathleen Madden
Ruth V. Madden
Stephen F. Maloney

David A. Marcoux, Jr.
George A. Marsh
Lawrence H. Martin
Ollis E. Matheson
Margaret McCarthy
Margaret C. McCarthy
Walter P. McCarthy
William J. McCarthy
Paul E. McDevitt
Ann J. McGuire
Charles D. McKinnon
Sigvard C. Melin
Gertrude M. Mellen
Viola Michaels
William H. Morris, Jr.
Louis Morrison
Mary C. Morrissey
Henry Mountford
Joseph N. Muise
Ethel L. Munroe
James A. Murphy
Margaret G. Murray
Thomas F. Murray
Anita A. Nardini
Dan M. Nixon
William Nowell
Ada M. Nunn
James H. O'Brien
Angus V. O'Hanley
Raymond N. Olsen
Athur O. Olson
Edward J. O'Neil
Joseph G. Orint
Charles J. Pabst, Jr.
Wilma M. Pacht
Ernest Pennell
Mildred Wells Pennell
Joseph E. Petrino
Clarence A. Poingdester
Arnold T. Polley
Edward F. Powers
Mae G. Quealy
James J. Quigley
William Ready
Hammond G. Reed
Charles A. Reid

Mary T. Reil
Stuart Reynolds
Irving P. Richard-
son, Jr.
Hilda Roberts
Robert Robertson
Arthur E. Roche
Arthur W. Rodday
Harry W. Rose
William C. Saltzman
Mary Sarno
Clarence A. Sawyer
Clifton J. Schaeffer
William B. Schmink
Leslie J. Scott
Gordon H. Sellon
Edward P. Shea
Stewart P. Sloane

Carlos C. S. Smith
Eugene B. Smith
Eleanor M. Spence
Walter H. Squires
Humbert J. Stasio
Ann M. Stiles
Gladys M. Stockwell
Oscar F. Stone
Norman W. Strickland
Helga G. Strong
John S. Sullivan
Margaret M. Sullivan
Gertrud M. Sundlie
Antons Sumskis
Priscilla S. Symington
Karl S. Tenney
E. Jane Terrell
Robert T. Thompson

Leonard C. Tims
Sylvia C. Topham
Thomas A. Trahan
D. Thomas Trigg
Arthur B. Tyler
Wightman S. Tyson
Maxine M. Vickery
William B. Wadland
John Wallace
Wilbar Whittemore
Myron O. Wilkins
Nelson E. Williams
Martha A. Winders
Warner Witherall
Marie B. Wolfe
Donald G. Wrenn
Lewis F. Wyant

*The following members were added in 1985:

1960
Edward P. Albaugh
Paul A. Alfama
Bernice M. Costello
Teresa A. DeStefano
Carol A. Devlin
Thomas F. Dooley
Franklin W. Faucette
James J. Flynn
Francis R. Fresina

Peter J. Hession
Allan J. Jones
Michael Kalambokas
Margaret F. Kane
John J. LaCreta
Anne W. Levis
Lawrence J. Lynch
Joseph R. Molloy
Eleanor A. Peters

Evelyn T. Pierson
Joan M. Plunkett
James F. Ryan, Jr.
Santina J. Salvoni
Paul W. Thielmann
Peter A. Wilson
Edwin Worthy

Cashiers and Auditors

Cashiers of the Shawmut Bank (1836–1985)

Drown, Thomas	1836–1846
Davis, Stephen G.	1846–1876
Stearns, James P.	1876–1894
Taft, Josephus G.	1894–1898
Barbour, Frank H.	1898–1912
Joy, Benjamin	1913–1917
Burnham, W. A., Jr.	1917–1918
Ryder, James E.	1918–1928
Wyatt, Stanley P.	1928–1947
Paterson, George M.	1947–1963
McGray, W. A.	1963–1968
Fischer, Richard E.	1968–1984
Nix, James E.	1984–

Auditors of the National Shawmut Bank, and the Shawmut Bank of Boston, N.A. (1916–1985)

Dunaven, Clarence E.	1916–1925
Crampton, Arthur W.	1925–1929
Grimm, George D.	1929–1954
Skeels, Clarence B.	1954–1962
Goodwin, George H., Jr.	1962–1970
Armitage, Donald	1970–1976
Nix, James E.	1976–1981
MacKinnon, Paul A.	1981–

General Auditors of Shawmut Corporation

Hansberry, Timothy J.	1973–1974
Nix, James E.	1974–1981
MacKinnon, Paul A.	1981–

Independent Auditors of Shawmut Association (1929–1965), Shawmut Association, Inc. (1965–1974), and Shawmut Corporation (1975–1985)

Lybrand Ross Brothers and Montgomery	1929–1947
Stewart, Watts, Bollong	1947–1957

Arthur Young & Company	1957–1961
Lybrand Ross Brothers and Montgomery	
(now Coopers and Lybrand)	1961–1971
Price Waterhouse	1971–

APPENDIX SEVEN

Directors of the Affiliated Banks of
Shawmut Corporation (as of April 30, 1985)

Shawmut Bank of Boston, N.A.

Joseph W. Bartlett	Partner, Gaston Snow & Ely Bartlett, Attorneys
William L. Boyan, Jr.	Executive Vice President, John Hancock Mutual Life Insurance Company
Melvin B. Bradshaw	Chairman and Chief Executive Officer, Liberty Mutual Insurance Companies
William F. Craig	Vice Chairman, Shawmut Corporation and President, Shawmut Bank of Boston, N.A.
Neal F. Finnegan	Vice Chairman, Shawmut Corporation; Executive Vice President, Shawmut Bank of Boston, N.A.
Paul Edward Gray	President, Massachusetts Institute of Technology
Stephen J. Griffin	Retired President, The Gillette Company
John P. Hamill	President, Shawmut Corporation and Executive Vice President, Shawmut Bank of Boston, N.A.
Colby Hewitt, Jr.	Chairman and Chief Executive Officer, Frank B. Hall & Co. of Massachusetts, Inc.
Herbert W. Jarvis	President and Chief Executive Officer, Sybron Corporation
John P. LaWare	Chairman of the Board and Chief Executive Officer, Shawmut Corporation and Shawmut Bank of Boston, N.A.
James M. Lydon	Executive Vice President, Boston Edison Company
John S. North	Executive Vice President and Chief Operating Officer, New England Telephone & Telegraph Co.
John B. Pierce, Jr.	Of Counsel, Gaston Snow & Ely Bartlett, Attorneys
William J. Pruyn	President and Chief Executive Officer, Eastern Gas and Fuel Associates
Kenneth G. Ryder	President, Northeastern University
William L. Saltonstall	Partner, Saltonstall & Co.
Winthrop A. Short	President and Director, Knapp King-Size Corp.

Eliot I. Snider	President and Treasurer, Massachusetts Lumber Co.
Muriel S. Snowden	Former Co-Director, Freedom House, Inc., Roxbury
Francis M. Staszesky	Former President and Chief Operating Officer, Boston Edison Company
D. Thomas Trigg	Former Chairman of the Board and Chief Executive Officer, Shawmut Corporation and Shawmut Bank of Boston, N.A.

Shawmut Bank of Bristol County, N.A.

James B. Barron	Chairman, President and Chief Executive Officer, Shawmut Bank of Bristol County, N.A.
Bruce A. Borden	President and Treasurer, Borden Insurance Agency, Inc.
Manuel Camara, Jr.	President and Treasurer, Manuel Camara, Jr., Insurance Agency, Inc.
Paul G. Cleary	President and Treasurer, Paul G. Cleary & Co., Inc.
John J. Dugan	President and Treasurer, John Dugan Buick-Pontiac, Inc.
Louis D. Finger	Vice President and General Manager, Fibre Leather Manufacturing Corp.
Malcolm W. Frasier	President, Franklin W. Hatch Co., Inc.
Murray L. Goldberg	President, M. L. Goldberg Co., Inc.
Philip M. Hawes	President, Hawes Electric Company
Leif Jacobsen	President, Jacobsen Fishing Co., Inc.
Gerald D. Kaplan	President and Treasurer, Kaplan Furniture Co. of New Bedford, Inc.
Matthew E. Lopes	President, New Bedford Floor Covering Sales Co., Inc.
Anthony M. Martin	D.D.S.
Mary H. Morss	Executive Director, Bristol County Development Council, Inc.
John P. Santos	M.D.
Aaron J. Siegal	Aaron J. Siegal, P.C., Attorney at Law
George L. Unhoch, Jr.	President, New Bedford Thread Company, Inc.
Lawrence A. Weaver	President and Treasurer, Crowley-Weaver Insurance Agency, Inc.

Shawmut Bank of Cape Cod, N.A.

Mylan J. Costa	President, Myre, Inc.
William G. Crockett	Treasurer, Crockett Mortgage Company

William W. DeWilde	Executive Vice President, Shawmut Bank of Cape Cod, N.A.
W. John Hinman	President, Shawmut Bank of Cape Cod, N.A.
Charles S. Innis, Jr.	Executive Assistant to the Directorate, Woods Hole Oceanographic Institute
Walter J. Meier	President, Chatham Jewelers, Inc.; President, MAT, Inc.
James E. Murphy	President and Treasurer, James E. Murphy, Inc.
Martin J. O'Malley, Jr.	Attorney at Law
Sumner Robinson	President, World of Watsons; President and Treasurer, Highland Motors Company, Inc.
Richard J. Vandermay, Sr.	Partner, Eastham Travel Agency, Inc.

Shawmut Bank of Franklin County

Channing L. Bete, Jr.	President and Treasurer, Channing L. Bete Co., Inc.
Arnold G. Blackstone	President and Chief Executive Officer, Shawmut Bank of Franklin County
Donald R. Castine	General Manager and Treasurer, F. L. Castine, Inc.
Domenic J. Ferrante	Retired President, Northfield Washed Sand & Gravel, Inc., Treasurer, Brattleboro Sand & Gravel, Inc., and Treasurer, Northfield Concrete Products Corp.
J. Nicholas Filler	Attorney, Treasurer and Director, Trudel, Bartlett, Barry, Filler & Wilson, P.C.
John W. Haigis, Jr.	President and Treasurer, Haigis Broadcasting Corporation
Robert S. Harper	Private Investments
Edward S. Harris	Vice President and Treasurer, Rodney Hunt Company
Walker J. Hosmer	Retired, Former Chairman of the Board and Former Chief Executive Officer, Millers Falls Paper Company
Robert E. Kaufmann	Headmaster, Deerfield Academy
Denham C. Lunt, Jr.	Chairman of the Board and President, Lunt Silversmiths
Robert S. Reid	President
Linwood L. Richards	President and Treasurer, Erving Motor Trans., Inc.
Delbert A. Witty	Attorney

Honorary Director
Denham C. Lunt

Eliot I. Snider	President and Treasurer, Massachusetts Lumber Co.
Muriel S. Snowden	Former Co-Director, Freedom House, Inc., Roxbury
Francis M. Staszesky	Former President and Chief Operating Officer, Boston Edison Company
D. Thomas Trigg	Former Chairman of the Board and Chief Executive Officer, Shawmut Corporation and Shawmut Bank of Boston, N.A.

Shawmut Bank of Bristol County, N.A.

James B. Barron	Chairman, President and Chief Executive Officer, Shawmut Bank of Bristol County, N.A.
Bruce A. Borden	President and Treasurer, Borden Insurance Agency, Inc.
Manuel Camara, Jr.	President and Treasurer, Manuel Camara, Jr., Insurance Agency, Inc.
Paul G. Cleary	President and Treasurer, Paul G. Cleary & Co., Inc.
John J. Dugan	President and Treasurer, John Dugan Buick-Pontiac, Inc.
Louis D. Finger	Vice President and General Manager, Fibre Leather Manufacturing Corp.
Malcolm W. Frasier	President, Franklin W. Hatch Co., Inc.
Murray L. Goldberg	President, M. L. Goldberg Co., Inc.
Philip M. Hawes	President, Hawes Electric Company
Leif Jacobsen	President, Jacobsen Fishing Co., Inc.
Gerald D. Kaplan	President and Treasurer, Kaplan Furniture Co. of New Bedford, Inc.
Matthew E. Lopes	President, New Bedford Floor Covering Sales Co., Inc.
Anthony M. Martin	D.D.S.
Mary H. Morss	Executive Director, Bristol County Development Council, Inc.
John P. Santos	M.D.
Aaron J. Siegal	Aaron J. Siegal, P.C., Attorney at Law
George L. Unhoch, Jr.	President, New Bedford Thread Company, Inc.
Lawrence A. Weaver	President and Treasurer, Crowley-Weaver Insurance Agency, Inc.

Shawmut Bank of Cape Cod, N.A.

| Mylan J. Costa | President, Myre, Inc. |
| William G. Crockett | Treasurer, Crockett Mortgage Company |

Shawmut Bank of Hampshire County, N.A.

Robert A. Aquadro	Treasurer, Aquadro & Cerruti, Inc.
Robert A. Borawski	President, Alexander W. Borawski, Inc. Insurance and Real Estate
Steven W. Brode	President and Treasurer, Blair, Cutting and Smith Insurance Agency
Judson C. Ferguson	Retired
Walter C. Jones	President, W. D. Cowls, Inc.
George B. May	Treasurer, Amherst College
Kenneth J. Parsons	Treasurer, Earl M. Parsons and Sons, Inc.
Thomas G. Sebastyn	President and Chief Executive Officer, Shawmut Bank of Hampshire County, N.A.
Stephen Whitcomb	Private Investments

Honorary Directors

Robert D. Hawley	Treasurer Emeritus, The University of Massachusetts
Wesley J. Wentworth	Real Estate Developer

Shawmut Community Bank, N.A.

Alfred F. Bonazzoli, Jr.	President, Bonazzoli Corporation
Gerard H. Boule	President, H. J. Boule Insurance Agency, Inc.
Christopher W. Bramley	President, Shawmut Community Bank, N.A.
George E. Fitts	Vice President, Fitts Insurance Agency, Inc.
Vincent E. Garino	Proprietor, Garino's Audio-Video, Inc.
Allen M. Glick	President, Crown Chevrolet, Inc.; President, Crown Oldsmobile-Toyota, Inc.; President, Crown Corporation, d/b/a/ Framingham Mitsubishi
James Golden	Trustee, J & K Realty Trust
Robert C. Hussey	Retired Executive Vice President, Shawmut Corporation
Walter I. Keyes	Partner, Keyes Associates
Paul Kwasnick	President, Mars Stores, Inc.
Donald G. O'Brien	President, D. G. O'Brien, Inc.
Ronnie E. Payne	Corporate Director of Purchasing, Digital Equipment Corporation
William G. Poist	President and Chief Executive Officer, Commonwealth Gas Company
Robert Tennant	President, R. L. Tennant Insurance Agency
James W. Walckner	Executive Vice President, Framingham Union Hospital

Donald F. Ryan	Senior Vice President, Massachusetts Mutual Life Insurance Company
John I. Simpson	President, Peck Lumber Company
Allen Steiger	Vice President of Finance, Albert Steiger, Inc.
Leonard A. Wilson	President and Chief Executive Officer, Shawmut First Bank
Adolph J. Yodlowski	Management Consultant

Honorary Directors

| Paul B. Buckwalter | Ralph E. Day | Robert G. DeCarlo |
| A. Ashley Carroll | Russell B. Day | Donald R. Taber |

Shawmut First County Bank, N.A.

Wayne T. Evans	General Director, YMCA
Henry N. Frenette, Jr.	Attorney, Keith, Reed, Wheatley & Frenette
Harvey E. Gates	President, Gates Clothing, Inc.
Ronald W. Mallette	President, Shawmut First County Bank, N.A.
David E. Marcello, Jr.	Chief of Surgical Services, Brockton Hospital
Edward J. O'Keefe	Former President, Shawmut First County Bank, N.A.
Richard C. Reed	Attorney, Keith, Reed, Wheatley & Frenette
Robert G. Sims	C.L.U. and Associates
John F. Spaulding	Retired President, Franklin Industries
Rudolf L. Talbot	Retired President, The Talbots, Inc.

Honorary Directors

Joseph Abusamra	Robert M. Keith	James J. O. Stone
Earle W. Carr	Chesterton S. Knight	George L. Wainwright
Charles C. Eaton, Jr.	Wallace J. McGrath	

Shawmut Merchants Bank, N.A.

Leonard Axelrod	President, Empire Clothing Co.
Jonathan Bangs	Attorney-at-Law, Peabody & Arnold
Randolph P. Barton	Trustee
Francis J. Bresnahan	Owner, M. H. Bresnahan & Sons
Arthur W. Delande	Chairman, Delande Supply Co., Inc.
Hollis French	President, Johnny Appleseed's Inc.
Joseph E. Lovejoy	Chairman, Ensign-Bickford Industries, Inc.
Philip H. McLaughlin	President, Shawmut Merchants Bank, N.A.
John G. Reed	President, Burbank Corporation
Howard Rich	President, Jerry's Department Stores, Inc.

Morton H. Sigel	President, Millbrook Distributors, Inc.
Harry I. Spencer, Jr.	Executive Vice President, Cashier and Secretary, Shawmut Worcester County Bank, N.A.
Herbert M. Varnum	President, Quabaug Rubber Company
Meredith D. Wesby	Director of Human Resources, Wright Line, Inc.

Honorary Directors

John Adam, Jr.	President Emeritus, The Hanover Insurance Companies
Robert J. Whipple	Fletcher, Tilton & Whipple, P.C.

APPENDIX EIGHT

A. Growth of Assets and Deposits of Shawmut Bank of Boston at Significant Moments in the Bank's History

Significant Dates	$ Assets	$ Deposits
1836 Founding Warren/Shawmut Bank	889,533*	169,532*
1865 Shawmut National Bank	2,201,768	516,845
November 7, 1898** Shawmut National Bank	15,648,313	13,833,425
1899 National Shawmut Bank	35,504,164	30,477,917
1928 Founding of Shawmut Association	246,611,389	174,064,408
1936 Centennial Year National Shawmut Bank	213,570,764	180,264,393
1965 Shawmut Association Reorganized Shawmut Association, Inc.	649,808,879	564,202,376
1975 Name Shawmut Bank of Boston, N.A., changed from the National Shawmut Bank of Boston	1,647,646,000	1,223,826,000
June 1985	3,531,962,000	2,239,225,000

* End of first full year of operation, 1837
** Last report of Shawmut National Bank. On November 22 Shawmut merged with nine other banks and changed its name to National Shawmut Bank.

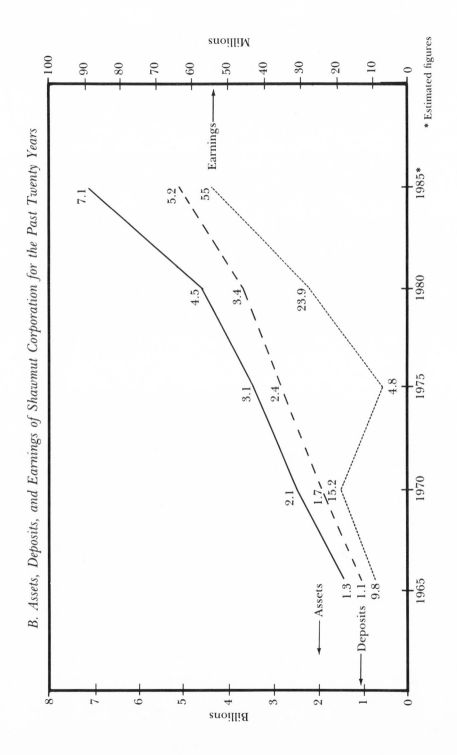

B. Assets, Deposits, and Earnings of Shawmut Corporation for the Past Twenty Years

* Estimated figures

Index

Wallace, John, 233–34, 255, 416–
18, 424–25, 428, 433
Waltham Citizens National Bank,
264, 367, 405–6
War of *1812*, 6–7; banking, 18–
19; debt accumulation, 18–19
Ware, William R., 351
Warren, Joseph, 34
Warren Bank, 30, 32, 370–71,
453; Albert Fearing's role in,
41–43; founding of, 23–30;
John Gardner's role in, 40–41;
incorporation, 26–28; name
change to Shawmut Bank, 34–
35; opening of, *1836*, 32; organizing leaders of, 25–26; Benja-
min T. Reed's role in, 28–40;
and Suffolk System, 33–34
Warren Charitable Trust, 233–34
Warren Insurance Company, 23–
25, 28, 30–32, 34–35, 42, 44–
45; *see also* Warren Bank
Warren National Bank of Pea-
body, 367, 408, 409, 411, 413
Waterfront Redevelopment Pro-
gram, 252
Webster, Frank G., 82, 84, 107,
127, 350
Webster and Atlas National Bank,
403
Wells, George W., 89
Whig party, 10, 25
Whig Young Men of Boston, 25
White, Frederick W., 235
White, James R., 270
White, Kevin, 330
White, Weld and Company, 192
Whitney, William, 38, 49
Whiton, David, 51–52
Whittier, Charles W., 351, 361
Wiggin, Rohl C., 165, 169, 233,
328, 408, 416
Wilkins, Myron, 171
Williams, Jeremiah, 82
Williams, Moses, 87, 105, 107
Williams, Richard A., 322
Willis, Parker H., 100

Wills–St. Clair Company, 136
Willys Overland Company, 136
Wilson, James G., 290
Wilson, Woodrow, 100, 114
Winchester National Bank, 167,
261, 367, 397, 435, 445
Winchester Repeating Arms
Company, 112, 125
Winslow, Walter, 351
Winsor, Robert, 82, 84, 86, 107–
9, 350
W. L. Douglas Shoe Company,
192
Woods, George, 91
Woodworth, Alfred S., 82, 88
Worcester Bancorp, Inc., 336,
368, 448–50
Worcester Bank and Trust Com-
pany, 129
Worcester County Institute for
Savings, 121
Worcester County National Bank,
121, 336, 368, 449
World Bank (International Bank
for Reconstruction and Development), 205, 210, 231
World War I, 110–13, 119–25,
218; branching privileges: during, 391–92; after, 172–73; economic effects of, 122–25; economic fluctuations after, 138–
39; exports after, 126–27;
housing boom after, 162; repa-
ration payments after, 195;
technological improvements
after, 159–60
World War II, 237; bank holding
companies after, 411; commercial loans during, 241; DFSC
profits after, 161; economic expansion after, 284; effect on
Shawmut Association, 403–4;
effect on textile industry, 207;
extension of credit after, 196–
97, loans during, 200–202
Wyatt, Stanley, 190
Wyman, Edward, 51